The Economy of Ireland

13TH EDITION

Policymaking in a Global Context

WITHDRAWN
THE LIBRARY OF
TRINITY COLLEGE DUBLIN

AUTHORISED: ∩K

DATE: 1/6/12

50744974

5 0 7 4 4 9 7 4

WITHDRAWN
FROM THE LIBRARY OF
TRINITY COLLEGE

The Economy of Ireland

13TH EDITION

Policymaking in a
Global Context

John O'Hagan

Francis O'Toole

Editorial selection and matter © John O'Hagan and Francis O'Toole 2017
Individual chapters © their individual authors 2017

All rights reserved. No reproduction, copy or transmission of this
publication may be made without written permission.

No portion of this publication may be reproduced, copied or transmitted
save with written permission or in accordance with the provisions of the
Copyright, Designs and Patents Act 1988, or under the terms of any licence
permitting limited copying issued by the Copyright Licensing Agency,
Saffron House, 6–10 Kirby Street, London EC1N 8TS.

Any person who does any unauthorized act in relation to this publication
may be liable to criminal prosecution and civil claims for damages.

The authors have asserted their rights to be identified as the authors of this
work in accordance with the Copyright, Designs and Patents Act 1988.

First published 2017 by
PALGRAVE

Palgrave in the UK is an imprint of Macmillan Publishers Limited,
registered in England, company number 785998, of 4 Crinan Street,
London, N1 9XW.

Palgrave® and Macmillan® are registered trademarks in the United States,
the United Kingdom, Europe and other countries.

ISBN 978–1–137–61106–2 paperback

This book is printed on paper suitable for recycling and made from fully
managed and sustained forest sources. Logging, pulping and manufacturing
processes are expected to conform to the environmental regulations of the
country of origin.

A catalogue record for this book is available from the British Library.

A catalog record for this book is available from the Library of Congress.

338·09415
N5 *12; 2

TRINITY LIBRARY

O   23 OCT 2017

DUBLIN

Contents

Contributors

Chapter 1
Jonathan Haughton has a B.A. from Trinity College Dublin and a Ph.D. from Harvard University. His current position is Professor of Economics, at Suffolk University Boston.

Chapter 2
Dermot McAleese has a B.Comm. and M.Econ.Sc. from University College Dublin, and an M.A. and Ph.D. from the Johns Hopkins University. He is Emeritus Whately Professor of Political Economy, at Trinity College Dublin.

Chapter 3
Philip R. Lane has a B.A. from Trinity College Dublin and a Ph.D. from Harvard University. His current position is Governor Central Bank of Ireland and Whately Professor of Political Economy (on leave of absence), at Trinity College Dublin.

Chapter 4
Micheál Collins has a B.A. from NUI Galway, an M.A. from University College Cork, and a Ph.D. from Trinity College Dublin. His current position is Assistant Professor, School of Social Policy, Social Work and Social Justice, at University College Dublin.

Chapter 5
Tara Mitchell has a B.A. and M.Sc. from Trinity College Dublin, and a Ph.D. from the London School of Economics and Political Science. Her current position is Assistant Professor, Department of Economics, at Trinity College Dublin.

Francis O'Toole has a B.A. from Trinity College Dublin, an M.Mang.Sc. from University College Dublin and a Ph.D. from Georgetown University. His current position is Head Department of Economics and Associate Professor, at Trinity College Dublin.

Chapter 6
Tara McIndoe-Calder has a B.A. and Ph.D. from Trinity College Dublin, and an M.Phil from Oxford University (Hertford College). Her current position is senior economist, Irish Economic Analysis Division, at Central Bank of Ireland.

John O'Hagan has a B.E., B.A. and M.A. from University College Dublin and a Ph.D. from Trinity College Dublin. He is an Emeritus Professor of Economics and Senior Fellow, at Trinity College Dublin.

Chapter 7
Michael Wycherley has a B.Sc. and MSc. from the University of Southampton and a Ph.D. from the European University Institute, Florence. His current position is Assistant Professor, Department of Economics, at Trinity College Dublin.

Chapter 8
Michael King has a B.A. and Ph.D. from Trinity College Dublin and an M.P.A. in International Development from Harvard University. His current position is Assistant Professor, Department of Economics, at Trinity College Dublin.

Chapter 9
Alan Matthews has a B.A. from Trinity College Dublin and an M.Sc. from Cornell University. He is an Emeritus Professor of European Agricultural Policy, at Trinity College Dublin.

Chapters 10 and 13
Ciara Whelan has a B.A. and Ph.D. from Trinity College Dublin. Her current position is College Lecturer, School of Economics, at University College Dublin.

Chapter 11
Eleanor Denny has a B.A., M.B.S. and Ph.D. from University College Dublin. Her current position is Associate Professor, Department of Economics, at Trinity College Dublin.

Chapter 12
Ronan Lyons has a B.A., M.Litt. and M.Sc. from Trinity College Dublin and an M.Phil. and D.Phil. from Oxford University. His current position is Assistant Professor, Department of Economics, at Trinity College Dublin.

Chapter 14
Anne Nolan has a B.A. and Ph.D. from Trinity College Dublin. Her current position is Associate Research Professor, Economic and Social Research Institute Dublin and Adjunct Associate Professor, at Trinity College Dublin.

Preface

IRELAND: AND THE UK, EU, USA AND BEYOND

Ireland has been one of the most interesting case studies in economics and more generally political economy in recent decades.

In terms of geography, however, Ireland with a population of less than five million is a very small country, only part of a small island to the west of Britain, which in turn is a somewhat larger but much more densely populated island to the west of mainland Europe. Ireland and the UK, with its population of over 65 million, have in essence a common labour market and huge trade and tourism flows in both directions. Ireland's relationship with its closest neighbour is crucial not only to Irish economic performance but also to continued peace on the island of Ireland. The island of Ireland consists of two political units, the larger portion of which forms the Republic of Ireland and the smaller portion Northern Ireland, which is part of the UK.

This book is about the economy of the Republic of Ireland, and the terms 'economy of Ireland' and 'Irish economy' refer to this economy, unless otherwise stated. Some reference is made to the Northern Ireland economy, but since Northern Ireland's overall economic policy is to a large extent determined in London, it is difficult to devote significant attention to policy in Northern Ireland without also reviewing UK economic policy. It is acknowledged, however, that there has been increased cross-border co-operation between the Republic of Ireland and Northern Ireland on the economic front since the Good Friday Agreement of 1998 and that the UK's (as opposed to just Britain's, or just England's) decision to trigger the process of negotiating its exit from the EU has given rise to many potentially profound economic and other uncertainties.

Moving beyond these small islands, the links, economic and cultural, between Ireland and continental Europe have strengthened considerably in recent decades, something that membership of the EU and associated educational and employment opportunities as well as low-cost air travel have facilitated. Ireland is also a member of the euro zone, with the euro having replaced Irish notes and coins in 2002. Irish people are now much more familiar than they were even 15 years ago with detailed political developments in Europe (e.g. French, German and Italian elections), and with European sporting and cultural events. In particular, Ireland operates increasingly within an agreed economic, political and social policy environment determined, with Ireland as a voting member, at an EU level.

Moving further afield, international competitiveness is a key determinant of Ireland's economic performance and more specifically Ireland's attractiveness to foreign direct investment. In particular, the scale of investment from the USA into Ireland in recent decades has been such that Ireland's industrial policy performance, and economic policy performance more generally, must be viewed against the twin backdrops of, and interactions between, EU policy (e.g. state-aid) and USA policy (e.g. corporation tax).

At a global level, the rise of China and India is an economic reality that has affected not just small countries like Ireland but also the two largest trading blocs in the world, namely, the EU and the USA. In particular, China's economic power is growing, and Mandarin is the mother tongue for by far the largest number of people in the world. As such, China's influence will soon extend well beyond the economic to the cultural and political spheres; indeed, at the time of writing, China's pro-globalisation stance contrasts sharply with the USA's apparent adoption of a protectionist stance.

FALL OF THE CELTIC TIGER AND RISE OF THE CELTIC PHOENIX?

During the period of Irish austerity and in particular in 2012, the unemployment rate exceeded 15 per cent, the numbers in employment fell below 1.85 million and the national debt to GDP figure was almost 120 per cent. Subsequently, the Irish unemployment rate has more than halved and in particular has dropped below 7 per cent for the first time since 2008. Although movements in the unemployment rate in Ireland are influenced greatly by migration, it is also the case that the employment figure has risen above two million for the first time since 2009 and, notwithstanding some significant problems with the usefulness of the GDP metric in an Irish context, the national debt to GDP figure has dropped below 80 per cent for the first time since 2009.

Forecasts from many informed commentators on the Irish economy, including the Central Bank of Ireland, suggest further significant increases in output and employment and further significant decreases in unemployment and the national debt to GDP figure. Indeed, Ireland's economic recovery has been deemed a 'Phoenix Miracle' by some and Ireland itself has been described as the 'Celtic Phoenix'. However, as readers know only too well, such labels can easily turn out to be afflictions as opposed to accolades.

NATIONAL AND INTERNATIONAL CHALLENGES

Ireland faces a number of important and foreseeable national and international challenges in the medium term and challenges that are global in nature must be addressed globally. Major global issues include: the environment and, in particular, the increasing danger of possibly catastrophic global warming; terrorism and, in particular, the possible use of biological and nuclear weapons; migration; the need for secure and safe energy supplies; continued large-scale global tax avoidance and evasion; and, increasing threats to the global trading environment.

From an EU perspective, more locally-based challenges include: the UK's future relationship with the EU, as well as possible contagion from Brexit; the future of the euro and the related issue of the continued very high level of indebtedness of Greece and some other EU countries; the future of the EU itself, with the growing possibility of the adoption of a multi-speed approach to future political developments; migration (into, as well as within, the EU); and, demographics.

From an Irish perspective, well recognised significant challenges include: the effect of Brexit on trade between Ireland and the UK as well as on the peace process; a possible future break-up of the UK itself; and, an arguably unhealthy reliance on multinational companies, shadow banking activities and perhaps related developments with regard to international tax competition.

On all of these global and international issues Irish interests and concerns are best voiced at an EU level and through the EU on the global stage. However, there are also many important national policy issues in Ireland that deserve focused Irish attention. Indeed, very many such issues are largely within Ireland's own remit and can be resolved, given the political will and an informed and realistic public debate. In this regard, the vociferous objections and pleadings of special interest groups must be challenged, especially by those whose job it is to sift and present information/arguments in a balanced way, so that informed timely decisions can be made and implemented. Of course, and crucially, it must be recognised that economic policy is exercised on the political field. Economists often forget that economic policy and politics are inseparable; having an apparently good solution to a problem is of little benefit if the solution cannot be implemented from a practical or political economy perspective. Of course, the political system in turn must somehow become more, as opposed to less, responsive to evidence-based discussions.

Taking housing policies as one example, prices have risen significantly in recent years, although not yet to the unsustainable levels of 2007. However, rents, particularly in the Dublin area, have risen to well beyond the levels of 2007. Fine-tuning policies focused on the demand-side of the sector (e.g. providing a subsidy to one group of potential consumers over others) is akin to replaying musical chairs with the same number of chairs but ever more participants. On the other hand, a suite of coherent policy options focused on the supply side of the sector offers at least the possibility of reducing the scale of the various and related housing crises.

The increasing cost of providing pensions, both in the public and private sectors, offers another national policy challenge. Postponing the necessary policy discussions and inevitable changes required, as arguably has been done to date, merely serves to reduce the available policy options. Arguably there is a time and a place for kicking certain 'cans down the road' but pensions' policy ticks neither box. In terms of public pay negotiations and, for that matter, any significant contractual arrangements involving the state, there seems much scope for explicitly addressing some of the inevitable uncertainties. Rather than specifying fixed terms, at least some room for particular and well-recognised contingencies could be built into contracts. For example, if the national economy performs much differently than initially expected/forecast, then the previously negotiated settlement can be adjusted automatically in a mutually beneficial manner. In a sense, just as we have learned the very hard way that bank bondholders must be bailed into any future bank losses, public sector workers or Irish residents more generally should be bailed into future failures (or successes).

However, and notwithstanding the above challenges, there is much reason for optimism. There is no reason why Ireland cannot continue to prosper in years to come and, in particular, remain one of the highest income countries in the world. Contrary to appearances at certain times, the country has a healthy, stable democracy and a well-established rule of law. There is also a welcome for diversity and difference in twenty-first-century Ireland that at least arguably wasn't present only a couple of short decades ago.

STRUCTURE OF BOOK

This book has evolved from an earlier book, first published over forty years ago. The Irish Management Institute published the first six editions, Macmillan published what, in effect, was the seventh edition, Gill & Macmillan published the next five editions and now Palgrave publishes its first but in effect the thirteenth edition of the book.

The tenth edition of this book was published in 2008 as Ireland entered the Great Recession, the eleventh edition was published in 2011 just after Ireland had, in effect, agreed to surrender much of its macroeconomic sovereignty to the Troika and was reeling from the austerity associated with the Great Recession and the Irish banking crisis. The twelfth edition was published in 2014 as Ireland began its rather dramatic economic recovery from the effects of this austerity. As such, 2017 marks a suitable time for pause and re-consideration and we believe that this book can facilitate in such a task.

The broad structure and purpose of the book have in essence remained the same over the years, but in terms of content there have been very significant changes, even since the last edition. Apart from standard updating, significant changes have been made to all chapters, to reflect the changing circumstances and policy issues facing the Irish economy. And five of the chapters are new or have new authors.

This book is not and never was concerned primarily with shorter-term economic issues. It generally takes a much longer-term historical perspective, a perspective that is salutary in reminding us that booms come to an end and in the more recent context that the bad times do not last forever. This book is also much more about general policy issues, thereby providing the context for debate be it in the short, medium or long term.

Section I provides the key policy background, namely, the historical evolution of the economy (Chapter 1) and a discussion of what are the key policy priorities and issues for a small regional economy such as that of Ireland (Chapter 2). In particular, it is essential to know what we want from the Irish economy before asking how we might achieve those aims and how well we are doing in achieving the objectives. These questions are examined in Sections II, III and IV.

Section II examines the implementation of policy. Chapter 3 sets out the appropriate role of the state, in terms of rationale, levels of government and size of the state sector. It also addresses the possible future of the euro zone in some detail. Chapter 4 examines how state involvement is funded and the principles underlying a good tax system, namely, efficiency, equity and administrative simplicity. A number of important categories of taxes as apply in Ireland are examined against these criteria and deferred taxation, or borrowing, is also considered. Regulation permeates our lives to an extraordinary extent and Chapter 5 examines the principles underlying good regulation and explores various types of regulation. Particular emphasis is placed on recent findings and policy suggestions from behavioural economics.

Section III consists of three discussions of Ireland's success, or otherwise, in meeting the objectives and associated policy issues outlined in Chapter 2, namely, employment and migration (Chapter 6), growth in living standards and output (Chapter 7) and distribution and poverty (Chapter 8). Much of the key statistical material of the book is presented in these three chapters.

Section IV contains a detailed discussion of policy issues and performance in the market and non-market sectors and builds on much of the earlier material. Chapter 9 looks not only at the agricultural sector but also at the issues of food distribution and consumption and the rising concern over security of supply and food safety. Chapter 10 examines the market sector perhaps of most importance to the success of the future economy, namely, manufacturing and internationally-traded services. Chapter 11 looks at the vitally important energy sector and its major environmental impact. Chapter 12 examines housing and related issues such as credit and highlights the crucial issue of housing supply.

The final two chapters deal with education (Chapter 13) and health (Chapter 14). Both of these in general non-market sectors are not only crucial to the well-being of the population at large but also to the future success of the economy. Both are also sectors of major economic significance in their own right, although assessing performance in either is fraught with difficulty. Both areas also are faced with the reality of possible future sweeping technological change impacting significantly on the delivery of outputs.

ACKNOWLEDGEMENTS

There are many people who have facilitated the publication of the new edition of this title and we thank the staff at Palgrave for their central role in bringing this book to the publication stage. In particular, we thank Aléta Bezuidenhout, Kirsty Reade and Amy Wheeler. We also thank Siobhán O'Brien in Trinity College for important help in this regard.

The book would not of course exist without the contributed chapters. As always, it was (mostly) enjoyable work liaising with each of the contributors, at each step of the process. In particular, it was rewarding to see chapters take shape and mesh into the overall structure of the book following comments, suggestions, banter and, at the extreme, simple dictate! Of course, the judicial use of dictate (while rather exhilarating in itself at times) comes with the disadvantage of the editors having to accept responsibility for any remaining errors and at least some responsibility for all views expressed. Attempted joking aside, we very much appreciate the input (and eventual cooperation) of each and every contributor.

We also thank the many lecturers and students who have used this book over the years. This has made the book both viable, despite the small size of the potential market, and a very satisfying experience, at least for us. The book is also read widely outside academia and outside these shores and we hope that this will continue to be the case. This is the type of book, and related course, which students seem to enjoy immensely and we are informed (reliably, we have decided to believe) that lecturers in many other colleges have also found this to be the case.

Finally, as the latest edition of this textbook goes to print, we feel that Ireland will continue to represent one of the most interesting political economy case studies in the world … for we hope all of the right reasons.

John O'Hagan and Francis O'Toole
Trinity College Dublin
May 2017

SECTION I

POLICY CONTEXT

CHAPTER 1

Historical Background: 1690 to Present

Jonathan Haughton

1 WHY ECONOMIC HISTORY?

Why take the trouble to study history, and particularly the economic history of a minor European island? Six good reasons spring to mind.

History tests theory. The propositions of economics are often best tested by exposing them to historical evidence. Was Malthus right when he argued that population growth would inevitably outstrip food supply? Irish experience, even during the Great Famine, suggests not. Do farmers respond to changes in the prices they face? Evidence from late nineteenth-century Ireland confirms that they do. Does emigration serve to equalise wages between Ireland and Britain? Data for this century indicate that, broadly speaking, it does. Cicero took this view of history, writing that 'the causes of events are even more interesting than the events themselves' – surely a view espoused by most academic economists!

History gives perspective. Standard economics textbooks typically provide a short-run and partial approach to economic problems. While this may be appropriate for tracing the immediate effects of a shift in demand, or a monetary expansion, it provides fewer insights on the fundamental determinants of economic growth or of income distribution, since these may only be observed over long periods of time. The historian Joe Lee has made the point forcibly, writing that 'while contemporary Irish economics can be impressive in accounting for short-term movements, it has contributed relatively little to understanding the long-term development of the Irish economy'. He argues that most economists are 'blind to either long-term perspective or lateral linkage' and that 'with the exception of a handful of superior intelligences, Irish economists are far more impressive as technicians than as thinkers'.

An important lesson from economic history is that it provides a sense of the fragility of economic growth, and of its intermittent nature. For instance, many look back to the 1960s as a golden era of Irish economic growth. Yet Kennedy, Giblin and McHugh, in their interesting study of Irish economic development in the twentieth century, argue that 'a sense of historical perspective would have

2

encouraged greater modesty about the achievements of the 1960s by recognising that they depended heavily on a combination of uniquely favourable external and internal circumstances'. Of course not everyone is convinced that history is good at giving perspective: in the view of Aristotle, 'poetry tends to express the universal, history the particular.'

History fascinates. While the study of any subject may be justified on the grounds of its intrinsic worth, economic history is particularly interesting. The visible remains of the past are everywhere – ports, houses, crooked streets, and ruined cottages. It is natural to wonder about their origins. Less visibly, our view of history informs our view of who we are, and what our culture stands for. These roots merit exploration. History also has its share of intellectual puzzles: Why were the Céide fields abandoned four thousand years ago? Why was economic growth in the 1950s so anaemic? How did per capita incomes rise faster in Ireland between 1850 and 1920 than anywhere else in Europe? Was the tariff regime of the 1930s a failure?

History debunks. Ideologues of all stripes invoke history to bolster their claims. When John Mitchel argued that 'The Almighty, indeed, sent the potato blight, but the English created the famine' he was revisiting history to support his nationalist position. Marxists turn to the land question as evidence of class conflict. An appreciation of history is essential if one is to make an informed judgement about the solidity of such ideas. Once again, Lee states it well, arguing that 'the modern Irish, contrary to popular impression, have little sense of history. What they have is a sense of grievance, which they choose to dignify by christening it history'. He concludes that 'it is central to my argument that the Irish of the late twentieth century have still to learn how to learn from their recent history'. Although written only a few years ago, this view may already be outdated, prey to what F.S.L. Lyons refers to as the dilemma of the contemporary historian – recent events may still be too close in time to allow for enough historical perspective. On the other hand, there is no such thing as a single correct historical perspective, which is surely the idea behind Oscar Wilde's quip that 'the one duty we owe to history is to rewrite it.'

History instructs policy. Ireland has tried laissez faire (1815–45); import substitution (1930–58); export promotion with foreign direct investment (1958–80). It has had budgetary discipline and chronic deficits, fixed exchange rates and floating, price controls, incomes policies, free trade zones, and public and private enterprise. Out of this varied experience there are lessons. While, in Santayana's famous words, 'those who ignore history are condemned to repeat it', the study of history is not merely to avoid making mistakes, but also to learn what works well and merits copying.

An interesting example of the relevance of history for policy is the 2011 book by Reinhart and Rogoff entitled *This Time is Different: Eight Centuries of Financial Folly.* Their exhaustive review of financial collapses in scores of countries over many decades shows that time and again governments, bankers, and others simply ignored the lessons of the past, rationalising their actions with the thought that no two situations are the same, things had changed, and this time was different. The Irish housing bubble that began in 2000 and collapsed in 2008, bringing down the country's entire banking system, is a case in point.

The Irish case has served as a positive role model too. Ireland's torrid economic growth in the late 1990s interested many in less-developed countries, which too are typically small open economies with a colonial past. Ireland in the twentieth century was a tardy bloomer, and a major theme of this chapter, indeed of this book, is to try to understand why.

History can be misused. Interpretations of history can have real consequences, for good or for bad, because they help form the world view of subsequent generations. George Orwell famously wrote, 'who controls the past controls the future: who controls the present controls the past.' The different versions of history taught in Protestant and Catholic schools in Northern Ireland, for instance, have contributed to an enduring communitarian divide. Nazi teachings on racial purity contributed to the horrors of the holocaust, but Hitler wrote, 'the victor will never be asked if he told the truth.' The antidote to the misuse of history is to inform oneself, to apply an enquiring mind even to received wisdom, in short, to develop some knowledge of history.

The main focus of this chapter is on how Ireland has developed economically. Crotty defines such development as 'a situation where (a) more people are better off than formerly and (b) fewer people are as badly off'. By this yardstick it is necessary to look at population growth, since an economy whose development is accompanied by massive emigration has in some sense failed. This parallels the suggestion of the 1948 Emigration Commission, which proposed that 'a steadily increasing population should occupy a high place among the criteria by which the success of national policy should be judged'.

Economic development also requires that incomes rise (growth), including, or especially, those of the least well off (equality), and this is presumably facilitated by an efficient use of resources (notably full employment).

The starting point, arbitrarily chosen, is 1690, with the consolidation of the Protestant ascendancy. The subsequent years are divided into sub-periods – growth and early industrialisation during 1690 and 1815, rural crisis between 1815 and 1850, the population decline that accompanied increasing prosperity from 1850 to 1921, the intermittent economic development between independence and about 1960, and finally the grand cycle of modern Irish economic growth, hesitation, boom, reverberation, bust, and rebirth stretching over the past half century.

2 FROM BATTLE OF BOYNE TO 1815

Eighteenth Century

At the time of the battle of the Boyne the Irish economy was predominantly rural, although it was no longer a woodland society. Population stood at a little under two million, roughly double the level of a century before, and was growing at an historically high rate of at least half a per cent per year. With the spread of population the forest cover was rapidly disappearing, giving way to both grazing and tillage. The largest town, Dublin, had about 60,000 inhabitants.

The country was an important exporter, especially of grain, beef, butter, wool and, to a lesser extent, linen. Presaging the situation of three centuries later, almost half of all exports went to Continental Europe, notably to France. Earnings from these exports were spent on items such as coal and tobacco, and a surplus on current account amounting to perhaps 10 per cent of exports allowed for the remittance of rents to absentee landlords. Petty, visiting the country in 1672, commented on the large number of people who rode horses, and the high standard of clothing relative to France and most of Europe. He also noted the shabbiness of the houses, of which he reckoned only a fifth had chimneys. The implication was that Ireland was not significantly poorer, and was possibly better off, than most of Continental Europe at that time, although less affluent than most of England.

Income was distributed unevenly. Land was owned by perhaps 10,000 landlords, and six-sevenths of the land was held by Protestants. Much of this was let out to farmers, who in turn frequently sublet small plots to cottiers, or hired casual labour. By one estimate, a little over half of the population constituted a rural proletariat, with minimal access to land and close to the margin of subsistence. The potato had been introduced early in the seventeenth century, but was only an important part of the diet of the poor, although its spread allowed for rapid population growth throughout the eighteenth century.

Growth and Structural Change
The essential features of economic growth during the period 1690 to1815 were a rapid recovery from the war, a period of relative stagnation (1700–20), 25 years of crisis that included two famines (1720–45), and a long wave of sustained and relatively rapid economic growth (1745–1815). The evidence for these is indirect, since few economic statistics were collected at the time, but trade data show a steady increase in exports, with relatively rapid growth between 1740 (£1.2 million) and 1816 (£7.08 million). The structure of exports changed, as shipments of cattle and sheep gave way to beef, butter, grain, and linen.

These changes were driven in part by policy. In 1667 the Cattle Act excluded Irish cattle, sheep, beef and pork from England. The country responded by exporting wool rather than sheep, and by searching for new markets for meat, notably the important provision trade, serving transatlantic ships and the West Indies, and the extensive French market. It also shifted resources from dry cattle to dairying, and butter exports grew rapidly. This process was speeded by the Woollen Acts, passed in 1699, which prohibited the export of wool from Ireland or England to other countries, and imposed a stiff duty on Irish wool entering England. More positively, the granting of duty-free access to England for linen helped that industry.

The significance of English laws for Irish economic growth is a matter of controversy. Writers in the nationalist vein have stressed the ways in which English law handicapped Irish growth, for instance by hampering the development of the woollen industry. However, Cullen has argued that the negative effects were minimal, as producers shifted rapidly and effectively into new lines of production.

The changes in the structure of production during the eighteenth century also occurred in response to an increase in the relative price of agricultural commodities, especially grain. Increasing urbanisation in Britain raised the demand for food, and Ireland was favoured as a source of supply during the Napoleonic wars. The most important effect of this improvement in Ireland's terms of trade (price of exports relative to imports) was to raise the incomes of farmers. Ireland continued to export grain until the late 1860s, when the falling costs of shipping, coupled with the opening up of the American mid-west, brought cheaper grain to Europe.

Agricultural structure was also influenced by the diffusion of the potato. An acre of potatoes could support twice as many people as an acre of grain. Moreover potato cultivation does not reduce soil fertility, and potatoes contain substantial amounts of protein and essential minerals. Cullen argues that as the eighteenth century progressed, cottiers increasingly ate potatoes instead of butter or oats, and sold these instead, using their earnings to buy other goods; thus the shift towards the potato is seen as 'related to commercialisation and the urge to increase cash incomes ... for luxuries'.

The expansion of potato cultivation contributed to the dramatic expansion of Ireland's population, from a little more than a million people in 1600 to over eight million by 1841. It was checked briefly by a severe famine in 1740–1, which was caused by a cold summer and led to as many as a quarter of a million deaths. But population growth accelerated after 1750: better nutrition reduced the death rate, and the availability of conacre may have contributed to a reduction in the marriage age. The population rose despite substantial emigration from the northeast, which began early in the eighteenth century, became self-sustaining, and may have been as high as 12,000 annually in the difficult years of the 1770s.

Industry

Industrial change was dominated by the rise of the linen industry, which Cullen calls 'perhaps the most remarkable instance in Europe of an export-based advance in the eighteenth century'. From a low base in the 1690s linen exports rose rapidly, accounting for a quarter of all exports by 1731. The first linen weavers were mainly skilled immigrants, especially Huguenots who fled France after 1685. Duty-free access to the English market helped, and in 1711 the Irish Parliament set up the Linen Board to regulate the industry, spread information, and subsidise projects. Based solidly in the rural areas, an elaborate network of merchants bought the raw linen and undertook the more capital-intensive activities of bleaching and finishing. By the early nineteenth century linen was increasingly spun and woven under the 'putting-out' system; cottiers would be provided with raw materials, and paid in cash for the amount they spun or wove.

Even as late as 1841 an astonishing one person in five stated their occupation as being in textiles, and most of these lived in rural areas. Fully a third of all counties reported in 1821 that more individuals were occupied in 'manufacture, trade and handicrafts' than in agriculture. It has been argued that this type of 'proto-industrialisation' is usually a prelude to full (i.e. factory-based) industrial-isation, fostering as it does entrepreneurial skills, monetisation of the economy, and commercial links. In the Irish case no such evolution occurred, although it is not clear why.

Other industries also expanded and modernised, notably those based on the processing of agricultural products, such as brewing, flour milling, and distilling. After 1800 the cotton industry flourished, albeit relatively briefly.

It is important to realise that the industrial revolution did in fact come to Ire-land, initially. The organisation of many industries was radically changed, with the establishment of breweries, textile factories, and glass works large enough to reap economies of scale. At first these factories were located where water power was available, but steam power was introduced early too. In the eighteenth cen-tury the road network was greatly improved and expanded, at first by private turnpikes and later by local government (the 'Grand Juries'). The first canals were built.

By 1785 Pitt and others saw Ireland as a viable competitor to English industry. But by 1800 this was not the view in Ireland, and it is ironic that the areas that most favoured union were Cork and the south, with their strong agricultural base; opposition was strongest in Dublin and the north.

Distribution of Income and Wealth
The benefits of economic growth in the late eighteenth century were not spread equally. The most evident rift was that between landowners and the large rural proletariat. Rents of a third of the gross output were probably normal. In 1687 Petty estimated rent payments at £1.2 million, of which £0.1 million was remitted to absentee landlords abroad. Rents thus came to approximately double the level of exports, or almost as much as a quarter of national income. It was this surplus, and tithes paid to the Church of Ireland, that financed the magnificent country houses, churches, Dublin squares, university buildings, paintings and follies that stand as monuments to the eighteenth century.

Most farmers were tenants of large landlords, and in turn rented land out to cottiers. Frequently such plots were confined to conacre (potato land), whose quality improved as they were planted in potatoes. Cottiers also performed work for the farmers to which they were attached. Labourers did not have even the security implied by access to a plot of land. The position of these groups did not improve in the 50 years prior to 1745. There then appears to have been a period of rising real wages, which probably stopped in the 1770s, and may never have resumed.

A second divide was between Catholic and Protestant. The Penal Laws placed restrictions on the right of Catholics to purchase land, to worship, to run schools, to vote, to take public office, to enter the professions, to take long leases, and to bequeath property. Barred from the professions and politics, able Catholics often turned their energies towards commerce, and the expansion of trade helped create a significant Catholic middle class. By 1800 the wealthiest Dubliner was Edward Byrne, a Catholic businessman. Presbyterians and Quakers, faced with similar restrictions, also turned to commerce and industry, with some success. Over time most of the restrictions were removed or fell into disuse, and by 1793 Catholics could vote and attend Trinity College, but could not stand for office or fill certain government positions. At times the friction boiled over, as reflected in the strong sectarian component of the insurrection of 1798.

The third divide was between town and country. Dublin grew to be the second town of the UK by 1800, with a population of about 200,000. Cork, basing its role on the profitable provision trade, had 80,000 inhabitants, or approximately the same population as a century later. Third came Limerick, with a population of 20,000; Belfast was still a minor town. That the country was able to support such a significant urban population, and to export increasing quantities of food, reflected a growing agricultural surplus and rising agricultural productivity.

3 FROM 1815 TO INDEPENDENCE

1815 to 1850

The period 1815 to 1850 was one of rural crisis, culminating in the disaster of the Famine. The crisis was reflected in rising emigration. This was also the period when Ireland most clearly failed to participate in the Industrial Revolution that was then in full spate in Britain.

The census of 1841 enumerated 8.2 million people in Ireland, a higher level than any measured before or since, and over half the level of Britain. Since 1750 the population had risen at an average rate of 1.3 per cent per year, which was well above the annual rates recorded in England (+1 per cent) or France (+0.4 per cent).

Yet by the 1830s the growth rate had fallen to 0.6 per cent, due almost entirely to massive emigration, mainly to North America; the Irish accounted for a third of the free transatlantic migration of the period. Without emigration, the pre-Famine population would have grown at a rapid 1.7 per cent per annum, due in part to a very high rate of marital fertility. Life expectancy at birth was 37–38 years, lower than in Britain or Scandinavia, but higher than in most of the rest of Europe.

Living Standards

On the eve of the Famine, Ireland was one of the poorest countries in Europe, as the comparative figures in Table 1.1 show. Per capita income was about 40 per cent of the British level, and contemporary visitors were particularly struck by the shabbiness of clothing and the poor state of rural houses.

Yet if the country was poor, it was also well fed, on grain, potatoes and dairy products. Peter Solar estimates that in the early 1840s potatoes and grain alone provided a substantial 2,500 calories per person for direct consumption,

Table 1.1 Real Product per Capita (UK=100)

	(1) 1830	(2) 1913	(3) 1950	(4) 1992	Population growth (%) 1919–92
UK	100	100	100	100	31[1]
Ireland (South)	40[2]	53[3]	51	73	13
Ireland (North)	–	58	68	–	27[5]
US	65	119	170	142	–
Denmark	61	80	99	112	57
Finland	51	47	66	96	60
Greece	39[4]	26	27	52	109
Italy	65	49	53	102	60
Portugal	68	22	23	61	54
EU-15	–	–	69	102	–

Sources: Adapted by author from: K. Kennedy, T. Giblin and D. McHugh, *The Economic Development of Ireland in the Twentieth Century,* Routledge, London 1988, pp.14–15; J. Lee, *Ireland 1912–1985,* Cambridge University Press, Cambridge 1989; and R. Summers and A. Heston, *Penn World Tables Version 5.1,* National Bureau of Economic Research, Cambridge MA 1995.
[1] GB only. [2] 1841, all Ireland. [3] 1926. [4] 1841. [5] 1984.

two-thirds of it from potatoes. Observers at the time generally thought that the Irish were healthy and strong; they grew taller than the typical Englishman or Belgian. Also compensating for low incomes was the wide availability of cheap fuel, in the form of peat.

Industry and Agriculture
It has become common to consider the 1815 to 1850 period as one of 'deindustrialisation', during which the importance of industry in the economy fell. This is only partly correct. For the island as a whole, industrial output appears to have increased. Large-scale and more efficient production methods were applied to milling, brewing, shipbuilding, rope-making and the manufacture of linen, iron, paper and glass; the road system was improved and reached a good standard; banks were organised along joint-stock lines. But rural industry declined. Thus, for instance, while Bandon boasted over 1,500 handloom weavers in 1829, the number had shrunk to 150 by 1839.

The first cause of rural deindustrialisation was that the woollen and cotton industries wilted in the face of competition from Britain. This prompted Karl Marx to write that, 'what the Irish need is ... protective tariffs against England'. On the other hand Ireland was not denuded of purchasing power or exports, for otherwise it could not have afforded to buy British textiles.

A second blow to rural industry was the invention of a method for mechanically spinning flax, which made hand-spinning redundant. It also led to a

9

concentration of the linen industry in the north-east. The weaving of linen was still done by hand, and was boosted by the development. In 1841 Armagh was the most densely populated county in Ireland, testimony to the importance of cottage-based textiles as a source of income.

Despite the rapid fall in prices after 1815, agricultural exports continued to rise, notably livestock and butter and, most dramatically, grain and flour. By the 1830s Ireland exported enough grain to feed about two million people annually, testimony to the dynamism of the agricultural sector, which increasingly used new technologies such as improved seeds, crop rotations, better ploughs, and carts.

The Famine

The most traumatic event of the period was the Famine. After a wet summer, potato blight arrived in September 1845 and spread over almost half the country, especially the east. Famine was largely avoided at first, thanks largely to adequate government relief. But the potato crop failed completely in 1846, and by December about half a million people were working on relief works, at which stage they were ended. The winter was harsh. By August 1847 an estimated three million people were being supported by soup kitchens, including almost three-quarters of the population of some western counties. The 1847 harvest was not severely harmed, but it was small because of a lack of seed. The blight returned in 1848, and in 1849 over 900,000 people were in the workhouses at some time or another. After 1847 the responsibility for supporting the poor had increasingly been shifted from the government to the local landowners who, by and large, did not have sufficient resources to cope. Noting that a few years later Britain spent £69 million on the (futile) Crimean war, Mokyr argues that for half this sum 'there is no doubt that Britain could have saved Ireland'. It is also unlikely that an independent Ireland, with a GNP of £85 million, could have done so without outside support.

As a direct result of the Famine about one million people died, representing an excess mortality of about 3 per cent per annum during the famine years (and 4 per cent in the north-western counties). Ireland was not the only country hit by the potato blight – excess mortality was comparable in the Scottish Highlands, and the excess mortality rates were 2 per cent in the Netherlands and 1 per cent in Belgium – but given its high dependence on the potato, Ireland was especially vulnerable, particularly its poorer and remoter districts. Three-fifths of those who died were young (under 10) or old (over 60), and labourers and small farmers were hit most severely. These unequal effects have led Cullen to argue, controversially, that 'the Famine was less a national disaster than a social and regional one'.

In the course of the Famine, the output of potatoes fell by about three-quarters, the use of potatoes for animal fodder ceased, and food imports rose very rapidly. As a result the amount of calories available for direct consumption barely fell, on a per capita basis. This gives credence to Amartya Sen's contention that famines are rarely caused by an absolute lack of food, but rather by a change in the food entitlements of major groups in society. So, for instance, labourers were unable to find employment when blight reduced the need for harvesting and planting potatoes; without income they could not buy food, and so became destitute.

Distribution
Pre-Famine Ireland probably had a 'very unequal distribution of income by West European standards'. According to the 1841 census, 63 per cent of the population had access to less than five acres of land, or were 'without capital, in either money, land or acquired knowledge'. Just 3 per cent were professionals and rentiers, and included the approximately 10,000 proprietors, or 0.12 per cent of the population, who owned at least 100 acres.

Rent, including payments in kind, accounted for about £15 million, or almost a fifth of the national income of £80 million. Presumably the bulk of this rent accrued to the wealthiest 3 per cent or so of the population, implying a very great degree of income inequality. Rough calculations suggest that this group probably had per capita incomes averaging over £100 per annum, compared to a national average of £10, and an estimated £4 for poor households.

By 1845 a rudimentary welfare structure was in place, with the completion of 130 workhouses having a total capacity of 100,000. In practice the numbers living in the workhouses rarely exceeded 40,000, except during the Famine.

There is no shortage of hypotheses as to why Ireland remained poor, and hence uniquely vulnerable by European standards to the chance failure of the potato crop. Thomas Malthus, writing in 1817, considered that population growth was running ahead of food production; however, the more densely-settled countries were not necessarily the poorest ones. Other writers blamed the insecurity of tenancy for low agricultural investment, although it is not clear how insecure tenancies really were. Some have pointed to agrarian violence, or the lack of coal deposits, or inadequate financial capital, or insufficient human resources (especially entrepreneurs), as barriers to economic development. None of these explanations is waterproof, and Ó Gráda wrote recently that 'exactly why comparative advantage dictated industrial decline for Ireland is still unclear'.

Fewer but Richer: 1850 to 1921
The 70 years following the famine witnessed enormous changes in Irish society and saw the emergence of the modern economy. Over this period per capita incomes more than doubled, and came closer to the British level, while the population fell by a third. A rural middle class emerged, replacing the landlords and squeezing out the rural labourers. Within agriculture, tillage declined, and the production of dry cattle increased. The north-east became industrialised.

The dominant demographic fact of the period is that population declined, from 6.6 million in 1851 to 4.2 million by 1926. Without emigration the population would have risen, by about 1 per cent annually in the 1860s, and by 0.5 per cent annually at the turn of the century, a decline largely explained by a falling marriage rate. Almost 2 per cent of the population left annually in the 1850s; the pace slowed markedly to less than 1 per cent after 1900. The early emigrants were drawn from all areas of the country, but in later years the bulk of the emigrants came from the poorer, mainly western, districts. Over the period 1820 to 1945 an estimated 4.5 million Irish emigrated to the USA, comparable in magnitude to the flows from Italy, Austria and Britain.

Living Standards

Astonishingly, between 1840 and 1913 per capita incomes in Ireland rose at 1.6 per cent per year, faster than any other country in Europe. Where Irish incomes averaged 40 per cent of the British level in 1840, this proportion had risen to 60 per cent by 1913. During this period Irish incomes came from behind, and then easily surpassed, those of Finland, Italy and Portugal.

Part of the explanation is statistical. The Famine, and subsequent high levels of emigration, removed a disproportionate number of the very poor; even if those who remained experienced no increase in their incomes, average income would have been higher than before. The poor were more likely to leave because the gap between Irish and foreign wages was greatest for unskilled labour. In 1844 the wages paid to a skilled builder in Dublin were 14 per cent *higher* than in London, but the wages paid to an unskilled building labourer were 36 per cent lower. A comparable gap persisted until at least World War I.

Incomes also rose because of dramatic increases in output per worker. The north-east became highly industrialised; in the rest of the country agricultural productivity rose rapidly. Almost all of the expansion of the modern industrial sector was in the north-east. While linen output increased slowly, it was increasingly concentrated in factories in Belfast and the Lagan valley: between 1850 and 1875 employment in linen mills and factories rose from 21,000 to 60,000 as power weaving replaced the cottage industry.

The manufacture of boilers and textile equipment needed in the mills helped diversify the industrial base, and provided the skills and infrastructure that were important for the growth of shipbuilding. Harland and Wolff, the celebrated firm that built the Titanic, grew from 500 workers in 1861 to 9,000 by 1900. The shipbuilding industry also provided an impetus for other upstream activities, including rope making, paint, and engineering.

Benefiting from 'external economies of foreign trade' – regular trade links with markets and suppliers, and a financial system geared towards supporting such links – Belfast rivalled Dublin in size by 1901, when it had about 400,000 inhabitants. Londonderry became the centre of an important shirt making industry, employing 18,000 full time workers and a further 80,000 cottage workers at its height in 1902.

By 1907, industrial activity in Ireland as a whole employed a fifth of the work force, making the country at least as industrialised as Italy, Spain or Portugal. Half of all industrial output was exported, Ireland had a worldwide reputation in linen, shipbuilding, distilling, brewing and biscuits, and the volume of trade per capita was higher than for Britain.

It is sometimes wondered why Ireland did not become even more industrialised, more like Clydeside than East Anglia. And related to this question, why did the north-east industrialise while by and large the rest of the country did not? Put another way, why did Irish labour emigrate, rather than capital immigrate?

There was no lack of capital, and indeed from the 1880s on Irish residents were net lenders of capital to the rest of the world, investing in British government stock, railways, and other ventures overseas. The banks may have been cautious at lending, but in this they were no different from their counterparts in England, where industrial development was rapid. Nor is there evidence that skills were lacking. The primary school system expanded rapidly, enrolling 282,000 pupils in state-subsidised schools in 1841, and 1,072,000 by 1887. Whereas 53 per cent of the population was illiterate in 1841, this fraction had fallen to 25 per cent by 1881 and 16 per cent by 1901. Enterprise may have been lacking, although clearly not in the Lagan valley. The absence of coal probably had some effect, not because this raised costs of production unduly, but because coal itself was a big business; in 1914 a quarter of the British labour force was directly employed in coal or iron and steel. Ireland was next door to, and had free access to, the world's most affluent market.

Perhaps the explanation rests largely on chance, the idea that once Belfast grew as an industrial centre, accumulating skills, capital and infrastructure, then it became an increasingly attractive location for further investment – an argument that might also be made about the unanticipated growth spurt of the 1990s.

Agriculture

Between 1861 and 1909 gross agricultural output rose by a quarter; since the rural population fell sharply, output per capita in agriculture more than doubled, a solid performance, but less impressive than that of Denmark, where output per male agricultural worker almost quadrupled over the same period.

This growth masks an important change in the structure of agriculture, which shifted from crops to cattle in response to a fall in the price of grain relative to cattle. Tillage, including potatoes, shrunk by two-thirds between 1845 and 1913. Farmers were not, as is sometimes supposed, slow to change or innovate. For instance, when circumstances demanded it they adopted the creamery system rapidly. And exports of eggs – traditionally a source of revenue for farmers' wives – were almost as valuable as cattle: by 1920, after improvements in the varieties of hens, Ireland had become the world's largest exporter of eggs. Faced with changing prices and technology, wrote Hans Stahl, 'the response of the Irish agriculturalist … was rational and normal'.

Distribution

Between 1870 and 1925 the landed proprietors 'surrendered their power and property', to an increasingly 'comfortable, educated, self-confident rural bourgeoisie', thereby effecting one of the most extensive land reforms in history, although it should be noted that a similar land transfer occurred a century earlier in Denmark, and half a century later in Finland, so the Irish case was by no means unique.

As late as 1870, 97 per cent of all land was owned by landlords who rented it out to others to farm. Just 750 families owned 50 per cent of the land in the country. About one landlord in seven lived outside Ireland, and another third lived outside their estates; the remaining half were not absentees. Two-fifths of all landlords were Catholic.

The agricultural crisis of the late 1870s meant lower agricultural prices and this, coupled with fixed rents, squeezed tenant farmers. By now they felt confident enough to agitate for the 'three Fs' – fair rent, fixity of tenure, and free sale of 'tenant right'. Michael Davitt's Land League forged a link with Parnell and the Irish party in parliament. Their efforts resulted in the Land Act of 1881, which established land courts to hear rent appeals. The courts reduced rents by an average of about 20 per cent, and later courts reduced rents by about another 20 per cent after 1887. In a formal sense this diluted the power of the landlord – Moody refers to it as 'dual ownership' – although it is noteworthy that during the same period real rents fell by comparable amounts in England.

Further efforts prompted legislation that provided tenants with government loans with which to purchase their land, including the Ashbourne Act of 1885, and the Wyndham Act of 1903, and paid 12 per cent bonuses to landlords who sold their entire estates. The result was that 'by 1917 almost two-thirds of the tenants had acquired their holdings'.

With rural depopulation, land holdings increased in size. The number of cottiers working less than five acres fell from 300,000 in 1845 to 62,000 by 1910. The same period saw the 'virtual disappearance of the hired labourer from Irish agriculture', as the number of 'farm servants and labourers' fell from 1.3 million in 1841 to 0.3 million in 1911.

The distribution of income can be considered in other dimensions too. Thus, for instance, Protestants maintained their share of national income. This largely reflected the growth of the industrial north-east, which was dominated by Protestant interests, and the fact that Catholics were more likely to emigrate (and more died in the Famine). Catholics did come to fill an increasing proportion of government and professional jobs, although not in proportion to their numbers. The Catholic Church itself grew rapidly, with a spate of church building between 1860 and 1900, and church going became much more common. The number of Catholic priests, nuns and other religious rose from almost 5,000 in 1850 to over 14,000 by 1900, making it one of the fastest growing professions during this period.

The small towns stagnated, and so did Dublin until late in the century. Kevin O'Rourke contrasts the dynamism of Danish agriculture after 1880 with the slow development of Irish agricultural production, particularly dairying, and suggests that the violence associated with Irish land reform, the diversion of talent from the business of farming to the politics of redistribution, and a deficit of community trust in Catholic parts of Ireland, help explain the difference. In contrast to the rest of the country Belfast grew rapidly. The zenith of its prosperity came during and immediately after World War I, with a boom in shipbuilding and engineering; as David Johnson put it, 'in economic terms the last years of the Union were the best ones'.

4 FROM INDEPENDENCE TO 1960

When it finally achieved independence, the Irish Free State could count some important assets. It had an extensive system of communications, a developed banking system, a vigorous wholesale and retail network, an efficient and honest administration, universal literacy, a large stock of houses, schools and hospitals, 3.1 million people, and enormous external assets. By the standards of most of the world's countries Ireland was well off indeed.

On the other hand the new state faced some serious problems. It had to establish a new government, the civil war had been destructive and had helped prompt 88,000 people to emigrate in 1921–22, the dependency ratio was high – Catholics marrying before 1916 had an average of 6.0 children per family – and the post-war boom had run its course. We now document its subsequent achievements, and evaluate its early performance as an independent country.

1921 to 1932: Agriculture First
The growth model pursued by the Cumann na nGaedheal government was based on the premise that what was good for agriculture was good for the country. Patrick Hogan, the Minister for Agriculture, saw the policy as one of 'helping the farmer who helped himself and letting the rest go to the devil'. This emphasis on agriculture was not surprising. In 1926 agriculture generated 32 per cent of GDP and provided 54 per cent of all employment. The government relied heavily on the support of the larger farmers. The expectation was that not only would agricultural growth raise the demand for goods and services from the rest of the economy, but would also provide more inputs on which to base a more substantial processing sector. The three major industrial exporting sectors at the time – brewing, distilling, and biscuit making – were all closely linked with agriculture.

The essential elements of the policy, which has come to be known as the 'treasury view', were free trade, low taxes and government spending, modest direct state intervention in industry and agriculture, and parity with sterling. Free trade was seen as essential if the cost of farm inputs was to be kept low.

The support for free trade was perhaps surprising given that Griffith had argued that one of the main benefits of independence would be that the country could grant protection to infant industries. On the other hand the government was cautious about making such changes, perhaps for fear of upsetting the financial community, whose opposition to protection was well known, or perhaps because they were, in the words of Kevin O'Higgins, 'the most conservative revolutionaries in history'. The government sought to deflect pressure for stiffer protection by establishing the Tariff Commission in 1926, and appointing members who were, in the main, in favour of free trade. The onus of proof was on any industry wishing to be protected, and the Commission moved slowly on requests, granting few tariffs other than on rosary beads and margarine.

Government spending was kept low, the budget was essentially balanced, and revenues came to just 15 per cent of GNP in 1931. This was a remarkable achievement, given that military spending had trebled during the civil war. One serious consequence was that welfare spending remained low, and in the absence of major government assistance, housing for the less well-off remained scarce.

Ideologically the government did not favour taking a very active role in promoting economic development. Despite this it intervened pragmatically in several ways. The Department of Agriculture was greatly expanded, although the impact of this on agricultural output has been questioned. The Congested Districts Board was replaced by the Land Commission, which transferred 3.6 million acres, involving 117,000 holdings, to annuity-paying freeholders during the period 1923 to 1937. Laws were passed to improve the quality of agricultural output, by regulating the marketing of dairy produce (1924) and improving the quality of livestock breeding by registering bulls (1925). The Agricultural Credit Corporation (ACC) was set up to provide credit to farmers. The government subsidised a Belgian company to establish a sugar factory in Carlow, and provided incentives to grow sugar beet.

A major innovation was the establishment of the Electricity Supply Board (ESB) in 1927. This, along with the ACC, represented the first of the state-sponsored bodies (SSBs) that were established during the ensuing years. The ESB successfully undertook the Ardnacrusha hydroelectric scheme – when it came on line in 1927 it was the largest hydroelectric plant in the world, and by 1935 it provided 80 per cent of the country's electricity. The completion of the project, boosted the country's prestige, and was the most visible accomplishment of the first decade of independence.

In due course state-sponsored bodies were set up in many fields, including air, train and bus transport, industrial credit, insurance, peat development, trade pro-motion, and industrial development. By the early 1960s, when the most impor-tant of these bodies had been established, they employed about 50,000 people, representing about 7 per cent of the total labour force. The SSBs were not the outgrowth of any particular ideology, but were rather 'individual responses to specific situations'. This, along with their ability to attract good managers, may help explain why they are generally considered to have been successful agents of economic development, especially in the first few decades after independence, when the private sector did not appear to be very enterprising.

Parity with sterling was the final ingredient in the development model pur-sued. Few countries at the time had floating exchange rates, and it seemed logical to peg the pound to sterling since 97 per cent of exports went to, and 76 per cent of imports came from, Britain. The Currency Act of 1927 established an Irish currency, fully backed by British sterling securities; until 1961 Irish banknotes were inscribed 'payable in London'. By linking the currency with sterling, the Free State gave up the possibility of any independent monetary policy, in return for greater predictability in trade with Britain and lower transaction costs.

The economic policy of the Free State in the 1920s was similar to the typical prescription given by the World Bank to less-developed countries in the 1980s: get the prices right, using world prices as a guide, reduce budget deficits, keep government 'interference' to a minimum, and follow a conservative monetary policy. Did it work?

The simple answer is 'in the circumstances, yes in most respects, eventually'. The young nation got off to a rocky start. Between 1920 and 1924 agricultural prices fell 44 per cent; the civil war, which only ended in 1923, arrested investment; after independence, a significant proportion of the skilled labour force left; and the recession in the UK after sterling's return to the gold standard in 1925 reduced the demand for Irish exports. However, between 1926 and 1931 real per capita GNP rose about 3 per cent per annum; exports rose 20 per cent, reaching a peak of 35 per cent of GNP in 1929, and a volume that was not exceeded until 1960. Industrial employment rose by 8 per cent.

1932 to 1939: Self-sufficiency, Economic War and Depression
Fianna Fáil came to power in early 1932, with an economic policy that differed in two fundamental ways from its predecessor; it was ideologically committed to a policy of greater economic self-sufficiency, and it reneged on paying land annuities to Britain. It also came to power during the darkest hour of the Depression, a time when most countries were erecting tariff barriers.

Why self-sufficiency? The case for limiting economic interactions with the rest of the world is more cultural than economic, but it attracted some intellectual support. John Maynard Keynes, lecturing at UCD in April 1933, said, 'I sympathize with those who would minimize ... economic entanglement between nations. ... But let goods be homespun whenever it is reasonable and conveniently possible'. Perhaps these oft-quoted remarks are out of context, for he went on to argue that only 'a very modest measure of self-sufficiency' would be feasible without 'a disastrous reduction in a standard of life which is already none too high'.

How self-sufficiency? The main instrument used was more and higher tariffs, which rose to a maximum of 45 per cent in 1936, dipping to 35 per cent by 1938. In Europe only Germany and Spain had higher levels by then; Irish tariffs were twice as high as in the US, and 50 per cent higher than in the UK. They were introduced piecemeal and so formed an untidy pattern that, in FitzGerald's view, had 'no rational basis'; Meenan considers that they fell more heavily on finished goods, and so provided an incentive for domestic assembly using imported raw materials. The pursuit of self-sufficiency would justify indefinite tariff protection; in this it differs from the views of Griffith, who saw a role for temporary protection to encourage infant industries to take root.

Self-sufficiency was also pursued by introducing price supports for wheat, which was instrumental in raising the acreage planted to wheat from 8,000 hectares in 1931 to 103,000 by 1936. Somewhat inconsistently, bounties were paid for exports of cattle, butter, bacon and other agricultural products in order to expand the volume of exports, and this resulted in a significant rise in the share of government spending in national income. To foster Irish involvement in industry the Control of Manufactures Act (1932) required majority Irish ownership, although in practice exceptions were usually granted upon request. The Industrial

Credit Corporation was set up to lend to industry, and issued £6.5 million in its first four years of operation.

It is difficult to assess the effect of the policy of self-sufficiency because it became inextricably tangled with the effects of the economic war. Previous Irish governments had recognised an obligation to pay land annuities to Britain, to cover the cost of money lent under the various pre-independence land acts. These came to about £5 million annually, or about one-fifth of government spending and almost 4 per cent of GNP.

On coming to office in March 1932, de Valera refused to continue the annuities. In July Britain retaliated by imposing special duties, initially at 20 per cent and later at 40 per cent, on imports of livestock, dairy products and meat, and also imposed quotas, including halving the number of cattle permitted to enter the UK. The Free State countered with tariffs on British goods, including cement and coal – surprising choices for a country bent on industrialisation. After these escalations tempers cooled.

Under the Cattle-Coal pacts Irish cattle had easier access to Britain, and Ireland agreed to buy British coal. Initially approved for 1935, the pact was extended and renewed in 1936 and 1937, and the Anglo-Irish Trade Agreement ended the 'war', with Ireland agreeing to pay a lump sum of £10 million and Britain ceding control of the 'treaty ports'. Given that the capitalised value of the annuities was close to £100 million, this was considered to be a major diplomatic and economic victory for de Valera.

The combined effects of protection and the economic war were initially dramatic. Industrial output rose 40 per cent between 1931 and 1936. Population stabilised, standing at 2.93 million in 1931 and 2.94 million in 1938 – the first period since the Famine when there had not been a substantial decline – but the amount of unemployment soared, almost quintupling between 1931 and 1934 to about 14 per cent of the labour force by 1935. In large part this reflected reduced opportunities to emigrate to the United States. Despite rapid industrial growth, agriculture stagnated, as exports fell sharply. Where exports and imports together amounted to 75 per cent of GNP in 1926, they constituted 54 per cent in 1938, although this decline pales beside the two-third reduction in trade that the US faced in the early 1930s. The existing manufacturing export industries also suffered some decline. By 1936 import-substituting industrialisation had run its course, and industrial output only rose a further 4.5 per cent between 1936 and 1938. It is widely accepted that the slow growth of the economy in the 1950s was largely because of the inefficiency of the industrial sector that developed during the 1930s.

One other event of this period merits a brief discussion. With the onset of the Depression, Britain erected tariffs on a wide range of items, including beer. This prompted Guinness to establish a brewery at Park Lane near London. Beer had been Ireland's single most important industrial export, and brewing had accounted for 30 per cent of manufacturing value added in 1926. Once the Park Lane brewery was established, there was little incentive to return to the earlier pattern of concentrating Guinness's production in Dublin. In this case British tariffs led to the establishment of an efficient new factory in England, at the expense of Ireland. It is possible that some Irish tariffs did the same in the other direction, although with a smaller internal market it is less likely to have been common. Using tariffs to promote investment and industry in this way has come under increasing scrutiny by economists in recent years, under the rubric of strategic trade policy.

Historical Debate: Was the Drive for Self-sufficiency a Mistake?
Joseph Johnston, writing in 1951, argued that but for the economic war 'our real National Income might well have been 25 per cent more in 1939 than it actually was and 25 per cent more today than it actually is. ... The process of cutting off one's nose to spite one's face is sometimes good politics, but always bad economics'. He might have noted that between 1931 and 1938 Irish GNP rose about 10 per cent, compared to 18 per cent in less-protectionist Britain. He might also have questioned how many industrial jobs were really created, noting that while the 1936 census enumerated 199,000 individuals 'involved in industrial occupations', this was only 11,000 higher than the number enumerated in 1926.

Johnston's estimate of a 25 per cent decline has been sharply questioned. Recent research, which tries to recreate what might plausibly have happened in the absence of tariffs, by constructing a computable general equilibrium counterfactual, suggests that the total cost of protection might have been 5 per cent of GNP per year, or £7–8 million annually during the late 1930s, of which perhaps two-thirds is attributable to the economic war. Against this, Ireland gained the treaty ports and received a £90 million write-off on its foreign debt. The expansion of the industrial sector may have provided experience in business management, which was valuable in later years.

Having built high tariff barriers, Ireland was slow to reduce them later, and the average rate of effective protection of manufacturing was still an exceptionally high 80 per cent in 1966. If some of the economic sluggishness of the 1950s was the result, then the protection of the 1930s may appear more damaging; perhaps had Johnston been writing in 1960 he would have been closer to the truth. One may also wonder whether a policy of more selective protection, perhaps along the lines favoured by Taiwan or South Korea, might not have proven more valuable.

1939 to 1950: The War and Rebound
The most important economic result of World War II was that it opened a wide gap between Northern Ireland and the Republic. Between 1938 and 1947 national income grew just 14 per cent, compared to 47 per cent in the UK and 84 per cent in Northern Ireland. Where incomes, north and south, were broadly comparable before the war, by 1947 incomes per head in the Republic had fallen to about 40 per cent of the British level, while in the north they had risen to close to 70 per cent. Why did the south perform so poorly?

Between 1938 and 1943 the volume of exports fell by a half, and imports fell even more. During this period industrial output fell 27 per cent, and industrial employment dropped from 167,000 to 144,000. The main reason was the scarcity of raw material inputs for industry, and the shortage of shipping capacity. Completely reliant on outside shippers until 1941, the government founded Irish Shipping, and moved rapidly to purchase ships, which soon proved their worth. Because of the difficulty of obtaining imports, the country built up significant foreign reserves, and by 1946 residents had external assets totalling £260 million, approximately equivalent to GNP in that year.

The total value of agricultural output fell during the war period, but net agricultural output, (i.e. total output less the cost of non-labour inputs), rose, by 17 per cent between 1938–39 and 1945. This reflected the drastic fall in the use of fertiliser and other inputs, and is generally acknowledged to have exhausted the soil significantly. The structure of agriculture changed, as the area planted in grain and potatoes almost doubled, due in part to the introduction of compulsory tillage.

During the war real GNP fell, especially initially. Living standards fell further as households, unable to find the goods they wanted, were obliged to save more. The stock of capital in industry became run-down. With emigration to the US blocked, population rose, by 18,000 between 1938 and 1946. The unemployment rate stood at over 15 per cent in 1939 and 1940, but declined thereafter to a little over 10 per cent in 1945. The decrease was due to a sharp rise in migration to Britain, reaching near record levels in 1942, as people left to work in factories and enrol in the armed forces.

The war was followed by a rebound, and per capita real GDP rose by 4.1 per cent per annum between 1944 and 1950. This occurred despite the fact that agricultural output stagnated, with gross volume falling between 1945 and 1950, and net output shrinking by 5 per cent. Not surprisingly, 70,000 people left agriculture between 1946 and 1951; yet during this period the unemployment rate fell and population increased. Much of this is attributable to the expansion of industrial production, which more than doubled during the same period.

Government spending rose rapidly in the early war years as the army was increased from 7,500 to 38,000 men. After the war, government spending grew far faster than national income, increasing its share of GNP from 23 per cent in 1945 to 39 per cent by 1951. In large measure this increase occurred as Ireland sought to emulate the 'social investment' of the Labour Party in Britain, by expanding welfare spending.

1950 to 1958: Decline or Rebirth?

It had become standard to consider the 1950s as a period of stagnation and failure. This is a half-truth. Between 1951 and 1958 GDP rose by less than 1 per cent per year. Employment fell by 12 per cent, and the unemployment rate rose. Irish GDP/capita fell from 75 per cent to 60 per cent of the EU average. Half a million people emigrated. Yet between 1950 and 1960 real product per capita grew at 2.2 per cent per year, possibly the fastest rate recorded up to then, and industrial output expanded at 2.8 per cent per annum. Output per farmer grew at a respectable 3.4 per cent per year. Rural electrification spread, and the housing stock improved appreciably. Was the glass half full or half empty?

The key to understanding the 1950s is to note that this was the decade when Europe rebounded; Ireland's performance looks disappointing only by the standards of neighbouring countries, not by historical standards. Much of the emigration reflected the lure of improving wages elsewhere, notably in Britain.

Why did output not grow faster in the 1950s? FitzGerald believes that the key problem was a 'failure to reorientate industry to export markets', considering that 'the naïveté of the philosophy that underlay the whole protection policy was not exposed until the process of introducing protection had come to an end'. By the 1950s Irish industry was supplying as much of the domestic market as it reasonably could, and in order to expand had no option but to seek markets overseas. But since much of the industrial sector could only survive because of protection, it was too inefficient to export successfully, although it was certainly strong enough to lobby against any liberalisation.

To help provide incentives to industries to switch to exporting, export profits tax relief was provided in 1956, and in 1958 the Industrial Development Authority (IDA), which had been set up in 1949, was granted more powers to provide tax holidays for export-oriented companies. The Shannon Free Airport Development Company was set up in 1959.

One might better view the 1950s as a period of transition rather than one of failure, much as it was in Taiwan and South Korea. It has been argued that the economy was in fact in the process of re-orientating itself towards export markets, but that any such change was bound to be slow. As J.J. McElligott put it in the 1920s, when warning of the dangers of protection, 'to revert to free trade from a protectionist regime is almost an economic impossibility'. Exports of manufactured goods rose quite rapidly, accounting for 6 per cent of all exports in 1950 but 17 per cent by 1960. Dramatic as this change was, the increase was from a very low base, and the export sector simply was not large enough to be a potent engine of growth.

An entirely different explanation comes from Kennedy and Dowling, who state baldly that 'the chief factor seems to us to be the failure to secure a satisfactory rate of expansion in aggregate demand', most notably unduly restrictive (in their view) fiscal policy in response to the balance of payment crises of 1951 and 1955. This argument provides an intellectual underpinning for the highly expansionary, and ultimately disastrous, fiscal policy experiment of the late 1970s and early 1980s.

Whatever the causes, the poor overall economic performance created a feeling of pessimism, and this in turn probably deterred investors. As T.K. Whitaker, then secretary of the Department of Finance, put it, 'the mood of despondency was palpable'. In 1958, at the request of the government, he wrote the report *Economic Development*, best remembered now for the optimistic note that it struck in pessimistic times. The report proposed that tariffs should be dismantled unless a clear infant industry case existed, favoured incentives to stimulate private industrial investment, and proposed expanded spending on agriculture. On the other hand it warned against the dampening effects of high taxes. With such measures, it suggested, GNP could grow 2 per cent annually, although it stressed that this was not a firm target. These measures were incorporated in the First Programme for Economic Expansion which appeared in November 1958, but generally not implemented.

Economic growth during the period of the first plan exceeded anyone's wildest expectations, reaching 4 per cent per annum instead of the anticipated 2 per cent. At the time much of this increase was attributed directly to the impact of the First Programme, and support for such indicative planning increased. The Second Programme, introduced in 1963 and designed to run to 1970, was far more detailed and ambitious, forecasting an annual increase in GNP of 4 per cent per annum; industry was to expand 50 per cent and exports 75 per cent during the plan period. When it appeared that these targets would not quite be met, the Second Programme was allowed to lapse. A Third Programme was produced, but quickly sank into oblivion, along with most of the enthusiasm for indicative planning.

5 SINCE 1960

Between 1960 and 2014, Ireland's real GDP grew at an annual rate of 4.4 per cent. This sustained effort increased output tenfold, and saw Ireland catch up economically with even the richest countries of Western Europe. Over the same period the population rose from 2.8 million to 4.6 million, propelled both by a high natural rate of increase, and net in-migration of over half a million between 1995 and 2009.

The experience of economic growth over this half century is summarised in Figure 1.1, where the dark horizontal line indicates the average growth rate. One is struck by the variability in the GDP growth rate from one year to the next, and by the rarity of recession. Although real GDP fell slightly in 1983 and 1986, there was no modern precedent for the sharp recession of 2008–09. After those lean years there is now a robust recovery.

There is more to be said about the pattern shown in Figure 1.1, which we now discuss in more manageable chronological pieces.

1960 to 1979: From Protection to Free Trade
Between 1960 and 1979 real output increased at 4.4 per cent per annum, the highest rate sustained until then. In-migration exceeded out-migration, contributing to population growth. Per capita incomes rose by 125 per cent, kept up with income growth elsewhere in Europe, and significantly outpaced growth in Britain or Northern Ireland.

This first wave of substantial economic growth has been largely attributed to the strategy of export-led growth that the government, heeding the recommendations of *Economic Development*, pursued; less publicised, but important nonetheless, were a notable improvement in the terms of trade (39 per cent better in 1973 than in 1957), expansionary fiscal policy, the boom in the nearby European economy, and the fact that solid institutional foundations had been laid in the 1950s.

Figure 1.1 Irish GDP growth, 1960–2014

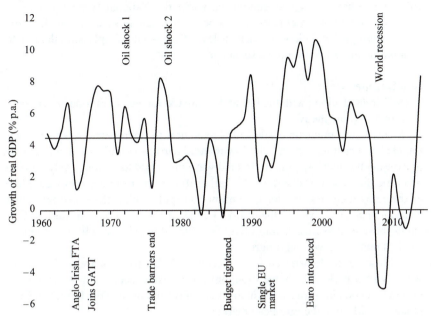

Source: Constructed with World Bank data from: *World Development Indicators,* http://databank.worldbank.org/data/reports.aspx?source=world-development-indicators [accessed February 2017].

The policy of export-led growth stood on two legs – trade liberalisation, and the attraction of foreign direct investment. Trade liberalisation called for reducing tariffs; these, by making inputs dearer and by drawing resources away from other sectors of the economy had worked to inhibit exports. Foreign investment, it was hoped, would bring new skills to the country, and help raise the overall investment, and hence growth, rate.

Trade liberalisation was begun in the 1960s as Ireland unilaterally cut tariffs in 1963 and 1964, negotiated the Anglo-Irish Free Trade Area Agreement in 1965, and subscribed to the General Agreement on Tariffs and Trade (GATT) in 1967. These moves also prepared for eventual membership of the European Economic Community.

With a panoply of tax breaks and subsidies, Ireland successfully, although at considerable expense, induced foreign companies to set up branches in Ireland, and by 1974 new industry accounted for over 60 per cent of industrial output. The 10 per cent tax on profits in manufacturing also made the country something of a tax haven, although it did require at least a fig leaf of manufacturing presence.

The final thrust of government policy was wage restraint, viewed as necessary, especially with a fixed exchange rate, to help keep industrial costs at a competitive level. In the 1960s government efforts amounted to exhortation, while in the 1970s wage bargaining was centralised under the National Wage Agreements. Given the option of emigration, the scope for manoeuvre here was small. If real wages were pushed below the British level they would simply stimulate faster emigration, and so could not be sustained.

Into Europe
In 1973 Ireland, along with the UK and Denmark, joined the European Economic Community (now the EU).

Membership immediately led to a reduction in trade barriers. The EU was founded as a customs union, with low internal barriers to trade and a common set of external barriers. By joining, Ireland was committed to trading freely with the other member countries, and by 1977 all tariff barriers had been removed. Many of the remaining, less obvious, restraints on trade within the European Union were dismantled as part of the effort to create a Single European Market. Officially these changes came into effect in 1992, although the full elimination of barriers remains a work in progress.

With lower trade barriers, it was recognised that some of Ireland's industry would wither under the competition, but it was also expected that Ireland would become a good platform from which companies from outside the European Community could serve the European market.

These expectations were met. While Irish exports amounted to 34 per cent of GDP in 1963, and 38 per cent in 1973, the proportion had risen to 94 per cent by 2002, one of the highest in the world. This burst of exports paralleled a similar increase in intra-EU trade that took place in the 1960s, and shows how even small reductions in the cost of trading can have a large impact on the volume of trade.

Membership of the EU also led to a net inflow under the Common Agricultural Policy (CAP), which subsidises farm prices. Higher farm prices help farmers at the expense of consumers, but as a net exporter of farm produce, Ireland was on balance a beneficiary.

Although the bulk of EU transfers to Ireland are farm-related, part consist of transfers from the 'structural funds,' including the Regional Development, Social, and Cohesion funds. In principle these funds might have added to investment and thereby boosted economic growth, but in practice they mainly appeared to have substituted for projects that the government would otherwise have had to finance; they thus made a more important contribution to living standards than to growth. Since 1973, gross receipts from the EU have exceeded €50 billion; net receipts peaked at 6.5 per cent of GDP in 1991, but by 2014 Ireland had become a net contributor to the EU budget, receiving €1.52 billion (of which 80 per cent went to farmers) and paying €1.69 billion.

1979 to 1986: Growth Interrupted
Between 1979 and 1986, per capita consumption in Ireland actually fell slightly and GDP rose very slowly. What went wrong?

Membership of the EU coincided with a fourfold increase in the price of oil (from \$3 to \$12 per barrel) that resulted from the first oil shock in late 1973; a sharp worldwide recession followed.

The government's response was thoroughly Keynesian. The higher price of oil meant that spending was diverted towards imports, thereby depressing aggregate demand for Irish goods and services. The solution adopted was to boost government current spending, and as a consequence the current budget deficit rose from 0.4 per cent of GDP in 1973 to 6.8 per cent by 1975. For a while the policy worked: despite a difficult international situation, GDP growth during the first six years of EU membership was robust.

Then came the mistake, the source of the failure of the fiscal experiment: successive governments were unwilling to reduce the budget deficit, and continued to borrow heavily, so the ratio of government debt to GDP rose from 52 per cent in 1973 to 129 per cent by 1987, by then easily the highest in the European Union. By 1986 the cost of servicing this debt took up 94 per cent of all revenue from the personal income tax. Although efforts were made to solve the problem by raising tax rates, especially in 1981 and 1983, these changes hardly increased tax revenue, suggesting that the country was close to its revenue maximising tax rates: the marginal tax rate on someone earning the average industrial wage was 73 per cent. Much of the additional spending went to buy imports, and the current account deficit widened to an untenable 15 per cent of GDP by 1981. Partly as a result, the Irish pound was devalued four times within the European Monetary System in the early 1980s. In 1986 an estimated IR£1,000 million of private capital left the country, anticipating a devaluation; the smart money was right, and the Irish pound was devalued by 8 per cent in August.

In 1987 the Fianna Fáil government introduced a very tight budget, cutting the current budget deficit to 1.7 per cent of GDP through reductions in real government spending that made Margaret Thatcher's efforts look gentle. Public capital spending, which had manifestly not boosted economic growth (at least in the short-term), was also sharply cut, especially on housing.

The 1987 reform worked, not only because it addressed unsustainable macroeconomic imbalances, but also because of deeper changes in economic policy that began to tackle structural problems. As late as 1980, a third of the workforce was employed by the public sector, including the 8 per cent of employment that was in public enterprises, some of which were thoroughly inefficient (Irish Shipping), or were largely sustained by their quasi-monopoly positions (Aer Lingus).

The first important move was the liquidation of loss-making Irish Shipping (in 1984), which signalled an end to the unconditional state support for public enterprises. The airline deregulation of 1986 was a remarkable success: between August 1985 (pre-regulation) and August 1987 (post-regulation), fares on the Dublin-London route fell by 54 per cent and traffic rose by 92 per cent. The number of visitors to Ireland rose from 2 million in 1987 to 3 million in 1990, with most of the increment carried by air. Emboldened by this success, several of the most visible state enterprises were privatised in the 1990s, including Greencore (sugar), Irish Life (insurance), B and I Line (shipping), and Telecom, followed later by three banks (TSB, ICC, and ACC), and the oil refinery. The retreat from state enterprise reflected a change in attitudes that increasingly favoured the private sector and that has, over time, led to a greater focus on making Ireland an easy place to do business.

In the wake of the 1987 reforms, economic growth resumed, as confidence (and investors) returned and exports boomed, thanks in part to the devaluation of 1986 and to continued wage restraint. By 1992, the ratio of public debt to GDP had fallen below 100 per cent, and the macroeconomic crisis was over.

Reflecting confidence in the new policy regime, sweetened with £87 million in IDA grants, Intel began work on a major plant in 1989 – it is now the company's largest manufacturing facility outside the USA – and this helped ease the way for the substantial inflow of foreign investment by major US firms in the 1990s. But the lessons of the failed fiscal experiment are important and have been largely internalised: fiscal rectitude is important for long-term growth, and taxes cannot be pushed too high.

From Sterling to EMS to Euro
In 1979, in a move that was hailed at the time as foresighted, Ireland broke the link with sterling (which dated back to 1826) and joined the European Monetary System (EMS). The reasoning was straightforward: Ireland had experienced inflation averaging 15 per cent between 1973 and 1979, necessarily the same rate as in Britain, and it was believed that the key to reducing the inflation rate was to uncouple the Irish pound from high-inflation sterling and attach it to the low inflation EMS, which was dominated by the deutschmark. Some also argued – correctly as it turned out – that sterling would appreciate with the development of North Sea oil, and that this would hurt Irish exports. Although over 40 per cent of exports still went to the UK in 1979, about a quarter went to the other EU countries, and so a change in exchange regime was considered feasible.

The adjustment to the EMS was slow and rocky. In the early 1980s inflation actually fell faster in the UK, which stayed out of the EMS, than in Ireland. The slow reduction in Irish inflation towards German levels meant that the Irish pound became overvalued, and had to be devalued within the EMS. The standard explanation is that wage demands – which often respond to recent inflation – were slow to change, so wage increases continued to be too large to be consistent with very low inflation. The lesson here was clear: economic growth and macroeconomic stability can easily be undermined if wage increases get out of line.

By about 1990 Ireland could boast of low inflation, a tight budget, and a falling ratio of government debt to GDP, and it looked as if, after a decade of relative economic stagnation, the decision to join the EMS was finally paying off. Then in late 1992 the EMS fell apart. High interest rates in Germany, resulting from that country's need to finance reunification, caused the deutschmark to appreciate. Sterling was devalued, and the Irish pound ultimately followed, because

32 per cent of Irish exports still went to the UK, and in the absence of a devaluation, Irish competitiveness in the important British market would be too severely compromised.

After the collapse of the EMS, it became clear that a regime of 'fixed but flexible' exchange rates is an oxymoron. Without a viable middle way between floating exchange rates and a single currency, the European Union opted for the latter. The schedule was set out in the Treaty of Maastricht, signed in 1992 and ratified the following year. As the decade progressed, it became increasingly clear that Ireland would qualify to join the euro. At the same time, the Single European Act came into effect in 1992, breaking down many of the remaining barriers to the movement of goods and people among the countries of the EU.

'Tiger' Years

Between 1994 and 2000 Ireland's real GDP rose by 10.2 per cent annually, and employment increased by half a million, from 1.2 to 1.7 million. The stunning economic boom was entirely unexpected. How did it happen? (See also Chapter 8 for a full discussion of this issue.)

Standard economic theory tells us that when economies apply more inputs – the factors of production (land, labour, capital, technology) – then output will rise. Yet during the Tiger years the investment rate was not especially high, and improvements in education and technology were not sudden enough to explain any upswing in economic growth. The puzzle deepens when one notes that despite this, not only did output per worker increase (by a strong 3.4 per cent per year), but employment rose sharply – in stark contrast to the abysmal record of job creation over the previous half century, when Irish employment hardly rose at all.

The simple solution to the enigma runs something like this: with relatively low taxes and macroeconomic stability, and the implementation of the EU single market by 1992 that assured the easy movement of most goods and services within the EU, Ireland by the early 1990s was an attractive destination for US companies wishing to serve the EU market. There was a substantial pool of available well-educated English-speaking workers, and a regime of low corporate taxation and industrial subsidies. This mix proved attractive to highly-productive export-oriented labour-using foreign firms, particularly in pharmaceuticals and high technology. It also had a quick direct payoff, and surprisingly large knock-on effects, boosting the large services sector as the economy found itself in a virtuous circle of expansion: as more households could count on steady earnings, the demand for services, including public services rose quickly, so employment spread to other sectors too.

By 2000, Ireland had caught up economically with its peers in the EU, and the country became the poster child of the benefits of economic integration. The unemployment then stood at 4 per cent, but the wave of American foreign direct investment had also subsided, as rising prices and a shrinking supply of available labour made the country less competitive.

Echo of the Boom

The initial boom might have run its course sooner had Ireland not joined the euro area in 1999. Ireland easily met the criteria for graduating to the euro, and the exchange rate was locked at €0.787564 per Irish pound on 1 January 1999. Ireland, like the states of the USA, no longer has the option of an independent monetary policy. This is not a radical break from the past; an independent monetary policy was not possible when the Irish pound was linked with sterling (1826–1979), and was severely circumscribed during the period of the European Monetary System. The main advantage of a common currency is lower transaction costs, and perhaps a steadier hand at the tiller; the cost is a reduced ability to respond when faced by an external shock or domestic rigidity – for instance, if export prices fall or wages fail to adjust.

Prior to the single currency, credit was more expensive in Ireland than in Germany or France, in part because of currency risk; with the advent of the euro, interest rates were essentially equalised across the euro zone, as money flowed from (low-interest) Germany to (high-interest) Ireland. Irish banks, flush with funds, lent freely; households, increasingly accustomed to higher wages and lower unemployment, took on more loans; the government expanded tax incentives for housing; and inexperienced Irish regulators believed this time was different. The result was a housing boom, sustained by a large inflow of workers from Eastern Europe (mainly Poland and Lithuania), which kept labour costs in check. Although rising prices made the Irish industrial sector less competitive – industrial employment contracted during this period – the expansion in the financial sector, made easier by the use of the euro, offset this to some extent. In 2005 the *Economist* rated Ireland as having the highest economic quality of life in the world, based on an index constructed using data on (among other measures) material wellbeing, health, political stability and freedom, and job security.

Collapse

The 'party' could not last. Household debt, which stood at €90 billion at the beginning of 2004, rose to €200 billion by mid-2008, and by 2009 represented a world-leading 215 per cent of disposable income. As early as 2000 the IMF warned that property prices in Ireland were too high and that a housing bubble was in the making; the growing chorus of warnings went unheeded, and house prices doubled between 2000 and 2006 before stabilising in 2007. The bubble burst in 2008, and by 2010 housing prices in Dublin were less than half of their peak level; by the end of 2012 a fifth of commercial loans and 13 percent of all mortgages were in arrears.

By 2009 the major banks were insolvent, and only survived because of a government guarantee to creditors, which in turn required the government to borrow heavily to pay the bill – injecting money into the two largest banks (Bank of Ireland, and Allied Irish Bank), nationalising Anglo Irish Bank, and shifting 'toxic' assets with a face value of €74 billion to the National Assets Management Agency (NAMA).

The collapse of the housing bubble coincided with a serious recession – world GDP fell by 0.6 per cent in 2009, the first decline since the end of the Second World War – and this ended any prospects of a rapid recovery for the Irish economy. By late 2010, faced with rapid withdrawals from the banking system, the government was obliged to accept a €85 billion rescue package from the IMF and EU, with its accompanying strictures on taxation and spending.

The result was a serious recession, as real GDP contracted by 4.5 per cent in 2008 and a further 4.7 per cent in 2009. A modest recovery in 2010 was largely offset by further shrinkage in 2011 and 2012. Unemployment reacted rapidly, rising from 5 per cent in early 2008 to 15 per cent by late 2010, where it stayed for almost two years. Emigration rose, and between 2010 and 2015 net out-migration totalled more than 150,000. The poor health of the banking system, overhang of public debt, sluggish recovery of the US economy, and anaemic growth in most of the EU (which anyway has a very limited capacity to boost fiscal transfers to regions that are in recession), meant that recovery was bound to be slow.

'Celtic Phoenix'

Rebounding in style, the Irish economy has surprised once again, with a total increase in real GDP of over 40 per cent since 2012. Some of this is statistical sleight of hand – in 2015, some airplane leasing companies moved to Ireland, which is the world leader in the field, immediately boosting the country's capital stock. But much of the recovery is real: the unemployment rate has fallen steadily from 15 per cent in 2012 to around 6 per cent by 2017, and household debt has fallen to about 60 per cent of GDP, in line with the EU average, but half the rate of 2010.

The return to growth reflects the perception that Ireland has been a model pupil at getting its public finances in order. It has been rewarded by improved access to world credit markets, and by early 2014 the government was able to borrow on international markets at an interest rate of just 3.5 per cent. In December 2013 the formal monitoring of government financial decisions by the 'troika' of the IMF, European Central Bank, and European Commission came to an end, leaving Ireland with slightly more room for manoeuvre in handling its public finances. Political continuity, and a series of pragmatic economic reforms, have also helped maintain international confidence in Ireland as a destination for investment.

6 A HUNDRED YEARS ON

On the centennial of the Easter Rising of 1916, the Central Statistics Office published a report entitled *Life in 1916 Ireland: Stories from Statistics*. It is worth stepping back for a moment to reflect on the enormous magnitude of economic and social change that has occurred, essentially within living memory.

We live longer, healthier lives. In 1916, out of every thousand births, 81 died in infancy; by 2016 the number was just four. The average person a century ago had a life expectancy of 54, and that has now risen to 78 (for men) or 83 (for women).

Deaths from bronchitis or tuberculosis were common, and are now extremely rare. The living also get married differently: in 2016, just 1 per cent of marriages consisted of civil ceremonies, a number that has now risen to 28 per cent.

We travel differently. Dublin had 96 km of tram lines, compared to 37 km today; and there were 964 train stations around the country, compared to 144 in 2016. But the number of cars has risen, from about 10,000 in 1915 to 2.0 million today, or more than one per household.

We have changed our occupations. In 1911, half of the workforce was in agriculture, compared to five per cent today. A quarter of all employment was in manufacturing, while the proportion has now fallen to nine per cent. And a tenth of workers were domestic servants, a group that has now almost vanished. The service sectors, including information technology, finance, tourism, education, and public administration have taken up the slack.

We are better educated. A hundred years ago, about eight per cent of the population was illiterate, and the rate was twice as high as this in Donegal. Although primary school was required, the attendance rate in 1916 was just 71 per cent compared to 94 per cent in 2012–13. Only 1,400 students sat the Senior exam in 1916, in sharp contrast to the 55,000 candidates for the Leaving Certificate in 2015.

We are more affluent. One compelling measure of this is the proportion of household spending devoted to food and beverages, which was 57 per cent in 1922, and 11 per cent in 2011. Potatoes were still important, grown on 172,000 hectares in 1916; by 2010 the area had shrunk to 12,000 hectares. An estimated 13,000 people migrated to Britain for seasonal agricultural work in 1914, to augment the low incomes they made in Ireland's western counties.

7 CONCLUDING OBSERVATIONS

The significant events of Irish economic history have been marshalled to support a number of different interpretations.

Nationalists emphasise the ways in which the links between the Irish economy and Britain have worked to Ireland's detriment. Writers in this vein have stressed the damage caused by the plantations, the Navigation, Cattle and Woollen Acts, the solid growth during the years of Grattan's Parliament, the lowering of tariffs in the years after the Act of Union, the ineffectiveness of relief efforts during later years of the Famine, and the costs of Ireland's inability to protect its industry from British goods during the second half of the nineteenth century. This approach has typically been used to lead to the conclusion that Ireland would be better off economically with independence.

Support for the nationalist interpretation waxes and wanes with the performance of the economy of the Republic. When independence did not bring a dramatic improvement in growth, and when the import-substitution policy of the 1930s created an inefficient industrial base which stagnated in the 1950s, the advantages of independence came to be seen as less obvious, especially as Northern Ireland appeared to be prospering at the time. However, from 1960 to 1980, when growth in the Republic was faster, and dependence on the British market reduced, the nationalist view became respectable again despite, or perhaps because of, the dismantling of tariff protection.

Outside the Irish context, this view is comparable to the approach of *dependency theorists*, who emphasise the harmful results of links between peripheral areas and the major industrial powers. The main weaknesses of this approach is that it has tended to neglect the potentially beneficial effects of links with the metropolitan area, and has overestimated the ability of independent states to make wise decisions, as exemplified for instance by Ireland's disastrous fiscal experiment in the late 1970s.

Membership of the EU has not made the nationalist view completely obsolete, but it has been stripped of its anglophobic character. There remains space for a nationalism, or perhaps localism would be a better term, to counteract the tendencies of the EU to regulate from the centre what would be better done at a much lower level of government. But Irish support for the EU is typically strong: in the Eurobarometer survey of autumn 2016, 55 per cent of those in the Irish sample said they have a 'positive' view of the EU, the highest rate among the 28 member countries.

Marxists stress the role of the conflict between different classes within the country. Thus, for instance, the Famine and subsequent emigration swept away the greater part of the rural proletariat, paving the way for the emergence of a rural bourgeoisie, which in due course wrested control over land from the aristocracy and provided the leaders of a conservative independent state. In this view the labouring class, whether agricultural or industrial, never achieved enough strength to effect significant social or economic change, and the indigenous capitalist class failed in its mission of creating a dynamic industrial base, thereby forfeiting its right to the perquisites that it continues to enjoy. The conclusion most commonly drawn is that the state needs to take a more active role in filling this entrepreneurial function. Foreign investment by footloose companies is seen as conveying few benefits.

The Marxist view fails to explain why largely non-class conflicts, such as that in Northern Ireland, can persist. It typically overstates the ability of the state and public enterprises to create sustainable jobs; once this prop falls, it is not clear what prescription for economic growth remains.

In reaction against the weaknesses of the nationalist and Marxist interpretations, most recent writers have tended to view economic events as having a significant life of their own, being 'substantially independent of political and constitutional issues'. Hence the role of the Cattle Acts, or the Act of Union, or the replacement of tenant farmers by smallholders, are seen as minor. Economic actors are believed to redirect their energies fairly quickly, and seize the available opportunities. This perspective, epitomised in the large body of revisionist writings of Cullen, could be labelled the *classical economics approach*. In the hands of a new generation of economists this approach to history has become increasingly quantitative.

This view too has its faults, in that it can go too far in neglecting political events and institutional arrangements. In the words of Douglass North, 'institutional change shapes the way societies evolve through time and hence is the key to understanding historical change'. North originally believed that inefficient institutions would be weeded out over time, but in his more recent writings he is less sanguine about this prospect. The *institutional approach* complements rather than supplants the classical economics view, and we have drawn on these two perspectives in writing this chapter.

In the mid nineteenth century Denmark was substantially better off than Ireland, despite facing a similar external environment – both depended on the British market, and both were open to free trade. O'Rourke suggests that Denmark maintained its lead, and (unlike Ireland) expanded its population because it had successfully introduced land reform a century before Ireland, and perhaps more importantly, achieved universal literacy much sooner. More recently, Irish decisions – such as membership of the EU, the adoption of the euro, and the maintenance of a lean public sector – appear to have paid dividends in the form of rapid economic growth. Institutional decisions do have consequences.

The most interesting lessons from Irish economic history are about growth strategies. Economic growth comes from a multitude of sources such as new technology, capital investment, education and training, land reclamation, enterprise, shifting prices, higher aggregate demand and chance. However, these are only the raw ingredients, and must be combined to sustain growth. It is easy to see these ingredients at work. The new technologies of the potato, railways, power weaving and computers have all been influential. Capital spending is essential at all times, although rarely needs to be above a fifth of GDP. Higher levels of education and improved training have boosted labour productivity. Chance brought the potato blight and two world wars. Land reclamation helped fend off famine in the early nineteenth century. Enterprise was at the heart of the introduction of shipbuilding in Belfast. A secular increase in wheat prices radically changed agriculture in the eighteenth century. Low aggregate demand reined in growth in the 1950s.

Recognising the role of these elements is important, but holds few lessons. The study of growth *strategies* is more illuminating. The policy of laissez faire need not guarantee growth, as experience from 1815 to 1850 demonstrates. Nor does a strategy of import substitution necessarily fare better, for while it may have been helpful in the short run in the 1930s, protection left a legacy of inefficient industry in the 1950s. An approach that favours agriculture-led development, such as followed by the Free State in the 1920s, may succeed in raising real incomes, but given the small size of the agricultural sector (2 per cent of GDP in 2012) it is no longer a realistic option. An industrialisation strategy based on attracting foreign capital also has some advantages, but is expensive to implement, and risks leaving a country more vulnerable to decisions outside its control.

32

As a practical matter Ireland has limited room for pursuing independent economic policies. Fiscal restraint is needed because persistent expansionary fiscal policy does not work well in a small open economy, as the experiment of 1978 to 1987 shows. With the euro in place, monetary policy is not an option. Industrial policy is increasingly circumscribed by the rules that have applied since 1993 to the Single European Market. Recognising the need for greater efficiency, the country has privatised or closed down several state-owned enterprises. Ireland now has only a little more autonomy than a typical state of the United States.

That leaves a narrower and more difficult field for local economic policy. The focus has shifted to the factors needed to maintain 'competitiveness' – what Michael Porter calls the 'microeconomic foundations of prosperity'. This includes bending to such tasks as gearing society to produce entrepreneurs, vitalising indigenous enterprise, providing adequate and appropriate education and training, evaluating public investment more thoroughly, introducing flexibility into the labour market, reducing the disincentives to do unskilled jobs, and fostering competition among firms. Affluence requires efficiency in the public arena – in the provision of services and the formulation and targeting of policy – in addition to efficiency by businesses.

Since wages in Ireland are closely linked with those in Britain and the European Union, once individuals have been equipped with education, economic policy has limited influence on the standard of living they will enjoy in Ireland. What it can still influence, perhaps more thoroughly than was commonly believed just a few years ago, is the number who enjoy that standard of living in Ireland rather than elsewhere.

Suggestions for Further Reading

The literature on Irish economic history is already enormous. A few suggestions for further reading are given here, and much of the information in this chapter comes from these sources.

General History
1   R. Foster, *Modern Ireland 1600–1972*, Allen Lane, London 1988.
2   J. Lee, *Ireland 1912–1985*, Cambridge University Press, Cambridge 1989.
3   F. Lyons, *Ireland Since the Famine*, Weidenfeld and Nicolson, London 1971.

Economic and Social History
1   R. Crotty, *Irish Agricultural Production*, Cork University Press, Cork 1966.
2   L. Cullen, *An Economic History of Ireland Since 1660*, Batsford, London 1972.
3   M. Daly, *Social and Economic History of Ireland Since 1800*, Educational Company, Dublin 1981.
4   K. Kennedy, T. Giblin and D. McHugh, *The Economic Development of Ireland in the Twentieth Century,* Routledge, London 1988.
5   J. Mokyr, *Why Ireland Starved*, Allen and Unwin, London 1983.
6   C. Ó Gráda, *The Great Irish Famine*, Macmillan, London 1989.

7   C. Ó Gráda, *Ireland: A New Economic History 1780–1939*, Oxford University Press, Oxford 1995.
8   C. Ó Gráda, *A Rocky Road: The Irish Economy Since the 1920s*, Manchester University Press, Manchester 1997.

Web references
1   Central Statistics Office. Mainly recent data, but some series stretch further back. www.cso.ie/en/
2   Wikipedia: The Irish economy. https://en.wikipedia.org/wiki/Economy_of_the_Republic_of_Ireland
3   Wikipedia: Economic history of the Republic of Ireland. https://en.wikipedia.org/wiki/Economic_history_of_the_Republic_of_Ireland
4   Wikipedia: Economic history of Ireland. https://en.wikipedia.org/wiki/Economic_history_of_Ireland

CHAPTER 2

Policy Priorities for a Small Regional Economy

Dermot McAleese*

1 INTRODUCTION

The policy priorities of a regional economy and a national economy are very similar. Both are concerned with achieving higher living standards, full employment, a fair distribution of income, and economic stability. Both worry about competitiveness. And the balance of payments has implications for both the region and the nation state, though as we shall see these implications are far more transparent in the case of a nation.

The main difference between a region and a nation is *the policy context*. A region has no independent currency and no control over its monetary policy. Its trade policy is determined by outside forces and balance of payments issues have to be radically reinterpreted. It has limited discretion in the use of fiscal policy. Seen in this context, a region's approach to policy has a dual dimension. First, it has to consider how to use its limited influence on policy developments where the key policy decisions are being made. In the case of the Republic of Ireland, this might be Brussels, Frankfurt, or Luxembourg depending on the issue being decided; in Northern Ireland, London would figure prominently. Second, in areas where they do possess policy autonomy, regions must ensure that this degree of policy discretion is used effectively.

As Ireland becomes increasingly integrated into the European economy, the Republic is losing many of the trappings of a national economy, especially given its very small relative size. The completion of the single market and the movement towards economic and monetary union constitute important turning points in this respect. Hence, the focus in this chapter is on the policy objectives from the perspective of a very small regional economy in the euro zone. This perspective is of special interest at present because the Irish Republic is a comparative newcomer to regional status, unlike say Northern Ireland or Scotland, and it has had to acclimatise itself rapidly to the economic limitations of regional dependence. At the same time, as a nation state, the Republic could, if it managed its economic affairs well, exert more influence at the centre of European policymaking than many European regions of much larger size.

The plan of this chapter is as follows. In Section 2 we explain why output growth is regarded as the primary priority of economic policy regardless of the size of the economy and how this output growth is related to employment. In Section 3 the limitations of output growth as a policy priority are analysed by taking account of the complex linkages between advances in material living standards and human welfare in the broad sense. Section 4 examines the goal of equity and the relationship between economic growth and happiness. In Section 5 we discuss various dimensions of economic stability, including price stability, as priorities of policy. Competitiveness is discussed in Section 6. The search for ways of restoring competitiveness has become the *leitmotif* of economic policy in Ireland in recent years, in particular since the country became part of the euro zone. Failure to recognise this fully for most of the 2000s was one of the factors behind the recessionary years 2008 to 2012. Section 7 concludes the chapter.

2 GROWTH AND EMPLOYMENT

Introduction

Rapid, sustained growth is a primary objective of economic policy. Fast economic growth means higher living standards, and is associated with an expanding and dynamic business environment. Slow or zero growth is perceived as stagnation. Confronted with the record of a slow growing economy, we instinctively ask what has gone wrong. Policymakers are always on the lookout for advice about ways of promoting economic growth. An advance in living standards is something that most people want, enjoy, and expect to be delivered.

Economic growth is desired for many different reasons. Affluent countries see growth as an essential contributor to ever-higher living standards, full employment, and healthy government finances (see Chapter 7). They also perceive faster growth as a way of maintaining their economic and military position relative to other countries. Not long ago, Americans worried about being overtaken by the Japanese; and the Japanese in turn worry about their economic standing relative to China. By contrast, governments of developing countries see faster economic growth as a means of escaping from poverty and material want, and in particular from the vulnerability and sense of inferiority that, rightly or wrongly, attaches to low economic development. For them, 'catching up' on the material living standards of the affluent countries is a key policy imperative. All countries appear to view growth as an indicator that resources are being employed efficiently, and faster growing economies are often taken as models for slower growing economies to copy and learn from.

Growth and Efficiency

Economics generally endorses the idea that efficiency and growth are related. Most fast growing economies are efficient, and most efficient economies tend to grow faster than economies of similar size and scale that are inefficient. The meaning of efficiency and growth in an economic sense is illustrated in Figure 2.1.

Imagine an economy that produces only two goods, X and Y. We set up a list of combinations of X and Y that the economy could produce if its resources were utilised in the most efficient way. In other words, for any given level of X, we find out the maximum amount of Y that can be produced in the economy. The curve showing various combinations of X and Y derived in this way is known as the *production frontier*. The production frontier is TT in Figure 2.1.

Figure 2.1 Production Frontier

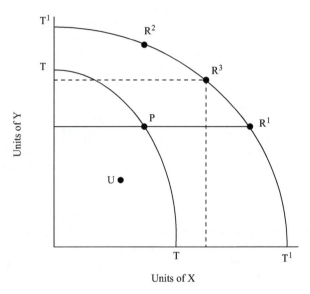

Provided production takes place on the production frontier, where resources are fully employed, more of good X implies less of good Y. In other words, in order to produce more of X, scarce resources have to be transferred from industry Y to industry X. One can go further and define the cost of X as the amount of Y that has to be sacrificed in order to produce one extra unit of X. This is called *the opportunity cost of X*. The opportunity cost concept has many practical applications and serves as a reminder of the obvious point that 'free' education, 'free' transport and other 'free' goods and services offered by the state are not costless. The resources used to supply these goods and services could have been used to produce automobiles or holidays instead. Hence the well-known maxim; in economics there is no such thing as a free lunch.

An *efficient* economy is one that operates on its production frontier (i.e. at a point such as P in Figure 2.1). At any point below the production frontier, society could have more of X and Y simply by moving to the frontier. Thus, by definition, a point such as U is not an efficient outcome. At that point, some productive resources are being either used inefficiently, or worse, not being used at all. At a point such as P it is not possible to make one person better off without leaving the other worse off. This condition applies to all such points on the production frontier and hence all are efficient. The choice between these points then is a question of distributional justice (see later).

Why Growth is Important

Over time growth, or pushing out the production frontier, will be the main force in determining living standards. A GNP growth rate of 4 per cent maintained for 17 years will result in a doubling of the original GNP level. Even a more modest 2 per cent growth rate will translate into a doubling of living standards every 33 years. Figures such as these indicate the potential gains from raising the growth rate. In terms of Figure 2.1 outward shifts in the production frontier will over time dominate the effects of movement to a given frontier from off-frontier points, such as U. However, since countries that are efficient normally grow faster than those that are inefficient, the objectives of efficiency and growth are in practice complementary.

To illustrate the benefits of growth, we can depict it as a series of outward shifts in the production frontier, such as that represented by the move from TT to T^1T^1. The T^1T^1 frontier shows the expanded range of options growth provides to society. Economic growth is a 'good thing', in so far as it enables the consumers in the economy to enjoy:

- More of X and the same amount of Y – at a point such as R^1;
- More of Y and the same amount of X – at a point such as R^2;
- More of both X and Y – at a point like R^3;
- Any other desired combination of X and Y – any point on the expanded frontier.

Growth extends the range of consumption possibilities, and people choose between these different possibilities through the market system, supplemented by government intervention.

The production frontier can be shifted outwards by two forces: first, increases in the *quantity* of productive factors and, second, improvements in the *productivity* of these factors. Since we are primarily concerned with growth per person rather than total growth, it is common to abstract from the increase in growth that is attributable solely to the increase in the population. Growth in living standards, or GNP per person, depends on (see also Chapter 7):

- The *amount* of productive factors at each person's disposal (the more machinery and the more hectares of land at the disposal of a worker the more will be produced per worker);
- The *productivity* of these factors of production (better machinery, better seeds and fertilisers, better technology);
- The knowledge, skills, and motivation of the workforce (see Chapters 6 and 13).

Growth and Employment

Full employment means that there is work available for everyone willing to seek it at prevailing pay levels. This is obviously a desirable objective of economic policy. There is a strong empirical association between full employment and economic growth and this explains why one of the major perceived benefits of faster growth is that it provides more job opportunities and reduces the unemployment rate.

Yet in strict logic there is no reason why growth should be a necessary condition for full employment. To see this, go back to Figure 2.1. Assume a situation where TT is fixed (i.e. zero long-run growth). At point U, there is unemployment. As noted above, this is an inefficient point, indicating waste of resources. The solution is to implement policies that address the unemployment problem. As more people are employed, we move towards a point like P on the production frontier TT.

The necessary policies might take any of the forms outlined in Chapter 6. Hence full employment can be regarded as an indicator of efficiency. In moving from U to P, there will be an increase in output and therefore some faster economic growth will be recorded. But once attained, there is no reason why full employment should not be maintained at P. Faster growth at that stage makes no difference one way or another. Hence the 'classical' conclusion: *full employment is always attainable irrespective of the level of output or of the growth rate of output.*

Intuition and empirical fact, however, suggest that full employment is easier to attain when an economy is growing. Also when growth declines, unemployment rises. For example, South Korea, long used to near zero unemployment rates, found itself facing unemployment of an unprecedented 7 per cent following the 1997–98 currency crisis. In a similar manner, Ireland's unemployment rate rose from 4 per cent to over 14 per cent following the post-2008 property crash and the collapse in its GDP. The amount of unemployment associated with the fall in output between 2008 and 2013 has varied across EU countries, with Greece (8 to 27 per cent), Spain (11 to 27 per cent) and Cyprus (4 to 16 per cent) being the most markedly affected. In Ireland's case, the collapse in the construction industry, an exceptionally labour intensive activity, was a key factor in generating job losses.

Thus, growth is desired not just for its own sake but for the indirect benefits it provides such as helping to keep unemployment low.

Growth of GNP per Person as a Policy Objective

The focus on income per person rather than total income (GNP) as the policy objective has profoundly important implications.[1] Suppose one had to choose between three growth profiles as indicated in Table 2.1.

Total GNP is increasing fastest in situation A. If total GNP were the policy objective, A would be the preferred situation. If GNP per person were the policy objective, situation C would be chosen. Ranking A and B would be more difficult. The only difference between them is that there are more people around in

A to share a given GNP per person growth rate. Suppose these additional people happened to be immigrants from Africa. The economy's faster growth means that they can be accommodated without impairing average living standards of the existing population; while at the same time the immigrants' living standards are much higher in the host country than they were at home. Also if the host country had a large national debt, this debt could be shared among a larger population. This would suggest a preference for A over B. But there may be other effects to consider, relating to the broader social impact of immigration and effects on income distribution. An influx of unskilled immigrants, for instance, would tend to reduce earnings of native unskilled workers, but would tend to benefit the middle and upper class generally by reducing the cost of unskilled labour that these more affluent people employ (such as domestic help, catering staff, construction workers). Clearly personal values and one's position in the income distribution ranking influence preferences between the various growth and population combinations.

Table 2.1 Growth: Illustrative Example

Growth Profile	Total GNP (% p.a.)	Population (% p.a.)	GNP per person (% p.a.)
A	5	3	2
B	4	2	2
C	3	0	3

In the above example, population growth is treated as if it were independent of GNP growth. A crucial question is whether and how population growth interacts with GNP and the consequential effect on living standards per person. Take, for example, a country such as Uganda with an annual population growth of 3.2 per cent. Its population has grown from 19m in 1990 to 36m in 2012 and it is estimated to reach 60m in 2030. Output growth of over 3 per cent will be needed simply to prevent living standards from falling.

Many argue that population growth at that rate has a negative effect on total GNP growth and hence can depress income per person. An expanding population of young people and large family size reduces national savings and consequently limits the volume of investment. Simultaneously, a burgeoning population puts pressure on a country's natural resources. If the rate of population growth interacts negatively with GNP per person, a vicious circle of economic decline can be generated. At the other end of the spectrum, excessively low population growth can be equally problematic. The 'greying' of Europe's population has led to concerns about the financial viability of pension schemes, escalating medical costs, ability to finance public debt and an erosion of social dynamism and innovation. Considerations such as these reinforce the case for using GNP per person, not total GNP, as the relevant policy objective.

Affluent households tend to have smaller families than poor households. Likewise, developed countries have lower population growth than poor countries.

Thus, since 1980, population has grown in higher-income countries by only 0.6 per cent per annum, compared with 2 per cent in low-income countries. Ireland too has experienced the same phenomenon. As Chapter 6 will show, with increasing prosperity its birth rate has declined. But have we become better off because of a low birth rate, or is the birth rate low because we are more affluent? There is no definitive answer to this question, but many governments in less-developed countries now believe that lower population growth would help to raise living standards and have introduced strong family planning programmes to encourage smaller family size. Irish governments have never gone as far in this direction as governments in developing countries such as India and China. One reason for this is that Irish people, unlike many in the present developing world, had the option of emigration.

Migration and Growth
The impact of emigration on living standards has long been a controversial topic. Some argued that a larger population would have raised living standards in Ireland. Patrick Pearse believed that the country could support a population of 30 million (see Chapter 6). A bigger population would mean larger domestic markets, greater economies of scale, higher productivity and, eventually, more growth. Higher living standards and a more dynamic local community would in turn induce skilled and talented Irish people to stay at home, thus reinforcing faster growth. This is a rather rosy view of what might have happened to living standards in the absence of emigration. Demographers, however, agree that if there had been no emigration since 1841, the population in the Republic would be in the region of 20 million instead of 4 million (see Chapter 6). Some argued that a growing population was a good thing in itself, irrespective of its effects on material welfare.

An opposite viewpoint was that emigration acted as a welcome safety valve, enabling the amount of land and capital per person remaining in Ireland to be increased, with beneficial effects on Irish productivity. At the same time Irish emigrants were able to find more productive employment and acquire valuable work-experience and skills abroad. A win-win outcome for all parties, just as predicted in John Kenneth Galbraith's famous dictum that 'emigration helps those who leave, the country they go to, and the people they leave behind'.[2]

Underlying this approach was the idea that the primary focus of economic policy should be living standards of the Irish people wherever they happened to live, not just of those residing in the Irish state. Thus the policy objective should be to encourage Irish people to go to where their productivity was highest and their material rewards greatest. According to this logic, Ireland's access to the comparatively prosperous labour markets of the USA, the UK, Australia, and Canada has been a tremendous boon and the Irish government's main responsibility is to provide education to its citizens and equip them to make maximum use of the opportunities open to them at home *and* abroad.

During Ireland's boom the focus of interest changed to the effects of immigration rather than emigration. For the first time in centuries foreigners came each year to work in Ireland. At a broad level, this change in demographic pattern was benign. Higher output growth involved both significant net immigration *and* an improvement in living standards. Then after 2008 the pendulum swung back and Ireland reverted to being a country of net emigration, but net immigration may be in evidence again today (early 2017). At a broader societal level migration, inward and outward, brings its own set of problems and opportunities that the policymaker must not overlook. Paul Collier in a major study of global migration concluded that the question is not really whether migration per se is good or bad, but rather how much migration there should be and who benefits from it. In his view, 'moderate' migration is mostly advantageous but 'runaway' or what used to be called 'catastrophic' migration can result in severe economic losses due to the breakdown of social solidarity and trust in the host countries.[3]

3 OUTPUT GROWTH AND WELLBEING

Optimal Growth, not Maximum Growth
While growth is a primary policy priority, it does not follow that the aim is simply to *maximise* growth. One reason for this is that growth involves a degree of intergenerational distribution. By cutting down on its consumption and investing more, any present generation can raise economic growth rates. Japan's average investment/GNP ratio during the period 1960 to 1995 exceeded the investment ratio in the EU and the USA by more than 10 percentage points (31 per cent as against 22 per cent and 18 per cent respectively). Not surprisingly, Japan's growth rate of 6 per cent per year was twice the rate of most industrial countries. China and some other fast growing emerging economies put aside as much as 50 per cent of their GDP for investment. By investing so much, the present generation sacrifices its material welfare in the interests of future generations. But for how long can, and should, this process be maintained? Clearly different societies place a different premium on the future relative to present living standards. Authoritarian societies are often able to achieve extraordinarily rapid growth, but at serious cost to the people who had to produce the necessary saving.

Another reason for not choosing maximum growth as a policy objective relates to its potential undesirable spillover effects. These became apparent in the early 2000s and again in the late 2010s in Ireland. Traffic congestion worsened markedly; water quality declined; hospital resources were overstretched. Another spillover effect was the inflow of job seekers from abroad. Initially the decline in emigration was widely welcomed. No less welcome was the inflow of former emigrants returning to a buoyant domestic market. These immigrants helped to sustain the boom by moderating pay growth and plugging vital gaps in labour supply.

Generally there is no problem with immigrants of similar nationality and background to the host country. Difficulties arise, however, when unskilled immigrants of more diverse background enter the picture, as was evidenced politically in the

UK and the USA in 2016. There is also the difficulty that, if immigration does not lead to a corresponding increase in public services, such as health and education, migrants (who have contributed substantial tax revenue to pay for these services) may be seen as the cause of overcrowding rather than under-provision (which can stem from many causes). Also there are income distribution effects to consider. Middle and upper-income groups gained from the entry of the unskilled into the Irish labour market, but those at the lower end of the income profile tended to lose out. Finally, excessively rapid growth can often lead to inflation and to escalating property prices. Inflation can cause many problems as we shall see below.

One important, intangible benefit of growth is the influence and power that it brings with it. We can learn from the dominance of the USA in the world economy how economic success and political and military power are closely linked. Also faster growth facilitates adjustment in a country's productive structure (from import-competing to export activities, for example) and enables desirable social change. A further advantage is that economic growth tends to boost a country's international reputation. Successful countries are listened to with respect. Economic success engenders a virtuous circle and a palpable air of self-confidence, as Ireland's experience during the Celtic Tiger boom demonstrated. Economic decline after 2008 led to the opposite: a severe reputational loss, exposure to criticism and mockery, all deeply discouraging to a country that had become used to taking praise and admiration for economic achievements as a matter of course. Fortunately the reverse process applied after 2013, with Ireland again being considered by some as the 'poster child' for the other peripheral economies of Europe.

These advantages and disadvantages must be weighed in determining a country's optimum growth rate. Choosing an optimum growth path requires careful consideration of the broader socio-political factors mentioned above, as well as of the limitations of GNP as an indicator of welfare, a subject to which we turn next.

Welfare: Limitations of GNP Measure
So far we have discussed economic growth as if growth, as measured by GNP in the numerator, were the main objective of economic policy. But it is well known that GNP is an inadequate indicator of human welfare. As one critic expressed it:

> The Gross National Product does not allow for the health of our children, the quality of their education or the joy of their play. It does not include the beauty of our poetry or the strength of our marriages; the intelligence of our public debate or the integrity of our public officials. It measures neither our wisdom nor our learning neither our compassion nor our devotion to our country; it measures everything, in short, except that which makes life worthwhile.[4]

GNP does not account for many of the things that make for the good life and some items are included in GNP that may worsen rather than improve human welfare. Three specific criticisms of GNP have been made on this account. First, GNP, as officially measured, places no value on leisure and on the (unpaid and therefore unrecorded) contribution of stay-at-home partners to the household economy. Second, some items are recorded as outputs although in reality they are inputs or costs. Also some outputs that add to quality of life – such as access to a good public infrastructure – are difficult to value properly in money terms. Third, GNP statistics take insufficient account of environmental issues such as pollution and resource depletion and of the broader issue of sustainability. In this section we focus on this third limitation given its growing national and international importance. In Section 4, we consider two further factors that bear on the relationship between material growth and welfare: income distribution and the elusive question of the relationship between growth and happiness.

Conventional GNP measures do not deal satisfactorily with environmental and ecological factors (see also Chapters 9 and 11). Higher GNP has implications for the environment on several levels that fail to be recorded in the statistics. Three aspects, in particular, merit attention: (1) higher levels of pollution, (2) depletion of natural resources and (3) global warming.

First, no deduction is made in GNP statistics for the higher levels of pollution and chemical waste that often accompany economic growth. Attempts have been made to compute 'green' national accounts that allow for these negative effects but there is as yet no consensus on how the pollution effects should be computed.

Second, depletion of a nation's stock of non-renewable resources such as oil and coal is not accounted for in GNP calculations. Even in the case of renewable resources, problems can arise if economic growth leads to their being exploited in excess of the replacement rate. For example, the serious decline in the water table caused by increased economic activity in the countries bordering on the Aral Sea in Northern China and Israel-occupied Palestine is ignored in the national accounts.

Third, economic growth is associated with deforestation, change in land use and most notable of all with burning fossil fuels. As a result the concentration of greenhouse gases has risen alarmingly – the current level is higher than at any time in the last 650,000 years and there has been an accompanying rise in world temperatures. Already, an increase of 0.6°C has been recorded since the mid 1970s. A change of this magnitude may appear small, but its effects over time could be enormous (see Chapter 10). Long-time lags between today's green gas emissions and future damage to climate and the environment mean that the adverse effects will not be reflected in GNP for many years. Although Ireland might not be as badly affected as other countries by global warming, we are expected in the interests of EU solidarity to pay carbon taxes (see Chapter 4), to restrain energy consumption and, in short, to become much more 'green' than before (see Chapter 11).

GNP and Human Development Indicators
Making growth in GNP per capita a primary objective is really short-hand for something much more complex. In evaluating a country's economic performance, account must be taken of the quality of the lifestyle enjoyed by the population as

well as the quantity of goods and services consumed. Thus, imagine two countries. One has a lower GNP per person than the other, but it happens to have a healthier, more literate and less crime-ridden society. In this instance, GNP is an inaccurate measure of the relative welfare of the two countries, and making GNP growth a primary policy objective may not be an appropriate response. Instead of economic growth, can we find a way of measuring human development and making it the primary policy objective?

Efforts have been made by several international bodies to develop a more comprehensive socioeconomic measure than GNP. One of the earliest and best known is the Human Development Index (HDI) published each year by the United Nations. The HDI is a composite index that combines standard GNP statistics with other important indices of welfare. The HDI is a weighted average of data on GDP/GNP per person, life expectancy, and educational attainment of the population (see also Chapter 7). (An 'adjusted' HDI has also been introduced that takes account of income distribution.)

As one would expect, such exercises lead to some changes in ranking. The 2013 *Human Development Report* reveals a HDI ranking higher than the GDP per person ranking for New Zealand, Australia, Germany and Ireland; the opposite is the case for Singapore, China, and South Africa.[5] Ireland is placed seventh of 186 countries in the HDI league; a position that flatters and is unlikely to last. By adding to the list of indicators, and measuring them in different ways, more radical alterations in ranking can be computed. Experimentation and analysis along these lines is continuing.

Yet, the limitations of GNP as a measure of welfare must not be exaggerated. For all its defects, a higher output per person gives society the *capacity* to achieve a better quality of life. This explains the close positive correlation between the HDI and total output per person. Also there is a strong positive correlation between GNP per capita growth and some important empirical measures of the quality of life. Countries with higher GNP per capita tend to be healthier and better educated than those with lower GNP per capita. They also tend to be better policed and are more secure in a financial and physical sense (see Table 7.1).

London is safer than Lagos, Manila, or Sao Paolo. Affluent Tokyo is one of the safest cities in the world. While many forms of recorded crime have increased since 1945, prosperity has tended to result in a reduction in crime and disorder. During the nineteenth century, industrial nations became less crime ridden as they became more industrialised. Indeed, as pointed out in Chapter 1, these two factors are interrelated: the rule of law and good governance are essential prerequisites of a prosperous market economy.

Faster growth makes it easier to reduce unemployment, to lessen poverty, to improve education and health services and to provide all the other good things that constitute prosperity. There are, of course, negative aspects of growth, such as erosion of community life, destruction of traditional values and, as discussed above, damage to the environment. Since the birth of the Industrial Revolution in the late eighteenth century, economic growth has had its critics, some of the most trenchant of whom have been economists. The tradition of scepticism, verging on hostility, towards growth remains active to this day. Despite these downsides, governments and those who elect them evidently believe that the positive effects of growth outweigh its negative effects, and both continue to accord it a high priority. Indeed, in periods of low economic growth, the electorates can turn on the democratic system as the cause of poor economic performance, and thereby generate considerable political instability, as was and still is the case in some EU countries in recent years. Flat-lining of living standards in the past decade is seen by many as one of the causes for the rise of populist political movements in both Europe and the USA.

4 EQUITY, INCOME DISTRIBUTION AND HAPPINESS

What is a Fair Distribution of Income?

GNP per person, being an arithmetic average of total output divided by total population, reveals no information about the distribution of resources within a society. It could rise, even though the majority of the population may be getting worse off. For example, if the income of the most affluent one third of a population rose by €50 billion, and the income of the poorest two-thirds fell by €30 billion, GNP would increase. But does it follow that society as a whole is better off?

Some argue that the long-run sustainability of growth depends on income being shared on an equitable basis. Successful policymaking requires change, and such change can only be achieved if the majority of people believe that they have a stake in the economy and will benefit from its continued growth. This issue has assumed increased importance in recent years: the rise of populist political movements alluded to above is not attributed solely to stagnant incomes but also to what is seen as the unfair distributional effects of globalisation.

But this still leaves open the question of what is meant by sharing income on an equitable or fair basis? Since Chapter 8 is devoted to this topic, a brief outline of the main parameters of this debate will suffice at this stage.

The value judgements underlying modern economics are derived from a philosophy of individualism and liberalism. *Individualism* means that what ultimately counts is the utility every individual attains and that the utility of each individual should be given an equal weight. *Liberalism* signifies that individuals should be free to decide what provides the greatest utility. Individual preferences are taken as given. The task of the economist, in this view, is to devise market structures that will enable individuals to satisfy their preferences, not to pass judgement on them.

Diminishing Marginal Utility Argument

Utility and income must be distinguished in this analysis. The standard assumption underlying economic reasoning is that the marginal utility of income is positive but decreases as income rises. Individuals always prefer a higher income to a lower one, but the intensity of this preference diminishes as income rises. A systematic relationship thus links utility to income. On the face of it, the individualist principle of treating the utility of every person equally, coupled with the assumption of declining marginal utility for all individuals, would imply that the total utility in society is maximised when income is distributed perfectly evenly. But there are two reasons why even committed utilitarians do not push the argument to the extreme of total income equalisation.

First, different people derive different amounts of satisfaction from the same income levels. Material wealth does not matter equally to all. However, utility is difficult (some would say impossible) to measure and compare among individuals. Hence it is simply not practicable to redistribute income on the basis of differences in capacity to enjoy income.

Second, the adverse effect on incentives to work and enterprise of policies to achieve greater equality may, up to a point, lead to a fall in total income. The more we try to increase equity by the redistribution of income, the more we reduce efficiency. In transferring income from the high-income group to the low-income group of society, the authorities levy taxes on income from employment and capital holdings. There can be unwelcome consequences of these taxes. Thus a rise in income tax can discourage work while capital taxes discourage investment and savings (see Chapter 4). In theory, both effects lead to a reduction in the amount of income available for redistribution. (The empirical importance of these effects varies and is much disputed.) The less well-off in society may well lose rather than benefit from such policies in the long run.

Rawlsian Perspectives
The assumption of decreasing marginal utility implies that when we take a given amount from the rich to give to the poor, the rich will suffer less of a utility loss than the utility gain enjoyed by the poor. If asked to choose between a perfectly equal distribution of income and an unequal distribution *of exactly the same total income*, a utilitarian would tend to favour the equal distribution. Egalitarian predispositions also emerge from other philosophies and schools of thought. Some argue that society should give the utility of the poor greater weight than the utility of the rich on grounds of need, regardless of fine points about diminishing utility. Others, such as the philosopher John Rawls, have pushed this line of judgement to the extreme, arguing that any economic change which increases inequality would be acceptable only if it makes the poorest better off also. This implies that the utility of the worst-off individual takes precedence over all others and that a fair distribution of income is one that makes the poorest person as well off as possible after taking all costs of income transfers into account.[6]

Irish policy objectives have a Rawlsian flavour. Successive governments have tended to prioritise social inclusion as a strategic objective in its own right, the primary objective being to ensure that the benefits of economic growth and related social improvements are shared by all sections of the Irish population. Social inclusion has been a major theme of agreements with the social partners (see Chapters 3 and 8). Does the same principle apply in the case of economic decline? Should the losses in income be shared by all sections of the population? Not much explicit consideration has been given to how the losses of economic decline should be shared – until 2008, this type of problem seemed almost inconceivable. It still dogs assessment of the policy performance of the Irish economy over the period 2008 to 2016 (see Chapter 8).

Equality of Opportunity
In opposition to the egalitarian presumption, Robert Nozick argued that the idea of fairness as an outcome cannot be justified. Fairness must be based on rules, not outcomes. Two rules are crucial: (1) the state must enforce laws that establish and protect private property and (2) private property may be transferred from one person to another *only* by voluntary exchange. Provided markets are open to competition and there are no major market 'failures' (a hugely unrealistic assumption), the resulting distribution of income is by Nozick's definition, fair. It does not matter how unequally this income is shared provided it is generated by people each of whom voluntarily provided services in exchange for market-determined compensation. The entrepreneur who accepts business risks and has succeeded deserves to be rewarded. Redistribution of these earnings is unjustified. By the same token, in times of recession, business losses are solely the responsibility of the entrepreneur and no government bailouts are justified. From this perspective the key issue is equality of opportunity, not equality of outcome. Indeed given an uneven distribution of skills, motivation, and willingness to work, equal opportunities will inevitably entail unequal outcomes.

Horizontal Equity
So far the discussion has focused on *vertical equity*. This refers to the proposition that differently situated individuals should be treated differently. The well off, in other words, should be taxed in favour of the poor because they can afford to pay these taxes with less pain. *Horizontal equity* is also important. The underlying principle is that people with the same incomes and same circumstances should be treated in a similar fashion. For example, families with the same number of dependants and the same income should pay the same rate of tax (see Chapter 4). Horizontal equity requires that property developers, farmers, and PAYE employees should be subject to the same tax unless there is a clear demonstration of different circumstances.

Perceived breaches of this equity principle can be a source of major grievance. By extension, people in different circumstances should not be asked to pay the same taxes. This principle is the motivating force of many income distribution policies (see Chapters 4 and 8). The case for regional grants and incentives, for example, is based on the idea that people in less developed regions do not enjoy the same access to infrastructure as those living in richer regions.

The relationship between equity and growth depends ultimately on individual attitudes and culture. Income inequalities are more acceptable and financial work incentives valued more in some societies than in others (see Chapter 8). The combinations of growth and equity attainable in a competitive market economy full of individualistic materialists will be different from those attainable in a cooperative economy run by and for ascetic altruists! In practice people have voted with their feet on this question. Comparison of income distribution before and after tax and state benefits shows that major transfers take place from richer to poorer income groups in all industrial economies (see Chapter 8).

Equity, Material Living Standards and Happiness
In recent years, the research agenda has been widened even further by tackling the much broader question of how GNP per capita, and its distribution in a society, is related to happiness. Do higher standards of living, whether defined on broad or narrow definitions of the term, translate into greater happiness? Economists have had a long abiding interest in this correlation. In the light of our discussion of GNP per capita as a measure of welfare and of the importance of income distribution, the reader will not be surprised that economic research has come up with some complex findings.

A first step is how to measure happiness? The main source of information comes from large-scale citizen surveys that ask individuals to report on how happy they feel, how satisfied they are with their lives and/or with their jobs. Sometimes this is supplemented by data on suicide rates and health status as proxies for (un)happiness. Defined this way, happiness is clearly dependent on many variables other than the level of income – contrary to the much-quoted adage that 'anyone who says money can't buy happiness doesn't know where to shop'. The key methodological challenge is to identify the specific contribution of increases in GNP per capita, and by extension individual income levels, to the happiness index.

Research over the past decade enables us to draw several broad conclusions.[7] First, for any one individual, more income leads to more life satisfaction, everything else being equal. Within a single country, at a given moment in time, those in the highest income groups are happier than those in the lowest income groups. Second, citizens of very poor countries tend to be happier as living standards increase. Studies of former Soviet Union countries, for instance, show a clear positive correlation between income per capita and reported happiness. Third, beyond a certain level of income, the average person does *not* become significantly happier as income increases. At an aggregate level there has been no increase in reported happiness over the past 30 years in Japan and Europe, with if anything a decline in the USA. This is called *the Paradox of Happiness*. Fourth, *relative* income matters as much, if not more, to most people than *absolute* income levels. People's definition of what constitutes an 'adequate' level of income seems to depend as much on the level of income enjoyed by their neighbour as on the absolute value of their own income (see Chapter 8). Fifth, virtually all studies show that being unemployed has a strongly negative effect on happiness. Joblessness depresses well-being more than any other single characteristic including divorce and separation. Not only those who are made redundant suffer, but the spread of job insecurity lowers welfare among those still in employment. For this reason, those working in the private sector tend to be affected more strongly by economic downturns than those working in the public sector.

In Ireland, the relationship between happiness (measured as percentage of the population who described themselves as 'very satisfied with their life') and material welfare is also decidedly weak. The annual *Eurobarometer* survey showed that 40 per cent of Irish people fell into the very satisfied 'happy' category in 1980. There is no evidence of the proportion of happy people rising since then, notwithstanding the huge increase in material income. Curiously, even after the trials and tribulations of the economy and society post 2007, Irish people were still ranked 8th in the EU27 in terms of life satisfaction according to the 2011 *Eurobarometer* Survey. A surprising 88 per cent of those surveyed described themselves as 'very satisfied' or 'fairly satisfied' with life. That state of satisfaction went hand in hand with a grim assessment of the situation of the national economy – 84 per cent described the national economic situation as 'very bad' (compared with an EU average of 26 per cent) and 72 per cent considered that the impact of the crisis on the job market was likely to get worse.

One element on the happiness spectrum *did*, however, change. The number of people who were acutely *dis*satisfied with their life declined consistently since 1990. The fall in Ireland's unemployment since that time was most likely a key factor in this development. Hence, to the extent that fast economic growth has helped to reduce unemployment, we can conclude that economic growth in Ireland may not have added much to the happiness of already happy people, but it made those at the bottom of the happiness league feel less dissatisfied.

Archbishop Whately, who established the Chair of Political Economy in Trinity College in 1832, took an interest in a related question of whether economic growth has an impact on moral behaviour. Unlike a modern social scientist he had to rely on deductive reasoning instead of mass opinion surveys. As a general rule, he concluded, 'advancement in National Prosperity, which mankind is by the Governor of the universe adapted and impelled to promote, must be favourable to moral improvement'.[8] Whately championed the cause of teaching and research in economics because he believed that economic growth would lead to moral improvement, and moral improvement would in turn bring as much 'happiness' as we can reasonably expect in this life. This is an alternative perspective on the GNP/happiness correlation that would no doubt prove controversial in modern Ireland.

The literature on happiness continues to grow. It is a subject that requires cross-disciplinary research involving economics, statistics, psychology and philosophy. As yet conclusions are tentative, but the general thrust of the findings suggests two conclusions. One is that it would be a mistake for economists in the twenty-first century to focus excessively on ways to increase the level of GNP per capita, or to accept too readily that slow economic growth necessarily indicates 'failure'. A second conclusion is that, as prosperity increases, more emphasis should be placed on the provision of public goods than on facilitating the output of more private goods and services. The 'well-being' of an individual includes much more than income. Access to decent public amenities, pollution-free air, good education, secure employment, a fair distribution of income and a crimeless environment contribute more to happiness than any monetary measure can adequately convey.

5 FINANCIAL STABILITY

So far we have outlined the advantages and limitations of using the level of GNP per person as an indicator of well-being and a policy objective. But the level of GNP is not the only factor that matters. The stability of that level also impacts on society's welfare. In a market economy, a boom that gets out of hand (as nearly all do sooner or later) leads to bust and with it a steep downturn that can have a devastating impact on people's lives. A well-run economy, therefore, must have regard to the objective of stability. Indeed stability and the rule of law are the sine qua non for all prosperous economies.

Economic and financial stability has three dimensions: first, macro-stability, which refers to the avoidance of boom-and-bust cycles; second, financial stability, which is concerned with the viability of the banking and financial system; and third price stability. The first two types of stability are examined in other parts of this book. In this chapter we focus on price stability. Note that the three types of stability are interlinked. Maintaining price stability for example can be one of the most effective ways of avoiding macro fluctuations; and ensuring macroeconomic stability lessens the risk of instability in the financial sector. As we shall see, for a regional economy like Ireland, price stability is a particularly important objective.

A small region will experience price stability only if the centre provides it. In the Republic's case the centre is Frankfurt, the headquarters of the European Central Bank, while for Northern Ireland the relevant policy centre is the Bank of England. Policymakers in the regional economy must therefore support the establishment of strong financial institutions at the centre.

What is Price Stability?
In the past, inflation was so rampant and endemic that price stability was largely understood as the absence of inflation. In recent times, the threat of deflation (declining prices) has become the more pressing threat to price stability. While deflation means that the purchasing power of the currency is increasing – good news for those with cash balances – it has serious damaging side-effects, especially on countries with large government debts and a heavily indebted private sector. Hence price stability is the objective; inflation and deflation must both be avoided.

Price stability is defined as the absence of any persistent and pronounced rise or fall in the general level of money prices. The general level of prices is measured by the Consumer Price Index (CPI). This index is defined by reference to the price of a fixed 'basket' of consumer goods. In the Republic, the selection of items for the basket is made using results of the national household budget survey. Every five years new weights and new items are introduced into the index.

The European Central Bank (ECB) defines price stability as year-on-year increases in the CPI of the euro zone *below but close to* 2 per cent, maintained over the medium term; the Bank of England adopted a similar definition in December 2003. The US Federal Reserve's target is also 2 per cent, but in September 2013 it announced its readiness to condone inflation of up to 2.5 per cent as long as the level of unemployment was above 6.5 per cent. The central banks of Sweden, Norway, New Zealand, and Canada have opted for a target inflation rate in the wider 1–3 per cent range.

Asset Prices, Price Stability and Central Bank Targets

The issue of whether *asset prices*, and in particular house prices and stock market valuations, should be included in the policy objective of price stability has been much debated in recent times. The issue arose because in many countries (Ireland, the UK, and Spain for example) house prices were rising well above the CPI rate for several years (see Chapters 7 and 12). While housing costs are included in the CPI (they have a weight of 7 per cent in the Irish CPI), the authorities in Ireland, and also in the UK, USA and Spain, took too little account of the implications of booming property prices on long-run disposable income.

An important matter then is whether a central bank should monitor asset prices as well as the CPI in assessing how well it is doing its job. It is clear that, with the benefit of hindsight, the answer is yes. Prior to the 2008 financial crisis, CPI prices were stable in the industrial world, clustering around an average of 2 per cent. Central banks grew complacent ignoring the fact that asset prices were escalating at extremely high levels. As we have learned, the ensuing collapse in asset prices inflicted terrible harm on the economy – as much as any deviation from price stability narrowly defined. Leaving asset prices to market forces and ignoring the damage they might cause was a grave mistake made by central banks. Asset prices are highly relevant to both price stability and to economic and financial stability.

It is now accepted that central banks should have acted pre-emptively, raising interest rates and/or curbing property loans when asset markets were in the grip of 'irrational exuberance' and boom-time psychology. Furthermore they should have been more vigilant in ensuring that banks remained liquid and solvent and did not lend too much in the good times (see Chapters 3 and 7).

In practice, this policy prescription is not always easy to implement. Asset bubbles are obvious in retrospect but not in prospect. Often they begin as rises in asset prices that are founded on fundamentals. The correct value of an asset depends on projections of future income flows from that asset that are difficult to evaluate objectively. Taking action to head off an asset boom requires clear lines of responsibility. (See Chapters 3 and 12 for a discussion of the reforms introduced in Ireland and the euro zone since 2008 to address this issue.)

In assessing the immediate danger of a price collapse one problem familiar to all those who have studied economic cycles is that of premature warnings. This applied in the Irish case, where early warnings of an asset bubble as far back as 2003 did not materialise and hence undermined the credibility of future warnings. The key point is that it is very difficult to identify, and to anticipate the consequences, of an asset price collapse, even with the support of a strong economics research team. In retrospect, we see that Ireland suffered a near-perfect example of what Nassim Taleb defines as a Black Swan: an event or combination of events that (a) lies outside the realm of regular expectations, (b) carries an extreme impact and that (c) can be explained retrospectively after the event but not prospectively.[9] Banks are particularly prone to Black Swans. They can hide explosive risks in their portfolios and in just one day can lose the profits of decades.

Why Consumer Price Stability is Important

Although asset prices have attracted much attention in recent years, it is useful to consider the arguments for price stability in the narrower context of the CPI.

Failure to achieve price stability impacts adversely on both economic growth and income distribution. As we have seen, deviations from price stability can take the form of inflation or deflation. Of the two, inflation has presented the more prevalent and persistent danger over time.

Deflation, defined as a persistent decline in the general price level, has been a rare phenomenon. The most traumatic case of deflation was the 25 per cent decline in USA prices during the Great Depression of 1929 to 1933. Another case has been the deflation in Japan after the mid 1990s. Japanese consumer prices fell in every year (save 2008) between 1999 and 2012. There was also great concern that the euro zone would experience deflation in the years 2008 to 2016, with price rises close to zero for several years, well below the stated target of close to 2 per cent per annum. The main worry is that deflation can prolong a recession by giving consumers and investors an incentive to postpone spending, and this appears to have been the case in the euro zone countries and elsewhere in these years.

With price rise now expected to exceed the target of 2 per cent per annum in the years ahead, attention has now turned again to the dangers of inflation. What are these? First, uncertainty about the inflation rate undermines the role played by money in economising on transaction costs. Fixed-price orders, leases and other explicit long-term contracts, fixed-time schedules for price changes and the broad general commitment to continuity of offers by suppliers are important ways of assisting forward planning. Uncertainty about the future price level shortens the time horizon of such agreements, thus imposing a welfare loss on society.

The haphazard nature of the income distribution effects of inflation can also lead to social unrest and general discontent as people find it increasingly difficult to estimate the growth in their real incomes and to predict what their real earnings will be in the future. In a period of 1 per cent inflation, people who receive pay increases of 4 per cent recognise clearly that they have gained in real terms. In a world of 15 per cent inflation, those receiving pay increases of 19 per cent are likely to be much less confident about how they are faring.

6 COMPETITIVENESS

Small regional economies like Ireland are largely 'importers' of price trends abroad. Thus if the CPI is rising in continental Europe and the UK at around 2 per cent, inflation in both parts of Ireland will also approximate 2 per cent. This is a valid generalisation over the long run. But it is not universally the case and significant short-run deviations between a region's inflation rate and the national/ area average do occur. During the period 1999 to 2008 Irish prices rose twice as fast as average euro-area prices. As a result, Ireland became one of the most expensive countries in the euro zone. The excess has been only partially reversed by price restraint (and an actual decline of 6 per cent in the Irish price level up to 2010). Theory indicates that there will be *mean reversion,* (i.e. that sooner or later price levels in Ireland will revert to the euro-area average), but serious damage to the economy will have been done in the interim.

Why do cost divergences occur between a country such as Ireland and the euro zone average and what can or should be done about them?

Price and Cost Divergences
One reason for the divergence in price trends stems from Ireland's rapid growth relative to the euro zone. Faster growth translates into higher pay. This is non-inflationary where productivity rises in line with pay. Thus a 5 per cent pay rise matched by a 5 per cent productivity increase leaves unit cost, and hence prices, unaffected. However, in those parts of the economy where productivity growth is relatively modest, employers will have to increase wages in line with other sectors (or else their workers will leave for better pay elsewhere). Hence unit costs and prices will tend to rise.

Second, changes in the euro exchange rate have had a strong effect on domestic prices. A 20 per cent decline in the value of the euro has been estimated to lead to only a 1 per cent rise in the average euro-zone price level. However, because of the Republic's higher trade dependence and the higher proportion of trade with countries outside the euro zone, the impact of such a depreciation of the euro on the Irish CPI is far higher.

Implications of a Loss of Cost Competitiveness
When a region's prices/costs rise relative to other regions, this is termed a loss of cost competitiveness. One immediate impact of such deterioration is a decline in exports as they become more expensive to foreigners. For the same reason, domestic goods become more expensive relative to imports and the import bill rises.

For a country with an independent national currency the next question is the effect of the deficit on the exchange rate. If the exchange rate devalues, this offers a short-run solution to the loss of competitiveness. But the resultant rise in domestic prices could set in motion an inflationary spiral, with devaluation causing domestic price increases, which lead to compensatory pay claims. This is the classic downside of devaluation as a policy response to deficits induced by cost-competitiveness problems.

In the case of a small regional economy, the exchange rate is fixed and it will not change in response to the region's loss of competitiveness. If Northern Ireland loses cost competitiveness and runs a deficit, this will not materially affect the value of sterling. Likewise the Republic's competitiveness will have no impact on the fortunes of the euro. In each case the region is too small to affect the bigger picture.

The region may thus be left with a situation where imports rise and exports lose momentum. This means that the region is spending more on foreign goods and services than it is earning from exports. In this sense, a deficit signifies that a country is 'living beyond its means'. The deficit will have to be matched by foreign borrowing, and the corresponding capital inflow will eventually have to be financed and repaid.

An adverse movement in a region's cost competitiveness cannot be indefinitely sustained. As regional prices increase, the region's cost structure becomes more and more out of line with its competitors. It will begin to lose export markets and will become less attractive as a location for investment. Borrowing abroad will become more expensive or even dry up entirely. Eventually growth will slow, labour demand will decline, and pay pressures will ease.

The speed of this process was a much debated issue in Ireland prior to the financial crisis of 2008. Ireland's price level had risen by 40 per cent above the euro-zone average. In a situation like this booming regions hope for a 'soft' landing, whereby rising costs will gradually be restrained to more sustainable levels over time. Unfortunately, the historical experience provides many examples of 'hard' landings where adjustment takes place abruptly, property markets collapse and unemployment rises. Ireland was to prove no exception to this rule. We suffered an exceptionally hard landing and the slow painful process of restoring competitiveness had to begin in earnest after 2008. With the economy recovering rapidly since 2013 the danger of hubris is already evident, with the consequences again of a severe loss of competitiveness if the warning signs are not heeded.

This suggests that the major concern of any region must be to safeguard its competitiveness, achieving its economic potential while moderating booms and avoiding busts along the way. The importance of avoiding deviations from competitiveness in a common currency union has long been accepted. In 2011, Angela Merkel the German chancellor floated the idea of a Competitiveness Pact among euro area members whereby price deviations from the euro-area average on the part of a member state would be monitored and would trigger a collective response to correct it. The aim would be to ensure much closer economic and fiscal coordination in the euro zone.

Thus for a small region like Ireland lacking an independent exchange rate and with largely downward-inflexible labour costs, domestic competitiveness policy is an instrument of critical importance.

Broad Definition of Competitiveness
Competitiveness has become something of a global preoccupation since the 1990s. Every region worries about it and governments everywhere feel compelled to do something to improve it. Practically every country in Europe has set up a competitiveness council. The *World Competitiveness Report*, and its rival, the *Global Competitiveness Report*, are published annually and attract worldwide publicity. Their findings are scrutinised with a fine toothcomb by development agencies and government commissions.

Competitiveness has been a well-established theme in economic debate in Ireland. In the Republic, the National Competitiveness Council was set up in 1997. Its *Annual Competitiveness Report* is a rich source of information on competitiveness indicators (see Chapters 7 and 10). The Council's remit is to examine key competitiveness issues and to make recommendations on policy actions required to improve Ireland's competitive position.

Competitiveness can be defined in a narrow sense or in a broad sense. The narrow definition focuses on trends in pay, productivity, and unit costs. These components are aggregated into a cost competitiveness index and movements in the index are tracked over time and compared with trends in competing countries. For many years, emphasis was placed on this narrow definition partly because of data limitations (information on the components of the broader definition has only recently become available) and partly because Ireland's performance on the cost-competitiveness definition was exceptionally poor.

The broader definition includes price and non-price factors such as product quality, reliability of supply, backup marketing services, and taxation, and extends to consideration of human resource development, business services, infrastructure and public finance and administration. A country's long-run competitive position can also be profoundly influenced by its policy towards research and development (R&D), and by its success in product innovation and technology. Innovation and R&D are the key ingredients of a region's infrastructure (see Chapters 7 and 9). Competitiveness authorities in both parts of Ireland currently use the broader definition of competitiveness.

Competitiveness is a relative concept. Success in the competitiveness league depends on how well an economy is progressing relative to others. It is possible for all countries to grow faster, to generate more employment, to export more; but by definition only some countries can become more competitive. In other words, the process of striving to be more competitive, in so far as it improves economic growth and efficiency, is a positive-sum game. But in terms of ranking in competitiveness leagues it is a zero-sum game, since one region advances in the ranking order only if some other region declines. Failure to recognise this point can lead to competitiveness becoming what has been called a 'dangerous obsession' instead of a stimulus to improved performance.

Strategy to Improve Competitiveness

Policies to improve competitiveness constitute the theme of many chapters of this book. These policies change over time and according to circumstances will differ across region and nation. To date the policy objective has focused on creating an environment that would encourage (see Chapters 7 and 10 in particular):

- The growth of export-oriented firms, especially Irish-owned firms;
- The retention and attraction of foreign direct investment in knowledge-based sectors and activities such as information technology, electronics, pharmaceuticals, biotechnology, and software;
- The development of linkages between existing and new green-field firms;
- A balanced location of economic activity within the island.

This ambitious programme has involved several policy dimensions and instruments, which will be analysed throughout the rest of this book.

Policy measures taken at the centre (Brussels/Frankfurt/Strasbourg) are becoming increasingly important. Monetary and exchange rate policy is the obvious example. The Centre also exerts major influence over fiscal, competition, transport and agriculture policy as well as state aids and taxation. The European Commission is concerned about competitiveness at the EU-wide level, and action taken to improve it will have important implications for Ireland (see later chapters).

The scope for regional policy initiatives, though declining, remains of crucial importance. A key fiscal incentive in the Republic is the 12.5 per cent tax rate for all corporate income from 2003. In addition, domestic authorities have some degree of discretion in the payment of capital grants, training grants, R&D support and so on. The extension of these fiscal and financial concessions to internationally-traded service industries has proved to be a significant incentive to the development of the Irish Financial Services Centre and the attraction of major multinationals to Ireland (see Chapter 10). Provision of a good physical environment and human capital structure (education) is also an intrinsic part of a strategy for improving competitiveness (see Chapters 7, 10 and 11).

7 CONCLUSION

The first priority of economic policy is to ensure high and rising standards of living. In practical terms, this means that economic performance is judged mostly by reference to changes in GNP per person. People want economic growth because of what it can do for them in terms of higher purchasing power and also because of the other good things that often accompany growth such as more employment, generous safety nets for the poor and greater security.

Growth is a primary priority, but there are limits to what it can deliver. Growth at any price is not a sensible objective, nor is the attainment of maximum growth, particularly when this would involve environmental damage, an excessively large increase in immigration, and other undesirable spillover effects. In setting medium-term targets, rather than targeting the maximum growth an economy can reach and then working out the implications of this for policy, we should instead be asking what growth we wish to obtain and work backwards from there.

GNP per capita has many limitations as an indicator of output and human welfare. It leaves out of account leisure, the environment, and global warming, and misclassifies many inputs as outputs. Another limitation is that GNP per capita neglects important indicators of human welfare such as education and health. Despite its many failings, however, the GNP per capita statistic serves as a remarkably good proxy for more sophisticated measures of human welfare, as comparisons between rankings based on GNP per head and the United Nations Human Development Index demonstrate.

Equity in the sense of a fair distribution of income and an adequate level of income to all individuals is an important policy objective. The issue of equity is indeed a central aspect of most economic problems. In the Irish political domain concerns with equity and income distribution often outweigh concerns with economic efficiency in discussion of policy alternatives. Policymakers seek to reduce social exclusion and long-term unemployment by widening opportunities for education and work. Care should be taken, however, when deciding on the degree of redistribution to avoid penalising the achievers and stifling economic growth. Protecting the vulnerable is good, but encouraging those who will lead the Irish economy to enduring good health must, for the next decade at least, be paramount.

It is also important to consider the 'wellbeing' or happiness of the community in the broadest sense when formulating economic policy. The weak association between GNP per person and happiness gives pause for reflection. There is some evidence that this relationship also applies when income is falling. With good management perhaps the painful effects of the loss of income can be moderated. This reinforces the need for policies that will seek to maximise societal welfare and that will deliver a full-employment, pollution-free, low-crime and safe society.

Financial stability is a policy objective that is both desired for its own sake and as a means to the end of attaining growth. There is now more conviction among politicians of the electoral advantages of running an economy in a way that maintains macroeconomic, financial and price stability. As a population ages, it is likely that the constituency in favour of stability will grow. Politicians seem increasingly content to leave monetary policy to independent central banks. Some elements of sovereignty in relation to fiscal policy have also been voluntarily relinquished. This new approach is helpful for price stability and good for the overall economy, since price stability and output growth complement one another in the long run.

Experience over the past few years has, however, taught a further important lesson. Price stability (in terms of consumer prices) is not enough. The authorities also need to pay careful attention to the evolution of asset prices. Stability of the financial system is an even more important objective that, we see in retrospect, was given all too little attention in the lead up to the banking crisis.

As we advance into the twenty-first century, we can expect competitiveness to occupy the high ground as a major secondary policy priority for the Irish economy. Competitiveness covers a wider spectrum of economic variables. Irish policymakers used to focus on standard comparisons between cost and price indicators here and those in competitor countries. These indexes continue to be relevant. Within the space of a few years, the Republic became a comparatively expensive location for visiting or doing business, and prices and pay rates converged towards the higher end of the European spectrum. The detrimental effects of this loss in competitiveness became apparent as the post-2008 crisis evolved. In the longer run, it clearly will be necessary to justify higher earnings by higher productivity. It is here that the broader definition of competitiveness comes into play. Competitiveness in this broader sense includes R&D, education, quality improvement, marketing and physical infrastructure – the intangible and often difficult to measure aspects that impact crucially on an economy's ability to perform well. Addressing this issue in a sense is the purpose of the rest of this book.

Endnotes

*   The author wishes to thank John O'Hagan for percipient and extensive comments on successive drafts of this chapter for this and previous editions.

1   See Chapter 7 for a discussion of the difference between GNP and GDP, an issue of particular importance in Ireland. In most countries they give the same numbers but in the case of Ireland GNP (income) is around 20 per cent less than GDP (output) and hence we will use GNP for the remainder of this chapter.

2   J. Galbraith, *The Nature of Mass Poverty*, Harvard University Press, Cambridge MA 1979.

3   P. Collier, *Exodus: Immigration and Multiculturalism in the Twentieth Century,* Allen Lane, London 2013.

4   R. Kennedy, quoted in *Finance and Development*, Washington, December 1993, p.20.

5   United Nations Development Programme, *Human Development Report,* 2013 (www. hdr.undp.org).

6   J. Rawls, *A Theory of Justice*, Harvard University Press, Cambridge MA 1971.

7   A readable and enlightening overview of the literature is provided in R. Layard, *Happiness: Lessons from a New Science,* Penguin Books, New York and London 2005.

8   R. Whately, *Introductory Lectures on Political Economy*, London 1831.

9   N. Taleb, *The Black Swan: The Impact of the Highly Improbable*, Penguin Books, London 2007.

SECTION II

POLICY IMPLEMENTATION

CHAPTER 3

National/International Levels of Government: Rationale and Issues

Philip R. Lane

1 INTRODUCTION

Chapter 2 established economic policy objectives for Ireland. The government is responsible for the pursuit of these goals, either directly or in tandem with its international counterparts. The government's ability to achieve its policy goals is supported by the special powers assigned to the state, most notably its powers of compulsion in terms of setting legislation and collecting taxes. In this chapter, the role of government in pursuing these policy objectives is addressed.

The rest of the chapter is organised as follows. Section 2 reviews the theoretical basis for government intervention in the economy. The allocation of responsibilities across different levels of government is described in Section 3, followed in Section 4 by a specific consideration of the very important single currency and the euro zone. In Section 5, the central role played by public expenditure and taxation policies is analysed. Section 6 addresses other policy instruments available to the government, while Section 7 discusses the economic and political factors determining the size of the government sector. Section 8 concludes the chapter.

2 RATIONALE FOR GOVERNMENT INTERVENTION

There are a number of classic arguments that provide a rationale for government intervention in the economy. The starting point is to recognise the absurdity of a no-government economy. A central authority and a *legal system* are necessary to permit the (implicit or explicit) contracts that govern all economic activity, for example through the design and enforcement of corporate and labour laws. Cross-country evidence and historical examples show that anarchy and the absence of a 'rule of law' result in very poor economic performance (and the emergence of private contract enforcement systems, such as Mafia-style organisations): the evidence from 'failed states' lends considerable support to these concerns.[1]

Put another way, we can interpret economic activity as an elaborate game: as with any other game, a set of rules and a referee are required. The state is responsible for designing and enforcing the rules that determine permissible behaviour on the parts of firms and consumers: the anarchic alternative would be unstable and highly deleterious for economic performance. Some rules of the game relate to ensuring that the level and mix of economic activity is not unnecessarily hampered by a lack of enforceable agreements (that is, contracts that can be protected through the legal system); other rules are intended to ensure that the game meets some minimum degree of fairness (for example, by ensuring that people can obtain some level of education and healthcare, independently of household income levels).

A second function relates to the efficient allocation of resources. A laissez-faire economy will not efficiently provide *public goods* (e.g. national defence). A pure public good is non-rival (it can be collectively consumed) and non-excludable (its benefits cannot be easily withheld from individuals): examples include the provision of national security and basic scientific research (a new mathematical formula can be used by everyone and, once published, is non-excludable). Non-excludability prevents market provision, since no one has an incentive to pay for a good if it can be freely consumed. The state must step in to support the provision of such public goods and raise the resources required by levying taxation.

Similarly, market prices do not reflect *external effects*, with the result that activities generating positive externalities are under-produced and those generating negative externalities are overproduced. A good that produces a positive externality is similar to a public good, in that some of its benefits are non-excludable and accrue to others than just the direct consumer. However, such goods may be rivalrous and may be partially excludable, so that some private provision occurs even if the level of production is inadequate.

The road network is a good illustration of a positive externality: the gain to building an extra kilometre of motorway increases the productivity of other parts of the road network that become more accessible. One obvious example of a negative externality is environmental pollution. A second example is provided by commonly-held resources such as fisheries, whereby individuals are not responsible for the maintenance of a sustainable stock. The government can promote the production of goods that generate positive externalities through a variety of mechanisms, including direct provision or subsidy schemes. In contrast, it may impose quotas or taxes on goods that generate negative external effects.

Other sources of market failure include *monopoly power* and *imperfect information*. The former means that prices will be too high and output too low relative to the competitive outcome (see Chapter 5). The latter means that many credit and insurance markets are missing or incomplete, since it is impossible for private firms to adequately evaluate projects, accurately calculate default risks and monitor the behaviour of individual agents. Such market failures provide a *prima facie* case for some kind of government intervention, either by direct provision or through subsidisation.

However, the desirability of actual intervention is tempered by 'government failure': it is not clear that, in many cases, governments can deliver a more efficient outcome than that generated by even imperfect markets. Electoral pressures; interest group lobbying; perverse incentives in administration; corruption; restrictive practices and inflexible procedures in the public sector; and inadequate management skills may all lead to welfare decreasing interventions in the economy. Accordingly, the optimal degree of government intervention must balance the prospective gains against potential implementation problems.

Even if free markets delivered a perfectly efficient outcome, *distributional considerations* would still justify government intervention (see also Chapter 8). The income distribution attained by a market economy is conditional on the initial distribution of endowments (both monetary and individual characteristics such as intelligence, good health and family background). Being lucky in one's choice of parents is an important determinant of success in a market economy: for example, in Ireland and elsewhere, educational attainment levels are highly correlated with family income levels and social background (see also Chapter 13). Moreover, economic outcomes have a random element. The weather influences the success or failure of many agricultural projects and many entrepreneurs recognise the role played by fortune in creating viable new businesses.

Accordingly, voters typically demand that the government redistributes income in order to protect the poorly endowed and the unlucky, with the redistribution function further reinforced by the increasing acceptance of rights-based frameworks that require sufficient material provision for each individual. However, the ability of the government to redistribute income is constrained along two dimensions. First, excessively high taxation depresses incentives, reducing the level of income and growth rates. Second, mobile factors (capital, highly-skilled workers) may leave jurisdictions that impose harsh tax burdens.

Finally, it should be clear that government performance is an important determinant of international competitiveness. An efficient government enhances the ability of domestic firms to compete in international markets, by reducing the taxation and other costs of attaining policy objectives; in international empirical studies, an efficient government is highly correlated with strong growth performance.[2]

3 LEVELS OF GOVERNMENT

Different levels of government can intervene in the economy. While the traditional focus has been on national governments, global, European and local levels of government are also increasingly important. A special form of governance at a

European level arises from the existence of the euro zone, a topic which will be given separate treatment in Section 4.

Global Governance

For some issues, global levels of government are best placed to deal with a given issue. Ireland participates in the World Trade Organization, is a member of the International Monetary Fund and World Bank, and subscribes to various international policy agreements, such as on climate change. Through its membership of the European Union, Ireland is also indirectly represented in global fora such as the G-20 set of meetings.

The driving force behind global levels of governance is that the globalisation of many economic activities enhances efficiency and is facilitated by a common set of international rules. For instance, it would be an extremely tedious procedure for each country to negotiate bilateral agreements with all its potential trading partners: the World Trade Organization and the various regional trade agreements greatly reduce the transaction costs in ensuring trade liberalisation.

Similarly, in tackling problems that are fundamentally global in character, non-coordinated national policy responses make little sense.[3] The most obvious example is the climate change problem: carbon emissions in each country symmetrically affect the global climate. However, similar considerations apply in the domain of public health: high levels of air travel mean that a virus that emerges in one area can quickly be transmitted around the world. To the extent that some security threats are global in nature (for example, the control of nuclear weapons and the risks posed by dissident groups that seek to disrupt global economic and social systems), there is also a global level to defence policies. Finally, large international income inequalities, especially the extreme poverty of the 'bottom billion' of the global population (primarily in sub-Saharan Africa) constitutes a global problem across many dimensions.[4] In addition to the ethical issues, it is in the self-interest of advanced economies to promote international development, in view of the inter-connections between extreme poverty, political instability, mass migrations, and public health.

Moreover, the globalisation of economic activity also makes national or regional policy actions less effective: for example, high tax rates or onerous regulations may prompt mobile factors to relocate to more business-friendly regimes. Conversely, national subsidies or tax breaks distort international location decisions, since a firm may opt to produce even in an inefficient location if it receives sufficiently high compensation from the host government. For these reasons, coordination of international policies can potentially restore the ability of governments to tax mobile factors and avoid undesirable 'subsidy auctions' in competing for footloose firms.

That said, the difficulty with international policy coordination is that there is not always consensus on the correct policy. Preferences may legitimately differ across countries on important issues such as: the appropriate level of taxation; the ideal level of social protection; and the optimal degree of risk aversion in food regulation. Accordingly, global governance arrangements are more easily achieved on technocratic issues such as elements of the world trade and financial systems, with less progress on social issues. For this reason, it is sometimes argued that the development of global governance has been unbalanced: much progress has been made on cooperation in economic policy but with less effective coordination of labour or environmental regulations. However, in the absence of a directly elected 'world government', it is unlikely that much progress can be made on controversial issues that are the subject of much disagreement both within and across countries.[5] Moreover, cross-country distributional issues also limit the scope for global cooperation. These factors mean that global levels of governance are likely to remain quite circumscribed in the absence of sufficient consensus on various issues across sovereign nations.

The ongoing struggle to implement a global plan to address climate change illustrates these tensions (see also Chapter 11). While there is a strong intellectual consensus on the need for urgent action to combat climate change, there are significant differences of opinion in terms of the balance of adjustment between advanced and developing economies, in view of their different cumulative contributions to carbon emissions. A fair global solution plausibly involves a significant transfer of funds from the advanced economies to the developing world, to compensate for the fact that the accumulated stock of carbon emissions has been primarily generated by high-income countries over many decades of industrial activity: achieving agreement on the scale of such redistribution will be difficult. A second problem is that it is difficult and costly to impose sanctions on non-compliant nations, so that any global initiative must rely on softer methods of promoting compliance – for example, peer pressure across member governments, plus monitoring by national and international 'civic society' groups such as Saving the Earth, Greenpeace and other activist organisations.

EU Governance

EU membership is the most important international commitment of the Irish government. Although the scale of inter-governmental cooperation at the EU level faces many of the difficulties encountered at global levels of governance, the scope for establishing common policies is much greater at the EU level. This reflects the very close economic and social ties across the member countries, plus the elaborate institutional structure that has been developed (European Commission, Council of Ministers, European Parliament, inter-governmental treaties) to promote and sustain policymaking at the EU level.

Moreover, since member states bargain over many issues, decision making is facilitated by the multi-dimensional nature of political relations among the member states: for instance, some undesirable regulation in one area may be accepted in exchange for a concession on another issue. In other cases, the level of disagreement may be so strong that coordination is not possible, with countries retaining independent national policies. Although a national veto still remains on some policy issues (e.g. tax rates), qualified majority voting now applies in many areas.

The 2016 Brexit vote means that Europe will now have to adapt to a new institutional setting in which the EU interacts with the UK on the basis of a new agreement, with the departure of the UK from the EU also likely to induce a re-assessment of the internal operation of the EU among the remaining member states.

Four Freedoms

In order to create a single market, EU law guarantees the 'four freedoms': the free movement of goods and services; freedom of establishment; the free movement of persons (and citizenship), including free movement of workers; and the free movement of capital. In addition, EU competition law also now sharply restricts national autonomy in industrial and competition policies, with EU-level monitoring of state interventions in domestic markets. In addition, large public contracts must be advertised at an EU wide level, rather than directly allocated to domestic firms.

In these ways, the EU can be interpreted as an international 'agency of restraint' that promotes more efficient allocations and depoliticises many economic decisions. The flip side is that the sharing of sovereignty at an EU level is perceived by many as representing an excessive loss of national influence over policy decisions. Indeed, the Brexit vote was driven to a significant extent by an expressed desire to 'take back control' over key policy issues, such as migration and trade.

A difficulty with international policy coordination is that there is not always consensus on the correct policy. Preferences may legitimately differ across countries on important issues such as: the appropriate level of taxation; the ideal level of social protection; and the optimal degree of risk aversion in setting various regulations. Since member states bargain over many issues, some undesirable policy outcomes in one sphere may be accepted in exchange for concessions on other issues. In other cases, the level of disagreement may be so strong that coordination is not possible, with countries retaining independent national policies.

Democratic Accountability

A common criticism of international policy coordination is that it leads to a 'democratic deficit', with decisions made at a level that is too far removed from ordinary voters. Although the 2008 Treaty of Lisbon introduced some reforms to improve democratic accountability, it remains an ongoing concern that EU institutions are perceived as too remote by the general European population. Moreover, the policy response to the European financial crisis during 2010 to 2012 underlined the lack of trust in EU-level institutions that are not directly controlled by national governments.

As a result, there is a tension in the operation of the EU between taking decisions through the official EU institutions versus inter-governmental negotiations. While the former may be more efficient, the latter ensures that national governments have a greater say in EU policymaking. For instance, the allocation of official loans is now controlled by the European Stability Mechanism (ESM), which makes decisions on the basis of unanimity among the member governments. Given the large sums controlled by the ESM, the inter-governmental nature of its governance underlines the limited autonomy acceded to EU institutions by the member states, with the main exception in the economic sphere being the exceptional independence accorded to the ECB.

Taxation

As indicated, many decisions concerning government spending and taxation remain at the national level, providing scope for significant variation in the level and nature of government intervention across member countries. Following the earlier discussion, harmonisation of tax rates on mobile capital is advocated by some member countries. However, there is little agreement on the appropriate tax rate: a high capital tax rate may be progressive and reduce pressure on other parts of the tax base but at the cost of a negative effect on growth performance, with countries having different preferences as to the optimal trade off across these dimensions.

Ireland currently resists pressure to harmonise corporation tax rates at a higher level. However, there is also a current proposal to design a common consolidated tax base, such that a multinational firm need only produce a single set of European financial accounts, with capital income taxed according to a formula that reflects its economic activities (such as sales revenues) in each country (for detailed discussions of this see Chapters 4 and 10). To the extent that this is a voluntary code, the impact on Ireland may be relatively minor but widespread adoption of a common tax base would limit the level of corporate income that is taxable in Ireland, in view of the export orientation of most multinational firms operating there.

Future Evolution

In terms of the future evolution of EU governance, one option is to take an incremental approach, with the scale and pace of EU integration adjusted to match the contemporaneous EU-wide political appetite for further integration measures. A second option is to deepen the extent of political integration, with more power ceded to EU-level institutions but matched by an increase in pan-EU democratic control, for example through more directly-elected positions. As with the development of any federal structure, this requires a sufficiently-strong consensus within the electorate of each EU member state that it is willing to accept the decisions made by EU-level politicians, even in scenarios in which the decision may be at odds with national-level preferences. It remains to be seen if such a strong level of EU political integration can develop in the coming decades.

Local Government

At the other end, some policy issues are being devolved from national to local and regional levels of government. Local government plausibly has an information advantage in designing and implementing policies that better reflect the preferences and needs of local residents. A closer relationship with the electorate may also improve the responsiveness and accountability of government. However, decentralisation also brings risks, especially if fiscal and functional responsibilities are not clearly allocated between the centre and periphery.

In Ireland, local government has traditionally played a very limited role. However, with the switch towards greater local financing and autonomy in the provision of services, the trend is for greater diversity in local government in Ireland. In principle, this can be supported by the new property tax, which provides a new source of locally-controlled funding (see Chapter 4).

The application of the subsidiarity principle is also more evident at the EU level: there is greater recognition that the EU should focus its energies on those policy areas where cooperation is most effective, with the return of some policy issues to national governments. For instance, with the move to direct payments in subsidising the agricultural sector, it is predicted that responsibility for the agricultural sector will be shifted from Brussels to national levels of government (see Chapter 9). In a related fashion, EU competition policy can now also be implemented by national competition authorities using national court systems.

Finally, in light of the improved political climate since the 1998 Good Friday Agreement, progress has been made for improved policy cooperation between the Republic of Ireland and Northern Ireland, with considerable scope for yet further integration. Significant scale economies can be achieved in areas such as tourism (e.g. with the creation of the all island Tourism Ireland marketing organisation) and network externalities can be better exploited by more efficiently integrating the transport and energy networks between the two jurisdictions. Moreover, the economic success of the Republic of Ireland has led to some reorientation of activity in Northern Ireland, with a greater focus on pursuing cross-border business opportunities.

Under the Good Friday Agreement, a number of inter-governmental agencies have been established to facilitate enhanced policy cooperation in areas such as environment, agriculture, education, health, tourism, and transport. The preservation of cross-border North-South cooperative mechanisms will be an important challenge in the UK-EU Brexit negotiations, especially in view of the challenges posed by the re-introduction of trade barriers and migration controls.

National Governments

In this section, we have shown that global, EU and local levels of government play important roles. However, by default, the primary level of government remains at the national level, since national boundaries define the most advanced current levels of democratic political systems.

Over the last thirty years, it has been recognised that globalisation and international (global and EU) levels of government makes it more viable for smaller nations to operate independently.[6] In the European context, the security provided by the dense level of EU integration means that smaller nations need not be part of a large multi-national political unit for national defence purposes, while international and EU trade liberalisation means that smaller nations need not be too worried about the economic costs of a small domestic market. Since the 1990s, Europe has seen the breakup of the former Yugoslavia into its constituent nation states and the Velvet Divorce by which the former Czechoslovakia broke up into the Czech Republic and the Slovak Republic. In September 2014, Scotland only narrowly rejected the option to become independent, while there are also strong independence movements in Catalonia and other semi-autonomous regions in Spain and persistent strains between the Flemish and French parts of Belgium.

4 SINGLE CURRENCY AND EURO ZONE

In 1999, a subset of eleven EU members, including Ireland, adopted the euro as a single currency. By 2017, nineteen EU members have joined the euro area, with further members expected to join over the next decade. In principle, a monetary union offers microeconomic efficiency gains and facilitates the development of a deep, liquid capital market. Moreover, a large currency bloc can provide insulation from destabilising speculative attacks on national currencies, permitting lower average interest rates and reducing the risk of financial crises.

Role of ECB

A core feature of European monetary union is that the member governments have delegated the operation of monetary policy to an independent agency – the European Central Bank (ECB). With each member state nominating members to the Governing Council of the ECB, decisions over monetary policy are made on a joint basis, with the primary goal of attaining price stability on an area-wide basis. This is in sharp contrast to traditional fixed exchange rate regimes, in which one country sets monetary policy and other countries must follow suit. At the same time, the institutional design of the euro zone is quite different to the setup in the United States in which the common currency (the dollar) is matched by an array of other federal features, including significant federal tax revenues, federal levels of government spending and federal deposit insurance.

The delegation of technocratic forms of government intervention, such as the conduct of monetary policy, to semi-autonomous institutions can be interpreted as a useful agency of restraint that ties the hands of political leaders that face enormous short-term pressures to adopt populist policies that may damage the economy in the long term. Democratic accountability is facilitated through several mechanisms: the mandate of the ECB is fixed by treaty; the President of the ECB testifies before the European Parliament on a regular basis; and the ECB is in regular dialogue with the European Commission and the euro zone meetings of finance ministers.

However, a 'one size fits all' monetary policy may itself be a source of instability if business cycles are not highly correlated across member countries. In the early years of EMU, Ireland fell into this category: in view of our high growth rates, interest rates were inappropriately low and excessive inflation was the result. In the other direction, countries such as Germany, Portugal, and Italy may have preferred a looser monetary policy during this initial period, in view of the relatively-poorer domestic performance in these economies.

In common with many other advanced economies, EU member countries were also insufficiently prepared to deal with the international financial boom that took hold during 2003 to 2007. During this period, easy global credit conditions contributed to excessive debt accumulation in some member countries. In Ireland and Spain, the private sector took on debt as national real estate bubbles took hold (see Chapters 7 and 12). In Greece and Portugal, the government was the primary borrower during this period. Model simulations show that the accumulation of imbalances would have been much less severe had active macro-prudential policies and more prudential fiscal frameworks been in place at the national level.[7]

Global Financial Crisis 2008 to 2009
The twin financial crises (global crisis in 2008 to 2009, euro zone crisis in 2010 to 2012) revealed the strengths and weaknesses of the design of the monetary union. At one level, a common currency provided a lot of insulation. The ECB cut interest rates sharply in late 2008 and early 2009 from 3.75 per cent to 1.00 per cent. This cut in interest rates provided substantial relief for indebted households and firms throughout the crisis. This has been further maintained in the aftermath of the crisis, especially through the extensive asset purchase programmes from 2014 onwards which have contributed to a relaxation in financial conditions in the euro zone.

In addition, the ECB provided general liquidity to the European banking system, substituting for the breakdown of the inter-bank wholesale market in 2008. The liquidity operations of the ECB provided extraordinary support to the troubled banking systems in the euro periphery and to overextended systemically-important banks in the core member countries, with an outflow of private capital from these entities partly replaced by an inflow of official funding from the ECB.

The 2010 to 2012 euro zone crisis also demonstrated systemic vulnerabilities in the design of the EMU institutional framework. Starting in late 2009, bond investors became sceptical about the capacity of the new Greek government to meet its debt obligations (which had been partly concealed by the previous government). In similar fashion to the various emerging market crises that had occurred in previous decades (such as the Asian financial crisis in 1997 to 1998), it was assessed that it was desirable to provide international official funding to Greece in order to avoid an outright debt default.

Official funding plays several roles. First, by allowing a country to meet its debt obligations, it limits the risk of contagion to other weak governments, with the fear that default by one country might elevate debt crises in other countries. Second, since banks are major holders of sovereign bonds, avoiding a default also limits the risk of a banking crisis, which in turn might trigger banking crises in other jurisdictions. Third, to the extent that debt default is typically associated with a period of exclusion from funding markets, it limits the scale of spending adjustment required in the defaulting country, smoothing out the costs of adjustment for the domestic population.

Euro Zone Crisis 2010 to 2012
The 2010 to 2012 euro zone crisis was magnified by several factors.[8] First, the scale of outstanding debts and the degree of weakness in banking systems was exceptionally large, since the easy conditions during the mid 2000s and the ability to borrow in the shared domestic currency meant that the scale of debt flows was unprecedented. This meant that there were few historical guides to the consequences of substantial debt restructuring. Second, the common currency meant that it was plausible that contagion dynamics across sovereign debt markets and banking systems could be unusually powerful. Third, the appropriate role of the ECB in countering speculation about 'redenomination risk' in sovereign debt markets was not spelled out in advance of the crisis, whereas there was greater familiarity about the potential role of national central banks in local-currency debt markets in relation to other advanced economies. Fourth, sovereign default is typically associated with contractionary impulses in the economy, which cannot be offset by a national currency devaluation inside a monetary union.

The EU and IMF combined to provide official loans to Greece in May 2010. Ireland also received official funding at the end of 2010, with Portugal following in 2011 and Cyprus in 2013; Spain also received a limited type of bank-related bailout in 2012. The scale of the Greek crisis was such that the official loans also had to be accompanied by a substantial restructuring of the sovereign debt held by private investors in 2012.

These bailouts were intended to provide bridge financing for a temporary period during which the recipient countries reduce their dependence on external debt, by cutting fiscal deficits and deleveraging banking systems. At the end of 2013, Ireland was able to exit the bailout programme and Portugal also returned to market funding in 2014. In contrast, Greece remains reliant on official funding sources to service its debts.

Since the governments underwriting the official funding face potential losses in the event of non-repayment, such programmes are accompanied by sets of conditions in relation to the pace of fiscal austerity and the extent of structural reforms. While a standard feature in IMF-led programmes, the process of EU member states setting policy conditions for other member states has been politically challenging.

Reforms
The trauma of the crisis has also triggered a set of reforms in order to avoid a future re-run. First, there is now a permanent institution to act as an intermediary for intra-EU official funding, with the European Stability Mechanism (ESM) established in 2012. The existence of the ESM in itself acts to reassure investors that self-fulfilling speculative attacks in sovereign debt markets are less likely, in relation to governments that are evaluated as fundamentally solvent.

Second, the new fiscal framework in Europe (detailed further below) is intended to deliver more disciplined fiscal policies, making it less likely that fiscally-driven crises can occur. Third, under the Bank Recovery and Resolution Directive (BRRD), the organisational structures of banks are now designed to make it easier to restructure or shut down a troubled bank, without requiring recourse to taxpayer funding. Fourth, risk taking by banks is less likely with the imposition of higher capital and liquidity requirements and under the common supervisory regime imposed by the Single Supervisory Mechanism (SSM). In addition, stronger and more resilient banking systems also imply that it is more feasible to tolerate sovereign debt restructuring events, further limiting the need for official funding programmes.

Between 2011 and 2012, market fears that adjustment pressures might prompt some countries to leave the euro led to a further broadening of the crisis, with speculators requiring extra risk premia to hold the debt of larger member countries such as Spain and Italy. However, the Outright Monetary Transactions (OMT) programme that was announced by the ECB in September 2012 successfully calmed the markets by providing reassurance that the ECB would intervene were the existence of the euro to be threatened by speculative pressures, at least in relation to sovereigns that met the conditions for an ESM official funding programme.

Additional innovations could further improve the stability of the euro zone. A common system of deposit insurance would weaken the links between national governments and national banking systems and make self-fulfilling bank runs less likely. In addition, state-contingent types of sovereign debt contracts could provide stabilisation by tying repayment levels to macroeconomic performance. Furthermore, insulation against national macroeconomic shocks would be enhanced if member states committed to some degree of risk sharing through a common revenue base, a common system of unemployment insurance or through joint debt issuance in the form of Eurobonds. However, such innovations require sufficient safeguards against moral hazard, by which governments take greater fiscal risks if downside risk is shared through insurance arrangements. Cross-border risk sharing also require a sufficient degree of trust among the member states and a willingness to tolerate ex post resource transfers from better-performing countries to worse-performing countries.

Implications for Ireland
Ultimately, the primary restriction on members of the euro zone is that devaluation of a national currency is not available in adjusting to macroeconomic shocks. At one level, this potential cost has to be compared to the benefits of monetary union as a stabilising mechanism in relation to financial shocks and common shocks.[9] At another level, the loss of the devaluation option puts a premium on limiting exposure to macroeconomic shocks. To this end, it is recognised that measures to attenuate financial cycles are especially important, in view of the high costs associated with credit and housing boom-bust cycles. Such macro-prudential

policies include additional capital charges on banks to limit credit growth and borrower-based measures such as limits on the size of mortgages in order to limit housing-related boom-bust dynamics. In Ireland, the Central Bank of Ireland is the national macro-prudential authority. Since 2015, it has imposed limits on the size of mortgages relative to house values (loan-to-value ratios) and relative to incomes (loan-to-income ratios) (for a discussion of this issue see Chapter 12).

5 PUBLIC EXPENDITURE AND TAXATION

There are three types of government spending: public consumption, transfers, and investment in public capital assets. The first category incorporates the provision of government services such as the civil service, education, health, the justice system and defence. The second include social welfare payments, payments to the EU central budget and debt interest payments. The third refers to spending on infrastructure (e.g. the road network) and on the buildings and equipment associated with the provision of government services.

Public Consumption
Education and healthcare are the major items of public consumption. We only briefly review these sectors, since they are covered in more detail in Chapters 13 and 14. Spending on education and healthcare is in part motivated by redistributive considerations, to ensure access for all to at least a minimal level of services. At an efficiency level, full private funding of education and healthcare would result in severe under-provision, especially for lower-income households, due to myriad asymmetric information and agency problems. In addition, wide access to education and healthcare confers positive economic and social externalities, which provides a rationale for public funding. Furthermore, leaving aside strict economic arguments, the operation of democratic political systems and the fostering of rights-based civic cultures are associated with the setting of minimum access criteria for education and healthcare services for all, regardless of ability to pay. Although these arguments justify public financing of the education and healthcare sectors, this need not involve monopoly public provision of these services: for instance, the state could provide vouchers to parents that could be used to pay fees at private schools or pay the insurance premia to private healthcare companies.

Transfers
The welfare budget is the largest component of transfer spending. Some transfers can be justified by imperfections in insurance markets. For example, private insurance schemes are unlikely to provide fairly priced protection against the risk of unemployment or the occurrence of debilitating medical conditions. However, the stronger motivation behind transfers is redistribution: voters are unwilling to allow the incomes of unemployed, the sick, or the old to fall below a minimum level (see Chapter 8 for a full discussion of this issue). In designing a welfare

system, there is a clear trade-off between the level of benefits and the need to provide incentives to seek employment (in the case of unemployment benefit) or to save privately for retirement (in the case of pensions).

Producer subsidies are another kind of transfer. Although these have been declining in recent years, subsidies are still used to attract multinational corporations and support local start-ups. One problem with producer subsidies is that behaviour is distorted: rather than focusing on innovation and maximising profitability, entrepreneurs may divert resources to lobbying the government for subsidies. However, the worst excesses of this kind of behaviour have been sharply circumscribed by stricter EU regulations on the allocation of state aids to industry. Most notably, the European airline industry has historically been a major recipient of state subsidies but the European Commission now regularly prohibits the protection of national champions. A second problem with producer subsidies is that Ireland competes with other EU countries for footloose firms: this bidding war may result in the successful country suffering a 'winner's curse', having to offer a subsidy larger than any potential benefits.

Public Investment
Public investment has two economic functions: the provision of (a) public inputs that directly raise the productivity of the economy; and (b) public amenities that improve the quality of life and are valued by the community. Of course, the same project may contribute to both objectives. For example, an improved road network not only improves economic performance but the elimination of traffic jams is to be welcomed for its own sake in terms of reducing stress levels. Conversely, cultural projects and sports facilities not only improve the quality of leisure time but may indirectly improve economic performance by making Ireland a more attractive location for internationally mobile workers.

The state plays a central role in ensuring the provision of infrastructure, such as the transport network or the planning framework for housing and urban development. Infrastructure is fundamentally characterised by external effects: the value of a network is greater than the sum of its parts. For this reason, the state plays a leading role in the planning and design of networks in transport, utilities, housing and urban development.

In addition to its planning role, the state also directly provides much infrastructure. For instance, although privately-funded toll roads and bridges can make a contribution to the overall transport network, public good and equity considerations mean that much infrastructural investment is financed by the state. For instance, markets may under-supply infrastructural assets to thinly-populated regions, whereas a government might deem it essential that all citizens have access to a minimum level of infrastructural assets. Direct provision also solves severe coordination problems: for instance, a laissez-faire system may see wasteful duplication in those areas likely to generate the highest toll revenues.

In the decade prior to the 2008 to 2010 crisis, infrastructural investment was very high in Ireland, in a bid to redress the severe infrastructural deficit that emerged from a combination of low investment during the 1980s and early 1990s and rapid economic and population growth. During this period, there was a rapid expansion in the transport network (national road network, Dublin Port Tunnel, LUAS tram lines, Terminal 2 at Dublin airport), while there were also many capital projects in the health and education sectors. At a broader level, there was also a new focus on government investment in 'knowledge' infrastructure (government investment in human capital and scientific research).

However, it may have been more effective to adopt a more gradual rate of increase in public investment. The pro-cyclical timing of the acceleration in public investment can lead to overheating in the construction sector, especially if it is already under pressure due to rising private investment activity. The scale of the increase in public investment may also run into administrative, planning, and legal bottlenecks that further reduce returns. Over the medium term, it is certainly the case that a stable level of public investment is far preferable to the 'stop-go' cycle that has historically characterised Irish public investment dynamics.

The flush state of the public finances up to 2007 meant that much of the investment was met by tax revenues. However, some of the investment took the form of public private partnerships (PPPs), while tolls have partially financed some road and bridge projects. Although private sources of finance during normal times are typically more expensive (since a highly-rated government can borrow at lower rates than private firms), it does enable the use of scarce private managerial talent to achieve social goals. Moreover, the PPP contract typically includes appropriate penalty clauses, such that the risk of cost overruns or time delays is potentially transferred to the private operator. There have been only a few PPP projects in Ireland, and the UK experience has been that the transfer of risk to the private operator has not always been successfully executed.

An important element in efficient provision of public infrastructure is that all projects are subjected to a comprehensive cost-benefit analysis. Economic analysis has a large part to play in such evaluations. However, especially with respect to the provision of public amenities, variation in individual preferences between private goods and public amenities means that evaluation of such projects also has to take into account social and political factors in addition to the economic dimension. In Ireland, full cost-benefit analyses have not been applied to all projects in a transparent manner, such that the rationale for some investment decisions is not always clear.

Furthermore, with the major downward shift in the projected growth of the Irish economy, the appropriate level of public capital is also smaller than previously estimated. Many projects that could be justified under optimistic growth scenarios are no longer sustainable, in view of the slower rate of population growth, lower activity levels and a higher level of public debt.

Taxation

Chapter 4 will focus on taxation and the public finances, so we will only briefly discuss the role of taxation as a policy instrument. At one level, the main impetus for taxation is to finance public expenditure and the design of the taxation system is accordingly targeted at collecting revenues in a manner that least distorts economic decisions while also respecting fairness considerations. However, there is a secondary role for tax policies in order to correct market distortions – such tax interventions can be neutral in terms of the aggregate tax burden by offsetting the revenues collected through a reduction in other taxes.

In relation to environmental protection, the role of taxation as a method to alter behaviour is widely recognised. For instance, Ireland was a pioneer in reducing usage of plastic shopping bags, through the introduction of a small levy in 2002 that quickly converted most of the population to the use of re-usable bags. Similarly, bin charges have induced households to recycle more and avoid unnecessary packaging. At a wider level, it is widely recognised that a carbon tax has a key role to play in reducing carbon emissions, both domestically and internationally (see Chapters 4 and 11).

Along another dimension, user charges may be required to ensure efficient use of congested networks. Examples include user charges for water and congestion charges for access to city road networks (as in London and Singapore). Designing a politically-acceptable scheme that assures access for low-income households is a difficult challenge, as demonstrated by the recent protests about water charges in Ireland.

Another form of tax intervention is the deployment of tax breaks to encourage certain types of activities. Tax breaks are also termed 'tax expenditures' to capture the idea that a tax break is often a substitute for a direct subsidy payment. In Ireland, tax breaks were widely used in the past to promote construction in selected locations. In addition, tax breaks have also been used to promote the arts, the film industry, and the bloodstock industry. In general, it is difficult to make the case for tax breaks – if an activity is evaluated as deserving of a subsidy it is more transparent to offer a direct subsidy rather than to provide indirect support through the tax system. Moreover, tax breaks are of most value to high-income households, such that the exploitation of tax breaks can lead to a regressive element in the tax system in relation to the highest earners. For such reasons, there is some political momentum to restrict the use of tax breaks.

6 OTHER POLICY INSTRUMENTS

State Financial Policies

In addition to direct public spending on goods, services and transfers, a government may acquire financial assets and financial liabilities. In Ireland, the National Treasury Management Agency (NTMA) has a primary role in acting as a financial agent for the state. Ireland was an early leader in establishing an independent debt management agency that could provide specialist expertise in debt issuance: the NTMA was established in 1990. In recent years, the independent status of the NTMA (and its ability to recruit at market salary levels, unlike the rest of the public sector) has meant that it has become the parent agency for more recently-established units such as the NPRF, NAMA and ISIF.

National Pensions Reserve Fund and Irish Strategic Investment Fund
One motivation is to build a reserve fund that can help finance anticipated future increases in public spending. The National Pensions Reserve Fund (NPRF) was established in 2001 in order to finance future state pension liabilities. Rather than exclusively using budget surpluses to pay down the public debt, the plan was to allocate one per cent of GNP each year to the NPRF that invests in a portfolio of financial assets. The intention was that the dividend income and capital gains on these assets could be employed to finance pension expenditures, as a partial alternative to raising future taxation.

However, the precise design of such a fund is critically important for its success and political acceptability. A major concern is the politicisation of investment decisions. At the extreme, this might involve discriminating between domestic projects on the basis of the political connections of entrepreneurs. Less obviously, it may induce the allocation of an excessive portfolio share to domestic over foreign assets, with lobby groups pressing the state fund to support domestic firms and workers.

This is a very difficult problem. On the one side, it is desirable to minimise political interference in the operation of the fund. On the other side, in a democratic society, the operators of a state fund must be politically accountable. Much of the international debate concerning the delegation of public tasks to independent agencies, such as central banks and industry regulators, is relevant here. An important principle is that the government defines the objectives of the agency but that the agency is given wide scope in the pursuit of these objectives, subject to the issuing of regular public reports justifying any deviations from targeted outcomes.

Under normal financial conditions, it should be clear that the correct investment approach for a state pension fund is to overwhelmingly hold overseas assets. First, this strategy minimises the politicisation problem. Second, it is a sensible hedge. Imagine if the state pension fund held domestic assets: in the event of a domestic downturn, the public finances would be hit not only by a decline in tax revenues but also by a contraction in investment income. By holding foreign assets, in contrast, 'tax base risk' is offset. Third, the state pension fund would be large relative to the domestic market but tiny in global terms such that investing overseas improves flexibility and liquidity in portfolio management.

The initial investment strategy of the NPRF largely respected these principles. Its equity and bond holdings were overwhelmingly international, with only modest holdings of domestic securities. However, it also had some involvement in funding domestic infrastructural projects, which increased the risk that the fund's strategy might be subject to political pressure.

However, a large proportion of the NPRF portfolio was converted into a bank rescue fund since late 2008. In order to relieve pressure on the government's direct balance sheet, the NPRF was directed to sell most of its assets in order to purchase equity claims in the main Irish banks. While these assets may provide a return to the NPRF in the coming years, such a crisis-related role was not in the original design of the fund. Rather, it became a 'rainy day' fund that could be rapidly deployed to assist in meeting the large fiscal costs of rescuing the banking system.

In 2014, the NPRF was succeeded by the Irish Strategic Investment Fund (ISIF) that maintains both a Directed Portfolio (the government's ownership stake in the banks) and a Discretionary Portfolio. In contrast to NPRF, the focus of ISIF is on commercial investment opportunities in Ireland that can have an economic impact through expansion of employment and output. While the switch from a foreign-focused portfolio to a domestically-focused portfolio might not be advisable under normal financial conditions, it is arguable that the damaged state of the domestic banking system meant that domestic economic performance could be significantly boosted by the greater availability of non-bank domestic sources of finance. The same logic has justified the creation of state development banks in many countries: for example, the state-owned KfW development bank takes on this role in Germany. However, as the economic recovery takes hold in the coming years, it will be important to assess the net impact of ISIF as traditional forms of finance become more widely available.

NAMA

The government created a major new financial vehicle to help resolve the banking crisis. The National Asset Management Agency (NAMA) was set up in 2009 in order to relieve the banking system of the development-related property loans that were the main source of bank losses. NAMA purchased these loans at steep discounts from the banks and initially held a huge portfolio of property loans. In cases where the debtor could not repay the loan, NAMA could sell the underlying property assets in order to maximise recovery of funds.

The vast bulk of NAMA financing took the form of government-guaranteed bonds. However, there was also a minor role for private-sector financing, such that NAMA is not counted as part of the main public balance sheet. Accordingly, NAMA provides an important example by which the government can engage in financial engineering to meet its policy goals. However, such measures are opaque and require extensive public monitoring in order to avoid the temptation to excessively use 'off balance sheet' devices to understate the true level of government intervention in the economy.

State-Owned Enterprises
Rationale
State-owned enterprises have historically played a major role in the Irish economy, ranging from Aer Lingus to the ESB. Government ownership in the commercial sector may be explained by a number of factors.

First, underdeveloped capital markets prevented private entrepreneurs from raising the finance required to build profitable firms in capital-intensive sectors such as transport. Second, rather than implement regulation of monopolies (as in the United States), European countries tended to favour government ownership of utilities such as electricity production and telecommunications. Third, state ownership was seen as facilitating the pursuit of social goals such as access to services and regionalisation. Fourth, the investment policies of state-owned firms might be viewed as a substitute for official public investment, such that the investment programmes of these firms might be politically directed rather than determined on efficiency grounds. Finally, in many countries, state-owned enterprises have facilitated political patronage, with decisions concerning employment and investment being manipulated for electoral purposes.

Privatisation
In recent years, there has been a global shift towards the privatisation of such state-owned firms (see Chapters 5 and 11). The development of sophisticated capital markets now allows private entrepreneurs to finance efficiently even large-scale ventures. Market liberalisation, sometimes mandated by EU law, has reduced fears of monopoly power in many sectors. Moreover, as indicated earlier in the chapter, the EU prohibition on state aid to rescue non-viable firms means that such firms can no longer be protected for political reasons. Finally, technological innovations such as in the telecommunications sector now make it more feasible to have multiple competitors even in 'network' industries (see Chapter 5).

Where monopoly power is likely to persist, governments typically now prefer to regulate private firms as an alternative to direct state ownership (see Chapters 5 and 10). Similarly, social goals (such as the provision of cheap postal services to remote areas) can be achieved by a combination of subsidies and regulation, without requiring actual government ownership. Finally, with accumulating evidence on the performance of privatised industries in other countries, ideological resistance to private ownership has weakened over time.

Another reason for the shift towards privatisation is that government ownership may actually be detrimental to performance. Managers and workers in a state-owned enterprise know that they need not seek to maximise profits, since there is no threat of loss of control to outside investors, and hence have a weak incentive to behave efficiently or control costs.

In addition, as indicated earlier, the government may direct state-owned enterprises to pursue non-commercial objectives, such as providing employment for supporters of the government or locating in disadvantaged or politically-favoured areas.[10] A decline in clientelism and an improvement in the transparency of the political system have weakened the incentive of the government to manipulate the semi-state sector to achieve such non-economic goals. Even in the absence of privatisation, there are benefits to de-politicisation of these enterprises. Commercialisation of many Irish state-owned enterprises occurred in the 1980s, with significant improvements in performance. More recently, the privatisation process gained pace, with the (full or partial) disposal of the government interest in firms such as Eircom, Aer Lingus and Bord Gáis.

In designing a privatisation process, the government faces several conflicts. To maximise revenues, the government should seek the highest issue price or permit a concentration of ownership among large shareholders but this may conflict with a political goal to broaden the shareholder base. In addition, the sale price can be enhanced by offering monopoly rights to the purchaser but this conflicts with other goals such as the promotion of competition and lower prices for consumers. To secure the cooperation of powerful unions, the government may feel compelled to offer sharply discounted shares to incumbent workers in the state-owned firms and insert worker protection clauses into the privatisation contract, even if this reduces the value of the firm. Of course, the privatisation process should be fully transparent, to prevent state assets being sold at artificially low prices to politically connected business interests.

Privatisation generates a one-time cash windfall for the government. However, it is important to understand that the net impact on the government's balance sheet is much smaller: by transferring ownership, the government no longer receives dividends from the firm, reducing future government revenues. That said, to the extent that the firm is worth more in private hands and the buyout of incumbent workers is not too costly, the net financial gain of privatisation to the government will be positive.

The 2011 Report of the Review Group on State Assets and State Liabilities recognised that there are considerable gains to improved commercialisation of state-owned firms and that some level of privatisation proceeds might be helpful in reducing the high level of public debt, while recognising the limitations laid out in the above discussion.[11] In 2014, the government announced the establishment of NewERA (as part of the NTMA), which provides financial and corporate advisory services in relation to state-owned enterprises.

Regulation and Competition Policy
The privatisation of firms with considerable monopoly power (such as traditional monopoly providers of telecommunications), together with the principle of operating the remaining state-owned firms (such as the ESB) on a commercial basis means that the role of regulatory agencies have taken on new prominence in recent years (see Chapter 5).

Ireland has a number of sectoral regulators (such as the Commission on Energy Regulation, the Commission on Communications Regulation and the Commission on Aviation Regulation) that seek to prevent abuses of monopoly power by monitoring market conduct and retaining powers of approval over the prices charged by firms in these industries. While regulators rely heavily on economic theory to identify instances of market abuse or excessive price mark ups, it is not always straightforward to establish the scope for greater competition in certain sectors or the best methods to encourage the entry of new firms if the market is excessively concentrated. Moreover, especially in network industries, incumbent firms may frustrate efforts to reduce barriers to entry, especially by making it difficult for new entrants to obtain access to key distribution channels.

Even in sectors with many suppliers, market inefficiencies may arise if mergers and acquisitions lead to a reduction in the number of firms or if incumbent firms collude (explicitly or implicitly) to raise prices or erect barriers to entry. Accordingly, the Competition and Consumer Protection Commission (CCPC) has an important role to play in ensuring open competition is preserved.

In addition to preventing abuses of monopoly power, the government also regulates many spheres of economic activity in order to redress other perceived failures of a laissez-faire system (see Chapter 5). Informational asymmetries justify safety regulations, since individual consumers are ill-equipped to evaluate products that potentially carry high risks (air travel, processed foods, machinery to name just three examples) – accordingly, the markets for such goods can only operate effectively under the assurance of government-approved safety regulations (see Chapter 5). Of course, the trade-off faced in such regulatory systems is ensuring that such standards are not distorted in order to discourage innovation, restrict entry by new firms or act as a barrier to international trade. Regulation is also employed in pursuit of social goals, to ensure that businesses do not operate in ways that are prohibited under the relevant social legislation.

Finally, regulation plays an important part in environmental policy. For asymmetric information reasons, a market system may not be able to ensure that all firms produce using environmentally-responsible techniques – accordingly, firms are monitored to ensure that production does not violate environmental standards. In relation to managing climate change, the allocation of carbon quotas is widely used as an alternative or a complement to a carbon tax. The relative merits of 'quantity' regulation (quotas) versus 'price' regulation (taxes) depend on the precise scenario but a hybrid system that employs both tools may be the prudent choice when faced with a very uncertain economic environment, which is surely the case in relation to the climate change phenomenon (see Chapter 11).

Social Partnership

The role played by the social partnership process in contributing to the success of the Irish economy has been widely debated (see Chapter 6). Social partnership refers to a consensus-based approach to policymaking by which the government seeks to obtain agreement from the trade union movement, employer federations and other representative groups on key policy decisions and also to establish national benchmarks for important private-sector decisions (such as the appropriate level of wages).

There are several factors that point to a potential role for social partnership. First, a decentralised approach to wage agreements suffers from an externality problem: individual firms and unions do not sufficiently take into account the national macroeconomic environment when setting enterprise-level or sector-level wages. Through a coordinating mechanism (national dialogue between the various representative groups), it is hoped that the feedback loops between wage dynamics, government fiscal policy and aggregate macroeconomic performance can be internalised. While this may not be feasible for very large economies, a social partnership approach might be achievable for smaller countries such as Ireland.

Second, it is arguable that social partnership can also make it easier to implement major reforms since significant changes are most likely to be successful if there is buy in from all relevant stakeholders. This factor helped to justify the progressive expansion of the scope of social partnership agreements from the late 1990s onwards to cover a wider range of policy areas.

However, in the other direction, a social partnership framework runs the risk of promoting the interests of 'insiders' (those belonging to organised units such as large trade unions, especially in the public sector) over the interests of 'outsiders' (those working in non-represented sectors; those not participating in the organised labour market). In addition, a consensus-based approach to policy formation can be a barrier to tough decisions, especially to the extent that the government is unwilling to challenge the 'veto' threat posed by individual participants in the social partnership process.

Between 1987 and 2007, there was a succession of national agreements that were negotiated between the government, trade unions, employer federations, and a host of other representative groups. However, the scope of the social partnership approach has narrowed quite substantially during the crisis. Widespread consensus across the social partners was not possible in view of the differing views as to the source of the crisis or the optimal path to resolve the crisis. Accordingly, the government opted to simply impose many fiscal measures, while the wide variation in conditions in the private sector meant that employers withdrew from a common approach to wage determination in favour of firm-by-firm settlements.

However, a core element of social partnership has survived in that there is a common approach to public sector reform that has been agreed between the government and most of the unions representing public sector workers. In return for limiting the scale of pay reductions and avoiding compulsory redundancies, the so-called Croke Park and Haddington Road agreements specify an extensive programme of reforms across the public sector. Such a reform programme may not have been feasible without the social partnership framework. As the economy recovers and momentum builds for pay increases across the economy, the potential value of new social partnership mechanisms may be recognised in addressing the risk that decentralised wage bargaining can lead to an excessive loss in international competitiveness.

7 SIZE OF GOVERNMENT: ECONOMIC AND POLITICAL FACTORS

In evaluating tax and expenditure policies, a fundamental question is the optimal size of government. If the size of government is too large, it makes sense to prune expenditure and cut taxation; conversely, increases in spending and taxation are required if the government is too small to achieve desired policy outcomes.

Of course, determining the optimal size of government is a difficult challenge and involves economic, political and social dimensions.

Trends and International Comparisons
Although the government can also exert much influence through legislation, regulation, social partnership, moral suasion, and financial engineering, measures of public expenditure and taxation are most widely employed as imperfect proxies for the size of government. However, there has been much interest in recent years in measuring other dimensions of government intervention in the economy. For instance, the World Bank's *Doing Business* survey ranks countries on many dimensions of government regulation and bureaucracy while the OECD maintains a comprehensive database on regulation in its member countries. As is shown in Table 3.1, Ireland scores quite well along some dimensions of these indices but its rank is relatively poor in areas such as the ease of enforcing contracts. Table 3.1 also shows that high rankings can be achieved under a variety of governance systems.

Table 3.1 Business Environment[1]: Ranking of Selected Countries

	Doing business	Starting a business	Protecting investors	Enforcing contracts
New Zealand	1	1	1	13
Singapore	2	6	1	2
Denmark	3	24	19	24
Hong Kong	4	3	3	21
Korea	5	11	13	1
Norway	6	21	9	4
UK	7	16	6	31
US	8	51	41	20
Sweden	9	15	19	22
Ireland	*18*	*10*	*13*	*90*

Source: Constructed with World Bank data from: *Doing Business Survey* 2017 (www.doingbusiness.org).
[1] In terms of government regulation and bureaucracy.

In relation to levels of public expenditure, Figure 3.1 shows the boom-bust cycle over 1995 to 2016 (see also Chapters 1, 4 and 7). From 1995 to 2001, the substantial growth in public spending could be broadly justified as a response to the large increase in trend output and income levels in Ireland, since a busier economy and rising living standards led to calls for higher public investment, increased public services and higher rates of public sector pay and welfare bene-fits. Since tax revenues were boosted by the spectacular growth in the economy, the expansion in public spending was combined with a sharp fall in the ratio of public debt to GDP.

During 2002 to 2007, these forces persisted, even though the large shift in the orientation of the economy towards construction meant that the forces driving economic growth were temporary in nature and were accompanied by an increase in risk indicators, such as spectacular expansion in the scale of private-sector debt levels and a deterioration in the current account balance (see also Chapter 7). With the crystallisation of these risks during the 2008 to 2010 financial crisis, there was a mismatch between committed levels of public spending and the underlying levels of trend income and output. During 2008 to 2013, there was a major austerity drive to bring down levels of public spending, with a sharp fall in public investment, significant reductions in public sector pay levels and a scaling back in the provision of many public services. With the dura-bility of economic recovery increasingly evident, the pressure to increase public spending is currently quite intense. A basic analytical problem is that it remains difficult to assess the trajectory for trend growth in Ireland, since the recovery from 2013 had largely been driven by cyclical 'bounce back' that does not indi-cate the future pace of economic growth.

Figure 3.1 Inflation-Adjusted Public Spending, 1995–2016

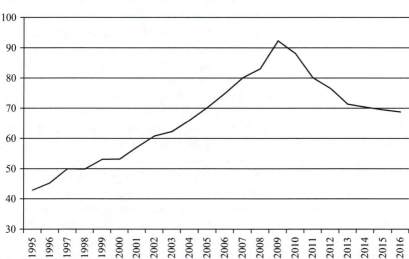

Source: Constructed with European Commission data from: *AMECO Online* database. Public spending calculated as sum of public consumption, public investment and transfers in billions of euro (deflated by 2016 CPI).

Causes of Variations in Size of Government

Wagner's Law

Many factors contribute to variation across countries and over time in government spending. First, across countries and over time, there is a clear positive correlation between the level of income per capita and the share of public expenditure in national income: this tendency is known as Wagner's Law. One reason is that public spending on healthcare, education and pensions may be interpreted as luxury items, with an income elasticity of demand greater than unity.

As incomes grow, voters demand more of these services, placing upward pressure on public spending. However, the damaging costs of excessive taxation place an upper bound on the sustainable level of spending on these items. The fiscal reforms attempted by many countries in recent years may in part be a result of having approached this upper bound. The increasing mobility of capital and skilled labour also places limits on the feasible size of government, by placing a cap on sustainable tax rates.

Baumol's Disease

Another driving force behind upward pressure on public spending is the so-called Baumol's disease, named after the American economist who proposed the hypothesis.[12] Baumol's hypothesis is that an economy can be divided into progressive and non-progressive sectors. Productivity gains in the progressive sector drive up wages, which must be matched by the non-progressive sector if it is to attract and retain workers.

Provision of education and healthcare services plausibly falls into the non-progressive sector, on the basis that productivity growth in such labour intensive sectors is limited. It follows that the implicit relative price of these services must rise, as wages increase without a compensating improvement in productivity. If the income elasticity of demand for these services exceeds the price elasticity of demand, the ratio of public spending to national income will increase, even if the volume of services provided is unchanged. Striking the balance between 'volume' and 'price' margins is a major challenge for policymakers in determining the composition of growth in education and healthcare spending (see Chapters 13 and 14). This is especially tricky, since it is difficult to determine the appropriate levels of pay for public-sector occupations, in view of the lack of strict comparability with private-sector occupations.

It is not correct to assume that productivity growth in publicly-financed sectors is impossible, as another factor behind slow improvement is the lack of competitive pressure to produce efficiently. Improved management, stronger cost controls and the outsourcing of some services may help in forcing more rapid productivity growth in these sectors. Moreover, recent technological change may enable new productivity gains. For example, Internet-based courses and learning aids may be feasible in many education sectors, while the electronic transmission of X-Rays and other medical information permits the remote provision of medical expertise. An important challenge for policymakers is to ensure such new technologies are exploited, even in the face of resistance from traditional suppliers, such as public sector unions. In 2011, a new Department of Public Expenditure and Reform was established in Ireland, with a mandate to drive productivity growth in the public sector.

Demographic Factors

Demographic factors also are important in determining the level of public spending. All else equal, countries with a large cohort of children will require a higher education budget. At the other end of the life cycle, many countries now face an increase in the proportion of old people in the population, with attendant growth in healthcare and pension expenditures. In addition, a high dependency ratio (a high ratio of children and elderly to the working-age population) also compromises tax revenues, since the working-age population is relatively low. Taken together, the combination of increased expenditure pressures and lower tax revenues means the political systems face difficult choices in determining the feasible scale of public spending in the face of demographic pressures. The problems associated with the greying of the population will progressively place upward pressure on public expenditure levels in Ireland over the next fifteen years (see also Chapter 6).

Automatic Stabilisers

Welfare spending fluctuates over the economic cycle, as the numbers of unemployed falls during expansions and rises during recessions. The operation of such 'automatic stabilisers' induces a natural countercyclical pattern in government spending: however, this may be attenuated by pro-cyclical shifts in the level of benefits: during booms, the level of benefits tends to improve. Together with the cyclical components in tax revenues, there is an overall counter-cyclical effect of automatic stabilisers on the budget balance with expenditure rising and taxes falling during recessions.

Political Economy of Public Spending

The preceding analysis generally assumes that the government acts to maximise social welfare. While the bulk of public expenditure may be usefully interpreted in this way, a substantial component is influenced by a more overtly political process, in which public expenditure allocations are the outcome of a contest between interest groups, public sector workers, and politicians. This process may produce outcomes that are contrary to social welfare: government failure may be as important as market failure in deviating from optimal outcomes.

Public Choice Theory

One reason why social welfare is not maximised is voter ignorance of the true costs of public expenditure. The Downs paradox (individual votes have no influence over the result of an election) suggests that it is not individually worthwhile for the electorate to learn much about the costs of different public spending programmes or the underlying forces driving public sector pay levels. In contrast, some groups have vested interests in specific areas of public expenditure (e.g. farmers and agricultural subsidies; public sector workers and public sector pay levels) and will act collectively to promote these specific public expenditures. In a famous book, the late Mancur Olson pointed out that such interest groups are easier to organise in a rich society and hence this problem will increase over time.[13]

The characteristics of the civil service bureaucracy can also contribute to government failure. Civil servants act as agents for the government in evaluating and monitoring the effectiveness of public spending. An influential hypothesis is that bureaucrats like to maximise the size of their departmental budgets, as this is associated with enhanced status and improved promotion prospects. With each department seeking to promote its own expenditure programmes, the net result is to place upward pressure on the level of public spending. Similarly, the political influence of a cabinet minister may be increasing in the size of her departmental budget.

However, centralised oversight of spending by the Department of Public Expenditure and Reform (backed up by the Department of Finance) can provide a significant counterweight: arguably, its focus is on holding back the overall level of spending.

Design of the Political System

Much current research is devoted to analysing the impact of the structure of the political system on public expenditure decisions. For instance, it is suggested that governments that are coalitions of parties with significantly different political philosophies and short tenures in office are less able to control public expenditure. Each party in a coalition has a veto on reductions in its favoured areas so that a prisoners' dilemma results – it is in the collective interest to control spending but no single party has the incentive to accept unilateral spending reductions. Short tenures make it infeasible to implement spending controls as it will not have the time to enjoy the benefits before the next election.

In such circumstances, it seems that fiscal control can only occur under 'crisis' conditions, with the public debt so high that there is no alternative to reform. Once fiscal control is established, fear of a return to instability may restrain expenditure for a period. However, memories eventually fade and the pressure for a relaxation on public spending may resume.

Another manifestation of politically-driven fluctuations in public spending is the impact of the electoral cycle on public spending: in the run up to elections, there is a tendency for public spending to increase (especially on visible projects) and taxes are reduced. The timing of these fluctuations suggests such spending has little basis in terms of social welfare but rather is directed at winning favour for the incumbent government.

Fiscal Framework and Rules

International evidence suggests that fiscal sustainability is facilitated by a formal fiscal framework that places a set of restrictions on the conduct of fiscal policy. A fiscal framework has several elements.

First, it may formalise the political process determining budgetary decisions, with fiscal control best achieved by a transparent system that places ultimate responsibility for fiscal policy on the finance minister than by a collegial and secretive system in which lines of responsibility are not clearly designated.[14] Second, it may provide a multi-year horizon for planning public spending, in order to avoid annual volatility in public spending levels.

Third, it may specify a set of numerical fiscal rules to guide the medium-term behaviour of fiscal policy. The set of fiscal rules typically sets some medium-term budgetary objectives, such as keeping the level of public debt below a ceiling value and a target for the structural budget balance over the cycle. In turn, each annual budget must be set within the confines of these rules.

Finally, it may include a watchdog role for an independent fiscal council, with the remit to monitor the quality of budgetary decisions. Such a council can improve the public debate about fiscal policy by providing a non-governmental source of objective analysis of the public finances. This role can be especially important during boom periods, since it is politically difficult to run large surpluses in anticipation of future rainy days. Having an independent fiscal council may provide some support for politically-difficult but economically-desirable fiscal decisions.

The EU Growth and Stability Pact provided a limited type of fiscal framework. It specified a debt ceiling of 60 per cent and a budget deficit ceiling of 3 per cent and also required governments to make an annual report regarding the state of the public finances. However, the original design of the Pact did not require governments to run sufficiently large surpluses during boom periods, nor was the level of external surveillance sufficiently robust to avoid the accumulation of fiscal vulnerabilities in some peripheral countries.

At an EU level, there has been a wave of reforms to strengthen the Pact. Under the new procedures, there is greater monitoring of budget setting across Europe under the 'European semester' fiscal process. In particular, budget plans must now be pre-approved at EU level, so that there is less risk of inappropriate budgets being implemented.

At a national level, the Fiscal Compact (and associated EU regulations) required that each member country adopted a Fiscal Responsibility Law, so that numerical fiscal rules are embedded in the domestic legislative framework. In addition, each country established an independent fiscal council to provide an objective opinion of the sustainability of the national budget plan and the macroeconomic forecasts that underpin budget plans.

In Ireland, the Irish Fiscal Advisory Council (IFAC) was established in 2011 and the Fiscal Responsibility Law was passed in 2012, following a constitutional referendum to transpose the European Fiscal Compact into the domestic legal framework. IFAC provides regular reports on Irish fiscal plans and also must endorse the official macroeconomic forecast. Through its reports, the political system and the wider public now have an independent window into the state of the public finances, rather than relying on the government to self-report.

8 CONCLUSION

The central theme of this chapter is that the state is a major economic actor. A well-functioning and effective government is necessary to achieve economic efficiency and redistribution objectives. The maximisation of societal welfare requires that the government choose the optimal mix of policy instruments to attain its desired policy objectives.

The analysis in this chapter gives some clues as to the likely evolution of the government's role in the economy in the coming decades. One global trend is a shift from the government as provider to a greater use of private inputs to achieve social goals. A second is the further decentralisation of some government functions to local levels of government. Currently, the trend towards greater internationalisation of the policymaking process is in question, with the rise of populist parties in many countries that seek to restore national autonomy in policymaking. The unfolding of the 'internationalisation versus populism' debate will be a major theme for the coming years.

Public expenditure policies remain the primary method by which the state intervenes in the economy. During the boom period, the decline in the public debt and an extremely favourable demographic structure meant that the government had considerable freedom in making spending decisions. However, the legacy of the crisis is a high level of public debt that will limit the government's flexibility in terms of spending and taxation plans.

Accordingly, it is important that rigorous evaluation procedures are employed to ensure that the state obtains value for money and delivers public services in an efficient and equitable manner. To this end, it is to be hoped that the new Irish Government Economic and Evaluation Service (IGEES) can provide the professional economic expertise to ensure that such evaluations are carried out to the highest possible standard.

Endnotes

1   See A. Shleifer and R. Vishny, *The Grabbing Hand: Government Pathologies and Their Cures*, MIT Press, Cambridge MA 1998.
2   See C. Jones and R. Hall, 'Why do some countries produce so much more output per worker than others?' *Quarterly Journal of Economics*, February 1999.
3   See J. Sachs, *Common Wealth: Economics for a Crowded Planet*, Penguin Press, New York 2008.
4   See P. Collier, *The Bottom Billion,* Oxford University Press, Oxford 2007.
5   See D. Rodrik, 'How far will international integration go?', *Journal of Economic Perspectives*, Winter 2000.
6   A. Alesina and E. Spoloare, 'On the number and size of nations', *Quarterly Journal of Economics*, November 1997.
7   P. Martin and T. Philippon, 'Inspecting the mechanism: leverage and the Great Recession in the Eurozone', *American Economic Review*, forthcoming.
8   See P. Lane, 'The European sovereign debt crisis', *Journal of Economic Perspectives*, Summer 2012; M. Brunnermeier, H. James and J. Landau, *The Euro and the Battle of*

Ideas, Princeton University Press 2016; M. Sandbu, *Europe's Orphan: The Future of the Euro and the Politics of Debt*, Princeton University Press, 2015.

9   P. Lane, 'Macro-Financial Stability under EMU', ESRB Working Paper No. 1, 2016.

10 See Shleifer and Vishny, *op. cit.*

11 See *Report of the Review Group on State Assets and Liabilities*, April 2011, at www. finance.gov.ie/viewdoc.asp?DocID=6805

12 W. Baumol, 'Macroeconomics of unbalanced growth: the anatomy of urban crisis', *American Economic Review*, June 1967.

13 M. Olson, *The Logic of Collective Action: Public Goods and the Theory of Groups*, Harvard University Press, Cambridge MA 1965.

14 See P. Lane, 'A new fiscal framework for Ireland', *Journal of Statistical and Social Inquiry Society of Ireland*, XXXIX 2010.

CHAPTER 4

Taxation: Measures and Policy Issues

Micheál Collins

1 INTRODUCTION

Taxation is a method for government to raise revenue by means of charges on persons or firms and can be collected nationally or locally. Governments collect taxes for two broad reasons. First, it provides revenue to run the state, as outlined in Chapter 3, and pays for the provision of public services, infrastructure, and the funding of redistributive policies. Second, taxation is used by governments as a corrective devise to alter the behaviour of individuals, firms or the economy as a whole. In such cases, governments can use taxation to, for example, discourage certain consumption choices, encourage investment in certain sectors, or reduce citizen's disposable income in an attempt to dampen the demand side of the economy.

In Ireland, the government via the *Budget and Finance Act* alters its taxation policies on an annual basis. However, the government's ability to choose freely these policies is limited by competitive forces, EU rules, rates in neighbouring jurisdictions and historical factors. In the case of the former, a small-open economy such as Ireland cannot easily alter its company taxation structures without having consideration of the taxation regimes in competing economies. Similarly, the government is limited by EU rules which require it to adhere to certain fiscal targets and it is restricted by EU single market rules from altering many of its consumption taxes. Past economic policies funded through government borrowing also reduce taxation choices as this debt must be serviced and repaid from current taxation revenues.

The plan of this chapter is as follows. In Section 2 we consider the principles of a good taxation system. Section 3 considers the operation and features of the taxation system in Ireland and reviews that structure in both historical and international contexts. In Sections 4 and 5 we evaluate the Irish taxation system first looking at taxes on income and then examining indirect, corporation tax, and property taxes. Section 6 discusses the issue of deferred taxation, namely borrowing, building on the discussion of this topic in Chapter 3. Section 7 concludes the chapter.

2 PRINCIPLES OF A GOOD TAXATION SYSTEM

In *An Inquiry into the Nature and Causes of the Wealth of Nations* Adam Smith set out a series of principles for the operation of a good taxation system.[1] Smith identified four maxims with regard to taxation in general stating that:

(i)   The subjects of every state ought to contribute towards the support of the government, as nearly as possible, in proportion to their respective abilities; that is in proportion to the revenue which they respectively enjoy under the protection of the state;

(ii) The tax which each individual is bound to pay ought to be certain and not arbitrary. The time of payment, the manner of payment, the quantity to be paid, ought all to be clear and plain to the contributor and to every other person;

(iii) Every tax ought to be levied at the time, or in the manner, in which it is most likely to be convenient for the contributor to pay it;

(iv) Every tax ought to be so contrived as both to take out and to keep out of the pockets of the people as little as possible, over and above that which it brings into the public treasury of the state.

Known as the *canons of taxation* these principles are generally summarised under the headings of equity, efficiency and simplicity and they have changed little since 1776. We explore each of these principles in turn below.

In the context of taxation, *equity* can usefully be explained via the concept of *ability to pay* which relates the quantum of taxes levied to an individual or household's economic resources. In general, an individual's economic resources are taken to be the flow of resources to them (their income) rather than their stock of resources (their wealth). What is known as *horizontal equity* implies that individuals with identical incomes should pay the same level of taxation while *vertical equity* implies that individuals with different incomes should pay different amounts. In practice this produces a *progressive* taxation system where as income increases an individual pays a higher *proportion* of income in taxes. The precise nature of that progressivity will depend on government choices regarding the structure of a taxation system.

The opposite of a progressive taxation system is a *regressive* one where as income increases the average rate of tax experienced by an individual decreases. When examining a taxation system over time we can also consider two other equity issues: *transitional equity* and *intergenerational equity*. The former reflects a challenge for tax policy reform, whereby adjustments from an undesirable structure to a more preferred outcome will in and of itself produce inequitable outcomes in the short term. Such transitional outcomes may be an unavoidable feature of enhancing equity. Intergenerational equity implies that ideally, each generation's taxes should cover its own expenses. Where a generation's expenditure exceeds spending, and unpaid public borrowing remains, one generation passes a burden of taxation on to another violating the principle of intergenerational equity.

The issue of *efficiency* in a taxation system arises because, in general, the imposition of a tax distorts what would have been the market outcome. It does so by imposing a wedge between the price received by the seller and the price paid by the buyer. This *tax wedge* alters the behaviour of these participants in the market. For example, say a farmer is willing to sell 50 apples at a price of 50 cent each and consumers are willing to purchase all his output at this price. If a 10 per cent tax is imposed on all fruit sales by government, this creates a wedge between the consumer demand price and the producer supply price. Consequently, both the consumer and the producer find themselves away from the optimal levels of demand and supply they would have chosen without the existence of the tax. Examples in relation to labour and other taxes are provided later.

The flow of resources from consumers to government as a result of the imposition of a tax causes an *income effect* whereby the purchasing power of consumers is reduced. Simultaneously, a *substitution effect* occurs as a result of consumers' response to the change in relative prices caused by the tax. An efficient tax is one where this substitution effect, also known as the *deadweight burden* of the tax, is minimised subject to raising the revenue target required by government. While different taxes will give rise to different sized substitution effects, in general efficient taxes are set with a negative relationship to goods price elasticity – low taxes where elasticity is high and higher taxes where price elasticity is low. Such an approach minimises the deadweight loss.

A further alternative are *lump-sum taxes* which are levied at the same amount on all taxpayers thereby implying no substitution effect. Such taxes can be difficult to implement and tend to be accompanied by undesirable outcomes when judged from the perspective of equity. Of course, these complications and deadweight losses could be completely avoided if the tax was not imposed in the first place. However governments need to source revenue from somewhere and the challenge, from an efficiency perspective, is to do so with minimal distortion.

A *simple* taxation system is one where the compliance and administrative costs of the taxpayer and tax authority are minimised given the requirement to raise sufficient revenue for the exchequer. Taxpayers face costs in understanding, completing and returning the appropriate tax payment given their resources. Tax authorities face costs in administering and policing the system. In general, these costs are positively correlated with the complexity of the taxation system. Therefore, a simple and understandable taxation system is likely to reduce costs for both government and citizens. It should also minimise the incentives for taxpayers to pursue various routes to minimise their taxation bill either legally (*tax avoidance*) or illegally (*tax evasion*). Increasingly, tax authorities are recognising the relevance of behavioural economics concepts in monitoring and enhancing compliance. A simple system combined with a greater appreciation of social norms and the unacceptability of tax evasion has been found to boost compliance at limited additional administrative cost.[2]

For a policymaker, the design of a 'good' taxation system which adheres to the above principles is challenging. In general, a balance has to be struck between the competing objectives of equity and efficiency while adhering to the desire to minimise complexity and raise sufficient revenue. Striking such a balance is not straightforward, for example an income tax incentive solely targeted at female labour supply may be more efficient than a population wide measure but it would not be equitable. Similarly, females, who on average live longer, should perhaps pay more social insurance contributions than males; again a policy proposal with efficiency merits but with problems when it comes to equity. Conversely, there may be equity merits in having low taxes on food, to assist low income households making ends meet; however better off households will also benefit raising questions of efficiency. Below, we outline the Irish taxation system and subsequently evaluate it relative to these principles.

3 IRISH TAXATION SYSTEM

Throughout this section and the remainder of the chapter various concepts and features of a taxation system are discussed. At the outset, some clarity on the meaning of these phrases is appropriate.

Governments can impose taxes *directly*, through the reduction of an individual's real income and the transfer of that revenue to government, or *indirectly* through the imposition of consumption taxes or user charges on goods and services. Therefore, direct taxes allow government greater ability to target taxation measures towards particular groups of specified earners and to pursue the aforementioned objective of progressivity. The *tax base* comprises that which is to be taxed and can include income, consumption, property, profits, and wealth. A *narrow tax base* will concentrate tax collection across a limited number of these areas while a *broad tax base* will include many if not all of them.

The *incidence of taxation* measures on whom a tax falls. This can be on producers or consumers, on those at particular income levels or situated in particular industries or regions. In this regard a distinction needs to be made between the legal and effective incidence; for example, brewers may legally have to pay the excise duty on alcohol but in practice it may be fully paid for by the consumer. The *tax rate* captures the scale of the charge imposed by government relative to a goods/services price or income level. Within income tax, we consider *average tax rates*, also known as *effective tax rates*, which summarise the overall proportion of an individual's income that is paid in taxation. This differs from the *marginal tax rate* which captures the proportion of the last euro in income that is paid in taxes. As such, marginal rates are always higher than average rates.

Occasionally, governments have chosen to address legacy tax evasion issues by establishing a *tax amnesty*. These tend to be time-defined opportunities for taxpayers to acknowledge hidden liabilities and settle their outstanding tax bills with the tax authorities without fear of prosecution. In behavioural terms, an amnesty offers an attractive opportunity to boost ongoing compliance and allows evaders to legitimatise their position; something that can be of particular relevance in the context of widespread evasion which would be administratively challenging to address. However, if amnesties become recurring events, they highlight the scale and potential for evasion and can therefore undermine compliance and the effectiveness of the tax administration system.

Tax Revenue: Historical and International Trends

The overall level of tax revenue in Ireland compared to the rest of the OECD and EU member states within the OECD is examined in Table 4.1. As taxation can be levied on all economic activity within a country, GDP is the international benchmark against which to assess the overall taxation burden. Irish data are compared against both GDP and GNP as these national income measures can diverge by as much as 20 per cent, and given some historical precedents to assess the tax burden against GNP (see Chapter 7). However, to do so only in relation to GNP would exclude some of the national tax base, specifically the profits of multinational corporations, and consequently overstate the comparable scale of the national taxation burden.

The table shows that over the period there was an international trend towards higher overall taxation levels within the OECD and its EU member states. During the period in Ireland, taxation first climbed and then fell driven by growth and fiscal policies of the 1970s and 1980s and the economic expansion and taxation reductions post 1990. The impact of the global recession (from 2008) saw overall taxation levels decrease once again, despite simultaneous decreases in national income. By 2014 Ireland's tax ratio had increased yet stood below average levels in the OECD and the EU.

Table 4.1 General Government Tax Revenue as a Percentage of GDP

	1970	1980	1990	2000	2010	2014
Ireland (% GDP)	27.6	30.1	32.4	30.8	27.1	28.7
Ireland (% GNP)	27.2	31.1	36.5	35.9	32.7	33.9
OECD EU[1]	28.8	33.8	36.8	37.2	35.8	37.4
OECD average	26.7	30.1	32.0	34.0	32.6	34.2

Source: Constructed with OECD data from: *Revenue Statistics 1965–2015*, OECD, Paris 2016.
[1] OECD EU represents EU member states who are also OECD members.

Table 4.2 shows the composition of tax revenue in Ireland and the OECD from 1980 to 2014. Internationally, the major trends across that period have been a shift away from specific consumption taxes such as excise duties, reductions in the proportion of taxes collected from personal incomes and an increase in the contribution to taxation revenue from general consumption taxes (e.g. VAT). Most of these trends have been reflected in Ireland. The exception has been a continued reliance on personal income taxes as the source of almost one third of taxation revenue. The increase in the relative importance of corporate taxes as a revenue source in Ireland is also notable and is reflective of the increasing role of that sector in the economy. Property taxes also increased over the period in Ireland and by 2014 accounted for 8 per cent of total revenues; revenue from this source decreased from a peak in 2007 as the number and value of property transactions declined when Ireland's property bubble burst.

Using budget data on the expected flow of taxation revenue to the exchequer in 2017, Table 4.3 shows that the main sources of taxation revenue in Ireland

Table 4.2 Composition of Tax Revenue (percentage of total)

	1980		2000		2014	
	Ireland	OECD	Ireland	OECD	Ireland	OECD
Personal income tax	32	31	32	25	32	24
Corporate income tax	5	8	12	10	8	9
Social security and payroll taxes	15	23	12	26	18	27
Property taxes (incl. stamp duty)	5	5	6	6	8	6
General consumption taxes	15	14	23	20	21	21
Specific consumption taxes	28	17	14	11	10	10
Other taxes	1	1	2	3	3	4

Source: As for Table 4.1.

Table 4.3 Structure of Ireland's Taxation Revenue, 2017

	%
Income Tax (including USC)	32.1
Value Added Tax	21.2
Social Insurance (employee and employer)	19.7
Corporation Tax	12.2
Excise Duties	9.5
Stamp Duties	2.1
Capital Gains Tax	1.1
Local Property Tax	0.7
Capital Acquisitions Tax	0.7
Customs	0.6
Total	€63,005m

Source: Constructed with Department of Finance data from: *Budget 2017*, Stationery Office, Dublin 2016.

are those related to personal income (including social insurance contributions by employees and employers), consumption taxes (VAT and excise duties) and corporate taxes. We examine each of these areas and consider the role of capital taxes, property taxes and other smaller sources of taxation revenue throughout the remainder of this section.

Personal Income Taxes

Within the current Irish income taxation system, an individual's gross pay from working is reduced by three taxation payments: income tax, the universal social charge (USC), and employee's pay-related social insurance (PRSI).

Income tax is charged at the standard rate of 20 per cent on earnings up to €33,800 and above this income is subject to tax at the higher tax rate of 40 per cent. The USC is structured so that income up to €12,011 is charged at 0.5 per cent, between €12,012 and €18,771 it is subject to a 2.5 per cent rate, between €18,772 and €70,044 it is subject to a 5 per cent rate and all income above this level is charged at a rate of 8 per cent.[3] PRSI is charged at a rate of 4 per cent on all income once earnings exceed €424 per week (€22,048). Below this, the PRSI rate rises in increments, from 0 per cent to 4 per cent, once weekly earnings exceed €352 per week (€18,304 per annum). Collectively, these three charges sum to the worker's gross taxation level. From this the employees' income tax credits are deducted to establish their income tax liability.

Employees in the PAYE system are entitled to two tax credits which reduce their income tax liability, a personal credit, and a PAYE credit. These can only be used against the employee's income taxation liability and cannot be used against the USC or PRSI. Entitlements to additional tax credits associated with family circumstances and certain tax breaks, can further reduce an individual's tax liability. Similarly, non-PAYE workers, such as the self-employed and company directors, will record higher average tax rates as they are only entitled to claim the personal tax credit and an earned income tax credit, which is worth less than the PAYE credit. In the past this difference has been justified on the basis of the greater ability that the self-employed and company directors have over work associated expenses they incur.

The Social Insurance Fund receives pay-related contributions from employees, the self-employed and employers. These contributions are used to fund the provision of social welfare payments to those in society who may need them – jobseekers benefit, illness benefit, maternity benefit, etc. Where the fund is unable to meet the cost of these payments it is absorbed by the exchequer. As indicated, employees contribute 4 per cent of their earnings to this fund once their income exceeds €424 per week (€22,048 per annum). Those who are self-employed pay 4 per cent of their profits (income) as PRSI once profits exceed €5,000 per annum. Employers also pay to support the provision of social insurance for their employees. Employers' PRSI is charged at a rate of 8.5 per cent of gross pay up to €376 per week and 10.75 per cent of gross pay above this meaning that the net cost of an employee to an employer is €108.50 or €110.75 for every €100 of gross income.

Consumption Taxes

Value Added Tax (VAT) serves as the primary source of consumption taxes in Ireland. Most goods and services are subject to VAT at one of three rates. The standard rate is 23 per cent and this applies to most goods and services. A reduced rate of 13.5 per cent applies to a number of broadly consumed goods including heating fuel and electricity. A third zero per cent rate applies to many foods, medicines, books, and children's clothing/footwear. In addition, some goods are deemed to be exempt from VAT and these include many services supplied in the public interest in areas such as health, childcare, and education. There is a technical distinction between goods and services which are exempt and those that are charged at zero per cent. This relates to the ability of companies and the self-employed to claim VAT paid against VAT collected on these goods and services.[4]

Excise duties are a further source of consumption tax revenue for the Irish government. These duties, which are strictly regulated within the context of EU free trade rules, are charged in addition to VAT and apply to mineral oils (petrol, diesel, home-heating oil), alcohol and tobacco. In the case of each of these goods, the combined charge of VAT and excise duties represents a large proportion of the retail price paid by the consumer. The inelastic nature of their demand also makes them attractive sources for additional exchequer revenue at Budget time. Excise duties are also charged on certain business premises and activities including betting, alcohol sales, restaurants, auctioneers, and bookmakers.

Environmental taxes represent a recent and growing area of consumption-related taxation in Ireland. In general these taxes are intended to elicit some behavioural change among consumers by encouraging them to reduce or modify their consumption patterns. A carbon tax was introduced in 2010 at a rate of €15 per tonne of CO_2 equivalent and the rate increased to €20 per tonne in 2012. This means that the rate at which the carbon tax is levied is linked to how much pollution a good produces (see Chapter 11). For example, the carbon tax upon its introduction increased petrol prices by 3.5 per cent, natural gas prices by 7.0 per cent, peat briquette prices by 10.1 per cent and coal prices by 11.8 per cent. Over time, the government has signalled that it will increase the rate per tonne of CO_2 equivalent which will drive up prices and revenue from this taxation source. Carbon taxes are charged alongside VAT and, where appropriate, excise duties.

User-charges, such as commercial and residential water charges, act as both a contribution to the cost of provision and as a form of consumption tax. In particular, adjusting prices from zero to even small nominal amounts tends to alter consumption behaviour and promote the conservation of expensive societally provided and subsidised resources.

Corporation, Capital and Property Taxes

Corporation Tax

The tax rate for most company profits in Ireland is 12.5 per cent. Companies operating in specified natural resource sectors (minerals and petroleum) alongside those who deal in development land are subject to a higher corporate tax rate of 25 per cent. Companies can reduce their tax liability below these levels through the use of various tax breaks and exemptions (see later).

Capital Taxes

Capital taxes are levied on the value of assets, or the increase in the value of assets. In Ireland there are two main forms of these taxes, capital gains tax (CGT) and capital acquisitions tax (CAT). CGT is charged on the capital gain (profit after associated transaction costs) made on the disposal of any asset and is levied on the person making the disposal. These gains are subject to tax at a rate of 33 per cent and the first €1,270 of annual gains is exempt from the tax.

CAT is levied on the increase in a person's or company's wealth arising through either gifts or inheritance. The tax is charged at a rate of 33 per cent of the market value of the gain over and above certain specified thresholds. These thresholds depend on the relationship between the person giving the benefit and the beneficiary. Transfers between spouses are exempt from CAT while there are generous thresholds for gifts/inheritances to children with a CAT liability only arising on values above €310,000. These thresholds reduce to €32,500 for transfers among closely related people (near relatives and siblings) and to €16,250 where wealth increases come from any other person. Gifts below €3,000 per annum between any two persons are also exempt from CAT. Special provisions also exist for business owners and farmers who wish to transfer assets to family members. Capital taxes do not arise on increases in wealth associated with payments for damages or compensation, most redundancy payments or lottery wins.

Property Taxes

For many years Ireland remained an exception within the developed world in that it did not have any form of recurring residential property tax for all dwellings. However, this changed with the introduction of the Local Property Tax (LPT) in 2013. The tax is value based and levied on the owners of a property as a percentage of the mid-point of the valuation band into which a property falls. For example, in 2017 a property valued at €180,000 would fall into the €150,000–€200,000 valuation band and would be taxed at a rate of 0.18 per cent of the mid-point of that band (€175,000); giving an annual tax bill of €315. The rate of the LPT is the same for all dwellings below a value of €1 million. Above that threshold, a so-called 'mansion tax' applies where owners pay 0.25 per cent of the value above €1 million in addition to 0.18 per cent of the first €1 million in value. The revenue from the LPT flows to local government and individual local authorities can adjust the tax on properties in their area by plus or minus 15 per cent. In 2017 five local authorities voted to reduce their LPT charge and three increased it.

Associating the tax with local government and local service provision is intended as a measure to strengthen local government and was recommended by the Commission on Taxation in its 2009 report.

Two other forms of property taxes exist and these are charged on property transactions (stamp duty) and businesses via local authority rates. Stamp duties arise on the sale of any residential property and are payable by the purchaser. It is charged at a rate of 1 per cent on the purchase price up to €1 million and 2 per cent on the excess of the price above this threshold. Notionally, the 'stamp duty' is a fee associated with the state's need to record and register these transactions; however it is predominantly a revenue raising source for the exchequer.

Local Authorities levy businesses that occupy commercial property in their area with an annual rates bill which is based on the value of that property as established by a central government agency, the Valuation Office. Within each local authority the level of the rate (known as the Annual Rate on Valuation or ARV) is determined on an annual basis by the elected council as part of its budgetary process. The annual rates bill for commercial premises is calculated by applying this ARV to the valuation of the property concerned and it is levied on the occupier of the building. There are exemptions available for unoccupied units and some educational and charitable institutions. These charges provide around one third of the funding for Ireland's local authorities.

Other Taxes
A series of other taxes also provide revenue to the exchequer. The government imposes small rates of stamp duties and charges on bank card transactions, cheques, stock market share transfers and many insurance policies. Deposit interest retention tax (DIRT) is collected at a rate of 39 per cent on the interest paid or credited on deposits of Irish residents in financial institutions. It is collected at source, meaning the financial institutions deduct the tax from the interest paid and pass these funds to the Revenue Commissioners.

Where a working individual receives some additional non-monetary benefit on top of their salary, they are liable for benefit-in-kind (BIK) tax. These benefits may include the private use of a company car, free or subsidised accommodation, preferential loans received from an employer, free meals and subsidised childcare among others. BIK is levied at a workers marginal tax rate thereby treating the benefit in the same way as additional income.

The purchase and annual registration of motor vehicles produces another source of tax revenue for government in the form of vehicle registration tax (VRT) and motor tax. VRT is imposed as a percentage charge on the initial purchase price of a vehicle and since 2008 the levy is based on its CO_2 emissions. There are exemptions and reductions for electric and hybrid vehicles while rates range from 14 per cent up to 36 per cent for the highest polluting vehicles. Motor tax is an annual charge on all vehicles and is similarly structured with low charges (less than €200) for low polluting and electric vehicles and increasing tax levels associated with higher levels of CO_2 emissions. The payment is collected by local authorities and is unrelated to the usage levels of the vehicle.

Since March 2002, an environmental levy has been charged on plastic shopping bags at the point of sale. The rate of the levy is set by the Minister for Housing, Planning, Community and Local Government and stood at 22 cent per bag in 2017. A similar environmental initiative is the Waste Electronic and Electric Equipment (WEEE) levy which applies to the sale of most medium to large size electronic goods and is intended to fund the recycling of the product. The WEEE is incorporated by retailers into the selling price of products. Revenue from both these levies is *hypothecated*, or specifically allocated to, an environmental fund to support waste management, litter and other environmental initiatives. They are two of the few sources of tax revenue in Ireland that are hypothecated rather than flowing to the exchequer and merged into the overall collection and allocation of state revenues.

Development levies are imposed on non-residential developments following a local authority's approval of a planning permission for that development. The levy is based on the public facilities, such as roads, water, sewerage and parks, which the development will benefit from. They are set by each local authority and additional levies can be imposed for developments nearby certain urban redevelopment and infrastructural projects which the state is funding and which by their existence will further increase the value and benefits derived from the development. A similar tax, intended to recapture some of the windfall gains enjoyed by landowners where their lands are rezoned as approved for development by local authorities, was introduced in 2010 following the property collapse but removed in 2015.

4 EVALUATION: TAXES ON INCOME

Ireland's income taxes climbed to high levels in the 1980s, then slowly dropped on foot of social-partnership agreements and economic growth during the 1990s and early 2000s, before climbing once again as the recession and economic collapse unfolded and decreasing as recovery emerged. These trends have seen the Irish income tax system being described as a 'residual tax source' which increases to compensate for deficits in levels collected elsewhere and reduces as revenues from other sources temporarily increase. [5]

Focusing on the years from 1997 to 2017, Table 4.4 reports the effective tax rates faced by two household types at either end of that period and in 2008, the year when income taxation levels reached their lowest point. Overall, the table reflects significant reductions in income tax across the period, with all household types experiencing large income tax cuts up to 2008. Over the eleven years from 1997 to 2008 a single employee on €60,000 received almost €10,000 in income tax cuts with their disposable income rising from €33,660 in 1997 to €43,500 in 2008. Over the same period the post-tax income of a couple earning €60,000 increased by €14,640, almost 25 per cent of their total gross income.

Table 4.4 Effective Taxation Rates on Gross Annual Earnings, 1997, 2008 and 2017 (%)[1]

Income Levels	Single person			Couple two earners[2]		
	1997	2008	2017	1997	2008	2017
€15,000	23.0	0.0	0.9	11.1	0.0	0.0
€20,000	28.5	4.4	7.2	15.9	0.0	0.0
€25,000	33.7	8.3	13.0	20.3	0.0	0.7
€30,000	37.1	12.9	15.6	22.2	1.7	2.1
€40,000	40.6	18.6	22.1	28.5	3.6	7.9
€60,000	43.9	27.5	31.1	36.6	12.2	15.3
€100,000	46.5	33.8	39.1	42.6	23.8	27.5
€120,000	47.1	35.4	41.3	43.9	27.2	31.2

Source: Author's calculations, based on, *Budget*, Stationery Office, various years.
[1] Calculations are for a PAYE employee on full PRSI. Total income taxation includes income tax, PRSI and health and income levies for 1997 and 2008. Levies were replaced by the USC for 2017.
[2] Couple assumes 65%/35% income division.

At the lower end of the income distribution, a policy commitment to remove all at or below the minimum wage from paying income tax saw rates reduce to zero per cent. A need to generate additional taxation revenue from Budget 2009 onwards, saw a series of reductions in tax bands, cuts to tax credits and the introduction of the USC.[6] Collectively, these changes rapidly raised effective rates once again although the effective rates for all earners remained well below the levels experienced in 1997.

Behind the overall trends in Table 4.4 are a series of issues on the functioning and impact of the Irish income taxation system. We examine these throughout the remainder of this section.

Tax Base
The tax base defines what types and levels of income are to be considered as subject to taxation. Currently, each of the three tax charges on income has a differently defined tax base. This occurs as there are different tax exemptions and reliefs for income taxes, PRSI and the USC. Of these three bases, the USC is the broadest including most forms of income and offering limited reliefs and exemptions. However, the simultaneous existence of three bases undermines the aforementioned desire for simplicity in the taxation system and policymakers have signalled a desire to consolidate the tax base further, most likely by aligning and eventually merging PRSI and the USC.

The narrowness of the income taxation base has been a subject of increasing attention in recent years. To illustrate this, we can use data from the tax system as structured in 2017. Under that structure, the combined effect of income tax rates and tax credits implies that a PAYE employee only begins to incur an income tax liability once their income has exceeded €16,500 per annum. Up to that point, their income incurs a tax rate of 20 per cent but this liability is cancelled out by their entitlement to tax credits totalling €3,300 per annum. They are however subject to charges under the USC and PRSI. Data from the Revenue Commissioners following Budget 2017 (October 2016) suggested that in that year 37 per cent of income earners were exempt from income tax while 43 per cent paid at the standard rate and 20 per cent paid at the higher rate.[7] While these figures include those in receipt of all types of income, including pensions, they reflect both the narrowness of the income tax base and the fact that there are large proportions of the Irish population living on, and earning, low incomes.

The structure of the income taxation system is such that not all forms of income face the same marginal tax rates. In particular, income from savings and capital gains are treated differently to earned income. As outlined earlier, DIRT is charged at a rate of 39 per cent and capital gains incur taxation at a rate of 33 per cent. The tax expenditure system (see later) also incorporates generous reliefs which complement these rates and allow investors to write off the capital costs of their investment over short periods of 7 to 10 years; even when the value of these investments is inflating.

Tax Wedge and Employment
The combined impact of taxation on the take-home pay of workers has impacts on their labour market participation decisions, both at the margin (working additional hours) and at the point of entry and exit. As an employee's income level increases, high marginal taxation rates emerge and form a widening wedge between their gross earnings and their take home pay.

Using data from the 2017 tax system, Table 4.5 shows that once income passes €33,800 the marginal tax rate reaches 49 per cent; meaning an employee takes home €51 out of every additional €100 earned. Marginal rates exceed 50 per cent once income passes €70,044. The table also highlights the existence of a number of steps in the structure of marginal tax rates in the Irish system. These emerge given the structure of tax credits, tax bands, PRSI thresholds, and the USC. Self-employed earners with incomes above €100,000 are subject to an additional USC surcharge of 3 per cent on all income above this threshold bringing their marginal tax rate to 55 per cent.

The presence of high marginal tax rates and the step-effect nature of their increases have knock-on implications for the wider economy. An employee on average earnings (€36,519 in 2015) may find it unattractive to take on additional work hours given these rates.[8] For others, particularly those earning near the marginal tax thresholds, there may be an incentive to reduce work hours or to leave the active labour market and become unemployed – becoming so called 'discouraged workers' (see Chapter 6). To reduce the labour market participation disincentive effects experienced by individuals whose spouse/partner is already at work most tax credits are *individualised*, i.e. they can only be claimed by the

Table 4.5 Summary of the Composition of Marginal Tax Rates for Irish Workers (2017)[1]

Income Range	Income tax[2]	PRSI[3]	USC[4]	Marginal rate
€0–€13,000	0%	0%	0.0%	0.0%
€13,001–€16,500	0%	0%	2.5%	2.5%
€16,501–€18,304	20%	0%	2.5%	22.5%
€18,305–€18,771	20%	0.8%	2.5%	23.3%
€18,772–€22,048	20%	2.7%	5.0%	27.7%
€22,049–€33,800	20%	4%	5.0%	29.0%
€33,801–€70,044	40%	4%	5.0%	49.0%
€70,045+	40%	4%	8.0%	52.0%

Source: Author's calculations, based on, *Budget*, Stationery Office, various years.
[1] Assumes a single PRSI employee aged less than 66 years with entitlements to the personal and PAYE tax credit only.
[2] The personal and PAYE tax credit eliminate any income tax liability up to €16,500.
[3] PRSI is charged on all income once earnings exceed €352 per week (€18,304 per annum). Between €18,304 and €22,048 PRSI is phased in; employees pay 4% on all earnings in excess of €20,048. The table reports the midpoint PRSI rate for each income range.
[4] Employees who earn less than €13,000 are exempt from the USC; once earning above this level the USC applies to all income starting at a rate of 0.5% up to €12,012.

person who is entitled to them and they cannot be transferred to another, even within the same household. Consequently, a female returning to work after having children will start earning with her own PAYE tax credit intact, although she is likely to have shared her personal credit with her partner.

High marginal tax rates may also dampen the entrepreneurial enthusiasm of high-income workers including the self-employed; although the economic evidence for this is limited. Likewise, they can serve as a disincentive in attracting high-skilled migrants to work in Ireland while simultaneously enhancing the attractiveness of emigration for skilled nationals. They also tend to be associated with increasing activity in the shadow or black economy where workers are paid in cash and do not declare their income to the Revenue Commissioners. While the scale of this activity is difficult to measure, the incentive for its emergence and growth is positively related to the marginal tax rate.

For government, it is difficult to avoid many of these marginal tax rate problems in a progressive tax system. Consequently, the challenge for tax policymaking is to balance the necessity of collecting sufficient taxation revenue against the disincentives inherent in high marginal rates which may undermine economic activity and as a consequence undermine tax revenue.

Reliefs and Exemptions
An individual can decrease their effective and marginal tax rates below the levels in Tables 4.4 and 4.5 by availing of tax reliefs and exemptions. These mechanisms,

formally known as tax expenditures, are incorporated by government into the taxation system as a means of incentivising certain activity or accommodating certain needs. Examples include tax relief on pension contributions, incentives to invest in film making, small business and property, a tax credit for blind employees and a tax credit for employing a home-carer. Revenue Commissioners data for 2014 show approximately 70 discretionary tax expenditures costing €7 billion in *revenue forgone* – revenue forgone measures the tax forgone by the exchequer as a result of the tax break. The need to reduce the quantity and scale of these tax breaks and to adopt more formal accounting and economic evaluation methods in recording, reviewing and extending tax breaks has been highlighted.[9]

The largest tax relief is on employee pension contributions costing €2.4 billion in revenue forgone each year. Employees avail of the relief by making contributions to their personal pension funds from their pre-tax income. Consequently, a higher rate of relief is available to employees on higher income tax levels than those on lower incomes. Overall, the ability to avail of tax breaks is directly linked to higher incomes. The more income a person has the more tax they are liable for and therefore the more tax they have available to be written down against various tax breaks. In 2014 a minimum effective tax rate of 30 per cent of income was set for earners with incomes of more than €125,000 in an attempt to minimise their use of tax breaks to reduce their tax bills – a 30 per cent rate is equivalent to the tax level faced by a single PAYE worker earning €57,000. While there is merit in the provision by government of certain tax breaks, the evidence for many is limited and in some cases it is clear that they lead to unnecessary and arbitrary market distortions.

Equity and Simplicity
As Tables 4.4 and 4.5 show the Irish income taxation system has a progressive structure. But the equity principle is undermined at the top of the income scale by the quantity and generosity of many tax breaks. Similarly, there are questions at the other end of the income distribution regarding the point at which income taxes should begin to be imposed on earners. The USC initially (Budget 2011) collected tax from all earners on all income once their annual income exceeded €4,004; this was subsequently increased reaching €13,000 (Budget 2017). Collecting tax at low income levels marked a significant alteration in the approach to income taxation in Ireland which previously had exempted earners up to the annual value of the minimum wage. The appropriateness of this policy reform can be judged against competing desires to protect the living standards of low-income workers and the need for exchequer revenue collected from a broad income tax base. Undoubtedly, the debate on both these issues is likely to continue for some time.

From a simplicity perspective, the compliance and administrative costs faced by most Irish taxpayers are low. As taxes are deduced from wages before they are paid, most employees have limited need for interaction with the Revenue Commissioners. For the self-employed, directors and other corporate tax payers, on-line tax return systems and electronic cash transfers have made tax returns and compliance considerably simpler than in the past. It is likely that over the next decade the entire administrative side of the tax system will move to exclusively electronic exchanges. However, as we have seen, the Irish income taxation system is far from simple and the existence of multiple bases, thresholds, exemptions and rates provides a complex system that most taxpayers would be challenged to comprehend.[10]

5 EVALUATION: INDIRECT TAXES, CORPORATION TAXES AND PROPERTY TAXES

While income and social security taxes comprise more than 50 per cent of the tax take (see Table 4.3), almost all of the rest of the exchequer's revenue is derived from taxes on consumption, company profits and property. The performance of each of these taxes in the Irish system is considered in this section.

Indirect Taxes
Value Added Tax (VAT)
As Figure 4.1 shows, VAT is a regressive tax that collects a higher proportion of income from poorer households. The high indirect tax rates recorded for those in the bottom decile are influenced by a number of individuals within this group who experience a temporary loss of income but continue to consume at pre-existing levels; they consequently record high indirect tax amounts relative to their low income. In Ireland, as in most countries where VAT or equivalent general sales taxes have been in existence for some time, there are multiple VAT rates. This

Figure 4.1 Indirect Taxes as a Proportion of Gross Household Income by Decile, 2009–10

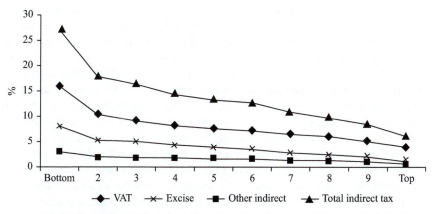

Source: M. Collins, 'Total Direct and Indirect Tax Contributions of Households in Ireland: Estimates and Policy Simulations', *NERI Working Paper No.18*, NERI, Dublin 2014.

contrasts to countries, including a number in Eastern Europe, who have over recent decades introduced VAT systems with only one or two rates. The Irish system is characterised by a large number of exemptions and goods and services charged VAT at zero per cent. As a result, the potential base for VAT in Ireland is narrower than it could be and consequently the standard and reduced rates (23 per cent and 13.5 per cent) are higher than they could be given the revenue raising constraints faced by government when setting these rates.

While the progression of VAT rates across categories of goods and services is for the most part negatively related to their necessity, the fact that the consumption of most goods and services increases as income rises results in higher income households benefiting more in absolute terms from the exemptions, zero-ratings and reduced rates. These benefits further undermine the equity of the tax and the complexity associated with their implementation and administration reduces the efficiency and simplicity of VAT. In general, such inequities and inefficiencies would make the case for reform of the VAT structure but the ability of government to do this is limited by strict EU rules which in effect only allow goods and services to be moved to the standard VAT rate irrespective of their current status.

Excise Duties
Excise duties on fuel, alcohol, and tobacco serve a dual function for government as both revenue generators and public policy tools to discourage consumption and reduce or minimise externalities such as pollution and health effects. The former is possible given that these goods are characterised by low price elasticities and consequently increases in excise levels produce limited demand effects and sizeable exchequer revenue effects. They are therefore a relatively efficient tax. Similarly, they are simple to operate with the tax revenue collected from distributors, importers, and retailers. However, these taxes do raise a number of questions when considered in terms of equity.

The involuntary nature of some expenditure, such as on fuel to heat the home or because products are addictive, makes excise duties difficult, if not impossible, to avoid. Furthermore, data from the Household Budget Survey shows that households at the lower end of the income distribution spend a greater proportion of their disposable income on fuel, alcohol, and tobacco – see Figure 4.1. Therefore, excise duties represent a greater burden to poorer households than better off ones, implying these taxes are regressive and violate the vertical equity principle. As the excise duty tax burden falls on households based on their consumption needs and addictions, households with similar incomes may pay significantly different amounts of total excise duties, violating the horizontal equity principle.

In terms of designing taxation policy, government needs to balance the problematic effects of these taxes against the objectives of revenue generation and discouraging certain consumption. The setting of excise duties are also influenced by levels in neighbouring jurisdictions as relatively high excise duties may result in a loss of the tax base as consumption shifts to purchases made outside the state. In recent years government has limited increasing the excise duties on tobacco and alcohol products as their levels in the Republic of Ireland were greater than those in Northern Ireland and the widening differential over previous years had shifted consumption and undermined the tax base.

Carbon taxes raise similar efficiency and equity issues when considered against the earlier principles given that they are collected and imposed in a similar way to excise duties. Studies prior to the introduction of the tax in 2010 suggested that the government should recycle some of the revenue from the tax to compensate low-income households whose consumption comprise a greater proportion of goods subject to the carbon tax than was the case for better-off households. It was argued that such an approach would cushion the effect of the policy reform while still encouraging households to alter their carbon consumption patterns. However, a compensating mechanism was not introduced to accompany the policy as the exchequer was unable to afford it in 2010. Similar issues also arise for motor taxation and it can be argued that these taxes fall heavier on rural households, large households and those living in areas with limited access to public transport.

Overall, for the most part reforms of indirect taxes have been driven by the desire for additional tax revenue rather than some other objective. Comparative European reports have highlighted Ireland as one of the countries that most frequently changes indirect taxation rates.[11] Furthermore, from the perspective of the overall taxation system, the fact that it is difficult to avoid the regressive nature of indirect taxes irrespective of their design and structure challenges government to ensure that the other elements of the tax system are characterised by a high degree of progressivity.

Corporation Taxes

The corporate profits of both indigenous and foreign owned firms in Ireland are taxed at a rate of 12.5 per cent. In international terms, Ireland's headline corporate tax rate is low, with only one other country in the EU or OECD possessing a rate below this level – Bulgaria with a 10 per cent rate.[12] Data for 2016 suggest that the Irish rate is ten per cent lower than the EU-28 average of 22.5 per cent and well below the top statutory rates on corporate income in Germany (30.2 per cent), France (34.4 per cent), the UK (20 per cent) and the United States (38.9 per cent).[13]

The effective tax rate faced by companies in these countries are likely to be below these headline rates as they can avail of various tax breaks such as for research and development, recruiting workers from disadvantaged groups or operating in regional or economically disadvantaged areas. In general, countries with higher headline corporate tax rates provide a greater array of corporate tax breaks. Estimates by the European Commission found that in 2015 the average EU-28 corporate tax rate reduced from a headline figure of 22.8 per cent to an effective average tax rate of 21.1 per cent. However, even taking account of tax breaks, the Irish corporate tax rate is low in international terms and regularly highlighted as a key incentive for new foreign direct investment.

In general foreign-owned firms benefit from Ireland's low corporate tax rate by locating a subsidiary in Ireland whose profits are subject to tax in Ireland with no taxes payable in the corporation's home country until the profit is repatriated there (see also Chapter 10). Upon repatriation, profits are taxed in the home country with a credit given for taxes already paid in Ireland. Companies are free to delay indefinitely the repatriation of these profits and as such benefit from an ability to use the portion of profit yet to be repatriated within their business. Shareholders also benefit from share price inflation associated with these higher profits and the benefits derived from the use of the additional funds. Irish subsidiaries also enjoy limited restrictions on their ability to engage in *transfer pricing*. This allows multinational companies to internally value sales between associated companies located in different countries and can be used to maximise the profit realised and taxable in lower tax jurisdictions such as Ireland. Such sales can comprise actual goods, or payments for intellectual property rights, and can often represent a large proportion of a firm's turnover.

The sustainability of Ireland's current corporate taxation model is under threat from a series of ongoing international reforms (see also Chapter 10). The ongoing OECD Base Erosion and Profit Shifting (BEPS) project aims to investigate and reform the international corporate tax system. At its core the BEPS has set out to establish whether and why the taxable profits of multinational companies are being allocated to locations different from those where their business activity takes place. The initial steps in this process have already occurred with further reform and increased transparency likely. Although reform will take some time, it carries notable implications for Ireland's corporate tax revenues.

Complementing the OECD BEPS process, there are a number of other corporate tax reforms with implications for Ireland. The impact of the post 2008 recession on the fiscal balance sheets of countries such as the United States focused attention on the need for governments to minimise tax leakages. As a result, incentives to repatriate profits have been introduced and a harder attitude is being taken to countries and territories that facilitate corporations not paying the tax they would be expected to pay. As these reforms continue to unfold, they are likely to cause a shift in the model of FDI investment and tax planning that has characterised some activity in Ireland over the last decade. Simultaneously, within the EU proposals for the establishment of a common consolidated corporate tax base (CCCTB) have been revived and are gaining support.[14]

While the debate on CCCTB is continuing, its emergence if agreed would require firms in all member states of the EU to calculate their profits in the same way, essentially imposing a uniform definition of how corporate income is defined and what can and cannot be discounted against it. The reform is also likely to require firms that operate in multiple countries to apportion their profits between those countries in accordance with a formula that weights the activities of the multinational in the different countries, rather than the company arranging its own internal balance sheet to maximise the profit it realises in the country with the lowest tax rate.

The problems reflected in Ireland's national accounts from 2015 underscore the scale and unsustainability of the current international corporate taxation system, one Ireland continues to gain from, but one which is inevitably reforming. While both the BEPS and CCCTB reforms seem logical, they would undermine the ability of firms to shift their profits and tax liabilities to Ireland and consequently reduce the flow of revenue from this sector to the exchequer. They also reflect a shift in the structure of corporate taxation, with the system edging nearer to that outlined earlier for VAT; one where there are national abilities to set and design tax rates and structures, but these will sit within an overarching international framework.

A further international threat comes from reductions in headline corporate tax rates of other countries. While Ireland's low corporate taxation rate has been a competitive advantage for some time, an increasing number of EU member states are cutting their rates to compete with Ireland, and others, for foreign direct investment. Governments in the USA and UK are also likely to pursue more aggressive corporate tax investment and retention strategies and it is highly likely that these changes will impact on the Irish economy including the tax take from the corporate sector.

Finally, despite the importance accorded to corporate taxes, and near universal political support to leave them untouched, there is limited economic evidence to suggest that there are no deadweight exchequer losses associated with having the rate at 12.5 per cent rather than 15 per cent or 20 per cent.

Property Taxes

A study by the OECD in 2009 used time-series data from its member states to establish a hierarchy of taxes with regard to their negative effect on GDP per capita in the following order from the most to the least harmful for growth: (i) corporate income taxes; (ii) personal income taxes; (iii) consumption taxes; and (iv) recurrent taxes on immovable property.[15] Notably, the Irish taxation system has only recently introduced a recurring domestic property tax, despite this being the least harmful form of taxation given the objective of economic growth.

Recommendations from the 2009 Commission on Taxation and requirements of the EU/ECB/IMF bailout set the context for the introduction of a Local Property Tax (LPT).[16] Political reluctance and fear of such a tax, spanning decades since the abolition of local authority rates on households in 1977, made it challenging for the tax to be implemented. At its most basic, the state did not possess a list of all the dwellings in the country, let alone details of ownership and the amenities they enjoyed. This is despite the fact that the state would have provided many of these households with tax breaks on their purchase, charged stamp duty on their transfer, paid universal transfer payments (child benefit, pensions) to their occupiers and collected various taxes from their occupiers. Despite delays, the commissioning of further reports, and the significant logistical challenges, the tax was implemented, more or less as the Commission on Taxation proposed, from mid 2013.[17] A key attraction of the LPT is that it provides a stable annual flow of resources to the exchequer based on an immovable tax base. This contrasts with the volatile flow of funds from transaction-linked stamp duties which had served as the main source of state property tax revenue.

Judged against the total amount of taxes collected (see Table 4.3) the LPT revenue is small at about 0.75 per cent of the total (€460m in 2017). From an efficient tax system perspective, it should grow over time, although it is unlikely to quickly exceed 2.5 per cent of the total tax take. There may also be regressive elements to the tax, where property owners are asset rich but have low incomes; although the LPT has been designed with a series of exemption and deferral mechanisms to counteract such outcomes. However, the intention is for the tax to fall on property, not income, and provide a flow of resources back to the exchequer and local government to reflect the cost of provision of local services and amenities enjoyed by occupants. Used correctly, an added benefit is that the LPT provides a new policy tool to keep a check on house prices and ensure they do not diverge from various earnings-to-price benchmark ratios as they did in the early 2000s.

6 DEFERRED TAXATION: PUBLIC DEBT

Imposing taxation on incomes, consumption, profits, and assets is not the only way that government can access finance to pursue its spending and economic management objectives. It may also borrow money by selling bonds and using the proceeds to finance public spending. In doing so, governments are engaging in *deferred taxation* as implicit in the selling of a bond is a commitment to pay interest over its lifetime and repay its value upon maturity. To do this, governments will have to raise future taxation revenue from current and future taxpayers.

The appropriateness of governments borrowing today on the basis of taxpayers paying in the future is linked to how governments use these borrowings. Where bond revenues are used to finance capital investments, such as hospitals, museums and transport infrastructure, the benefits derived from the provision of these facilities will flow to the future taxpayers who will service and repay the borrowing. As such, deferring taxation, so that beneficiaries finance the provision of government investments while they experience their benefits, has a logical basis.[18]

Conversely, governments should finance day-to-day, or current, spending from current taxation revenue thereby balancing the exchequer's current account. Current account deficits, where they occur, should only be associated with attempts to stabilise the economy in the short run and governments should cancel this effect out by running current account surpluses in other periods. Financing current account deficits from borrowing serves as an inappropriate transfer of avoided current taxation burdens on to future taxpayers.

The scale of public debt is measured relative to a country's national income with the EU and European Central Bank regarding a gross debt to GDP ratio of below 60 per cent as being optimal. As Figure 4.2 shows since 2000 Ireland has transformed from a low debt country into one with high levels of public debt. In 2000 Ireland ran a fiscal balance of 4.9 per cent of GDP meaning that taxation revenues covered all current and capital spending and provided almost 5 per cent of GDP as an exchequer surplus. By 2007 Ireland's debt to GDP ratio reached a level of 24 per cent of GDP; a debt burden regarded as very low and suggesting that the nation's debt was small, manageable and of limited long-term economic significance. If anything, such a low debt level reduced the need for higher future taxes as its servicing and repayment would inflict limited fiscal strain and given GDP growth, the debt burden would be further eroded.

The simultaneous collapse in the construction and banking industries from 2008 had significant knock on effects for exchequer revenue and spending. Taxation revenue from employees' incomes and spending rapidly contracted as did revenue from housing related VAT and stamp duty. The concurrent international recession also decreased trade, corporate activity, and corporation profits. Between 2007 and 2010 annual taxation revenues fell by just over €15 billion or 25 per cent. Exchequer spending also increased to fund higher social welfare needs and to pay for capital injections into various banks.

Figure 4.2 Ireland's National Debt as a Percentage of GDP, 2000–2020

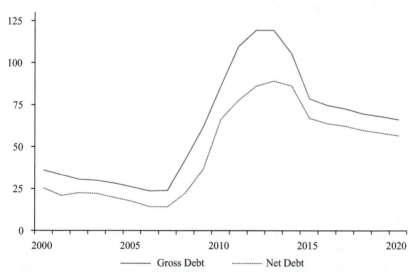

Source: Constructed with International Monetary Fund data from: *World Economic Outlook Database.* www.imf.org [accessed February 2017]. Data is available free of charge from the IMF at www.imf.org/external/pubs/ft/weo/2016/02/weodata/index.aspx

By 2010 Ireland's exchequer deficit reached record levels with the nation borrowing over 30 per cent of GDP in one year; a figure associated with both a large exchequer deficit and once-off rescue costs for Anglo Irish Bank. Ongoing budget deficits and low economic growth saw Ireland's gross debt levels peak in 2013 at 119 per cent of GDP. As Figure 4.2 shows, Ireland net debt level peaked at a lower level (89 per cent) in the same year. The net debt measure discounts cash balances and other financial assets held by the exchequer, including cash-on-hand at the National Treasury Management Agency (NTMA) who regularly stockpile borrowing in advance to minimise the exposure of the exchequer to turbulent bond markets.

Economic recovery, combined with exceptional increases in national income measures and low debt servicing costs, have seen both debt measures decline since 2013. By 2015 gross debt had fallen below the euro zone average (92.5 per cent) to 78 per cent of GPD and is expected to fall further to 2020.

This growth in debt carries a series of structural and policy implications for Ireland in the coming years. In a number of countries independent fiscal councils have been established to act as a watchdog for the fiscal health of nations and to comment publicly on the appropriateness of government's taxation and spending decisions before and after they are announced (see Chapter 3). In Ireland this has seen the creation of the Irish Fiscal Advisory Council (IFAC). However, the scale of Ireland's debt level will necessitate ongoing higher taxation levels relative to those that existed over most of the decade since 2000. Questions have also been raised regarding the sustainability of retaining and servicing certain elements of this debt, in particular that related to the rescue of banks, given the different European rules which applied to the Irish bank bailouts and subsequent ones in other member states.

The fact that future Irish taxpayers will pay for the fiscal and economic mistakes of the first decade of this century violates the logic of intergenerational deferred taxation discussed at the start of this section. The phenomenon of imposing this debt on future generations has also given rise to a consideration to create constitutional checks on governments' fiscal policy decisions.

7 CONCLUSION

This chapter has provided an overview of Ireland's taxation system, setting it in the context of economic theory, its features and operation and the nation's future liabilities. In a given year the taxation system, including tax expenditures, is a €70–80 billion system and it is clear that in the years ahead the system will face significant challenges and reforms.

Central to these will be the need to generate the additional revenue required to close Ireland's exchequer deficit and begin to repay the debt accumulated in the years since 2008. As part of doing this, the chapter has highlighted the opportunities and needs for a broader tax base and reforms targeted at enhancing the simplicity, efficiency, and equality of the tax system. These reforms will also need to address the backdrop of long-term unemployment and tackle any tax-related disincentives to labour market participation and where possible use taxation policies to enhance growth and recovery. A further backdrop will be reforms at a European level relating to corporate taxation structures, broader international corporate tax developments and the ongoing management and monitoring of fiscal policy (see Chapters 3 and 11).

The cumulative effect of revenue needs, deferred taxation, international reforms, and economic recovery in the years ahead will necessitate that taxation policy and taxation reform will serve as recurring public policy themes for the foreseeable future.

Endnotes

1   A. Smith, *An Inquiry into the Nature and Causes of the Wealth of Nations*, Strahan and Cadell, London 1776.

2   A good overview is provided by T. Weber, J. Fooken and B. Herrman, 'Behavioural economics and taxation', *European Commission Taxation Papers N.41*, Brussels 2014.

3   The USC does not apply to individuals with a gross annual market income of less than €13.000.

4   There are a total of six VAT rates in the Irish system. Additional rates of 4.8 per cent apply to agricultural livestock, horses and greyhounds, a rate of 5.4 per cent applies to certain agricultural outputs, and a second reduced rate of 9 per cent applies to a number of labour intensive and cultural services such as restaurant and catering services, hotel/B&B lettings, hairdressing and admissions to cinemas and theatres.

5   See M. Collins, 'Ireland's income taxation system: a social policy perspective' in G. Tobin and C. O'Brien (eds.) *Irish Tax Policy in Perspective*, Irish Taxation Institute and Department of Finance, Dublin 2016.

6   The USC was preceded by an income levy and health levy which were subsequently merged and increased in Budget 2011 to create the USC.

7   See Department of Finance, *Budget 2017*, Stationery Office, Dublin 2016.

8   Central Statistics Office, *Earnings and Labour Costs Annual 2015*, Stationery Office, Dublin 2016.

9   M. Collins and M. Walsh, *Ireland's Tax Expenditure System: International Comparisons and a Reform Agenda*, Policy Institute, Trinity College Dublin, Dublin 2010.

10 A comprehensive explanation is available on the websites of the Office of the Revenue Commissioners www.revenue.ie and the Irish Taxation Institute www.taxireland.ie

11 See European Commission, *Study to quantify and analyse the VAT gap in the EU-27 member states*, Brussels 2013.

12 Cyprus also has a rate of 12.5 per cent. This rate increased from 10 per cent as part of its economic collapse and rescue in 2012/2013.

13 Eurostat, *Taxation Trends in the European Union*, Eurostat, Luxembourg 2016 and OECD Tax Database.

14 See CCCTB proposal and background documents on the commission website at https://ec.europa.eu/taxation_customs/business/company-tax/common-consolidated-corporate-tax-base-ccctb_en

15 OECD, *Going for Growth*, OECD, Paris 2009.

16 Commission on Taxation, *Report 2009*, Stationery Office, Dublin 2009. EU/IMF, *Ireland Memorandum of Understanding on Specific Economic Policy Conditionality*, Dublin 2010.

17 See J. Kennedy and K. Walsh, 'The local property tax – a case study in designing and implementing a new tax' in Tobin and O'Brien, 2016, op.cit.

18 See A. Hillman, *Public Finance and Public Policy – Responsibilities and Limitations of Government* (2nd edition), Cambridge University Press, New York 2009.

CHAPTER 5

Regulation, 'Nudging' and Competition

Tara Mitchell and Francis O'Toole*

1 INTRODUCTION

This chapter examines from both the national and international perspective the general policy area of regulation as well as the specific policy area of competition policy. Many regulatory themes are examined and many regulatory examples, including some controversial issues, are raised, but the reader is warned in advance that comprehensive 'solutions' are not provided in a separate section at the back of the book; in particular, reasonable (as well as unreasonable) people may differ profoundly with respect to the appropriate manner in which many regulatory issues should be addressed.

Regulatory Scope

The field of regulation which spans disciplines such as economics, ethics, law, management, political science, public policy, social administration and sociology, requires a suitably wide definition, such as 'the intentional use of authority to affect behaviour of a different party according to set standards, involving instruments of information gathering and behaviour modification'.[1] A set of formal rules with respect to health and safety in the workplace provides an example of a so-called command-and-control type regulation while the use of taxes (e.g. a carbon tax) and subsidies (e.g. a subsidised flu vaccine for health workers or older people) that aim to alter behaviour provides an example of an incentive-based regulation. Informational requirements with respect to the publication of leaving certificate results obtained in secondary schools or whether or not the seller of a particular financial product is a tied agent represent supply-of-information type regulations.

However, specific uses of name and shame or nudge techniques by official agencies can also be viewed from a regulatory perspective. In the context of the official use of the name and shame approach, allowing a Financial Services Ombudsperson to name offending financial institutions or allowing the relevant Revenue authorities to publish summary details on tax cheats generally raise few major public objections but opening up the sex-offenders registrar to greater public scrutiny is a much more controversial topic. Similarly, but in the context of policy nudges, designing the presentation of the school lunch menu in a particular health-friendly manner seems a sensible nudge as does encouraging organ donor registration and designing tax return forms in as compliance-facilitating a manner as possible but a government agency being involved in designing campaigns (e.g. letters and emails) so as to maximise private donations to charities (and hence perhaps reducing demands on the public purse) could be seen as over-stepping some boundary.

As already demonstrated by the above examples, the regulatory remit certainly extends well beyond standard economic examples and into broader social policy-based areas such as: gay marriage; surrogacy; gender X (or intersex); the rights and responsibilities (and even definition) of parents; gene therapy; domestic and foreign adoption; genetically modified (GM) foods and food safety issues more generally; the wearing of the Muslim hijab or burqa or the Catholic habit; internet gambling, and, the 'markets' for sexual services or illicit drugs or even the 'market' for votes and the associated policy debates with respect to voter registration and limiting corporate or private donations to political parties.[2]

Competition Policy

Competition policy provides one important example of a regulatory policy. At the national level, Irish competition policy aims to ensure that markets produce pro-competitive outcomes such as lower prices and higher quality products for buyers, as well as appropriate returns for sellers. As such, competition policy discourages anti-competitive practices such as price-fixing or market-sharing and blocks mergers that would lead to a so-called substantial lessening of competition. However, competition policy also encourages pro-competitive agreements such as product standardisation agreements between rivals.

At the European Union (EU) level, competition policy is implemented by the European Commission and focuses attention on business practices that may affect cross-border trade within the EU. At the global level, the World Trade Organization (WTO) provides a stage for the negotiation of trade agreements between governments. The WTO encourages reductions in trade barriers as well as non-discrimination in the implementation of any remaining trade barriers but also has the authority to interpret and enforce the underlying existing trade agreements which cover goods, services and intellectual property.

An important distinction can be drawn between the traded and non-traded sectors of the economy in terms of competition policy, in that the enforcement of competition policy within the traded sector of the economy is facilitated often by the threat as well as the reality of imports, while in contrast the enforcement of competition policy within the non-traded sector of the economy is more dependent on the national competition policy agencies and/or national courts. However, the creditability associated with the threat of imports is in turn related to the effective implementation and enforcement of both EU competition policy and WTO trade agreements. In addition, the existence of large scale imports does not rule out the possible existence of local retail markets; for example, the large scale importation of many grocery and pharmaceutical items into Ireland does not rule out the possibility that a specific community could be vulnerable to being exploited by one supermarket or one pharmacy, especially in the presence of restrictive planning regulations.

Within competition policy, recent high profile issues include: the European Commission's decision (August 2016) to require Apple to repay €13b of (illegal) state aid plus interest to Ireland (and/or possibly some other countries); and, the proposed introduction of minimum retail pricing for alcohol in Ireland (as well as in some other countries such as Scotland). Within the context of the WTO's enforcement of international trade agreements, many disputes fall under the heading of export subsidies and/or dumping (i.e. predatory pricing), whereby products are exported at below cost prices in order to gain (and later exploit) market share unfairly.

Natural Monopoly
A natural monopoly exists in a market if it is technically more efficient, i.e. cheaper, for one firm, as opposed to two or more firms, to supply any relevant level of output. In particular, there are significant economies of scale and direct (i.e. 'in the market') competition between firms would be inefficient as economies of scale opportunities and hence significant cost savings would be foregone.

The setting up of a costly infrastructure such as a natural gas network or a national (inter-city) rail network provides an illustrative example of a natural monopoly. Recent prominent natural monopoly policy issues in Ireland include: the appropriate regulation of the collection and disposal of Dublin's household waste, encompassing the controversial Poolbeg incinerator/waste to energy project; the setting of landing and take-off fees at Dublin Airport by the Commission for Aviation Regulation (CAR); and, the setting of distribution prices (but not retail prices) for natural gas by the Commission for Energy Regulation (CER).

Regulation: Sectoral Importance
The importance of regulatory and competition policies is felt throughout the economy. For example, the EU Nitrates Directive which imposes limits on the amount of nitrogen (from animal manure or fertiliser) that can be used in farming highlights the specific importance of regulatory policies to the agricultural sector (see Chapters 9 and 11). In addition, very significant controversy was caused in Ireland by the attempted imposition of a ban on non-commercial turf-cutting on raised bogs which arose as a result of EU conservation laws. These two examples also demonstrate the importance of transnational regulatory policy and the need for co-ordination with respect to Irish and EU sectoral regulations.

Within the manufacturing sector, policies with respect to corporation taxes have been responsible for the location of many foreign-owned manufacturing plants in Ireland, for example in the IT and pharmaceutical sectors. The recent controversies surrounding Ireland's relatively low corporation tax rate (12.5 per cent) and, in particular, Apple's apparently much lower 'effective' rate again demonstrates the importance of transnational regulatory policy but also highlights the possible existence of tensions between the goals of national (i.e. Irish) and international (e.g. EU, USA and OECD) regulations (see Chapters 2 and 10 in particular).

Within the services sector of the economy, the importance of regulatory policy, both domestic and transnational, was more than aptly demonstrated by Ireland's banking crisis. The re-capitalisation and re-structuring of the Irish (as well as the UK) banking sector also demonstrates the importance of competition policy, both nationally and internationally. While competition policy was arguably trumped in the short run by the immediate needs of financial stabilisation (e.g. the merger of AIB and EBS in an Irish context), it is clear that a suitably designed and implemented competition policy offers significant long-run benefits (e.g. protection from a possible banking duopoly).

Chapter Outline

This chapter attempts to address many of the issues mentioned above. Section 2 provides an overview of regulation, addressing possible explanations and/or justifications for, and theories of, regulation and focuses specific attention on the risk-based approach to regulation. Section 3 reviews the insights offered by behavioural economics, and explores the policy implications of the associated literature which covers the overlaps between economics and psychology. In particular, this literature highlights clearly the importance of the manner in which choices are presented. The way in which these insights can be used by participants in the private sector should arguably be regulated, e.g. providers of payday loans should be forced to quote interest rates in a manner that is understood by their potential customers. The manner in which these insights can be used by public sector agencies should also arguably be regulated.

Section 4 focuses attention on the specific regulatory policy example of competition policy and provides a number of illustrative examples while Section 5 addresses the specific policy area that intersects both regulation and competition, namely, the regulation of natural monopolies and networks such as the electricity transmission and natural gas distribution grids. Section 6 offers some concluding comments.

The above outline and the previous examples make it clear that an understanding of regulation is essential for an understanding of policy issues in both the Irish market and non-market sectors. As such, it should be no surprise to readers of the rest of this book to re-encounter many of the above themes, for example in discussions surrounding food safety, labour markets, distributional issues, energy, education and health.

119

2 REGULATION: PRINCIPLES AND ISSUES

Reasons for Regulation
Information and Co-ordination
There are a number of plausible reasons for the existence of regulations. At a very general level, informational and co-ordination problems could justify, or at least explain, the existence of many regulations. For example, basic fire safety standards are set to protect the vast majority of individual users of, say, cinemas, hotels and public transport as individually very few of these users would be in a position to assess the appropriateness, or otherwise, of the fire safety precautions taken by others.

A similar argument holds with respect to the existence of regulations regarding, say, maximum taxi fares. For example, a fare of €100 might well be acceptable to an individual (rich) tourist attempting to get from an airport to the city centre on a very cold night but it is generally regarded as inappropriate to take advantage of the tourist's initial informational deficiency when arriving in a new city. Indeed, many forms of regulation are responses to what are seen as informational problems, as it is argued that markets often under-provide relevant information. For example, what is the real price of an advertised 1 cent airfare or how can one individual compare the costs of different loans? The latter question is addressed in the USA by the Truth in Lending Act (2001) which insists that all lenders must quote the annual percentage rate (APR) to potential borrowers; APRs can then be (to at least some extent) compared across different loan options.

Other regulations surrounding information requirements in at least some jurisdictions insist that car manufacturers provide fuel efficiency information, brewers of beer provide alcohol content information, cigarette packets display graphic health warnings, food products carry nutritional information and that league tables with respect to school performances are produced and published. In addition, various regulations insist upon what might be termed minimum standards, as opposed to just the provision of information, e.g. travel agencies and operators enter into various forms of travel bonds and retail banks must keep a certain proportion of their retail consumers' deposits in liquid assets. These minimum standards are at least arguably a policy response to underlying informational deficiencies.

Spillover Effects
Economists tend naturally to view the existence of (non-priced) spillover effects, or externalities, as providing an explanation for the existence of many regulations. Technically, externalities imply the existence of a divergence between private costs and social costs (or private benefits and social benefits), i.e. the existence of external costs (or external benefits). Within the standard example of pollution – a negative production externality – without suitable regulations a producer does not have to internalise the (external) cost of the pollution that the production process imposes on others.

A similar argument holds with respect to the placing of restrictions on the consumption of tobacco products although of course reasonable people can differ with respect to the appropriate limits of such regulations. For example, should an adult be allowed to smoke at home or in a car in the presence of children or should adults be allowed to choose between a smoking and non-smoking pub/restaurant? Indeed, the appropriate level of regulation of electronic cigarettes (e-cigarettes) is controversial.

Of course, informational and spillover explanations for regulations do not always separate out easily. For example, the requirement for drivers (and businesses more generally) to hold at least third-party insurance is commonly justified by the belief that drivers (and society more generally) should be protected from the results of mistakes of another driver, even if each individual driver is allowed to rationally (or otherwise) decide not to protect himself or herself from his or her own actions. The existence of this regulation can be understood via the information explanation (how would one know which drivers are insured) and/or by the spillover explanation (why should you have to pay for my mistake).

Another possible example is provided by retail planning guidelines with respect to the location and scale of various types of retail developments (e.g. shopping centres) at or near a town centre which set the rules by which business people make important (and often not easily reversible) investment decisions.

Unequal Bargaining Power and Wider Social Policy

The reality of the existence of unequal bargaining power also explains the existence of many regulations. For example, although at least some users of industrial saws or chain saws may well be prepared to work without safety guards, many other users would prefer not to be put in a position where they had to actively request the installation of such (perhaps expensive) guards and hence perhaps not be employed in the first place (as a result of their rather 'conservative' approach to safety matters).

Arguably, the same argument applies with respect to the use of minimum wage legislation; at least some workers and employers would be prepared to transact at a lower wage but society in effect does not allow such 'voluntary' transactions. However, at least some people might regard the setting of some safety requirements and labour restrictions as being excessively interventionist. Indeed, some people argue for less regulation in the 'markets' for sexual services or so-called recreational drugs but most people would feel very uncomfortable if a less interventionist position was used to justify the straight-forward buying and selling of votes or vital organs (such as kidneys) or even people (e.g. babies).

More generally, it is clear that many regulations are explained on broader social policy grounds as opposed to on what might be termed market failure grounds. For example, anti-discrimination legislation is difficult to explain on market failure grounds alone; indeed, some market proponents might insist that the market system would eliminate such discrimination. The existence of universal service obligations with respect to a basic daily postal delivery service (and at no extra cost to the recipient living alone in a very isolated location) or the proposed (in 2014) 1 per cent levy on all insurance products in Ireland to create a distress fund in order to cover those most at risk of flood damage (who were not offered flood insurance by the insurance market) can also be seen as addressing social policy objectives. Indeed, in at least the latter case, arguably there is no market failure at all as it would be irrational for an insurance business to offer affordable flood insurance if flood damage is almost guaranteed.

While information, co-ordination, spillover effects and unequal bargaining power or more generally social policy grounds can be used to explain the existence of very many regulations, it is not so easy to explain the existence of many other regulations, such as the ban on private health insurers from offering discounts to non-smokers without stretching concepts of co-ordination failures, spillover effects and social policy objectives beyond their usefulness. In addition, the above-mentioned proposed explanations may not be able to explain the non-existence of arguably sensible regulations, for example, with respect to you being required to inform (up-front) any potential partner of at least some of your particular/peculiar health and personality 'characteristics' prior to the potential partner makes a potentially irreversible investment in you. As such, there is merit in examining plausible over-arching theories of regulation.

Regulation: Theories and Strategies
Theories
There are a number of overlapping theories of regulation. From an economics perspective, it is tempting to focus particular attention upon the distinction between the public-interest approach to regulation on the one hand and the interest-group and private-interest approaches to regulation on the other hand.

The public-interest approach to regulation highlights the claimed equivalence between the regulator's interests and the broader public interest. As such, the regulator may be said, in a somewhat paradoxical sense, to be disinterested; the public interest is somehow ascertained (say, with respect to food safety), and the regulator acts in a purely technical manner so as to achieve the desired end-state. In particular, there is no allowance made for any underlying power struggle between, say, the regulated parties (e.g. producers and sellers of food) and the parties for whose benefit the regulations are being put in place (e.g. consumers of food). This approach may be particularly appropriate at least some times in the context of basic food safety, where the differences between the two groups may well be minimal and the issues to be debated rather well-defined, but what about in the context of the appropriate regulation of genetically modified (GM) foods?

In contrast, the interest-group and private-interest approaches highlight the private incentives of groups and individuals, respectively. Within the interest-group approach, attention is focused on the relationships between groups and the state. Within the context of these evolving relationships a competition or battle is seen to take place between various different conceptualisations of what is in the public interest. From an Irish perspective, the evolution of social partnership could be analysed from this perspective.

The private-interest approach also referred to as the economic theory of regulation or public choice, goes further and insists that the individual incentives confronting each rational agent or actor must be considered if regulation is to be understood. For example, it is claimed that regulatory capture, a process in which regulators over time appear to begin to represent the interests of the regulated, as opposed to society more generally, can only be understood if particular attention is paid to the incentives of the employees of regulatory agencies. It is these employees who interact with, and begin to depend upon the regulated entities (e.g. with respect to the provision of data within a particular format by a certain date).

From the public choice perspective, unless particular safeguards are put in place, it is hardly surprising that implicit understandings between these individuals and even their respective organisations begin to develop. For a very plausible example, consider at least some aspects of the Irish banking crisis, where the interests of individuals and financial institutions somehow appeared to become blurred with the interests of the state.

In addition to the above interest approaches to regulation, there are other approaches which can be considered on their own merits or in conjunction with the interest approaches. For example, at particular times in history, it is clear that the force of ideas can drive regulatory developments. At a macroeconomic level the Keynesian revolution could be viewed as a prime example of a shift in ideas with very significant policy implications, while at a more microeconomic level (albeit one with macroeconomic consequences), there was a shift towards privatisation in the UK and deregulation and market liberalisation in the USA during the early 1980s.

Strategies
Assuming the need for a regulatory response, various options exist with respect to the appropriate form of regulation, e.g. command-and-control (e.g. a no smoking indoors within work places rule); production and/or consumption taxes (e.g. the imposition of a carbon tax); quotas, perhaps supported by a system of tradable permits (e.g. fishing or even pollution); or, simply naming-and-shaming (e.g. tax evaders or negative inspection reports for nursing homes or, albeit perhaps less likely – but more horrifying – evaluation reports by students on individual lecturers). Even within the context of a standard externality, say insufficient take-up of the flu or more controversially the MMR and HPV vaccines, alternative and very different regulatory strategies can be followed, ranging from subsidising consumption of the vaccines to compulsory vaccination.

In contrast to these various measures, some market enthusiasts simply highlight the need to specify property rights very clearly so as to facilitate negotiations and market-based transactions between all affected parties. For example, if anglers have the right to clean water, anglers will be paid by the polluters for any pollution that the anglers choose to allow and if the polluters have the right to pollute the water, the anglers will pay the polluters to restrict the level of pollution to the appropriate level.

Almost all regulatory strategies suffer from some disadvantages. For example, command-and-control tends to be inflexible in that, say, in the context of pollution reduction the adoption of a tradable permit system would be more efficient in that those most able to reduce pollution could transfer (at an appropriate price) the right to pollute to those least able to reduce pollution. In addition, command-and-control, as well as at least some other regulatory strategies, can suffer from what is termed creative compliance, e.g. the introduction of a maximum waiting period for hospital admission is often closely followed by the introduction of, in effect, a waiting list for the waiting list. Another example is arguably provided by President Trump's early signing of an executive order (directed at generals and security advisors) calling for a plan to defeat Isis within 30 days. Assuming that the 30 days limit refers to the plan, as opposed to the actual defeat, it seems clear that the generals and security advisors have at least some wiggle room with respect to the definition of a plan.

More generally, there has been a move away from regulating by rule (which can be associated with a rather narrow understanding of regulation) and towards what might be termed market-based systems of regulation, e.g. where the regulator highlights the goals and allows maximum flexibility to the regulated with respect to attaining the goals, e.g. limit global temperature increase to less than two degrees (Celsius) or to reduce emissions in the EU by forty per cent. However, in the presence of serious or catastrophic risk (e.g. nuclear energy or some financial systems), it may not be appropriate to rely simply on the market system and the assumed rationality of all economic actors.

Risk-Based Regulation

The concept of risk has become an organising concept in regulatory matters, particularly with respect to allocating regulatory resources (in terms of the regulators) and perhaps even with respect to compliance efforts (in terms of the regulated). The adoption of a risk-based approach to regulation requires the estimation of both the probability of, in some sense, failure (to achieve the regulatory goal) and the impact of this failure in numerical or financial terms and the appropriate ranking of the subsequent adjusted or weighted risks. The resulting risk ranking varies from 'close to unacceptable' (e.g. nuclear energy) through 'as low as reasonably possible' (e.g. treatment of sex offenders within the community) to 'acceptable' (e.g. speeding). The appropriate regulatory strategy can then be assigned, e.g. command-and-control in the context of nuclear energy safety through perhaps mandatory registration in the local police station in the context of sex offenders to perhaps installation of speed cameras and/or speed bumps in the context of speeding.

While the risk-based approach to regulatory strategies has proved useful in dealing with certain types of risk, e.g. workplace accidents, environment and retail financial services, the approach suffers from a number of implementation problems.

First, there is the underlying fundamental problem of uncertainty versus risk, with the distinction being that only the latter can be estimated in any meaningful manner. As such, often uncertainties (perhaps with very significant potential impacts) tend to get omitted from the analysis. Arguably, GM Foods might provide such an example although the formal recognition of the existence of uncertainty in a particular context should not imply simple prohibition, as for example, it is unlikely that physicists would be able to prove comprehensively (especially to the armchair sceptic) that the Large Hadron Collider (LHC) in CERN is absolutely incapable of giving rise to a black hole sufficient in scale that would allow it to consume the LHC, France, Switzerland, the earth and the universe(s).

Second, arguably the risk-based approach to regulatory strategies also facilitates what might be termed the blame-shifting game. Take, for example, the mandatory registration of sex offenders at the local police station. In the event of repeat offending, to what extent, if any, are those at the local police station responsible? This example also highlights the apparent lack of evidence with respect to the actual rate of recidivism in the first place. Indeed, given the more general (acknowledged) absence of evidence, is it really possible to implement the risk-based approach to regulation to any degree of satisfaction in the first place?

Third, and even when there is a significant degree of evidence available, it is clear that society, for good or bad, has not responded fully to the risk-based approach to regulation. For example, it is clear that an excessive amount of impact-adjusted risk is accepted by society with respect to road transport and an insufficient amount of impact-adjusted risk is accepted by society with respect to rail and air travel. Perhaps more controversially, it appears that the same could be said with respect to childhood obesity and radon gas (where society appears to accept too much impact-adjusted risk) and smoking and nuclear energy (where society arguably appears to accept too little impact-adjusted risk, although the jury is still out with respect to the long-term effects of the Fukushima and other nuclear accidents).

3 BEHAVIOURAL ECONOMICS, NUDGING AND PATERNALISM

Behavioural Economics: Biases
Behavioural economics uses insights from psychology to analyse how individuals make choices and the possible policy implications and applications of same. In particular, behavioural economics highlights biases that impact significantly and consistently on the decision-making process such as: anchoring, framing, inertia, loss aversion and myopia.[3] Until recently, the standard economics approach would have ignored these biases, seeing them as short-run phenomena that, in theory must wash out in the long run.

Anchoring focuses on the importance of the order in which questions are asked. For example, consider the possible impact of reversing the order of the following two questions: (i) how happy are you; and, (ii) how many really close friends do you have? It seems likely that the stated (or perhaps even actual) level of happiness would fall considerably when one is tempted into anchoring the response against a (presumably) smallish number of really close friends.

Framing highlights the importance of presentation. For example, consider any standard quantity discount system where the mean price paid by the consumer falls as the quantity purchased increases. One can present this scheme as being a *loyalty discount* scheme (where the consumer is *rewarded* for loyalty) or as being a *disloyalty penalty* scheme (where the consumer is *penalised* for being disloyal or unfaithful); it seems very likely that more will be sold using the former marketing approach.

Inertia (or the status quo bias) refers to the tendency to stick to one's original choice which in many cases is the initial default option. For example, if the default option is that one must actively opt in to a basic retirement plan as opposed to actively opt out of a basic retirement plan it seems clear that less people will be enrolled.

Loss aversion refers to the, in general, greater level of unhappiness associated with a particular loss (say, €100) compared to the happiness associated with the same gain (i.e. €100). For example, studies suggest that the prospect of winning €200 just about compensates for the (equal) prospect of losing €100.

Myopic (or short-sighted) behaviour refers to the tendency to over-value (under-value) the present (future). For example, a small reward today might be chosen over a much larger reward tomorrow. Many would instinctively defend this choice as being rational (which it very may well be) but an underlying tension or apparent inconsistency of preferences is suggested if the same individual reverses the choice when, say, the same choice is put off for 24 hours; for example, perhaps you would choose €10 today over €12 tomorrow but you would also choose €12 the day after tomorrow over €10 tomorrow?

Many of the above biases centre on the architecture of choice. Under standard rational choice theory, the order in which options are presented or the way in which they are framed should not matter as they do not change the information that decision makers have and hence should not change their choices or indeed their underlying preferences. However, behavioural economics has shown that these factors frequently do influence the choices that individuals make and therefore they should not be ignored by policymakers.

Behavioural Economics and Policymaking
There are two main ways in which policymakers can use insights from behavioural economics to inform policy. First, firms may try to manipulate the choices that consumers make by presenting options in particular ways and policymakers may want to introduce regulations to prevent firms from acting in this way and thereby protect consumers. Second, governments themselves may want to

influence the decisions that individuals take and may use knowledge of behavioural economics in order to so do. From society's perspective there may be certain choices that are preferred (e.g. tax compliance) and the government may manipulate the choice architecture such that it makes it more likely for individuals to make those choices.

In 2009, Cass Sunstein, one of the authors of *Nudge*, was appointed the Director of the White House Office of Information and Regulatory Affairs ('OIRA') with the aim of informing regulatory policy with behavioural insights. Not long afterwards (in 2010), David Cameron, the UK Prime Minister, established the Behavioural Insights Team in the UK; this group consults with government departments on how to incorporate lessons from behavioural economics into policymaking. The Financial Conduct Authority in the UK has also been at the forefront of using behavioural insights to design policy and recently set up a Behavioural Economics and Data Science Unit. While not at such an advanced stage as the UK, the Netherlands, Germany, France and Denmark have all put together specialised teams to incorporate behavioural insights into policymaking and Finland and Austria are currently in the process of so doing.

At the EU level, the Joint Research Centre has been carrying out research on behavioural economics and recently established the EU Policy Lab with the aim of supporting policies with evidence from behavioural sciences. The OECD has also recognised the importance of behavioural economics for policymaking and has produced a Consumer Policy Toolkit.

Ireland does not yet have a dedicated behavioural insights team but the Irish Government Economic and Evaluation Service (IGEES) has been drawing actively on behavioural insights to inform policies and have been formally testing out the effectiveness of various approaches.[4]

Policymaking and Nudging

Preventing Manipulation of Consumers by Firms

Consumer protection legislation which recognised the potential impact of behavioural biases on consumer decision-making (without explicitly labelling it as such) has been in place for some time. In Ireland, the Consumer Protection Act (2007) has a number of regulations aimed at protecting consumers from being manipulated by sellers of goods and services. In particular, it prohibits misleading advertising and states that 'advertising is seen as misleading if it involves false, misleading or deceptive information that is likely to cause the average consumer to act in a way they might otherwise not.' For example, a seller cannot claim that a product is on sale at a discounted price if it was not available at the stated original price for a reasonable length of time. This is to avoid the anchoring effect whereby, regardless of the actual price being charged, consumers may be more inclined to buy a product if they believe that they are getting it at a reduced price.

The European Commission relied more explicitly on behavioural insights in the design of The Consumer Rights Directive which came into effect in Ireland in June 2014. This regulation was particularly aimed at protecting consumers in on-line interactions with sellers. Recognising the impact of defaults, the directive limits the use of pre-ticked boxes in consumer contracts. It also introduced a 'cooling-off' period whereby consumers can get out of a contract if they feel that they did not make the right decision in the moment.

The European Commission also drew on behavioural insights for its competition policy decision related to Microsoft in 2009. Microsoft had been setting Internet Explorer as the default browser within Windows. The European Commission was concerned that because of the influence of default settings on consumers this practice would reduce competition in the market for browsers. The decision required Microsoft to provide users with a 'Choice Screen' for a web browser rather than having Internet Explorer set as the default browser in order to allow/force consumers to make an active choice; the Commission subsequently imposed a fine for €561 million on Microsoft for non-compliance with this decision.

The USA has also been active in introducing legislation to protect consumers from manipulative behaviour by firms. President Obama signed the Credit Card Accountability Responsibility and Disclosure (CARD) Act into US law in May 2009. The aim of this Act was to protect consumers from practices by USA credit card companies that were considered to be unfair. The Act introduced new rules regarding the kind of information that companies were required to provide to consumers, including requiring calculations to be presented on credit card bills showing the time and cost of repaying the balance through minimum monthly repayments and the cost for repaying over 36 months. Certain types of 'hidden' fees were also banned. In particular, it may not be sufficient to require firms to present consumers with full information; policymakers may also need to regulate the form in which the information is presented. For example, OIRA has drawn a distinction between 'summary disclosure' and 'full disclosure' of information. Summary disclosure is intended to simplify and standardise information and may be mandated for certain products at point of sale in order to help consumers make decisions. Consumers may struggle to make optimal decisions in particular in markets in which they sign contracts for the on-going supply of services, e.g. contracts with telecommunications or utilities providers. Various departments in the USA and UK have been seeking to introduce MyData/MiData initiatives to provide consumers with access to historical data on their individual usage of a particular service in order to help them determine if their current contract is optimal for them.[5]

Altering Choice 'Architecture'
The examples given above have all been in reference to situations where policymakers are trying to protect consumers from manipulation by firms. However, there are also many examples of policies that are designed to alter the choice architecture in order to increase the likelihood that the decisions that individuals make are in line with the ones preferred by the policymakers. One of the most widely cited examples of the effect of defaults is the case of organ donation.

Research has suggested that changing from an opt-in scheme to an opt-out scheme can increase significantly the rate of organ donation. There are multiple reasons why this may be the case. Organ donation is a complicated moral issue and the type of decision that most people are likely to delay making for as long as possible. In addition, the setting of the default itself may signal to people what is considered to be the social norm and hence the appropriate choice. A number of European countries have now adopted opt-out schemes based on this research. Rather than forcing a particular default on citizens, the UK has instead adopted a policy that forces individuals to make an active decision. Now in order to get or renew a driver's license, it is necessary to state your preference regarding organ donation. There is some evidence to suggest that forcing an active decision can increase organ donation rates by a similar amount to adopting an opt-out scheme but more research is needed in this area.

Another area where policymakers have tried out different approaches is with policies related to points for drivers against the backdrop of trying to deter dangerous driving. However, countries differ in the type of system used. The system in Ireland is incremental, whereby drivers receive penalty (or demerit) points for each infraction and will lose their license for a certain length of time if they exceed the maximum allowable amount of penalty points. In contrast, a number of other countries use a decremental system. In this system, drivers start with a certain number of merit points which they lose every time they commit a traffic violation. If they lose all of their merit points then their license is revoked. Behavioural economics suggests that this system might be more effective as it draws on the power of loss aversion. Again, more research is needed in order to verify which system is more effective in practice.

Finally, a market that policymakers often intervene in is the market for cigarettes; in many countries, cigarette packets are required to carry health warnings. Since the vast majority of people are aware of the health risks associated with cigarettes it is likely that these warnings are driven by behavioural, rather than informational, concerns. Ireland is the first European country to go further and introduce legislation mandating plain packaging for cigarettes; this legislation is due to come into effect in mid 2017. The aim of this regulation is to make cigarettes less appealing by reducing the importance of branding and making health warnings on the package even more salient; arguably the impact of the regulations may even alter the (apparent) taste of cigarettes. The UK and France have also introduced similar legislation.

Libertarian Paternalism
Using regulation to prevent consumers being manipulated by firms seems a fairly uncontroversial idea. It is also easy to put forward an argument that justifies the government redesigning the choice architecture in order to influence decisions in the case of externalities, e.g. vaccination. However, there are many cases where behavioural insights are also being used to regulate internalities. These are situations where there is at least arguably an internal conflict between the short-run

preferences of a particular individual and that individual's long-run welfare, e.g. encouraging healthy eating or contributions to pension funds. Arguably, this regulation of internalities is paternalistic. On the one hand, governments are protecting consumers from being manipulated by firms but on the other hand governments are protecting consumers from being manipulated by ... themselves.

In addressing this tension, Sunstein and Thaler argue in favour of libertarian paternalism. They suggest that governments should not restrict the choices that individuals can make but that, where appropriate, governments should manipulate the choice architecture in order to 'nudge' individuals into making better decisions. Given its potential policy importance, for example, with respect to organ donation or retirement pensions, this is a very important argument. Very rational decision makers should not be influenced by the choice architecture and therefore since their choice set is not restricted, they will be no worse off as a result of the attempted nudge. But those individuals who are affected by behavioural factors may be better off as a result of this government intervention. This of course rests on the assumption that government officials know what the optimal choices are for these individuals and for society. This can be problematic when individuals have different (heterogeneous) preferences and also when government officials themselves suffer from behavioural biases. Sunstein and Thaler counter these arguments by claiming that no matter what governments do, a choice architecture always exists that will influence the choices of citizens. Indeed, it can be argued that it would be wrong not to respond to the importance of the architecture of choice as this apparent 'non-decision' (i.e. not to 'interfere') would actually represent a decision to not make people better off, i.e. in effect a decision has been made to make people worse off. For example, if school children tend to almost automatically pick the first option on the school menu, surely it is reasonable (indeed, necessary?) to dedicate that position on the menu to a healthy option? If organ donation is significantly higher under opt-out, as opposed to opt-in, surely it is reasonable to change the default for organ donation? If savers are myopic, surely it is reasonable to push them into increasing their pension contributions automatically as their income increases, as well as opting them into the pension scheme in the first place?

For many people, there are limits to this (libertarian) paternalist approach. For example, at least some might feel somewhat uneasy if an official agency sets out with the goal of increasing charitable giving by utilising the insights offered by behavioural economics.[6] Possible mechanisms include: offering individuals the opportunity to opt in to increased future donations; using personalised messages or offering prizes; using prominent individuals as examples to follow; and, getting the timing right by, for example, making the request in early December. The increased private donations may well reduce the immediate need for public expenditures but perhaps public expenditure was a more efficient and effective form of support for these (presumably deserving) charities in the first place? Indeed, arguably it is possible that the short-run significant increases in charitable donations might be offset by uncertain long-run reactions by the contributors, as the extra contributions must come from some part of their budget.

4 COMPETITION POLICY

Competition policy provides one very important example of regulatory policy at both the domestic (Irish Competition Law) and international level (e.g. EU Competition Law). Competition policy attempts to regulate competition between businesses by, for example, making cartels illegal and discouraging anti-competitive actions by a dominant firm (e.g. refusal to deal) but encouraging efficiency-enhancing agreements (e.g. product standardisations agreements) even between competitors.[7]

Competition policy enthusiasts do not suggest that unfettered competition between competitors (i.e. the unregulated market system) is a panacea for all of society's issues of resource allocation. For example, visions of completely uncontrolled competition between, say, competing household waste collection trucks in a housing estate touting for business on a daily basis, competing buses speeding towards the same bus stop and competing hospitals out in ambulances hunting for prospective clients, merely highlight the need for a rational policy approach to, and a specific regulatory framework for, competition, i.e. competition policy must be seen as a subset of regulatory policy.

The most important concept in the area of competition policy is that of significant market power. From the perspective of an individual firm, the presence of significant market power indicates the ability of the firm to raise price significantly above the cost of production for a significant period of time. In contrast, the absence of significant market power indicates the presence of an effectively competitive market. As such, the role of a suitably designed competition policy is to encourage the existence of competitive markets by discouraging anti-competitive conduct that give rise to the presence of significant market power (e.g. a merger between the two largest competitors in an already highly concentrated market).

Perfect Competition, Monopoly and Contestable Markets

There are three market structures that are particularly important for an understanding of the economics of competition policy: perfect competition; monopoly; and contestable markets. Perfectly competitive markets have the characteristic of being (allocatively) efficient, as firms are forced by the pursuit of their own self-interests to price at marginal cost (i.e. $P = MC$) and hence to produce the correct amount from society's perspective. Price (P) represents the economic value placed by society on the marginal or last unit of the product produced, while marginal cost (MC) represents the economic cost to society of producing that marginal or last unit. The equivalence between price and marginal cost suggests, at least in the absence of externalities or other market failures, that neither too little nor too much of the product has been produced, i.e. the correct amount of the product has been produced.

In contrast, a monopolist produces a level of output at which price is greater than marginal cost ($P > MC$), and hence produces too little when viewed from society's perspective. However, it is also argued that the monopolist's excess economic profits do not just represent a transfer from consumer to producer, as profit-seeking activities (or, rent-seeking, as it is generally referred to) dissipate these profits over time. In particular, prior to the creation of the monopoly (e.g. markets for various mobile telephony services), firms will involve themselves in socially unproductive activities in order to increase their chances of being the chosen one, while once installed, the incumbent will involve itself in unproductive activities, when viewed from society's perspective, in order to sustain its monopoly position.

Notwithstanding the strength of the above arguments against monopoly, there are also economic arguments in favour of monopoly. First, some economists and other social scientists view monopoly's excess profits as the short-term reward necessary for sustaining the competitive process in the long-term; IBM, Microsoft, Intel and perhaps Google provide at least somewhat plausible illustrative examples. Second, it is argued that a monopolistic market structure may be more conducive to the pursuit of innovation and research and development which require significant levels of up-front and risky investments; the pharmaceutical sector provides a possible example. Third, in the presence of significant economies of scale, it may well be appropriate to place a limit on the number of firms allowed to enter a market; indeed, in the extreme case of a natural monopoly, the appropriate number of competing firms is one (see Section 5 for further details).

More generally, the competitive process is facilitated by the presence of potential competition. Potential competition focuses attention on the ability of potential entrants to dissuade incumbent firms from attempting to take advantage of (i.e. abusing) their market position. In the extreme case of a perfectly contestable market, potential competition can perfectly simulate perfect competition, even in a monopoly situation. The incumbent firm is forced to price at marginal cost, as any divergence between marginal cost and price would allow an equally efficient entrant to enter with a price below the incumbent's price but above marginal cost and to exit if/when the incumbent reacts.

It is sometimes claimed that competing on a specific airline route provides an example of an almost perfectly contestable market, as the entrant's plane and other investments (e.g. a web-based reservation system) can be withdrawn and used elsewhere at little additional cost. In contrast, it would be difficult for an entrant to withdraw, without incurring substantial sunk costs, after attempting to compete with respect to the provision of a rail network or an electricity grid. Indeed, the latter examples represent natural monopolies as opposed to contestable markets; natural monopolies, in contrast to contestable markets, require hands-on regulation often by a dedicated regulator.

Competition Law
Objectives
Competition law addresses a number of specific concerns. First, and most importantly, anti-competitive agreements between firms (e.g. price-fixing or market-sharing agreements), are prohibited. In this regard, the courts generally

distinguish between horizontal agreements (i.e. agreements between firms at the same level of the production and distribution chain) and vertical agreements (i.e. agreements between firms at different levels of the production and distribution chain). Horizontal agreements are generally discouraged, as the effect of such agreements is often to dampen competition, to the almost inevitable detriment of final consumers; allowance is made for considering certain classes of potentially beneficial, or pro-competitive, agreements (e.g. research and development joint ventures or product standardisation agreements). In contrast, vertical agreements are treated on a case-by-case basis, as an agreement between, say, a manufacturer and a retailer that enhances the efficiency of their relationship does not necessarily come at the expense of final consumers; indeed, it seems likely to benefit final consumers.

Second, the anti-competitive creation of a position of market power, or what is formally referred to as a dominant position, as well as the abuse of any existing market power is also prohibited via abuse of market power or dominance legislation. Third, competition law also contains a pro-active approach to proposed mergers, acquisitions or takeovers, as a reactive approach would at times require the equivalent of the unscrambling of eggs.

EU Competition Law

EU competition law takes precedent over national competition law, provided that there is a significant effect on inter-state trade. This can be of practical and political significance as EU competition law arguably has not one but two policy goals: competition and the pursuit of the single internal market. EU competition law also limits the freedom of member states to intervene in the process of competition, through the actions of public undertakings (e.g. state-owned bodies) or private undertakings granted exclusive rights by member states. The state has limited exemptions from the application of EU competition law but only with respect to 'services of general economic interest'; at present the provision of the standard state pension system offers a generally accepted example of the application of this exemption.

Under the Treaty on the Functioning of the EU (TFEU), member states are also prohibited from granting state aid that would distort competition. Two prominent examples provide proof of the importance of the rules on state aid. First, the continued existence of a special low rate of corporation tax for manufacturing and internationally traded services (as opposed to non-internationally traded services) in Ireland would have fallen foul of these rules on state aids and hence the relatively low rate of 12.5 per cent is applied across all sectors. Second, the various recapitalisations and forced mergers of Irish banks and financial institutions had to be approved on a case-by-case by the European Commission as otherwise state-supported financial institutions would arguably have been unfairly advantaged for example by being able to offer superior deposit rates.

The European Commission enforces EU competition rules, the General Court hears appeals against Commission competition decisions, and the (European)

Court of Justice hears further appeals on points of law. However, in the pursuit of a policy of increased subsidiarity national courts and/or member states' competition authorities have been allowed and encouraged to directly enforce EU competition rules since May 2004; the increased similarity between national competition laws and Community competition law facilitated this shift.

Regulation and Competition Policy Examples
Apple
In 2014, the European Commission opened an investigation into whether or not two tax rulings issued in 1991 and 2007 by tax authorities in Ireland related to Apple were in breach of EU state aid rules. The concern of the Commission was that Apple received preferential treatment from the Irish government and hence had an unfair advantage in the market. Apple had two Irish incorporated companies, Apple Sales International and Apple Operations Europe. The Irish tax rulings in question allowed these companies to attribute large portions of their sales profits to head offices which had no geographic location (i.e. they were not tax 'resident' in Ireland or anywhere else) and therefore paid no taxes on these profits. Crucially, the investigation had nothing to do with Ireland's 12.5 per cent corporation tax, merely the non-imposition of any corporation tax on two companies incorporated in Ireland.

In 2016, the European Commission ruled that Ireland gave illegal tax benefits to Apple. In the opinion of the Commission, the 'head offices' of these companies existed only on paper and therefore could not have generated the profits that were attributed to them. According to the Commission, 'profits must be allocated between companies in a corporate group, and between different parts of the same company, in a way that reflects economic reality'.[8] The ruling determined that this had not been the case with the treatment of Apple in Ireland. The Commission ruled that Ireland must recover €13 billion (plus interest) in unpaid taxes from Apple covering the period of 2003 to 2013. The end date of 2013 is determined by the date that the Commission first requested relevant information from Ireland and the Commission only has the power to seek the recovery of (illegal) state aid for a period of ten years, hence the start date of 2003.

The Irish government and Apple have both lodged legal appeals against this decision but a final judgment is almost certain to be some years away. The Irish government maintains that the Commission misunderstood Irish tax law and in particular that the Commission failed to demonstrate that Apple received preferential treatment. The central argument appears to be that any of Apple's competitors – if in an equivalent situation – could have availed of a similar tax 'arrangement'. In addition, it is possible that some attention in the appeal(s) will be focused on a rather unusual aspect of the Commission's decision, namely that the amount of state aid to be recovered by Ireland from Apple is to be reduced somewhat if other relevant countries require Apple to make additional tax payments or charges on the economic activities that gave rise to the profits, for example, sales of iPhones in Europe and/or payments to Apple in the USA for related research and development costs.

Below-Cost Selling and Minimum Retail Pricing of Alcohol
The Restrictive Practices (Groceries) Order (1987) prohibited retailers from selling many grocery products (e.g. milk, alcohol) for a retail price below the relevant suppliers' net invoice price. Fears of predatory pricing by the large retail multiples, where price wars which would eliminate the smaller competitors would be followed by the charging of excessively high prices, were used to defend this provision. However, and crucially, off-invoice discounts (e.g. rebates) were not taken into account when defining the net invoice benchmark, i.e. retailers were 'forced' to impose a mark-up that was at least equal in size to off-invoice discounts. Under the Order, the Office of the Director of Consumer Affairs fined Dunnes Stores and Tesco over €2,000 for selling baby food products below cost in 2004. The Groceries Order was rescinded in 2006 but only after much debate and recrimination.

More recently (2012) Scotland passed legislation allowing for the introduction of a minimum retail price for alcohol, initially to be set at 50p per unit of alcohol. However, the Scottish Whisky Association and a number of European wine-exporting countries (e.g. France, Spain and Italy) brought proceedings against the legislation, arguing, for example, that the policy, if implemented, would discriminate against imports in a manner that could not be justified on public health grounds. As an alternative to the setting of a minimum retail price (or a ban on below-cost selling) of alcohol, many economists favour a targeted increase in excise duty with the potential for the extra revenue raised being used for health promotion; in contrast, the introduction of a minimum price of alcohol increases profits within the drinks sector.

In 2015 the (European) Court of Justice issued a rather subtle ruling. The Court of Justice ruled that while introducing a single internal market-restricting minimum retail price was not in principle precluded, the introduction of such a restriction must be proportionate (to the policy goal being pursued). In particular, the Court of Justice went on to note that in this specific case a general increase in taxation on alcohol appeared to be more proportionate than the introduction of a minimum retail price of alcohol and hence the latter appeared to be contrary to EU law. The Court of Justice then sent the case back to the Scottish court for further examination of all relevant specific evidence and final decision.

Moves towards the implementation of the Public Health (Alcohol) Bill in Ireland continue at the time of writing (February 2017); this Bill also contains a provision for the introduction of a minimum retail price of alcohol. It seems that future legal challenges to the implementation of this provision will have to be countered by reasons as to why the introduction of a minimum retail price for alcohol (as opposed to a general increase in taxation on alcohol) is justified in the specific Irish context.

Meanwhile in Scotland, the Court of Session decided recently (October 2016) that the introduction of minimum retail price of alcohol was not in breach of European law; an appeal to the UK Supreme Court was allowed subsequently (December 2016) and perhaps more intriguingly (given the backdrop of Brexit) an associated or further appeal to the European Court of Justice might be possible.

5 REGULATION OF NATURAL MONOPOLY AND NETWORKS

Specific sectoral regulation is required in the case of natural monopolies as the latter represents an extreme form of market failure, in that the relevant market cannot function efficiently without a significant level of direct and on-going regulation. The provision of an electricity transmission, or natural gas, grid, the provision of a water, waste water or railway network, the provision of a national daily delivery postal service and perhaps the provision of a national fibre-optic broadband network represent some examples of natural monopolies, many of which have been referred to as public utilities in the past in Ireland. Other possible examples include the provision of a local, regional, or national bus service or the provision of a local household waste collection service.

Pricing and Competitive Tendering
A natural monopoly exists if there are very significant economies of scale. In such a case, an individual firm's marginal cost (MC) and average cost (AC) curves decline continuously and the firm's marginal cost (MC) curve will be below its average cost (AC) curve. As the number of firms increased, the average cost of production would also increase, dramatically. Regulators can apparently achieve allocative efficiency by insisting that the natural monopolist produces a level of output at which price is equal to marginal cost. There are, however, at least two significant problems with this proposed solution.

First, the regulator may not have enough information to be able to determine the output level at which price would be equal to marginal cost; it would not necessarily be in the natural monopolist's interest to provide the regulator with the appropriate information. Second, even if the natural monopolist produces the allocatively efficient level of output, it will sustain losses, as pricing at marginal cost implies pricing below average cost as the marginal cost curve lies below the average cost curve in a natural monopoly.

One possible solution to this latter problem is for the regulator to provide the natural monopolist with a subsidy to offset the losses associated with achieving allocative efficiency. However, these subsidies must be financed by increased taxation elsewhere, which, in turn, causes other inefficiencies. It may also be difficult politically to be seen to provide a monopolist with a subsidy, although subsidies have been provided to public entities such as Bus Éireann and Irish Rail in Ireland for many years.

Setting price at average cost, where the natural monopolist makes neither excess profits nor losses, avoids the problem of having to subsidise the natural monopolist, but at the expense of sacrificing allocative efficiency. Average-cost pricing regulation also suffers from the problem of dampening cost-reducing incentives. In practice, average-cost pricing is often adapted so as to encourage cost-reducing innovations by allowing scope for some 'excess' profits. This type of regulation, adjusted average-cost pricing is referred to as rate of return regulation.

Rather than attempting to regulate the natural monopolist on an on-going basis, it may be preferable to auction the right to be the natural monopolist; this is often referred to as competition 'for the market' (as opposed to competition 'in the market'). The auction can be done on the basis of bidders committing to charging a certain price and providing a particular level of service to customers in the future. The results of this process are likely to be close to the results obtained by average cost pricing regulation, as bidders would find themselves forced to offer lower and lower (quality-adjusted) prices until almost no net excess profits could be expected.

Public Ownership, Privatisation, Market Liberalisation and Regulation
Rather than the state attempting to regulate the natural monopolist, many governments in the past, particularly within Europe, simply elected to be the (natural) monopolist. Within an Irish context, airport management, airline ownership, electricity, natural gas and public transportation provided examples of state ownership of enterprise. The distinctive feature (and advantage or disadvantage depending on one's political perspective) of this approach is that the objective of the natural monopolist is no longer the maximisation of profits or even the covering of costs. Opponents of state ownership of enterprises generally point to this so-called soft budget constraint, with management and workers it is claimed, being united in their efforts to extract public funds for 'their' enterprises. However, EU restrictions on state aids to public-owned enterprises have removed at least some of the force of this argument.

A movement away from public ownership and towards privatisation began in the early 1980s. The experience in the USA in the late 1970s and early 1980s was one of market liberalisation or deregulation, e.g. aviation, telecommunications and inter-state trucking. Within a European context, the UK government led by Margaret Thatcher was at the forefront of the privatisation movement, e.g. British Telecom (1984) and British Gas (1986), which created a large number of new holders of shares, with the value of these shares increasing significantly.

However, many of the large privatisations within the UK were subsequently followed up by the setting up of specialist independent regulatory agencies (e.g. Ofcom), as the process of competition failed to take off in what were markets still characterised by at least some elements of natural monopolies. Indeed, the ultimate lesson from the UK privatisation experience was that the creation of market conditions conducive to competition was at least as important as the formal ownership structure.

Within the Irish context, after successfully selling its stake in Irish Life (1991), the Irish state privatised Telecom Éireann (later eircom, still later eir). Initially, the privatisation proved to be a political success as eircom's share price increased by over 20 per cent above its floatation price. However, the share price then fell, and remained, for the rest of its (initial) existence as a public limited company, considerably below its floatation price. From an economics perspective, the success, or otherwise, of the privatisation of eircom should be judged primarily by the effect of the privatisation on the process of competition within the Irish telecommunications sector and on the quality-adjusted prices paid by final consumers. However, from a political perspective, the fall in eircom's share price, combined with Ryanair's attempted acquisition of Aer Lingus only days after Aer Lingus' part-privatisation (2006), had significant political economy repercussions for future possible privatisations in Ireland, e.g. Voluntary Health Insurance (VHI). In addition, the issue of privatisation became linked to attempts to reduce Ireland's growing national debt.

The various regulatory agencies in Ireland have on-going important decisions to make with respect to pricing and investment decisions within the particular elements of markets that are naturally monopolistic, e.g. Commission for Aviation Regulation (CAR). In the context of a downstream natural monopoly (e.g. fixed-line telecommunications in the past), the level of the resulting consumer price was at least highly visible, while in the context of an upstream natural monopoly (e.g. transportation of natural gas or electricity transmission), the level of the access price charged to downstream firms is less visible and hence may be less politically sensitive, but still of crucial importance, particularly if the upstream firm itself also operates in various downstream (e.g. retail) or upstream (e.g. power generation) markets.

Irish Water
Economic Considerations
The recent creation of Irish Water (Uisce Éireann) and its subsequent regulation represents an interesting case study from a political economy perspective. Irish Water (while technically a subsidiary of Ervia, the commercial semi-state body also in charge of Ireland's natural gas infrastructure) is a vertically integrated semi-state company which provides public water and waste water facilities; Irish Water has taken over these responsibilities from over thirty local authorities. The CER is the economic regulator of the water sector and hence Irish Water; Irish Water is also accountable to the Environmental Protection Agency (EPA).

Before the recent (attempted) introduction of water charges, Ireland was the only country in Europe not to have a direct charge for domestic water use; the cost of the water system was borne by the taxpayer. Providing water that is safe to drink directly into homes across the country and removing waste water is a costly business and especially so in Ireland where the public water infrastructure is very old and badly in need of repair and updating. Leaks are widespread and very substantial by international comparison, imposing a high cost on the taxpayer and on the environment.

The high cost of providing water systems to domestic users, including the environmental costs, has been recognised by the European Commission in the Water Framework Directive of 2000. This directive requires member states to introduce a system to recover the full cost of the water systems from water users. The directive states that water pricing should be designed in line with the 'polluter pays' principle in order to create an incentive for users to use the water systems efficiently. Economic theory suggests that this is the most efficient way to fund water systems as it gives users a direct incentive to conserve water. If consumers must pay the full cost of water used, then they would be expected to only consume an amount of water for which the benefits of consumption outweigh or match the cost. It is still possible to address equity concerns within this type of system, either by providing a certain allowance of water at no charge and charging for water used in excess of that allowance or by providing low-income households with a lump-sum subsidy or grant to cover the expected cost of water. The latter option is the most efficient as it keeps in place the incentive to conserve water at all usage levels.

Ireland was initially granted a derogation from compliance with the EC Directive based on Article 9 (4) which states that a member state may decide in 'accordance with established practice' not to introduce charges. However, in 2010, as part of the agreement for the Economic Adjustment Programme for Ireland with the EC, ECB and IMF, the then coalition government committed to introducing water charges in Ireland. In 2011, the new coalition government committed to the continuation of this policy. In 2013, Irish Water was established and began the widespread installation of water meters. The first water charges came into effect in 2015 for households connected to the public water/wastewater networks.

Political Considerations

While the economics of water charges are arguably relatively straightforward, the politics have been anything but straightforward. A significant proportion of the Irish public resisted the introduction of water charges; a series of significant public demonstrations in opposition to water charges occurred throughout 2014 and 2015. In addition, a significant portion of households did not register to pay the charges. Indeed, water charges became a key campaign issue in the 2016 election which led to the election of a minority coalition government; one condition of support for this minority government was that water charges were to be suspended and the system reviewed.

Why did the Irish public react so strongly to the introduction of water charges? There was a significant behavioural reaction to the introduction of a new tax in return for an already established product; when one is used to getting something arguably for free, it is hard to start paying for it directly. Some people also argued that as water is essential, it is a human right and hence that there should be no charge. While food and shelter are also essential for life and not free, there are important differences between these necessities. For example, food has been provided in a fairly competitive market and consumers are used to paying for food. In contrast, there are significant infrastructural requirements involved in providing water and waste water facilities and the associated natural monopoly national network requires significant and on-going interventions. Historically, much of these interventions have been financed by central exchequer funding. However, one should not exaggerate the distinction as various local authorities have imposed water charges in Ireland in the recent past and very many communities in Ireland organise and pay for private/community-based water schemes (as well as waste water/septic tanks).

Perhaps the major reason for the reaction was the timing of the attempted introduction. Water charges were introduced during a time of austerity when there had already been a number of tax increases and cuts to public services. The public arguably saw water charges as simply just one tax too many. In particular, the government was not suggesting that general taxation would be reduced in return for the introduction of water charges and hence the charge of double taxation seemed apt.

Water charges were suspended in July 2016 for a period of nine months and an Expert Commission on Domestic Public Water Services was established. The European Commission's apparent position is that Ireland is no longer exempt from imposing user charges under the Water Framework Directive as, since committing to introduce the charges in 2010 and subsequently introducing them, it is no longer considered 'established practice' in Ireland not to charge for water. The Expert Commission published their report in November 2016.[9] The Expert Commission has recommended a structure whereby all households receive a free water allowance (based on household size and 'normal' usage) but pay a direct charge for water in excess of that allowance; as such, direct water charges would only apply to the excessive/wasteful use of water services. It remains to be seen whether or not the European Commission and the Irish public will find this proposed solution acceptable. The issue of water charges in Ireland appears likely to remain politically charged.

6 CONCLUDING COMMENTS

The purpose of this chapter has been to provide the reader with a broad overview of the area of regulatory policy. In particular, this chapter has attempted to address various explanations for regulations, theories of regulation and approaches to regulation or regulatory strategies while at the same time discussing a number of specific types or examples of regulations in Ireland and the EU, including competition policy and the regulation of natural monopolies and networks. This chapter concludes with some brief comments on the evolving EU regulatory context and on the balance between the rules-based and principles based approaches to regulation.

EU Regulatory Context

In many regulatory policy areas such as the environment, agriculture, health and safety, competition and public utilities, the most important regulatory forum has moved from member states to the EU (see Chapters 2 and 3). As such, the discussion above is increasingly conducted at, and relevant to, an EU and even wider level debate (e.g. international trade negotiations). The growth of the European regulatory state has been facilitated by both demand and supply side factors. On the demand side, multinational firms increasingly sought out a one-stop regulatory shop, for example with respect to environment regulations while on the supply side, national regulations required an international forum in order to address regulatory spillover effects, for example with respect to environmental policy.

The EU Parliament's increasing powers with respect to the other two EU political institutions (namely, the Commission and the Council of Ministers) appears to have increased the EU's legislative mandate. In addition, the existence and decisions of the (European) Court of Justice as well as the on-going re-balancing of powers between the Parliament, Commission and Council of Ministers have increased accountability and control within the EU and have to at least some extent addressed past accusations with respect to there being a democratic deficit at the heart of the EU.

There are now a significant number of European regulatory agencies, which in general deal with narrowly defined policy areas, similar in standing to the European Food Safety Authority (EFSA) which was established in 2002 (see Chapter 9). The current highly Europeanised food safety regime has EFSA at the hub of the equivalent national organisations. EFSA champions food traceability and food science more generally and conducts prior risk analysis on behalf of the Commission, with the Commission being responsible for the formal making of decisions. For another example of Europeanised regulation, see the discussion above with respect to EU competition law, although it should be noted that in that context EU competition law can be implemented/enforced by the national courts, i.e. enforcement can take place in the locality although the policy is decided at the centre.

Rules-based or Principles-based Regulation?

While interesting debates can be held between followers of a rules-based approach to regulation and a principles-based approach to regulation, it is crucial that such a debate be informed by specific details of the proposed implementation of either approach. For example, given that a principles-based approach confers a significant level of discretion on the regulators and on the regulated entities, it is imperative that issues such as regulatory capture be considered.

Similarly the adoption of a rules-based approach does not avoid the need to consider important issues such as creative compliance. In addition, while the need for evidence-based policy decision-making is generally supported at least at a theoretical level, it seems less well recognised that its application may be in some tension with the desire to eliminate apparently unnecessary 'red tape' by reducing the need for, and amount of, form-filling. However, perhaps the biggest regulatory lesson from Ireland's recent experiences with the banking and fiscal crises is that in the absence of certain minimum agreed ethical standards very few assumptions of the 'public interest' kind can be made with respect to how interested parties may behave.

Endnotes

* The authors acknowledge many very helpful comments and suggestions by John O'Hagan. Any remaining errors and all views expressed remain the responsibility of the authors.

1 J. Black, quoted in R. Baldwin, M. Cave and M. Lodge (editors), *The Oxford Handbook of Regulation*, Oxford University Press, Oxford 2010, p. 12. For an excellent textbook on regulation, see R. Baldwin, M. Cave and M. Lodge, *Understanding Regulation: Theory, Strategy and Practice*, Second Edition, Oxford University Press, Oxford 2012.

2 Michael Sandel questions the moral limit of markets by highlighting some provocative USA-based examples of the current reach of markets, e.g. $6,250 ($25,000) for the use of a surrogate mother in India; $20 per hour to get someone (e.g. a homeless person) to represent you in a queue at Congress; $2 given to a child for each book read; and an unknown 'donation' for admission to a prestigious university; see M. Sandel, *What Money Can't Buy: The Moral Limits of Markets*, Farrar, Straus and Giroux, New York 2012.

3 See R. Thaler and C. Sunstein, *Nudge: Improving Decisions About Health, Wealth and Happiness*, Penguin Books, New York 2009, and D. Kahneman, *Thinking, Fast and Slow*, Allen Lane, New York 2011.

4 See K. Purcell, 'Applying Behavioural Economics in Irish Policy', Irish Government Economic & Evaluation Service, Department of Public Expenditure and Reform, Staff Paper 2016.

5 See P. Lunn, *Regulatory Policy and Behavioural Economics*, OECD Publishing, Paris 2014 (pp. 42–3).

6 See Cabinet Office: Behavioural Insights Team and CAF Charities Aid Foundation, 'Applying behavioural insights to charitable giving', 28 May 2013.

7 For a comprehensive review of the economics of competition policy (also known as antitrust economics), see S. Bishop and M. Walker, *The Economics of EC Competition Law: Concepts, Application and Measurement*, third edition, Sweet & Maxwell, London 2010.

8 See the European Commission Press Release, 30 August 2016, 'State aid: Ireland gave illegal tax benefits to Apple worth up to €13 billion'.

9 See 'Report on the funding of Domestic Public Water Services', Expert Commission on Domestic Public Water Services, November 2016, available at www.oireachtas.ie/parliament/media/committees/futurefundingofdomesticwaterservices/Report-of-Expert-Commission-on-Domestic-Public-Water-Services.pdf.

SECTION III

Policy Issues at National Level

CHAPTER 6

Labour Market and Migration

Tara McIndoe-Calder and John O'Hagan

1 INTRODUCTION

The experience with regard to employment and unemployment has been the truly remarkable 'story' of the Irish economy in recent decades. Table 6.1 illustrates clearly the dramatic changes that have taken place, in particular since 1995. Who could have predicted the scale of the change in the time between then and 2008? Employment in 1995 was just 233,000 higher than in 1971; the only period in which there was a significant increase in employment up to this was during the 1970s, when over 100,000 net new jobs were created. Between 1995 and 2008, however, 865,000 net new jobs were created, quite an extraordinary increase in employment in such a short period. The decrease in unemployment during the same period, as seen in Table 6.1, was equally remarkable.

Equally dramatic was the decline in employment between 2008 and 2012. Over 310,000 net jobs (the difference between all jobs created and jobs lost) were lost in this short period with the unemployment rate rising from 5.7 per cent in 2008 to 15.0 per cent in 2012. However, between 2012 and early 2017 more than 200,000 net new jobs were created bringing the total level of employment almost back to the peak level of 2008, with unemployment down to 6.7 per cent in just four years. The question now is will this upward swing continue or is the Irish labour market going to be inherently unstable given the connectedness of its labour market to parts of the wider global labour market and the uncertainty applying to the latter in terms of what has happened in the UK and USA in 2016?

Sections 2 and 3 examine the issues of population and labour supply and emphasise the critical role that migration plays in this regard, a factor that perhaps marks Ireland apart from other OECD countries. Section 4 looks at the issue of employment, its growth, and composition. Section 5 examines Irish performance in relation to unemployment, both over time and compared to other countries. The rest of the chapter examines the various factors that may influence the level of employment, and hence the level of unemployment, in a small open economy such as that of Ireland. Section 6 examines three factors that impinge on job creation, arising from the Single European Market and globalisation: namely

144

Table 6.1 Employment and Unemployment: Ireland's Changing Fortunes

	Employment (millions)	Unemployment rate (%)
1971	1.049	5.5
1980	1.156	7.3
1986	1.095	17.1
1995	1.282	12.2
2005	1.945	4.8
2008	2.147	5.8
2012	1.836	15.0
2016[1]	2.048	6.7

Source: Constructed with CSO population data from: *Quarterly National Household Survey (QNHS)*, Stationery Office, Dublin various issues.
[1] Quarter 4.

increased competition for goods and services; increased mobility and especially migration of labour across national boundaries, and, technological change. As the section highlights, the adaptability and skill levels of the labour force are the key issues in responding to these global pressures.

A major reason for the different responses in different countries to the phenomena of migration, technological change and the globalisation of trade relates to the *flexibility* of the labour market, this is the subject matter of Section 7. Issues such as the wage-setting process and the effects of employment legislation on employment creation are discussed in some detail. The effects of prolonged payment of unemployment and related benefits and the effectiveness or otherwise of active labour market policies in dealing with unemployment will also be examined in Section 7. Section 8 concludes the chapter.

2 POPULATION AND MIGRATION

Population Change and its Components

The size of the population has major emotive significance in Ireland; not surprisingly given the huge reduction in population in Ireland following the Famine (see Chapter 1). As a result, the size of the population has in a sense become an objective of policy in itself. Figure 6.1 outlines the trends in population dating back to 1841. The population of the Republic of Ireland in pre-Famine days was over 6.5 million. The decline in this population size in the post-Famine period is all too obvious: a fall of over two million in 20 years. Given the high birth rate at the time the population should in fact have increased substantially were it not for death and emigration.

Population continued to decline up to 1926; almost 50 years later there was no increase on the 1926 level, when the population in 1971 still stood at under three million. Since then population size has increased by almost 1.7 million with most of this increase occurring between 1991 and 2016; the population in 2016 in fact exceeded its level in the 1850s for the first time. This for many is seen as a positive development and reflects a reversal of a demoralising decline that had persisted for almost a century and a half. It is noteworthy that even during the recession years population continued to increase, up by almost 300,000 between 2006 and 2014.

Figure 6.1 Irish Population 1841 to 2016 (millions)

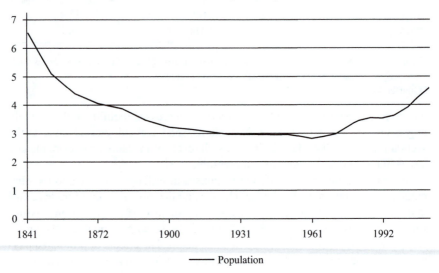

Population

Source: Constructed with CSO data from: www.cso.ie/multiquicktables/quickTables. aspx?id=cna13

To put these trends in context, Figure 6.2 plots the ratio of the Irish population (Republic) to that of the UK (less the Republic) from 1851 to 2015. It can be seen that in 1851 the Irish population accounted for 23 per cent of that of the UK, even though the Irish population had fallen by over one-fifth from its level prior to the Famine. By 1871 it had fallen to just around 15 per cent of the UK population, due to continuing population decline in Ireland and a rising population in the UK. By 1921 it had fallen to just 6.9 per cent: due to continuing emigration and population decline in Ireland and a large increase in the population of the UK: the UK population almost doubled between 1851 and 1921, compared to a decline of nearly seventy per cent in Ireland in the same period (see Chapter 1).

The low point came in the mid 1960s, when the Irish population dipped to under 5.3 per cent of the UK population. By 1995 it had risen to 6.2 per cent and today stands at around 7.2 per cent of the UK population, the highest level since the start of the twentieth century. But of course still way below the level of 1851.

Figure 6.2 Irish Population as a Percentage of UK (excluding Republic) Population, 1851 to 2015

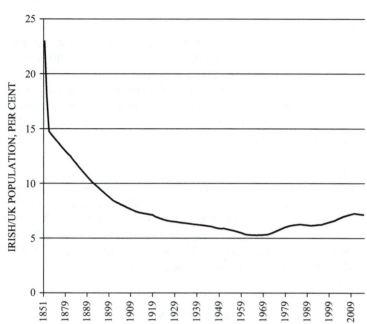

Source: Constructed with CSO data from: www.cso.ie/en/releasesandpublications/er/ pme/populationandmigrationestimatesapril2016/ and ONS at: www.ons.gov.uk/people populationandcommunity/populationandmigration/populationestimates/bulletins/annual midyearpopulationestimates/2015-06-25

Change in the total population of a country is comprised of three components: the number of births, the number of deaths and the level of net migration. The difference between the number of births and deaths is known as the natural increase and in most countries the natural increase translates directly into a population increase. This has not been the case in Ireland, where in the past the change in population has 'tracked' much more closely the trend in migration than that of the natural increase.

The number of births per annum reached a peak in the 1970s and declined significantly after that; it increased again in the 2002 to 2006 period, and reached a new peak in the period 2008 to 2012. Although these later increases were more a reflection of the increase in the size of the child-bearing female population than of any large increase in the birth rate it will have a positive impact on the overall demographics in Ireland as increasing numbers of young people become available to enter the work force. The number of births has decreased since then, now running at around 65,000 per annum. There is little variation in the number of deaths (around 30,000 per annum), which means that the number of births is what drives changes in the natural increase, the latter now running at around 35,000 per annum.

Migration

While there have been significant changes in the natural increase, they are slight compared to the huge swings in net migration that can occur: 40,000 outflows per annum throughout the whole of the 1950s, a similar number in some years in the 1980s, to net annual immigration of 2,000 in the early 1990s, around 26,000 per annum in the late 1990s and 48,000 in the 2000s, with net emigration again in some recent years of 30,000 per annum or more. The year to April 2016 saw a return to net inward migration of 3,100.

Gross and Net Flows

The *net* immigration figure is the balance between two flows, *gross* outflows, and gross inflows of people (see Figure 6.3). Looking first at gross inflows, immigration increased steadily, up from 40,000 in 1996 to over 100,000 per annum between 2002 and 2006. Large immigration continued in 2007 and 2008, but immigration flows reduced considerably thereafter, rising again in 2015 and 2016, with over 79,000 immigrants recorded in 2016.

Figure 6.3 Migration Trends, 1985 to 2016 (thousands)

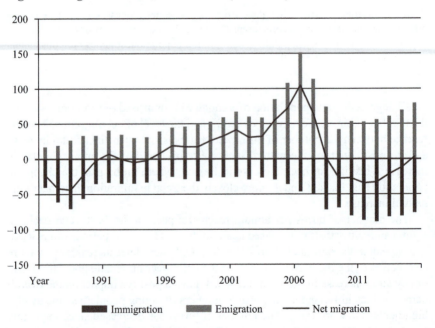

Source: Constructed with CSO data from: www.cso.ie/en/releasesandpublications/er/pme/populationandmigrationestimatesapril2016/

The overall migration trends since 1985 are well captured in Figure 6.3. This figure highlights the fact that net migration arises from two much larger flows namely immigration and emigration. There were substantial movements in both but the real swings are in the net figure, as can be seen in the solid line. This line swung from a large negative in the years up to 1992 to a very large positive by the mid 2000s, followed by a large negative up to 2015.

Origin and Destination Countries
Initially the increase in immigration was due primarily to returning Irish nationals, who accounted for around half of total gross immigration between 1996 and 2000 (see Table 6.2). In absolute terms the immigration of Irish nationals continued after 2000 at the levels of the period 1996 to 2000, but there was also a large inflow of non-Irish nationals, initially from 'Rest of the World' (mainly Africa, but according to the 2011 census more latterly predominantly from America – including Latin America, Canada and the USA – and Asia) and, since the enlargement of the EU in 2004, a further huge increase of non-Irish nationals from 'Rest of EU', mainly Poland and the Baltic states. This was arguably one of the most obvious changes in Irish society in this period, i.e. the increasing number of non-Irish nationals who to this day make up a significant share of the country's population and labour force. The evidence for this is clear to see, not only in Dublin but across the country, including many small rural towns. Even in the years 2011 to 2016 there were substantial inflows of people from outside Ireland and the UK (Table 6.2), especially from the Rest of the World in 2016.

Table 6.2 Estimated Migration Classified by Nationality, 1996–2016 (percentage of total)

	Irish	UK	Rest of EU	Rest of World	Total (thousands)
			Immigration		
1996	45.2	21.2	12.8	20.9	39.2
2006	17.5	9.2	58.1	15.2	107.8
2011	36.7	7.7	32.2	23.3	53.3
2016[1]	26.6	5.7	27.7	40.1	79.3
			Emigration		
2006	42.5	6.1	34.2	17.2	36.0
2011	52.1	5.7	29.9	12.3	80.6
2016[1]	41.7	3.4	30.5	24.3	76.2

Source: Constructed with CSO data from: www.cso.ie/en/releasesandpublications/er/pme/populationandmigrationestimatesapril2016/
Note: Figures for nationality of emigrants not available prior to 2006.
[1] Preliminary.

There was substantial out-migration also over the entire period. It was of course until recently less than gross in-migration and substantially so in some years, but nonetheless the persistence of out-migration during the boom years is noteworthy. For example, even in 2006 there was out-migration of 36,000 people, over 15,000 of them Irish nationals (Table 6.2). Between 2006 and 2011 the level of out-migration more than doubled. By 2016 though, immigration again exceeded emigration, albeit by a small amount.

Composition by Age
Table 6.3 provides an age breakdown of migrants over the period 2002 to 2016, which is of relevance to the later discussion. The most remarkable feature up to 2008 was the huge proportion of total immigrants in the active age groups of 15–24 and in particular 25–44. This means that the vast bulk of the immigrants came here for work, with few young dependants. Most of the dependants were probably attached to Irish nationals returning home with small numbers associated with the immigration of non-Irish nationals. This means that, many immigrant workers were of prime family-formation age and may have had children since they arrived in Ireland.

Migrant mobility is a function of many factors including: migration motives, for example employment; ease of migration, requirements for costly visa applications for non-EU citizens; and family ties to home and destination countries. Despite emerging family ties to Ireland, migrant motives are still likely to be largely labour related, the lack of visa requirements for EU nationals means the decision to leave can be reversed in the future with little cost if

Table 6.3 Estimated Migration Classified by Age Group, 2000–2016 (percentage of total)

	0–14	15–24	25–44	45–64	65 and over	Total (thousands)
			Immigration			
2000	13.5	31.9	44.5	7.6	2.3	52.6
2005	9.5	28.8	53.0	7.2	1.4	84.6
2010	4.3	41.4	45.0	4.8	4.6	41.8
2016[1]	15.6	24.8	52.2	5.4	1.8	79.3
			Emigration			
2000	0.0	80.5	17.3	0.4	2.3	26.6
2005	7.1	48.6	36.1	5.1	3.1	29.4
2010	2.9	38.6	52.7	4.2	1.6	69.2
2016[1]	8.3	41.6	43.7	5.1	1.4	76.2

Source: As for Table 6.2.
[1] Preliminary.

circumstances change whilst visa requirements for non-EU nationals means that without employment these migrants often lose the right to remain in Ireland. Thus migrants are still likely to be fairly mobile, reinforcing the point made earlier that many of the immigrants could go elsewhere if employment prospects turn down.

The increased share of young (0–14 years) immigrants since 2010 likely reflects the relative increase in Irish nationals and those from the rest of the world as opposed to EU nationals over this time period and must be balanced by the larger outflows of people over much of this period.

It is apparent that well over half of the out-migration between 2008 and late 2010 was accounted for by non-nationals mostly from 'Rest of EU' and that the vast bulk of this occurred in the active age groups of 15–24 and 25–44. It is interesting to note in fact that even in 2005 around 25,000 people in these age groups emigrated, but of course there were around 85,000 immigrants in that year thereby reflecting a very fluid migration situation in these age groups.

Composition by Educational Level
Another interesting dimension to migration patterns relates to the educational level and principal economic status of the migrants. Table 6.4 shows that the bulk of the *net* migration in both the recession and recovery years was among the less well-educated groups, in response chiefly to the huge decline in employment in construction (see later). There has been net outward migration among those with less than third-level qualifications since 2009.

Table 6.4 Estimated Migration Classified by Educational Attainment, 2000–2016 (percentage of total)

	Higher secondary and below	Post-leaving cert	Third level or above	Not stated	Total (thousands)
			Immigrants		
2009	31.7	9.4	47.0	12.0	69.1
2012	31.6	7.1	55.7	5.3	44.9
2016[1]	27.8	6.1	57.1	9.1	66.9
			Emigrants		
2009	45.3	9.6	35.0	10.0	69.7
2012	38.3	8.3	47.4	5.8	82.2
2016[1]	35.9	6.4	45.7	12.1	70.0

Source: As for Table 6.2.
Note: Figures refer to those 15 years and over only.
[1] Preliminary.

Throughout the period 2009 to 2016 close to 75 per cent of immigrants came for employment or as students with the majority of these coming for work. With over half the immigrants having at least third level education, this indicates that the jobs being created domestically were disproportionately skilled rather than unskilled. Additionally, close to half of the emigrants during this period emigrated to jobs with a further quarter leaving to study.

Migration to and from Ireland continues to be large, and is driven primarily by labour market concerns with new data showing emigrants being well placed to move directly to work abroad. This has long been a known characteristic of the Irish migration experience.

3 LABOUR SUPPLY

Labour supply in any country is determined by three factors: the total size of the population, the proportion of that population of working age, and the proportion of the working-age population seeking or in work. This is illustrated by the identity:

(1) $$L = (P) . (Pa /P) . (L/Pa)$$

where L is the size of the labour force, P the size of the population, and Pa the size of the population of working age. The labour force, in turn, comprises of those in employment (E) and those unemployed (UE). Hence:

(2) $$L = E + UE$$

We have already looked at P in Equation 1 and now turn to a discussion of the other two components of L, the working-age population (Pa/P) and labour force participation rate (L/Pa).

Working-Age Population (Pa/P)
The working-age population as a proportion of the total population is also given by one minus the non-working age group as a proportion of the total population. The non-working age group is made up of two cohorts, the young (those aged 0 to 14) and the old (those aged 65 and over).

As a result of the fall in the birth rate in the 1980s and 1990s, there was a later fall in the population aged 15 and under. However, because of the high birth rate prior to this, and more important the trends in migration observed above, there was a large increase in the population aged 15–64, and especially in the prime working-age population, 25–64. As seen, a large proportion of the immigrants were of prime working age, thereby pushing up the population in this age group disproportionately. The number of people aged 25–64 rose from 2.18 million in 1991 to over 2.91 million by the year 2006; this is a very large increase in such a short period and had a marked effect on Ireland's age dependency ratios.

Figure 6.4 Young and Old Age Cohorts as a Percentage of Total Population, 1926–2046 (actual and projected)

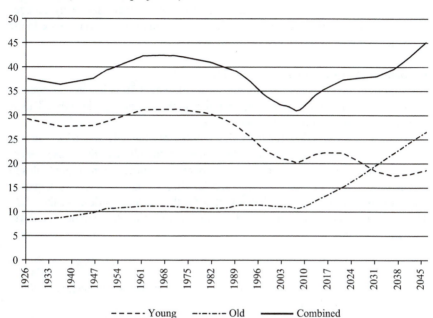

Source: Constructed with CSO data from: www.cso.ie/en/media/csoie/releases publications/documents/population/2013/poplabfor2016_2046.pdf

Figure 6.4 highlights these changes in the composition of the population since the foundation of the state. The proportion of the population aged 0 to 14 increased significantly between the mid 1930s and the early 1960s, pushing the overall dependency rate (those in the age groups 0 to 14 and 65+) up significantly in this period. From the mid 1980s to the mid 2000s though the share of those aged 0 to 14 decreased very significantly but as can be seen in Figure 6.4 rose again in the ten years to 2016.

In contrast, the share of those aged 65+ of the population showed minimal change between 1926 and 2006, but this changed in the period 2006 and 2016 and is set for further, possibly dramatic, changes in the next thirty years, as can be seen in Figure 6.4. With the aging of the population the dependency ratio could increase by then to levels not seen since the mid 1950s, with huge consequences for the state's finances (Chapter 3), distribution policy (Chapter 8) and policy in relation to housing (Chapter 12) and health (Chapter 14).

Labour force projections over the coming three decades entail substantial assumptions regarding fertility, mortality, migration, education duration (especially for the young) and labour force participation rates. Small deviations in these from the assumptions used by population modellers can yield large changes in the actual path of the labour force. Whilst the assumptions used are reasonable, the very fluid population movements Ireland has experienced for many decades are very unpredictable and may lead to an attenuation of the steep increase in the dependency ratios as envisaged in Figure 6.4.

Participation in Labour Force (L/Pa)

An important factor when examining the employment situation in any country is the proportion of the working-age population that actually seeks work. This is known as the labour force participation rate.

Table 6.5 provides data for Ireland, a number of other EU countries, and two countries of particular interest to Ireland (namely the UK and the USA); where possible these will also be used as the comparator countries in the other tables in this chapter.[1] As can be seen in Table 6.5, in 2015 the labour force participation rate for men in Ireland was well below that for the other countries, bar the USA. The rate for women was considerably lower than for the other countries shown, bar again the USA.

Table 6.5 Percentage Labour Force Participation Rates[1] in Selected OECD Countries, 2000 and 2015

	Men		Women	
	2000	2015	2000	2015
Ireland	80.0	77.6	56.3	62.8
Denmark	84.2	81.6	75.6	75.3
Germany	78.9	82.1	63.3	73.1
Spain	80.4	80.9	52.9	70.0
UK	84.1	82.8	68.9	72.5
USA	83.9	78.5	70.7	66.9

Source: Constructed with OECD data from: http://stats.oecd.org/Index.aspx?Dataset Code=LFS_SEXAGE_I_R
[1] Ratios refer to persons aged 15–64 years who are in the labour force divided by the total population aged 15–64.

Irish participation rates increased substantially in the ten years to 2008 and then fell during the recession to levels previously seen in the early 2000s. The recovery has not seen a return to pre-crisis participation rates, especially for men and the young, despite strong, broad-based employment growth. This remains a puzzle and suggests that the large increase in the years 2004 and 2007 was perhaps linked to the construction boom. There is room for an improvement in

the participation rate but this may require substantial up-skilling and other institutional improvements.[2]

A noteworthy feature is that female participation rates are increasing in most
countries, Ireland being no exception. Following a substantial increase up to
2000, the rate increased further in Ireland, up from 56.3 to 62.8 per cent by 2015.
However, as mentioned the rates for Ireland are well below those for four of the
countries listed in Table 6.5. It is difficult to predict how much further this participation rate will grow in Ireland, but with the lower birth rate, and if employment
prospects continue to improve, it could increase to British and German levels if
not to those in Denmark. If this happened, it would lead to a large increase in the
labour force arising from this factor alone.

Conclusion

A consideration of migration trends is central to any discussion of labour supply
in Ireland. It, more than any other factor, determines changes in the size of the
population and the growth of the labour force. As seen earlier, more than half of
those added to the Irish population on an annual average basis between 1996 and
2008 were as a result of net inward migration. Between 2008 and 2012 the trend
of net outward migration began to exert a marked downward pressure on population growth and for the years ahead it will be what happens on the migration
front that will largely determine labour supply. The increases in the labour force
participation rates of females aged 25 to 64 may be dwarfed by the changes in net
migration, but, if they rise to British or German levels, in themselves they could
also have a marked bearing on the growth of the labour force in years to come.

Labour supply of course is partly determined by labour demand (see Chapter 7)
and it is the interaction between the two that will determine actual as opposed to
potential labour supply.

4 EMPLOYMENT: GROWTH AND COMPOSITION

Overall Employment

Table 6.6 clearly illustrates the tiny size of the workforce in Ireland: around 2.0
million in 2016, as opposed to 18.2 million in Spain, 30.5 million in the UK and
142.6 million in the USA. Given that there is an effective common labour market
between Ireland and the UK, it is important for labour policy purposes to bear in
mind the relative sizes of these two labour markets in particular.

As seen in Table 6.1, employment in Ireland has increased dramatically since
1995, albeit with a major dip between 2008 and 2012. Only Spain, of the EU
countries, experienced similar large increases in employment.

Ireland up to 2005 had a much greater increase in potential labour supply
than any of the other countries. Hence unemployment would have remained at
a very high level and the position of net immigration may have been translated
into substantial net emigration without this growth in employment. Much of the

Table 6.6 Employment and Proportion of Active Age Group in Employment in Selected OECD Countries

	E (Employed millions)		E/Pa (%)	
	2016	2006	2013	2016
Ireland	*2.0*	*68.7*	*60.5*	*65.1*
Denmark	2.7	77.4	72.5	74.8
Germany	40.5	67.2	73.5	74.8
Spain	18.2	65.0	54.8	59.7
UK	30.5	71.6	70.5	73.5
USA	142.6	72.0	67.4	69.3

Source: Constructed with OECD data from: http://stats.oecd.org/index.aspx?queryid=36324

early immigration after all was due to the return of people who had emigrated in the depressed labour market conditions of the 1980s. Much of the immigration in the 2000s though, as seen earlier, was due to immigration of non-Irish nationals. In both cases, however, it was a response to improved labour demand in Ireland.

The last three columns in Table 6.6 show the ratio of total employment to population size aged 15–64 years for each of the countries listed. Despite the rapid growth of employment in Ireland up to 2016, just 65.1 per cent of the population aged 15–64 were in employment in 2016, lower than that experienced by many OECD countries in the same year; substantially below the figures for Denmark, Germany and the UK, but a lot higher than that for Spain.

It could be argued therefore that the employment increase in Ireland in the years up to 2016 was strongly associated with a huge increase in the labour force, an increase that was simply bringing Ireland towards, but still well below, international norms in terms of the proportion of the total working-age population in employment. In fact, the figure was as low as 58.8 per cent in Ireland in 2012.

Part-Time and Temporary Employment
An important issue relating to employment in some countries, including Ireland, is the extent to which it consists of part-time employment and/or temporary employment. The available data suggest (Table 6.7) that the level of part-time employment as a proportion of total employment is low throughout the countries examined. In this regard Ireland is not out of line with its OECD counterparts. Similarly, there appears to have been no significant increase in part-time employment, especially amongst men, in the period up to 2015.

There is a marked gender difference in relation to part-time employment, as can be seen in Table 6.7. Only 12.3 per cent of total male employment in Ireland

Table 6.7 Incidence and Composition of Part-time and Temporary Employment in Selected OECD Countries,[1] 2015

	Part-time employment (% of total employment)			Temporary employment (% of total employment)
	Men	Women	Total	
Ireland	*12.3*	*35.4*	*23.3*	*8.7*
Denmark	15.0	25.8	20.0	8.6
Germany	9.3	37.4	22.4	13.1
Spain	7.2	23.1	14.5	25.1
UK	11.9	37.7	24.0	6.2
USA[2]	12.4	25.2	18.4	–

Source: As for Table 6.6.
[1] Part-time is usual hours of work of less than 30 per week. No comparable data available for USA.
[2] Part-time is usual hours of work less than 35 per week for the USA.

in 2015 was part time, whereas 35.4 per cent of female employment was part time. These percentages vary considerably from country to country, but on balance the position in Ireland was not unusual.

What is more important perhaps is the extent to which part-time employment is involuntary, i.e. chosen by the individual only because they could not get full-time work. The evidence suggests that most part-time employment is in fact voluntary, reflecting therefore a desire for such employment; largely it seems from female employees entering the labour force and with a preference for part-time work as it fits better with family and other commitments. The gender imbalance here though probably points to underlying social norms *requiring* that women fulfil domestic duties disproportionately to men. The 'choice' to work part-time may have long term consequences for labour market outcomes, for example part-time arrangements contribute to the gender pay gap and impact career advancement of women.[3]

A different but related issue is the extent to which employment is in temporary work. This is a much debated topic in labour market economics as some economists believe that an increasing proportion of jobs will have to be temporary if labour markets, especially in Europe, are to be sufficiently flexible to cope with an employment crisis, a topic that will be returned to later. As seen in Table 6.7, temporary employment in Ireland in 2015 accounted for just 8.7 per cent of dependent employment a figure which compares favourably with the other countries listed. As such there is no evidence that employment here is overly based on temporary employment.

Although experiences across the OECD vary, it does appear that younger and less educated workers disproportionately fill temporary jobs. On the other hand, temporary workers are a diverse group who work in a wide range of occupations and sectors. There is no evidence that this is a particularly acute problem in the Irish context, and this may be due to the relative weakness of employment protection laws in Ireland whereby employers have sufficient flexibility to avoid the need to resort to temporary contracts, unlike is the case perhaps in Spain (see later).

Sectoral Composition of Employment

Table 6.8 outlines the composition of employment in Ireland from 1999 to 2016 and it shows some large and important changes over the period.

The once central position of the agricultural sector has truly diminished (see Chapter 1) and now accounts for around 5.0 per cent of total employment (down from around 12.0 per cent only 17 years ago). There are now more people employed in accommodation and food services than in the total agricultural sector, reflecting the increased importance of tourism to the Irish economy and the marked trend towards eating out by people in Ireland (see Chapter 9). The numbers employed in the health sector are the same as in total manufacturing and the numbers employed in education are almost 50 per cent higher than in agriculture.

Table 6.8 Employment by Sector, Ireland

	(000s)			
	1999	2008	2012	2016[1]
Agriculture, forestry and fishing	136.4	116.0	87.1	109.7
Industry and Construction	445.0	537.5	331.3	397.4
of which:				
Industry	308.0	291.4	231.7	259.1
Construction	137.0	246.1	99.6	138.2
Services	1016.8	1486.3	1416.0	1533.6
of which:				
Accommodation and food service activities	104.1	128.7	120.0	148.0
Financial, insurance and real estate activities	68.9	107.1	99.3	101.5
Education	101.7	147.4	146.3	156.1
Human health and social work activities	118.5	222.8	244.4	257.5
Other services	623.6	880.3	806.0	870.5
Total	1607.2	2147.3	1836.2	2048.1

Source: Constructed with CSO data from: *QNHS*, at: www.cso.ie/en/qnhs/releasesand publications/qnhspostcensusofpopulation2011/
[1] 2016 figures are Q4.

The figures in relation to employment in construction tell the story of the overheating and subsequent contraction of the economy: doubling between 1994 and 1999 and again between 1999 and 2007 before falling by fully two-thirds in the six years to 2013 (see Chapter 7). This is truly a roller-coaster in employment terms which in turn is reflected in the overall employment situation.

The services sector as a whole is almost four times the size of the industrial sector and six times that of the manufacturing sector. As can be seen in the final column in Table 6.8, employment in all of the services subsectors grew between 1999 and 2008, but in particular in administrative and support services and health. Between 2008 and 2012 there were further increases in employment in some services sectors but in particular in health, whereas there were declines in most other sub-sectors.

5 UNEMPLOYMENT: EXTENT AND FEATURES

International Comparisons

Table 6.9 provides the key information on recorded unemployment rates in Ireland and selected OECD countries. The unemployment rate is given by UE/(E + UE).

As seen in Table 6.1 already, the unemployment rate in Ireland was at a record low in 2005 and as seen in Table 6.9 was at a level to compare with the best in Europe (well below that for Germany and Spain in fact). The relative picture changed little by 2006, although Germany experienced a rise in its unemployment rate, to double that in Ireland. By 2011 the relative picture had changed utterly. The unemployment rates in Ireland and Spain had sky-rocketed, whereas it declined substantially in Germany. Five short years later large changes were in evidence (see Table 6.9). The unemployment rates in Germany, the UK and

Table 6.9 Standardised Unemployment Rates in Selected OECD Countries[1]

	As a percentage of the labour force			
	2000	2006	2011	2016 (Nov)
Ireland	*4.7*	*4.7*	*14.9*	*7.3*
Denmark	4.6	4.0	7.5	7.5
Germany	7.8	10.4	5.9	4.1
Spain	13.9	8.5	21.5	19.2
UK	5.5	5.4	8.0	4.8
USA	4.0	4.7	9.1	4.6

Source: As for Table 6.6.
[1] All series are benchmarked to labour force survey based estimates and have been adjusted to ensure comparability over time.

the USA were below five per cent, the Irish rate had halved but in Spain was still above 19 per cent. Thus using this measure of labour market performance Ireland has done quite well, even compared to Denmark and certainly compared to Spain.

Comparison/Measurement Problems

Standardised Unemployment Rates

The discussion above is based on the assumption that the data can be used for valid comparison both across countries and over time. Is this the case? There are three main issues of concern here. The first is whether or not all countries are using the same methods of defining and compiling data on unemployment; the second is whether or not over time there is a consistent series for Ireland and elsewhere; the last is whether or not there are certain categories of persons that are not, and perhaps cannot be, included by any country but which should be included in any discussion of labour market slack (i.e. where labour demand is less than labour supply) in an economy.

In relation to Ireland, there are two main sources of data on unemployment: the Quarterly National Household Survey (QNHS) and the Live Register. The QNHS provides data on the internationally recognised measure of unemployment and defines somebody as 'unemployed' if their response in the survey makes clear that they did not work even for one hour for payments or profit in the previous week, actively sought work in the previous four weeks, and are available to start work within two weeks. As such, it does not include so-called discouraged workers, those who have given up hope on the job search, a phenomenon which can vary in its impact in different countries and hence disguises comparison of the 'true' level of unemployment.

The QNHS definition is then a strict measure of unemployment and much more so than the Live Register measure. It is the QNHS data therefore that are used for international comparison, as the methods adopted in arriving at these data are considered to give the more accurate indicator of the underlying level of unemployment in a country. These data are also used in this chapter, unless indicated otherwise.

Invalidity/Disability Benefit Issue

There are also many people unable to work through invalidity or disability; the proportion of the working-age group in this category has grown significantly in some EU countries in recent years, with some commentators suggesting that some of the decrease in unemployment in the 2000s, in the Netherlands and the UK in particular, could be linked to this development.

As the OECD states, too many workers leave the labour market permanently due to health problems and, indeed, expenditures on disability programmes in many OECD countries far exceed expenditures on other income-replacement programmes for working-age persons (such as unemployment benefits).[4] A large number of OECD countries have seen substantial increases in the share of disability beneficiaries in the working-age population. It appears that vulnerable groups such as women, young individuals and the low-skilled are most affected by this trend.

Helping disabled people find and keep jobs is a major challenge for all OECD countries including Ireland especially given that the potential personal, social, and financial benefits are very significant. Although it is costly to leave disabled people outside the labour force, no country has so far been successful in crafting policies that will help disabled people participate in the paid labour force. The OECD suggests various broad areas for improvement including: individual benefit packages with job search support, rehabilitation and vocational training; new obligations for disabled people including, for those who are capable, a requirement to look for work; involving employers and trade unions in reintegration efforts; and more flexible cash benefits, depending on job capabilities and changes in an individual's disability over time.

Long-Term and Youth Unemployment
Apart from the level of unemployment, its composition is also of considerable interest to economists, for reasons alluded to already. The most important consideration in this regard arguably relates to its composition between short-term (less than 12 months) and long-term (12 months or more) unemployment.

Long-term unemployment (LTU) in Ireland rose significantly between 1980 and 1990. The long-term unemployment rate was only 2.8 per cent of the labour force in 1980, rising to 8.3 per cent in 1990. As Table 6.10 shows, a marked decline took place in LTU between 1990 and 2000. The reductions were remarkable; the numbers in absolute terms were down to just over a quarter of their level in 1990, the drop in the LTU rate was even more dramatic, falling from 8.3 to 1.6 per cent, below the level pertaining in 1980.

This picture remained largely unchanged up to 2008, when the first rise in LTU on all counts was recorded. Between 2008 and 2012 there was a dramatic

Table 6.10 Long-Term Unemployment in Ireland, 1990–2016

	Number ('000s)	Unemployment rate (%)	Long-term unemployment rate (%)
1990	110.2	12.9	8.3
2000	28.6	4.6	1.6
2005	31.6	4.7	1.5
2010	140.2	13.9	6.4
2012	199.6	15.0	9.3
2016[1]	79.7	6.7	3.7

Source: CSO, QNHS, *op cit.* and CSO, *Statistical Yearbook of Ireland,* CSO, Dublin 2000.
[1] 2016 figure is for Q4.

worsening of the situation, with the LTU rate rising from 1.5 per cent to 9.3 per cent in four years and the numbers in LTU increasing over six fold. The LTU problem of the 1980s and early 1990s had returned to Ireland in a few short years, although a significant decline did take place between 2012 and 2016 (Table 6.10). The long-term unemployment rate though was still at 3.7 per cent in 2016 and in many ways this could be the most worrying legacy of the economic crisis of the years 2008 to 2012.

Table 6.11 provides data on LTU as a proportion of total unemployment for the countries shown. The trends here reflect the earlier discussion. Despite making a lot of progress in reducing long-term unemployment in the first part of the 2000s, all of the countries in Table 6.11 saw increases in the share of LTU in total unemployment between 2006 and 2011. This was especially true for Spain, Ireland and the USA. The shares in both Ireland and the USA decreased between 2011 and 2015, with the percentage for the USA again the lowest for all of the countries listed. Again the picture for Germany stands out, with large decreases not only in unemployment but also in the share of LTU in total unemployment.

Table 6.11 Long Term Unemployment in Selected OECD Countries (percentage of total unemployment)

	2006	2011	2015
Ireland	*31.6*	*59.3*	*57.6*
Denmark	20.8	24.4	26.9
Germany	53.0	47.9	44.0
Spain	21.6	41.6	51.6
UK	22.4	33.5	30.7
USA	10.0	31.3	18.7

Source: As for Table 6.5.

Another major concern with regard to the composition of unemployment relates to youth unemployment (see Table 6.12). These data relate the numbers not in employment, education or training (NEET) to the total population in the age groups 15–19 and 20–24. Thus, they include not just numbers unemployed but also those on disability benefit, those doing domestic un-paid work and discouraged workers.

What is shown are not unemployment rates but 'inactivity rates'. These are more meaningful though than unemployment rates, which relate the numbers unemployed to the sum of those unemployed and those in employment, and not the total population in that age group. As such, youth unemployment rates can occur for say Spain, for example, of close to 50 per cent, when as seen in Table 6.12 there is only closer to 25 per cent of that age group not in employment, education or training.

Table 6.12 Percentage Youth Inactivity (neither employed nor in education or training)

	15–19 year olds		20–24 year olds	
	2008	2015	2008	2015
Ireland	*8.5*	*8.0*	*14.6*	*19.8*
Denmark	4.0	3.7	8.2	12.4
Germany	3.7	2.5	14.0	9.3
Spain	11.2	9.1	19.0	27.2
UK	9.8	8.7	18.3	15.6
USA	7.6	7.0	17.2	15.8

Source: Constructed using OECD data from: https://data.oecd.org/youthinac/youth-not-in-employment-education-or-training-neet.htm

The data presented in Table 6.12 are quite striking. Just under one fifth of all those aged 20–24 in Ireland are not in education, training or employment, the second highest of the countries shown but nevertheless closer in size to the experience of the UK and USA than Spain. The figure for Ireland did increase dramatically, from 14.6 per cent in 2008 to 26.1 per cent in 2011, but has since declined in line with the return to education for many in this age group as well as the improvement in the labour market since 2012. In Germany the figure is as low as 9.3 per cent, but the figures for the UK and USA are also high, although both these countries have seen declines in inactivity in the 20–24 year old group between 2008 and 2015. The great worry of course is that some of these people have been out of the labour market for more than a year and hence already belong to the long-term unemployed or long-term unwell.

6 ADAPTING TO NEW TECHNOLOGY, AND INCREASED TRADE AND MIGRATION

What causes employment levels to rise and fall, in any country including Ireland? First, there are arguments relating to global factors such as increased competition in international trade, technological change and greater freedom of movement of labour, especially in the EU, and hence a potentially large increase in migration. These are factors that would affect every country in Europe, but some to a greater extent than others. How each country fares largely depends on the skill level and adaptability of their labour forces in the new circumstances. These issues will be discussed in this section. Second, there are structural arguments relating to such issues as the role of unions and wage bargaining/setting, employment protection legislation and the taxation and social welfare systems. These issues will be discussed in Section 7.

Single Market, Trade, and Technological Change

Given the extent of Ireland's trade, factor and corporate links with the world economy, it is inevitable that the increasing globalisation of economic activity has, and will have, a major effect on economic activity and employment in Ireland (see Chapter 1 and later chapters). Added to this is the deepening of the Single European Market and the removal of barriers to free trade in services, mergers and acquisitions and capital flows with the consequential implications for economic activity, competition, and employment in Ireland. Ireland's entry into the euro zone in the late 1990s was a further major commitment to the benefits and challenges of the Single Market. It appears that these challenges were never properly understood at the time and that this was a key cause of the drop in employment between 2008 and 2012.

It is generally believed by economists that an increasing intensity of trade and integration will lead to higher incomes, but that it will also lead to the displacement of labour in some activities and the expansion of labour in other activities. The net impact on employment should be positive as long as labour and product markets function well and wages are reasonably flexible. Thus, if decreased overall employment result from increased trade intensity and competition it is not trade or competition *per se* that is causing the problem but the functioning of the labour and product markets, a topic that will be returned to in a later section. The evidence, according to the OECD,[5] supports such an argument. This indeed is the reason why Ireland has adopted such a pro-trade liberalisation stance in the last 45 years.

Increasing international trade and economic integration may also have an impact on innovation and the absorption of technological change. It is argued by some that labour-saving technologies are, at least in part, introduced in anticipation of and/or in response to the increased competition both on domestic and foreign markets that arises from the increased globalisation of trade and European integration. As such, the effects of increased international integration and technological change are difficult to separate in practice.

Technology is central to the process of growth (see Chapters 7 and 10): it allows increases in productivity and thereby real incomes. But does it destroy jobs and in the process create unemployment?

Fears about widespread job losses associated with the emergence of new technology are not new and are in the aggregate largely unfounded.[6] They date back to at least the time of the Industrial Revolution when the Luddite movement in England destroyed new machinery in the early nineteenth century for fear of job losses at the time. It is true that technological change involves a process of job destruction in some older occupations, firms and industries, but it also involves a parallel process of job creation in new and emerging sectors and occupations. There are many historical examples of predictions of large-scale technological unemployment being followed in fact by large net expansions of jobs, the experience in the last two decades or so with regard to the IT sector in the USA being the most recent striking example.

Nonetheless, fears arising from the negative effects of increased globalisation on employment had a huge effect on voters in elections in the UK and USA in 2016, even though there were record low levels of unemployment in both countries. Many of the jobs though leading to low unemployment were in low-wage occupations and this arises from the fact that globalisation has led to many losers, if not in terms of employment then in terms of income.

Fears that robots will lead to a large drop in net jobs persists, despite evidence to the contrary. The *Economist* took the striking example of the 'truck driver' in the USA: there are around 1.8 million of them at present.[7] However, if self-driving vehicles become a reality, then it could apply to trucks first, potentially reducing the number of drivers required by over 1.2 million. What in those circumstances would happen to the many drivers who have very little formal education and with no disposition to acquire one? Is it realistic to argue that they will find other jobs created by new and/or different demands? That is where life-long learning and training comes into the picture. Note in this case that it is primarily innovation, not globalisation that is causing the potential large-scale labour problem and that innovation can take place in a large closed economy, unrelated to changes in the extent of globalisation.

Table 6.13 Average Annual Hours Actually Worked per Worker[1] in Selected OECD Countries

	2000	2008	2015
Ireland	*1,574*	*1,504*	*1,475*
Denmark	1,407	1,389	1,407
Germany	1,360	1,340	1,304
Spain	1,705	1,668	1,643
UK	1,680	1,642	1,663
USA	1,836	1,797	1,795

Source: Constructed using OECD data at: http://stats.oecd.org/Index.aspx?DatasetCode=LFS_SEXAGE_I_R
[1] Average annual hours per employee.

Technology and trade then do not necessarily lead to any decrease in the level of employment, but they allow for a decrease in the annual hours of work per employee, thereby allowing for increased per capita incomes *and* increased voluntary leisure time. The average working year has declined steadily over the last 100 years and this trend is continuing, as seen in Table 6.13.

For all countries listed (bar Denmark), average annual working time decreased between 2000 and 2015, and more so in Ireland. The other finding in Table 6.13 is the significant variation across even developed countries in the average annual working time. In particular it can be seen that of the countries listed, the figure was highest for the USA, at 1,795 hours in 2015, and 1,663 hours in the UK, 30 per cent more than in Germany. This is an issue that is discussed in Chapter 7 when comparative living standards are examined. From a labour supply point of view, the question is to what extent the variation in hours is a reflection of work preferences or slack labour demand. Those supporting the USA model argue for the latter whereas Europeans tend to argue that the former applies.

While Ireland's adoption of new technology will be discussed in later chapters, particularly Chapter 10, it is worth noting here that there are four key technology areas that will influence the country's success in IT: infrastructure, competitive market conditions, education and training and access for all. It has been, and will be, the country's ability to take appropriate action on all four fronts that will allow Ireland to absorb and adapt to the new technology: the ability to do this in turn will be the key to employment, not only in manufacturing but more important perhaps, given its scale, in the services sector as well (see various later chapters).

Labour Market Integration

Labour market integration is a highly contentious aspect of economic integration in Europe. Popular opinion, especially in periods of high unemployment, holds immigrants responsible for high unemployment, abuse of social welfare programmes, street crime, and the deterioration of neighbourhoods. Economic theory predicts that in a world of no unemployment there will be both winners and losers resulting from labour migration. Without migration, however, the worldwide allocation of productive factors is inefficient. Improving the overall efficiency of the world economy through migration then leads to a net gain which must be split between the home and foreign country.

In the situation where there is no unemployment and workers initially earn better wages in the domestic economy than in the foreign economy, migration will result in labour flowing from the foreign to the domestic economy. This may push down wages at home, harming domestic workers while benefiting domestic consumers and owners of capital. The opposite happens in the foreign economy. Wages there tend to rise as some foreign labour moves to the domestic economy; thus, remaining foreign workers are better off while foreign consumers and the owners of capital are made worse off. The net outcome is positive for the efficiency reasons outlined above, but serious distributional issues arise.

For most European economies labour is comprised of both highly-skilled and low-skilled workers. Recognising this distinction allows a more nuanced understanding of the dynamics of labour market integration under net-inward or net-outward migration. It is in this context that one may view immigrant labour as a complement or substitute for domestic labour. If immigrant labour is a complement to native workers, immigration will raise the demand for native workers resulting in higher wages, higher employment, and an unambiguously favourable impact on unemployment.

But it is perceptions that matter when it comes to immigration, as the UK referendum on leaving the EU and elections in the USA in 2016 demonstrated. Many people had the perception that the number of migrants living in the UK was two to three times the actual number. Further, while the decision to leave the EU was based largely on these perceptions, it was very often the case that the highest percentage vote to leave the EU was in areas with least migrants. Besides, most of the immigrants in the UK had come from outside the EU. One major issue though in relation to migration is related not to employment but to ensuring that expenditure on public services and infrastructure keeps pace with the increase in population resulting from migration, something which does not appear to have happened in the UK. If public services and infrastructure are not upgraded then the problem is this and not immigration per se, unless one believes that there is some 'optimal' population for an area. How then could one explain the fact that so many people want to live in large densely populated cities rather than in less populated areas, Ireland included?

The empirical evidence for Ireland suggests that over the period 2000 to 2008 although the skill make-up of immigrants was higher than that of the native population, immigrants tended to fill low-skilled jobs and thus acted as complements to the skilled Irish workforce, even if this meant that migrants achieved a low occupational attainment relative to their educational attainment. In addition, preliminary evidence suggests (see Table 6.3) that recent immigrants are still mobile and that many have returned to their home countries as employment in construction collapsed. In this way the ease of movement between Ireland and the new European member states helped to ease the adverse unemployment impacts of the downturn in Ireland between 2008 and 2012.[8] Throughout the recovery the skill attainment of immigrants continued to be high, close to 60 per cent of immigrants between 2012 and 2016 had tertiary qualifications (Table 6.4). It remains to be seen whether migrants continue to act as complements to the existing skill profile in Ireland.

Education, Training and Skills Adaptability

Over the last 20 years the structure of work in the industrialised world has, for the reasons mentioned above, been changing. There has been a shift in demand away from low-skilled, low-wage jobs towards high-skilled, high-wage jobs. The change in the nature of work arises not only from the transformation of jobs by technology and international trade but also from the 'natural' sectoral changes that have occurred with regard to the composition of employment. Allied to this, because of immigration, there was a marked transformation in labour supply in many sectors.

The skills required in services are different to those needed for industry and hence the declining industrial workforce cannot be automatically transplanted into services jobs. The new wave of employment creation leads, as mentioned earlier, to a transformation of the competencies required from the workforce. Not only do they need different qualifications and skills but the continuously changing nature of work also requires them to have a high degree of flexibility that was not necessary in the past when permanent, stable positions were the norm.

The skills of the labour force then have to be altered to take account of the changing environment and nature of work that accompany this structural shift. In the absence of this adjustment, mismatch can, and may have, become a serious problem in the labour market.[9] Evidence for this is reflected in repeated statements of serious skills shortages in parts of the EU.

It is for these reasons that the EU has placed special emphasis on upgrading the skills and competencies of the labour force, as part of the search for a solution to maintaining and increasing employment. Not all persons have acquired adequate initial education and training before they enter the labour market and these are the people most likely to experience long-term unemployment in Ireland and elsewhere in Europe. The first priority then must be to reduce through preventive and remedial measures the number of young people who leave school without some qualification (see Chapter 13).

The next concern is to ensure that those who have acquired satisfactory initial qualifications make the transition to employment and this may be assisted by a more employer-led approach to education, particularly vocational education. Last, and of most relevance perhaps in relation to the issues discussed in this section, is the need to emphasise continuing education and training (see Chapter 13), as individuals need the opportunity to upgrade their knowledge and competencies to prepare themselves for the changes brought about by increasing international trade, migration and technological change. The challenges in 2017 are pressing in identifying the areas for employment growth and ensuring the skill levels of the Irish labour force match the resulting employment opportunities.

7 FLEXIBILITY IN LABOUR MARKET

It has been mentioned already that structural rigidities in labour markets, especially in those of many countries in Europe, may largely explain why unemployment was and is at such high levels in some countries. Putting it more positively, it is argued that it is the countries with flexible labour markets that have experienced the lowest rates of unemployment in the 2010s. There are several dimensions to the structural rigidity and labour market flexibility arguments and some of the key ones are looked at here.

First, wage and price adjustments are examined, with attention devoted to work-place relations and product market competition. Second, quantity adjustments (which refer to barriers facing the movement of people in and out of jobs) are analysed. Policies to enhance quantity adjustment include reforms of employment protection legislation and active labour market policies. Last, the effect of the tax and social welfare system on the working of the labour market will be examined briefly.

Wage Adjustments
Price formation in the labour market is, by necessity, different from that in other markets. This is because wages are not simply a price of one type of product among others, but determine to a large extent the well-being of the majority of people in modern society. Societies' concern about social justice and the distribution of income therefore becomes integrally linked to wage-setting (see Chapter 8). Because of this, distinct social arrangements and institutions intervene in every country in the market-clearing role of wage adjustments. However, even if the operation of the price system for labour is different than for that of products, the effects of prices being too high are the same, i.e. wages above market-clearing levels will result in excess supply and therefore lower levels of employment than would otherwise be the case.

Work-Place Relations
The response of wages to market conditions has to be seen against the background of the institutional arrangements, particularly those relating to work-place, or the more commonly used term of industrial, relations and the role of trade unions, in the labour market in each particular country. These arrangements have been partly designed to encourage stable employment relationships and to avert the income insecurity that can accompany rapid price adjustments in the market for labour, as happened in the USA in the 1980s. However, in so doing, these arrangements may encourage anti-competitive behaviour in the labour market and, as in all markets this will result in lower demand because prices are not set at their clearing rate. This of course must be set against the advantages for employees of the protective industrial-relations arrangements and the potential advantages for employers, in that these arrangements may strengthen cooperation by workers and prevent the harmful behaviour that may be inherent in a more atomistic wage-setting environment.

Given the above, it is generally recognised that income restraint by trade unions and individual workers is essential to employment creation in Ireland and that there *is* a trade-off between pay and employment. In the multinational high-tech sector of the economy, pay moderation can lead to more employment in the medium to longer term, through increased profitability and its effect on investment-location decisions. In the more traditional labour intensive parts of the traded sector there is likely to be a substantial trade-off between pay and employment, as in many cases pay moderation is essential in this sector, simply to retain existing jobs. In the sheltered private sector, pay moderation is necessary to underpin the competitiveness of the traded sector and also to generate increased employment in this sector. Last, in the public sector, given a fixed budget, there is a very direct and almost immediate trade-off between pay and employment.

The usual indicator of perceived industrial relations problems is the level of unionisation of the labour force in a country. There are a number of interesting facts though in this regard emerging from Table 6.14. First is the huge variation in trade union membership across countries, from as low as 10.7 per cent in the

USA to 66.8 per cent in Denmark. Surprisingly perhaps trade union membership is also low in Germany and Spain but relatively high in Ireland and the UK. As such, it is almost impossible to draw any firm conclusions between the rate of unionisation and unemployment. Ireland's unionisation density is falling faster than in the comparison countries examined here and has fallen steadily during the recent recession.

Table 6.14 Union Membership in Selected OECD Countries (percentage of employees)

	1999	2009	2014
Ireland	*38.7*	*33.1*	*27.4*
Denmark[1]	74.0	67.7	66.8
Germany[1]	25.3	18.9	18.1
Spain[1]	16.8	17.6	16.9
UK	30.1	27.3	25.1
USA	13.4	11.8	10.7

Source: As for Table 6.5.
[1] Latest available figures are from 2013 for these countries.

In relation to the wage-bargaining process, there is a degree of corporatism in the Irish labour market with a large proportion of wages having been determined by national wage agreements in the past (see Chapter 3). Ireland therefore appeared to have adopted the preferable system of wage bargaining (i.e. centralised) for such a small country where participants are more likely to take wider economic interests into account.

In recent years though the position in Ireland has changed dramatically and many now question the desirability of centralised wage setting, at least if it does not recognise the reality of competition in product markets in a single currency area and thereby the limitations of passing on wage increases into prices. As such, nation-wide collective bargaining has been effectively abandoned although it still applies across the public sector, with the so-called Croke Park and Haddington Road agreements put in place in recent years. As of 2017 there were signs of increasing tensions over pay in the work place, especially in the wider public sector and it remains to be seen how they will be addressed.

There is now a worry though about the power of public sector unions operating through or outside these agreements: while the overall level of unionisation might be low, it can still be high in the public sector, thereby giving that sector excessive wage-bargaining power perhaps, endangering not just employment but also a fair income distribution within Irish society (see Chapter 8) and indeed the level of public services provided. This was evident in 2016 and will become an increasingly contentious issue in 2017 and beyond.

There is emerging evidence that one part of the labour market is especially flexible with regards to wage setting behaviour, namely those starting work for the first time, and that (public and private sector) employers have utilised this in Ireland over the past ten years. This may in part be attributable to the abandonment of centralised wage setting, which itself is likely to have mitigated the unemployment effect of the recession. However, the wage flexibility of new hires will result in workers doing the same job being paid different wages, with attendant distributional effects.[10]

Competition in Product Markets

Imperfect competition in product markets can also affect the wage level and thereby the level of employment and unemployment. If there is an absence of competition in product markets, firms have an option of choosing 'supra-normal' profits ahead of increased employment. They also have the option of retaining the entire surplus for themselves or sharing it with existing employees. The latter will happen if the workers have bargaining strength or the rents may be willingly shared with workers to encourage efficiency and to boost work motivation, i.e. the employers may be prepared to pay what are called 'efficiency wages'.

The solution to reducing the distortionary effects of imperfect product market competition on labour market outcomes is clearly to remove the opportunity for producers to earn rent, and this calls for a strict and tough competition regime, a topic that is covered at some length in Chapter 5. More important, the opening of the EU market to increased competition, internal and external, has greatly reduced the potential for such imperfect competition. Besides, entry into the euro zone has removed the exchange-rate option for dealing with excessive wage rises: employers and employees must now 'live' with the euro exchange rate, which is determined elsewhere. The potential benefits of course are reduced exchange-rate risk, more transparency of prices, less transactions costs and increased employment levels overall.

The main concern now perhaps relates, as discussed earlier, to the public sector, where for some time the tax-price of its services can be shielded from any immediate effect on employment in the public sector. In time though the higher tax price for public services must be paid for out of taxation thereby impacting on Irish competitiveness and ultimately therefore on Irish employment, tax revenue and public sector employment. Wage, and related pension, negotiations still take place at the level of the whole public sector and in recent years there has been a realisation that in return for this much greater work flexibility and public sector reform will be required. Many though question the low scale of the latter.

Minimum Wage

A national minimum wage (NMW) was introduced in Ireland in 2000. Although the ESRI predicted that this would decrease employment and increase unemployment and inflation, 95 per cent of firms surveyed a year later viewed the NMW as having had no impact on the numbers of employees they had subsequently hired.

Those paid less than the NMW are concentrated in sales and personal services, which reflects a wider concern that younger female and non-national workers are most likely to experience low pay.

Many studies have shown that the adverse impact of minimum wages on employment is modest.[11] This however depends on the level of the minimum wage and how it interacts with the tax system. The important thing in this regard is to ensure that work pays better than remaining on social welfare benefits and also that high rates of labour taxation do not apply at low income levels (see Chapter 4). An employer considering hiring a low-skilled or inexperienced worker is likely to compare the worker's expected productivity with the *sum* of the minimum wage and employer-paid social security contributions when deciding whether or not to hire.

The minimum wage, relative to median income is about average in Ireland. As shown in Table 6.15, in 2015 this ratio was 0.44 for Ireland, compared to 0.49 in the UK (our main competitor market), and 0.36 in the USA. This ratio though has come down significantly for Ireland between 2000 and 2015, much more so than for any other country listed. Germany introduced a minimum wage only in 2015.

Table 6.15 Ratio of Minimum to Median Wage for Full-Time Workers in Selected OECD Countries

	2000	2009	2015
Ireland	*0.67*	*0.47*	*0.44*
Germany[1]	n/a	n/a	0.48
Spain	0.36	0.39	0.37
UK	0.41	0.46	0.49
USA	0.36	0.37	0.36

Source: As for Table 6.5.
[1] There was no minimum wage in Germany before 2015.

Employment Protection Legislation

Employment protection relates to the 'firing' and 'hiring' rules governing unfair dismissal, lay-off for economic reasons, severance payments, minimum notice periods, administrative authorisation for dismissals and prior discussion with labour representatives. A number of benefits are argued to justify employment protection legislation: encouraging increased investment in firm-specific human capital, reducing contracting costs by setting general rules and standards, and early notification of job loss to allow job search prior to being laid off. As against this, employment protection legislation imposes constraints on firms' behaviour that can raise labour costs and adversely affect hiring decisions. It may also provide strong incentives for employers to use forms of employment (e.g. short-term or even zero hour contracts) that do not involve high firing costs.

Labour security legislation does not only affect the actions of employers, it also influences the bargaining power and, hence, strategy of the insiders. With the legislation in place, workers' fear of job loss will be diminished and they will push for higher real wages. This will then have an impact on labour demand. Labour security legislation therefore could cause labour demand to be inflexible both directly (i.e. through employers' immediate decisions) and indirectly (i.e. through its promotion of higher real wages). In fact, employment protection laws are thought by many to be a key factor in generating labour market inflexibility.

It appears clear though that a certain level of employment protection is jus-tified to protect workers from arbitrary or discriminatory dismissals. However, the OECD believes that dismissals that are required on economic grounds must be allowed and that the provision of more explicit, long-term commitments to job security should not be imposed on all firms but decided on a firm-by-firm basis. Whether and to what extent reform is required clearly depends on the country-specific circumstances.

A related issue is that the emphasis is now increasingly on employment secu-rity rather than job security, that is on guaranteed employment as opposed to employment in a specific job. The best way to ensure this is to increase adapt-ability and employability, as discussed earlier. After all, labour reallocation is an important driver of productivity growth, in that less productive firms tend to destroy jobs and more productive ones create jobs and empirical evidence shows that the process of firm birth and death, as well as the reallocation of resources from declining to expanding firms, contribute significantly to productivity and output growth.

Attempts have been made to construct various summary indicators to describe the 'strictness' of employment protection in each country, including Ireland. Given the complexity of constructing such indicators, they are inevitably some-what arbitrary, but nonetheless are indicative. An OECD study ranking countries according to 'strictness' of protection in the areas of individual dismissals of reg-ular workers, fixed-term contracts and employment through temporary employ-ment agencies showed in 2015 that employment protection was ranked relatively low as a problem in Ireland (see Table 6.16). This applied in particular to tempo-rary employment and less so to regular employment as can be seen.

However, compared to the USA, Ireland, and indeed most of Europe, have much more strict employment protection, with scores of 0.26 for the USA in relation to regular employment in 2013 (0.25 for temporary employment), against figures of 2.20 and 1.38 in Denmark, and 2.05 and 2.56 in Spain. Indeed the important figure relates to regular employment, where the figure of 1.40 for Ire-land is much higher than in the USA and most important perhaps the UK (1.10). Over time it can be seen that the level of employment protection in Ireland has remained the same for regular employment but increased significantly for tempo-rary employment, up from 0.25 in 2000 to 0.63 in 2013.

Table 6.16 Employment Protection in Selected OECD Countries (strictness indicators, 0–6)

	Regular employment		Temporary employment	
	2000	2013[1]	2000	2013
Ireland	*1.44*	*1.40*	*0.25*	*0.63*
Denmark	2.13	2.20	1.38	1.38
Germany	2.68	2.68	2.00	1.13
Spain	2.36	2.05	3.25	2.56
UK	1.26	1.10	0.25	0.38
USA	0.26	0.26	0.25	0.25

Source: As for Table 6.5.
[1] OECD data updated only periodically.

Taxation

Payroll taxes, such as employers' social security contributions, raise the costs of employing labour over and above the wage paid. Taxes on income and employees' social security contributions reduce the return to working (see Chapter 4). These taxes therefore are important because they directly affect the rate of return from decisions to enter the labour market and thereby affect the supply of labour. They may also influence the choice between working in the shadow economy and declared paid employment.

These taxes may have an even greater impact on employment and unemployment through their influence on wage determination and therefore on the demand for labour. Cuts in real wages through the imposition of increased personal income taxes or social security contributions may be resisted by workers and compensated for by higher nominal wages – but at the cost of higher unemployment. Likewise, an increase in employers' social security contributions can also result in unemployment when workers resist offsetting wage cuts. In the light of increased competition, both within the EU Single Market and globally, though, the scope for such resistance by trade unions and workers is significantly reduced, as discussed earlier.

Reductions in average tax rates at low levels of earnings are clearly an important way of increasing the income differential between being in and out of work, for the groups for which this is the most serious problem (see earlier). It appears that particular attention needs to be devoted to social security contributions in this regard, not just to the level of these contributions but also their structure: employers' taxation not only influences the amount of people that are employed but may also influence the type of worker that is hired.

The level at which social benefits are withdrawn, as seen in Chapter 4, is also another important aspect of the problem. A feature of many tax and benefit systems, including that in Ireland, is that they can embody very high marginal tax rates for those on low incomes, especially those with large families, as benefits are reduced and earnings are taxed.

Unemployment Payments

The rationale for unemployment insurance payments is 'to relieve people who have lost a job through no fault of their own from immediate financial concerns, and thus allow efficient job search. Unemployment benefits also act as automatic stabilisers in an economy, for example they boost consumption when the economy is weak and unemployment is up; and dampen it when the economy is growing and unemployment is falling. Insurance benefits, therefore, have an economic efficiency as well as a social equity objective'.[12] In relation to unemployment assistance payment schemes, which apply in Ireland after twelve months and effectively for an indefinite period, the social or equity role, in reducing poverty among unemployed people and cushioning the adverse effects of high and rising unemployment, becomes paramount.

As a result of the above, there would be strong political objections to resist any cuts in unemployment benefits or assistance and this clearly 'flavours' any debate on the causal connection between unemployment benefit/assistance and unemployment. However, the possibility of such a causal connection, and its extent, must be addressed, as it has been recently in countries such as France and Italy, where unemployment persisted, at high levels, for more than a decade and led to a build-up of large-scale long-term unemployment and a 'hand-out' dependency. A similar problem has arisen in Ireland since 2008.

Few economists question the fact that there *is* a link between the benefit system and unemployment. At the simplest level, unemployment payments may create an option of leisure and low income, which some people might choose in preference to full-time work and a higher income. However, such payments could affect employment in many other ways. First, receipt of such payments may prolong intervals of job search, even for those who seek to work. Second, because unemployment payments reduce the cost of becoming unemployed, employed people may take a tougher stance in industrial relations disputes or in collective bargaining over wages (see earlier), thereby exacerbating the high real wage problem. Last, payments may increase employment in high turnover and seasonal industries, by subsidising these industries relative to those which provide long-term contract jobs.

As seen in Table 6.17, unemployment benefits, in the initial phase of unemployment, as a percentage of previous earnings (net of tax) – the net replacement rate (NRR) – increased markedly in Ireland between 2001 and 2014: the figure for Ireland is higher than the equivalent rate in the UK but substantially lower than comparator countries, including the USA. The NRR is substantially higher in Ireland and the UK for the long term unemployed than for the initial phase of unemployment, especially when social assistance 'top ups' are included. This is in stark contrast to the USA, and indeed Spain, where NRRs are much lower for the long-term unemployed when compared to benefits at the initial stage of unemployment. Long-term unemployment benefits do not differ substantially from short-term benefits in Denmark and Germany. So again the evidence of the employment effects of unemployment payments is mixed. It is noteworthy though that the net rates have not changed substantially between 2001 and 2014 for any of the countries listed, bar Ireland.

The adverse effects of unemployment payments may, however, result not so much from the existence and level of these payments, but more from the entitlement conditions, the administration of the system and other institutional background factors. For example, payment of unemployment benefits is conditional upon the claimant being available for, and willing to take, full-time work. If this condition is not effectively implemented, people *not* in the labour force (i.e. not available for or not seeking work) may register as unemployed simply to collect unemployment payments. If this condition is strictly enforced and payments stopped if it is not met, then the distortionary effects of unemployment payments could be substantially reduced. A related issue is that the employment agency must not only enforce this condition but must also facilitate effective job search, the final topic to which we now turn.

Table 6.17 Unemployment Payments in Selected OECD Countries (unemployment benefit/previous earnings)[1]

	Initial phase of unemployment			Long-term unemployment		
	2001	2009	2014	2001	2009	2014
Ireland	*0.39*	*0.53*	*0.49*	*0.69*	*0.80*	*0.70*
Denmark	0.86	0.82	0.84	0.82	0.80	0.79
Germany	0.60	0.60	0.59	0.58	0.50	0.48
Spain	0.76	0.77	0.78	0.32	0.32	0.32
United Kingdom	0.20	0.19	0.20	0.59	0.55	0.53
United States	0.62	0.60	0.61	0.09	0.10	0.09

Source: Constructed using OECD at: Tax-Benefit Models www.oecd.org/els/benefits-and-wages-statistics.htm
[1] Net replacement rates for single earner, previous earnings = 67% average wage; including cash housing assistance and social assistance "top ups" if available.

Active Labour Market Policies[13]

Issues

The OECD as far back as 1994 was unequivocal concerning the changes that needed to be effected across OECD countries in benefit administration. They suggested, for example, much more in-depth verification of eligibility, much better matching of workers to job vacancies and fieldwork investigation of concealed earnings and related fraud. A more fundamental problem they claimed

176

was making unemployment payments, especially to the long-term unemployed, effectively conditional on availability for existing vacancies. In particular, they stressed that the long-term unemployed should be expected to take, and unemployment payments made conditional on taking, even low-status jobs. As the OECD noted, much may depend upon achieving a social, political, and analytical consensus on this, rejecting the opposite idea that modern economies should be able to afford to make work optional.

The real concern here is that if people are allowed to drift into long-term unemployment, as happened in Ireland in the 1980s and in the early 1990s, and again after 2008, that the problem becomes more difficult to overcome. At an individual level long-term unemployment may lead to significant deskilling and demotivation. At a macroeconomic level, and partly as a result of this, the long-term unemployed may not be regarded as 'employable' and in a sense may cease to be part of the labour market. Thus they in effect exert no downward pressure on the wage-setting process that might bring about equilibrium in the labour market.

A similar problem has arisen in recent years in relation to groups receiving *non-employment* benefits. As discussed earlier, the numbers on some non-employment benefits have grown. These benefit recipients represent a large share of the potential workforce and if their numbers are not reduced employment rates will remain low for years to come in many OECD countries. The pattern in relation to non-employment benefit recipients suggest, the OECD argues, that there could be a high pay-off to extending activation measures, currently available to the unemployed, to persons receiving these non-employment benefits. Recent experience demonstrates that there is considerable scope to apply activation strategies to persons receiving non-employment benefits, albeit with appropriate modifications for the specific characteristics of each group.

Solutions

What was being suggested above is effectively a much more active approach to labour market policy on behalf of the employment service in each country. The purpose of active labour market policies is threefold: first to mobilise labour supply, second to improve the quality of the labour force, and third to strengthen the search process in the labour market. They are particularly appropriate for those experiencing long-term unemployment (and many of those on long-term disability benefit), because as mentioned many of them are effectively not participating in the labour force. Because of the deskilling and demotivation that has taken place, they need assistance with education and training, and because of demotivation and the indefinite nature of unemployment and related payments the search for jobs may not be as active as might be desired.

Active labour market policies can be classified into four categories: first, there are state employment services (e.g. placement and counselling); second, there is labour market training (i.e. for unemployed and employed adults); third, there are youth measures (e.g. remedial education, training or work experience for disadvantaged young people); and last, subsidised employment (i.e. subsidies to increase employment in the private sector, support for the unemployed persons starting their own enterprises and direct job creation in either the public or non-profit sector).

In the last decade or so many countries increased both the number and variety of instruments used to activate jobseekers. Job placement efforts have been enhanced, there is a greater emphasis on testing and monitoring work availability, there is earlier intervention in the unemployment spell and participation on programmes is compulsory and there is more efficient administration of public employment services. There is considerable evidence that these measures have made a significant impact on the numbers in long-term unemployment in several countries, including Ireland in the past. However, such measures are costly, and on-going evaluation of the cost-effectiveness of each programme needs to be undertaken.

The OECD in 2009 carried out a comprehensive evaluation of active labour market policies in Ireland.[14] The report was very critical of certain aspects of the unemployment service and also commented on the tendency for the implementation of administrative reforms to be slow. While dealing with the banking and fiscal deficit problems understandably took precedence in economic policy between 2008 and 2012, it is noteworthy that no serious action was taken until 2013 to deal with the long-term unemployment problem. The *Pathways to Work* initiative though has apparently transformed the Department of Social Protection in Ireland from a passive benefits provider to a public employment service that is now actively assisting job seekers to return to work. It may also be partly responsible for the more than halving of the long-term unemployment rate between 2012 and 2016 described earlier.

8 CONCLUSION

The outstanding economic policy failure in the last forty years in Ireland was the inability to increase employment in the 1980s, despite the huge increase in the potential labour force in this period. The result of this failure was a dramatic increase in the unemployment rate and emigration of almost 200,000 people. More seriously, perhaps, the sustained failure to increase employment meant not only that the high level of unemployment persisted into the mid 1990s, but also that an increasing proportion of that total drifted into long-term unemployment and, in many cases therefore, effectively left the labour market.

The outstanding policy success of the last forty years on the other hand, indeed of the whole post-Independence era, was the increase in employment between 1995 and 2006, which facilitated the corresponding huge reductions in unemployment and the dramatic switch from large scale emigration to significant immigration. In a very short period the disastrous failures of the 1980s had been turned around into one of the most remarkable success stories in terms of employment growth in the Western world.

The employment growth between 2004 and 2008 though was partly transitory, based as it was on unsustainable increases in building activity. Between 2008 and end 2010 all of the employment increases of this period had been reversed. The credit-based building boom could not be maintained and a large drop in employment in construction and related activities was inevitable; it was the speed and scale of the decline that surprised commentators most. Besides, since the early 2000s, Ireland steadily lost competitiveness, especially in terms of wage costs.[15] By 2008 this loss of competitiveness had become acute, especially in the context of Ireland being a member of the euro zone. Problems on this front, which had been disguised during the credit-fuelled boom between 2004 and 2008, came home to roost in 2009.

The boom in employment in the 1995 to 2008 period of course followed decades of failure to provide jobs for people in Ireland, the result being large-scale emigration in the 1950s and again in the 1980s. This resulted also in extraordinarily high unemployment levels in the decade 1985 to 1995. Potential labour supply had been increasing rapidly in Ireland from 1980 and a large employment increase was required to absorb this growth in supply; without it there was initially, and would have continued to have been, large-scale emigration and high levels of unemployment.

The country, in other words, for the first time in its history provided employment to those who needed it. This has been the norm in other small European countries such as Denmark, the Netherlands, and Norway for decades. Indeed, the unemployment rate in Ireland was in 2008 higher than in these three countries and the proportion of those of working age in employment in Ireland lags well behind that for these countries. Much progress has been made, but more has to be achieved and the failures of the past on the employment front must not be repeated.

That is the challenge that lies ahead. Employment levels are in 2017 back at pre-crisis peaks and hence the employment boom which took place between 1995 and 2008 has resumed, after a major downturn. The question is will it last.

The spectre of emigration still haunts the Irish psyche, and has done ever since Famine times. The costs of emigration now of course do not compare with then, or even the 1950s and 1980s, yet the question remains why can an independent state like Ireland not provide employment for its own nationals? It is true that emigration of Irish nationals continued during the period 1993 to 2004 and many returned with enhanced experience and skills. The scale of the out-migration of Irish nationals though increased substantially again between 2008 and 2012 and the worry is that the boom of the last four years may peter out and lead again to the resumption of large-scale emigration. Given its history, that is not for people in Ireland an unreasonable fear.

Endnotes

1   The OECD does outstanding research work in relation to data on employment, and related matters, and employment policies, both in general and by member country and this chapter draws extensively on such work. Its key publication is the annual,

Employment Outlook, which includes general chapters, detailed research reports, and detailed statistical tables.

2   S. Byrne and M. O'Brien, 'Understanding labour force participation', Research Technical Paper, 01/RT/2016, Central Bank of Ireland, Dublin 2016.

3   See http://ec.europa.eu/justice/gender-equality/gender-pay-gap/causes/index_en.htm for a review of the causes of the gender pay gap.

4   OECD, *Employment Outlook*, OECD, Paris 2009.

5   OECD, www.oecd.org/trade/benefitlib/, 2017.

6   For a review of the implications for employment of recent dramatic technological change, see 'Learning and earning' (Special Report), *Economist*, 14 January 2017.

7   Op cit.

8   Extensive work on various aspects of immigration in Ireland is undertaken at the ESRI. See for example publications at: www.esri.ie/publications/search_for_a_publication/search_results/index.xml?TopicSearch=9

9   See OECD, 'Skills use at work: why does it matter and what influences it?' *Employment Outlook*, OECD, Paris 2016.

10 R. Lydon and M. Lozej, 'Flexibility of new hires' earnings in Ireland', Research Technical Paper, 06/RT/2016, Central Bank of Ireland, Dublin 2016.

11 See OECD, 'Recent labour market developments with a focus on minimum wages', *Employment Outlook*, Paris 2015.

12 OECD, *Jobs Study: Part II*, OECD, Paris 1994, p.171.

13 A comprehensive review of these policies is contained in OECD, 'Activation policies for more inclusive labour markets', *Employment Outlook*, OECD, Paris 2015.

14 OECD, *Activation Policies in Ireland*, OECD Social, Employment and Migration Working Papers, *Employment Outlook*, OECD, Paris 2009.

15 O'Brien, D., 'Measuring Ireland's price and labour cost competitiveness', *Quarterly Bulletin*, Central Bank of Ireland, January 2010.

CHAPTER 7

Growth in Output and Living Standards

Michael Wycherley

1 INTRODUCTION

Thirty years ago Ireland was one of the poorest countries in Western Europe and showed little sign of catching up, indeed, the tendency since independence had been for average incomes in Ireland to fall relative to the rest of Western Europe. Employment had been reasonably stable at around 1.1 million since at least the 1940s despite population growth. Then in the twenty years after 1987 employment in Ireland almost doubled and output per person rose to a level amongst the highest in Europe. The past ten years has seen both employment and output per person fall back and then recover, with employment just over two million towards the end of 2016 and output per worker remaining above the Western European average.

This chapter will build on Chapter 1 in particular and attempt to explain this pattern of prolonged rapid growth (by European standards) followed by a significant stumble and subsequent recovery, and will seek to cast some light on the prospects for future income, output and living standards.

The basic story is that between about 1990 and 2000 Ireland experienced rapid growth driven by enduring improvements in productivity. After about 2000 growth remained high relative to other developed countries for a while but now it was increasingly driven largely by inward migration and the expansion of credit, particularly for construction. Growth based on ever higher debt proved unsustainable and from about 2007 the process of the previous seven years went into reverse as Ireland struggled to deal with the resulting debt burden. Growth resumed in about 2013 and long-run growth in the future seems likely to be much closer to that of other developed countries.

The measurement and comparison over time of output, incomes and living standards is not always straightforward, and Section 2 begins by discussing some of the issues involved and some ways of assessing these three different but related metrics. The section goes on to outline the position in the second half of the 1980s and how it changed over the subsequent thirty years (Chapter 1 provides a longer historical perspective). More detailed analysis of the sources of Irish economic growth is provided in Section 3, broken down into three sub-periods for quantitative analysis. Section 4 explains some of the factors behind the rapid Irish productivity growth between 1990 and 2000. The economic performance over the following sixteen years is addressed in Section 5, while Section 6 provides a brief outline of Ireland's future economic prospects and Section 7 concludes.

2 INCOME, OUTPUT AND LIVING STANDARDS

GDP and GNI per capita
The normal way to compare income and output across countries and across time is to look at Gross National Income (GNI) or Gross Domestic Product (GDP) per capita at constant prices and in purchasing power parity terms. Constant prices controls for variations in prices over time (e.g. due to inflation) and purchasing power parity controls for variations in prices and exchange rates across countries. GNI per capita is the value of the total domestic and foreign output claimed by residents of a country divided by the number of residents. GDP is the monetary value of all goods and services produced in a country in a given period. The difference between GNI and GDP is the value of goods and services produced in a country that accrue to foreign residents minus that produced outside the country that accrues to residents of the country. For example, profits from a factory owned by foreign residents will be included in GDP as they stem from domestic production, but will not be included in GNI as they accrue to foreign residents. For most countries the differences are relatively small and stable, and GDP is often preferred since it can be easier to measure. However, Ireland has relatively high levels of foreign investment and of profits reported by foreign owned firms (see Chapters 3 and 10) so that it has a large and varying gap between GDP and GNI, and hence both GDP and GNI will be provided for Ireland where possible and appropriate.

Figure 7.1 illustrates Ireland's relative economic performance in both GDP and GNI per capita. The comparison is with Denmark, as a similarly small open economy, the UK as its nearest neighbour, and with the EU-28 average included as well. The overall Irish story is similar whether GNI or GDP is used. By Western European standards, Ireland was a poor country in the 1980s but saw rapid growth from the late 1980s or early 1990s so that by the mid-2000s it was well above the EU average. Despite a fall back and recovery in the last ten years Ireland appears to have established a new equilibrium as one of the higher income EU countries. Irish GDP per capita rose from about the same as GNI per capita in 1980 to about 16 per cent higher in 2000 where it has roughly remained since. This increase reflects the growth in the importance of foreign firms and foreign investment to the Irish economy discussed earlier, which has made the estimation of domestic output increasingly difficult as multinationals headquartered in Ireland report significant profits and output here whilst employing relatively few people in Ireland. The sudden substantial swings, both up and down, in the

182

Figure 7.1 GDP or GNI Per Capita in Constant PPP

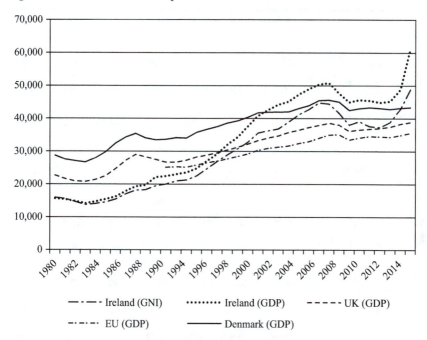

Source: *World Development Indicators* from the World Bank, http://data.worldbank.org/ data-catalog/world-development-indicator

economic activity that multinationals report as taking place in Ireland has further exacerbated the problem.

Other Measures of Well-Being

As the saying goes, there is more to life than money, and it follows that there are other indicators of living standards apart from average income. These are often correlated with average incomes, but there can be significant variations in the quality of life across countries with similar average income levels. This is because things like health, education and environmental conditions vary across countries for many different reasons. Table 7.1 provides a selection of quality of life indicators for Ireland and other countries (see also later chapters). There are a number of noticeable features, firstly the Irish quality of life appears to have improved on all of these dimensions, and secondly the numbers appear to indicate broadly similar standards of living across these countries, with the exception of India, a developing country. Hence it seems that average incomes may be a good proxy for living standards and confirming that Irish living standards have improved significantly.

The story so far has looked at per capita means rather than the distribution or the overall aggregate state of the economy. Chapter 8 looks at poverty and the distribution of income in more detail, and unsurprisingly absolute poverty has declined as average incomes have risen.

Table 7.1 Indicators of Quality of Life

	Ireland	UK	US	Denmark	EU	Spain	India
				1990			
Life expectancy	74.7	75.9	75.2	74.9	74.8	76.8	57.9
Internet Access per 100 people	0.0	0.087	0.785	0.069	0.097	0.013	0.0
Mobile phone subscription per 100 people	0.71	1.95	2.08	0.65	2.88	0.14	0.0
Fertility rate	2.11	1.83	2.08	1.66	1.67	1.36	4.04
Human Development Index	0.77	0.77	0.86	0.80	n.a.	0.76	0.43
				2011			
Life expectancy	80.7	81.0	78.6	80.3	79.8	82.5	66.5
Internet Access per 100 people	74.9	85.4	69.7	71.6	89.8	67.6	7.5
Mobile phone subscription per 100 people	108	124	94	121	129	113	62
Fertility rate	2.03	1.91	1.90	1.58	1.75	1.34	2.62
Human Development Index	0.909	0.901	0.911	0.92	n.a.	0.87	0.60

Sources: World Development Indicators from the World Bank, http://data.worldbank.org/data-catalog/world-development-indicators except for the HDI, which comes from the UN http://hdr.undp.org/en/content/human-development-index-hdi. The EU refers to EU28.

Aggregate Output

The large swings in Irish economic growth evident in Figure 7.1 indicates greater volatility in aggregate output in Ireland than in most other developed countries. This has posed a challenge for policymakers, although it's also possible that policy has contributed to this volatility. The surprisingly high volatility of Irish aggregate output has been associated with substantial changes in both per capita output and in the Irish labour force. The changes in the Irish labour force have been unusual, both compared to Irish history and to the changes in other European countries.

Irish demographic and employment changes are covered in more detail in Chapter 6, but a brief outline is provided here because of its relevance. The population of Ireland rose sharply between 1981 and 2011, going from 3.5 million to 4.6 million people. This was partly due to the natural increase from the high Irish fertility rate and a relatively young population, but it was also due to inward migration. During the 1980s there was net outward migration of almost 170,000 people, then during the 1990s there was net inward migration of 70,000 people followed by 400,000 in the 2000s.

The Irish labour force rose from 1.3 million in 1990 to 2.2 million in 2011, for three possibly interconnected reasons. First, there was the increase in the population, which all else being equal would be expected to increase the Irish labour force. Second, there was an increase in the proportion of the population of working age (i.e. between the ages of 15 and 64) from 61 per cent to 67 per cent. This was partly down to the age profile of immigrants, but also down to the ageing of the Irish population. Third, there was the increased participation of women in the labour force. The share of men between 15 and 64 participating in the labour force remained broadly stable at generally a little under 80 per cent. By comparison the share of women of this age in the labour force went from 42 per cent to 61 per cent over the period, and this change saw the labour force going from 34 per cent to 44 per cent female. The large increase in the labour force didn't lead to an increase in unemployment (although unemployment did vary over the period), and employment went from 1.2 million to 1.8 million and then increased further after 2011, passing 2.0 million in 2016.

The combination of rapid growth in both per capita income and population corresponded with a large increase in total output in Ireland. As Figure 7.2 shows this was not a smooth process, although a broad narrative can be provided. The second half of the 1980s saw the economy recovering from the recession of the early to mid 1980s before slowing down somewhat in the early 1990s. The mid 1990s saw an acceleration in growth that slowed around 2001 before picking up again and then declining dramatically from 2007 with an economic recovery

Figure 7.2 Irish Annual Growth Rate (%)

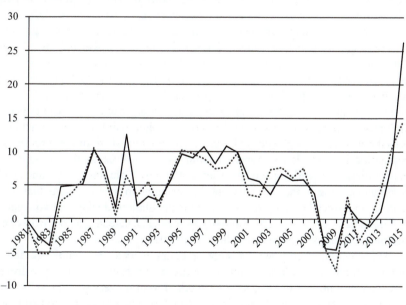

Source: World Development Indicators from the World Bank, http://data.worldbank.org/data-catalog/world-development-indicators

beginning around 2013. Very high growth in 2015 (over 20 per cent growth in GDP in the first quarter) was largely down to accounting changes which changed the reported geographic ownership of various multinational activities rather than any change in the economic activity occurring in Ireland. However, quarterly GDP and employment data makes clear that Ireland was indeed seeing a strong recovery over the years 2014 to 2016.

The average Irish annual growth rates between 1991 and 2015 of 5.0 per cent (GNI) or 5.5 per cent (GDP) compare very favourably with most developed countries. The EU saw GDP growth of 2.6 per cent, the UK and the US did slightly better with growth of 2.8 per cent and 2.7 per cent, respectively, partly because 1991 was the trough of a recession for both of these countries, with output low relative to potential. The Irish growth rate was most comparable to that of the East Asian "tiger" economies of Vietnam (6.9 per cent), Thailand (4.0 per cent), South Korea (4.8 per cent), Singapore (4.9 per cent), the Philippines (4.4 per cent) and Malaysia (5.6 per cent). This is especially true if comparing growth between 1991 and 2006, which saw Irish economic growth of 6.9 per cent and led to the Irish economy being dubbed the 'Celtic Tiger'.

Decomposing Growth in GNI per Person

Table 7.2 illustrates the contribution of changes in the labour supply to the growth in Irish GNI. The breakdown into three periods of before 2000, 2000 to 2007 and after 2007 is indicative rather than precise as things don't generally change abruptly when going from one period to the next. The choice of 2000 in particular is somewhat arbitrary as the ending of the first Celtic tiger period has been variously dated. However, it is clear that there were two periods with different sources of growth.

The second column of Table 7.2 gives the annual growth rate of GNI, the third column the annual growth rate of population. Subtracting one from the other gives the fourth column, the growth rate of GNI per capita. GNI per capita can rise because output per hour worked goes up (column five) or because the total number of hours worked per capita goes up. Hours worked per capita can go up because hours worked per worker go up (column six), a higher fraction of the labour force is employed (column seven), a larger share of the working age population is in the labour force (column eight), or because the proportion of the population of working age has risen (column 9). Columns five to nine can be combined as long as they are adjacent. For example to see the change that is due to the labour force being a larger share of the population add the last two columns (0.8 per cent in 1991 to 2015). Similarly to see the change in GNI per worker add columns five and six (2.7 per cent in 1991 to 2015).

As economic theory would suggest hours worked per employee fell as incomes went up. Aside from this there are a few features specific to Ireland that are worth noting. Output per hour worked went up very sharply in the early Celtic tiger period but the decline in the growth rate between 2000 and 2007 was masked by the increase in the labour force. After 2007 the labour force declined, both in absolute terms and as a percentage of the population, which exacerbated

Table 7.2 Labour Force Participation, Hours Worked and GNI per capita

Dates (1)	GNI (2)	Population (3)	$\dfrac{GNI}{Population}$ (4)	$\dfrac{GNI}{Population} = \dfrac{GNI}{hours}+$ (4)	(5)
1991–2015	5.0	1.1	3.8	3.8	3.6
1991–2000	7.5	0.8	6.6	6.6	4.3
2000–2007	5.4	2.1	3.2	3.2	2.4
2007–2015	1.9	0.7	1.2	1.2	3.9

	$\dfrac{hours}{worker}+$ (6)	$\dfrac{worker}{labour\ force}+$ (7)	$\dfrac{labour\ force}{adults\ 15\text{–}64}+$ (8)	$\dfrac{adults\ 15\text{–}64}{population}$ (9)
1991–2015	−0.9	0.3	0.6	0.2
1991–2000	−1.3	1.4	1.1	1.0
2000–2007	−0.5	−0.1	1.2	0.2
2007–2015	−0.9	−0.6	−0.4	−0.7

Source: GNI and population from World Bank *World Development Indicators,* http://data.worldbank.org/data-catalog/world-development-indicators. Hours per employee, employment, and labour force from the OECD, www.oecd.org/std/labour-stats/

the effect on output of a lower share of the labour force being employed, despite possibly reducing the increase in unemployment. The apparently rapid increase in GNI/hour after 2007 is largely due to very high growth in 2014 and 2015, as over the period 2007 to 2013 the growth rate of GNI per hour was slightly less than in 2000 to 2007. The sources of growth will be examined further in the next section.

3 EXPLAINING ECONOMIC GROWTH

The previous section described Irish economic growth over the last thirty years, however there was very little attempt to explain the sources of this growth. What was behind Irish economic growth between 1991 and 2000 and why a slowdown was inevitable will be addressed in this section.

Table 7.2 shows that understanding changes in output per hour worked is important for understanding Irish economic performance and a basic question is how much of these changes are due to workers using more machinery or other factors of production and how much is due to a more efficient use of existing factors of production. To address this question we need to impose more structure on the data. If the supply of all factors of production went up by ten per cent we might expect output to rise by ten per cent, but the supply of factors of production usually change by different amounts. If the skill level of the work force goes up by five per cent and the quantity of machinery goes up by ten per cent how much should we expect output to rise? Obviously this depends on the importance of each of these factors in the production process, and to approximate this economists typically use a production function, which tells us how much output we should expect for given quantities of each factor of production.

The problem of estimating the impact of changes in factor supply is made worse by changes in output without any apparent change in the use of factors of production. Increases in output without any change in inputs are typically seen as improvements in what is called Total Factor Productivity (TFP). TFP is an estimate of how efficiently factors of productivity are used, and cannot be directly measured. Instead TFP is obtained as a residual from the production function. If our data tells us that the workers are five per cent more highly skilled, ten per cent more machinery is employed and output is eight per cent higher, and our production function tells us that these changes in skills and machinery should imply six per cent higher output, then the remaining two per cent higher output is attributed to TFP. Therefore estimates of TFP depend significantly on the exact production function employed.

To complete our understanding of the sources of economic growth we need not just a production function, but also an explanation for the supply of the factors of production. Combining these two features gives us a model of the economy that we can use to explore the sources of economic growth.

Solow Model

The workhorse model of economic growth was developed in the 1950s by Nobel Prize winning economist Robert Solow. It has remained in use because it clearly answers two important questions, at least given certain assumptions. The first question the model addresses is whether growth comes from accumulating machinery or from improvements in productivity. It demonstrates that, given a production function with a diminishing marginal product of the reproducible factors, long run growth in per capita income is caused by improvements in TFP, not to simply using more of the reproducible factors. For example, if doubling the amount of machinery per worker doesn't double output per worker then long run growth cannot be due to more investment in machinery but must be due to more efficient use of machinery. This is because if each extra unit of machinery increases output by a little bit less than the previous unit, then eventually so much machinery is accumulated that the final extra unit of machinery produces just enough extra output to replace itself when it wears out. This implies there is an upper limit to the amount of machinery that can be employed in the long run without improvements in efficiency; so long-run growth cannot be driven by investment in machinery, unlike short-run growth.

An example of this might be increasing the number of tractors owned by a farmer without increasing the number of workers. The first few tractors might increase output substantially, but eventually no more tractors can be employed simultaneously due to shortages of drivers or land and any extra tractors are only occasionally used to cover maintenance and repairs. Each extra tractor increases annual output but by progressively less. Eventually, as the number of tractors increases, any extra tractors are hardly used at all and end up rusting away as it's not worth the cost of maintaining them. So output per worker cannot grow indefinitely through buying more tractors. However, improvements in the quality of tractors, for example through greater reliability or new uses for tractors, allows output to be higher without needing extra tractors.

The savings rate and rate of change of the work force affect the income level for a given level of TFP but once steady state is achieved they don't affect the growth rate as this is driven by the growth in TFP. A higher savings rate implies more capital and so higher income for a given level of TFP. For example, if a farmer reinvests a higher fraction of his or her revenue into tractors rather than buying convertibles this will imply a larger number of tractors for a given level of technology, and so higher output, but not permanently higher growth in output. A higher rate of increase in the workforce tends to reduce the level of output for a given level of TFP. This is because more of the investment is used to equip the new workers with the same amount of capital as existing workers rather than to add to the capital stock per worker or replace worn out capital.

The second question that the Solow model can answer is whether we should expect poor countries to grow more quickly and converge to the income levels of rich countries. The answer that it provides is that it depends. Countries that are poor relative to their savings rates, levels of TFP and population growth rates should grow more quickly than countries that are rich relative to their levels of these things. However, as savings rates, levels of TFP and population growth rates vary across countries it is not necessarily the case that poor countries in general grow more quickly than rich ones. In economists' terminology, the Solow model predicts conditional convergence, it does not predict absolute convergence, and this prediction appears to match the empirical evidence.

The simplest version of the model assumes that the labour force, employment and hours worked are given exogenously and that the economy is closed, i.e. that investment comes only from domestic savings and not from overseas. Both of these may have been approximately true for countries such as the US in the past, but they are much more debatable assumptions for Ireland, as the data in Table 7.2 illustrates for the labour input. However, although relaxing these assumptions complicates the model it does not change the basic results.

Since all the interesting results are derived in terms of units per worker and there are no economies of scale it follows that varying the number of workers does not change the result that a steady state level of capital per worker exists, so that long-run growth in output and consumption per worker continues to be driven by changes in TFP. Similarly, changes in the rate of population growth do not change the result that countries which are poor relative to their steady state should grow more quickly, although different rates of population growth can affect the steady state level.

Similarly, allowing foreign investment does not change the result that long-run growth is caused by productivity growth or that countries which are poor relative to their steady state should grow more quickly. What allowing foreign investment does is to increase the speed of convergence, as countries can now borrow from abroad to increase the capital stock rather than having to rely on domestic savings.

An open economy also possibly changes the steady-state capital stock through investment being disconnected from domestic savings. Investment occurs where the rate of return is highest, not where the savings rate is highest, so the effect of opening the economy could be to increase or decrease the capital stock.

With a closed economy the relatively fast population growth in Ireland would imply relatively low capital per worker, as the limited pool of investment is aimed at equipping the extra workers rather than adding to the capital available to existing workers. For a small open economy such as Ireland, the pool of investment is effectively limited only by its ability to earn a return similar to that available in other countries so output per worker is less related to population growth and Ireland is likely to have higher average incomes than if the economy were closed to foreign investment.

Having established a framework for analysis we can now address some questions about Ireland's economic growth. What were the sources of Irish economic growth, how far was Ireland's rapid growth simply down to starting from a low base and what are the prospects for the future?

Proximate Sources of Irish Economic Growth

The Solow model makes clear that, in the long run, growth is due to improvements in TFP but that in the short run growth can occur through the accumulation of capital. Table 7.3 shows the growth of GDP as well as the measurable inputs into production (the capital stock and hours worked). The table uses a standard production function[1] to calculate the improvement in TFP needed for the level of GDP in each period to be produced with the amount of capital and labour employed. The second part of the table uses the same production function to examine how much of GDP growth was due to changes in each of the capital

Table 7.3 Sources of Growth

	Growth of				% of GDP growth due to		
	GDP	TFP	Capital	hours worked	TFP	Capital	hours worked
1990–2015	130	85	83	29	64	21	15
1990–2000	69	44	33	25	60	16	24
2000–2007	36	10	39	20	27	36	37
2007–2015	24	31	11	−16	128	15	−43

Sources: GDP and Capital Stock from DG ECFIN AMECO. Hours from *OECD Economic Outlook.*

stock, hours worked, and TFP.[2] For example, the capital stock grew by 83 per cent between 1990 and 2015, and this lead directly to 21 per cent of GDP growth over the period, which was 130 per cent. So, if TFP and hours worked had seen zero growth, while the capital stock had grown by 83 per cent then GDP would have grown by 27 per cent, which is 21 per cent of 130 per cent.

GDP at constant prices more than doubled between 1990 and 2015, and over 60 per cent of this was directly due to improvements in productivity as captured by TFP. It is important to keep in mind that, while 36 per cent of growth was due to increases in the capital stock and total hours worked, at least some of these increases were due to higher productivity leading to higher wages and return on capital. As the Solow model makes clear, long-run growth in per capita output is due to productivity change, which in turn causes more investment and possibly immigration.

Also noticeable from Table 7.3 is that 1990 to 2000 saw higher annual growth than 2000 to 2007 and more of this was due to productivity improvements. In 2000 to 2007 growth fell and productivity growth was less than half as important in explaining GDP growth. In other words there appears to be two different Celtic tiger periods. Between 1990 and 2000 Ireland saw high growth driven largely by productivity improvements, from 2000 to 2007 growth was lower and was driven much more by simple factor accumulation. The second Celtic tiger period ended around 2007 after which growth fell further due to a decline in total hours worked and less investment. Annual productivity growth after 2007 averaged about the same as during the latter stages of the Celtic tiger, although a closer examination shows a decline over 2007 to 2009 and then a recovery.

The Solow model predicts faster growth by countries that have relatively little capital, while leaving productivity growth unexplained. The importance of productivity change in explaining Irish economic growth during the first Celtic tiger period suggests that this wasn't a simple case of conditional convergence as might be implied by the Solow model. This is supported by the observation that Irish GDP per capita had shown no sign of converging to UK levels before the late 1980s, remaining stable at around 65 per cent of the UK level from the late 1960s. However, the speed with which capital, labour and output grew once productivity growth had accelerated can be explained by a straightforward extension of the Solow model that allows capital and labour to move across countries in response to changes in their rates of return.

What appears to have driven Irish economic growth in the period 1990 to 2000 was a process of convergence in productivity and it is to the drivers of this that we turn next.

4 IRISH PRODUCTIVITY SUCCESS: 1990 to 2000

The rapid growth that Ireland experienced between 1990 and 2000 was largely due to total factor productivity growth. Growth in the labour supply and the capital stock also contributed, but improvements in productivity were a significant cause of higher investment and employment.

There is a large literature on the sources of productivity growth, but to summarise very briefly, productivity growth depends on the development of better products or more efficient ways of producing existing products. Both of these depend upon the generation of new ideas and then the integration of these ideas into the economy. The ideas can be new to the world or just the local economy, having been developed elsewhere and then adapted to local conditions. This ability to adapt ideas first created elsewhere implies that there ought to be some sort of conditional convergence in productivity. Countries that are surprisingly far below the world productivity frontier should find it easier to improve their productivity by adapting ideas in use elsewhere than countries which are at the frontier and so have to develop new ideas. Conditional rather than absolute convergence is implied because countries will differ in their ability and incentives to develop or adopt ideas.

There are many factors that influence the development of new or better ideas, what follows is a non-exhaustive discussion of some of the factors that have been important for Ireland.

Education
A more highly skilled workforce would be expected to be more productive and may well be better at innovation, so the development of the Irish education and training system is likely to be important. Irish education is examined in greater detail in Chapter 14, but a brief overview of the particularly relevant features is given here. Ireland introduced universal secondary education only in 1968, which was late by Western European standards. This took time to have much impact on the labour force, and for a long time older workers weren't particularly well educated by European standards. Coupled with the steady rise in third-level attendance from around the same date and the relatively young population, by the late 1980s Ireland had an increasingly well-educated population. Comparing Ireland with the UK, in the 1980s and 1990s Irish adults typically had around 10 years of education compared with an average of about 9 years in the UK, although the gap has subsequently closed. It's interesting to note that Irish women have typically been more highly educated than Irish men, so the increase in female labour force participation has tended to further increase the average education level of the workforce.

The current Irish school system provides good if not great outcomes, with standardised tests of 15–16 year olds administered by the OECD producing scores of 523 in reading literacy (compared to an OECD average of 496), 522 in science (501) and 501 in maths (494). As in many countries third-level enrolment has risen, with the share of the labour force with third level education going from around 20 per cent in the early 1990s to around 40 per cent in 2014, numbers that are similar to those of the UK.

Unfortunately the links between education and income and between education and growth are not straightforward, so it is difficult to quantify the importance of education to Irish economic performance. However, it seems likely that educational change contributed to Ireland's productivity convergence, but that further substantial improvements will be hard to achieve.

Research and Development

An obvious measure of the inputs into the creation of new products and processes might be research and development spending or the number of people engaged in research. However, the link between the inputs into research and research output is not straightforward. Furthermore, the link between scientific discoveries and economic growth is also not a direct one, with discoveries taking time to introduce to the market and this not necessarily being accomplished by the countries doing the original research. This is particularly true in a small open economy, which can benefit substantially from research done elsewhere without necessarily being able to contribute much in absolute terms to the global technology frontier except occasionally in specialised areas.

Nevertheless the evidence is that Irish research and development expenditure as a fraction of GDP roughly doubled over the 1980s and 1990s, which given the growth in Irish GDP implies very rapid growth in the expenditure on research. Similarly, the number of researchers employed in Ireland as a proportion of the population tripled over the period. This was accompanied by a more than doubling of the number of Irish patent applications. The evidence on Irish research and development expenditure in particular must be treated with caution given the importance of multinationals and the issues with correctly valuing their activities in different jurisdictions. The issue of correctly valuing the activities undertaken by multinationals in Ireland is a general one that has been referred to before and in other chapters. It is particularly acute when the activity is intangible and the revenues are in the form of delayed royalty payments as it is difficult to prove that the key breakthrough that generated the payments didn't occur where the tax on these payments is lowest.[3]

So there is evidence of a significant increase in the amount of research and development undertaken in Ireland, which probably both contributed to and reflected the increasingly high productivity and high technology nature of the Irish economy. However it is hard to quantify the contribution of this to Irish economic growth, and Ireland continued to spend less than the EU average on research and development, even given the small size of the Irish economy.

Competition

Productivity growth requires more than just the development of new products and processes, it needs them to be introduced to and disseminated through the economy. There is evidence that competition amongst firms is essential to this process. If firms have a guaranteed market then there are only limited incentives for them to become more efficient or to introduce better products. In addition, having a variety of firms in the market allows for a range of products and processes, with competition amongst firms allowing the most efficient to grow and prosper whilst the least efficient struggle, giving rise to what is sometimes called creative destruction.

Chapter 5 examines Irish regulation and competition policy in more detail but it seems clear that the late 1950s to at least the early 1990s saw an increase in the degree of competition in the Irish economy. The increasingly outward orientation of the Irish economy contributed to this as Ireland successively abandoned protectionism, joined the EEC, saw the introduction of the European Single Market and benefited from technological and institutional changes making it easier and cheaper to move goods around the world.

Foreign Investment
The Industrial Development Authority was set up in 1949 and soon focused on attracting foreign direct investment. Historical, cultural and linguistic ties to the USA probably helped Ireland attract investment from there, and this became increasingly valuable as changes in transport and communications made it easier to manage operations abroad, leading to an expansion of foreign direct investment around the world. Simultaneously the coming of the European Single Market in the early 1990s led many non-European firms to set up facilities in Europe and Ireland was an obvious destination for USA firms.

Underlying the encouragement of foreign rather than domestic investment is the belief that foreign investment comes with productivity benefits. Multinational firms tend to be more productive than purely domestic firms, and Irish productivity lagged behind that of countries such as the USA and the UK. If foreign firms established themselves in Ireland then Irish productivity should increase, and hopefully this would spill over to domestic firms. These spillovers could occur through greater competition but also by observation of the methods of the foreign firms, the training they provide to workers or by the impact on the suppliers or customers of the multinational. Chapter 10 looks in more detail at foreign direct investment into Ireland and the available evidence is that it did indeed increase the productivity of the manufacturing sector and that spillover effects have benefited Irish firms.

Role of the State
The government sector in Ireland is small by Western European standards and this enables relatively low marginal tax rates, particularly on corporate income and profits, encouraging foreign investment. The small government sector was made easier by the small military budget and relatively young population (see Chapter 3).

It is possible to point to 1987 as a turning point in the role and size of the state. The government promised lower taxes if wages and industrial disputes were restrained, which differed sharply from the European norm where governments typically promised higher social insurance benefits in return for wage restraint. This created a dynamic where there was a small state sector, relatively few public sector workers and only limited support for raising taxes. The importance of national wage agreements can be overstated though; labour unrest abated in most of Western Europe at this time and actual wage increases bore little relation to those in the national agreements.

At the same time as the state sector was being constrained, taxes and welfare payments were being reformed. The goal was to ensure that people would be better off in employment than relying on state benefits and this has mostly, if not entirely, been achieved.

The increasing involvement of EU institutions in the Irish economy may have also had an effect by spreading good practice and encouraging more careful policymaking through the need to explain decisions to outsiders.

Summary

During the 1990s Ireland moved from having GDP and GNI per capita below the EU and UK to well above these levels. This was driven largely by improvements in productivity. It is hard to be precise about why this happened, but perhaps a better question is why Irish productivity only started converging to the Western European average from around 1990.

It seems likely that there was a happy confluence of events. Changes to the global economy sometimes referred to as globalisation and the Information Technology revolution were underway. The reduction in the importance of distance and increase in the importance of education these entailed would particularly suit small, open, highly educated countries. Reforms of the Irish economy both then and some decades earlier were starting to have an effect and meant that Ireland was particularly suited to the coming global changes. At the same time Ireland had cultural, linguistic and personal links with the USA, which made it a natural destination for USA investment in Europe, especially given Irish membership of the euro. International direct investment into Ireland raised Irish wages and productivity and spilled over into local firms, enabling Ireland to rapidly close the productivity gap.

5 BOOM, BUST AND RECOVERY: 2000 TO 2016

Labour Market

After 2000 Ireland saw a decline in economic growth (Figure 7.2) and a shift in the sources of growth, with improvements in productivity being much less important than before (Table 7.3). This should not be surprising, Ireland had caught up with the Western European average so there was less scope for productivity improvements through copying what was being done elsewhere. What is surprising is the very rapid (by Western European standards) increase in population and total hours worked between 2000 and 2007 (Table 7.2).

Historically the Irish labour market is unusual in the extent to which labour mobility in and out of the country was legally possible and culturally accepted. Even when the goods market was relatively closed (before about 1960) Ireland had been part of a wider labour market with the UK. The size of the Irish labour force and the level of Irish wages and unemployment have tended to respond to events in the UK economy. For example, when UK demand for labour increased workers moved from Ireland to the UK, reducing Irish unemployment and putting upward pressure on wages in Ireland. The responsiveness of the Irish labour supply to changes in the demand for labour from outside the country was unusual and got stronger as travel costs fell and the education level (and so wages) of Irish migrants rose.

Chapter 6 looks at the Irish labour market and the role of migration in more detail, but it is clear that the improvement in Irish productivity lead to an increase in the demand for labour in Ireland, which lead to an inflow of migrants to Ireland along with the return of some previous Irish emigrants. The accession to the EU of a number of relatively poor Eastern European countries in 2004 reinforced this process, especially as many other EU countries imposed temporary restrictions on migration from the new members.

Property Sector
After about 2000 the change in the sources of growth from productivity improvements to increases in the workforce was accompanied by a change in the sectors that were seeing growth. Increasing incomes lead to higher domestic demand for both tradeable and non-tradeable goods and upward pressure on prices. The introduction of the euro in 1999 meant that the nominal exchange rate was fixed, so when higher domestic demand led to higher domestic prices Irish producers of tradeables were less able to compete with foreign firms. With the growth in productivity slowing, the higher domestic demand resulted in a shift in output towards the non-tradeable sector, particularly construction (Figure 7.3), with demand for tradeable goods being increasingly met by imports.

Figure 7.3 Irish Construction Industry (thousands)

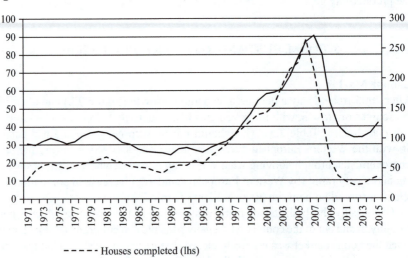

- - - - - Houses completed (lhs)

———— Employment in building and construction (rhs)

Sources: Houses completed from the Department of the Environment, Heritage & Local Government, Ireland. Employment from DG ECFIN AMECO, https://ec.europa.eu/info/business-economy-euro/indicators-statistics/economic-databases/macro-economic-database-ameco_en and *OECD Economic Outlook*, various issues.

The property sector is explored in more detail in Chapter 12, but it is important to discuss the impact the sector had on the rest of the economy here. Growing Irish prosperity in the 1990s had led to rapidly rising house prices by the end of the decade as can be seen in Figure 7.4. Nominal house price inflation is the change in the price of the average house, whilst real house price inflation is how much higher house price inflation is than overall inflation. Rising property prices lead to a positive wealth effect and a rise in government revenue through asset price related taxes such as stamp duty. These led in turn to higher private consumption and government spending.[4]

Figure 7.4 Irish House Price Inflation (%)

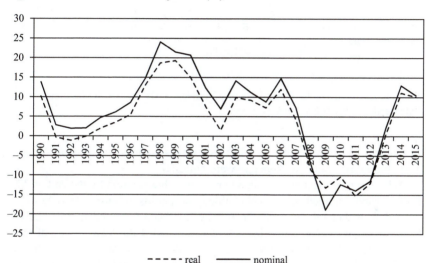

- - - - - real   ———— nominal

Sources: Derived from tables in *Oxford Economics,* www.oxfordeconomics.com/

Credit Market

The rapid growth in the property sector was partly because property was seen as an investment good as well as a consumption one, so people were willing to borrow to finance house purchases to an extent that they might be reluctant to for other goods, especially as house prices were increasing rapidly. Rapid credit growth fuelled the expansion in private consumption and property investment, especially from 2003 (Figure 7.5), much of which was provided by local banks. The simultaneous decline in the current account balance reflected Irish borrowing from abroad as Irish banks increasingly relied on international wholesale markets for funding, with a mix of short-term interbank funds and international bond issues. This was made easier by the reduction in exchange rate risk that accompanied the euro. The introduction of the euro also meant that Ireland had given up its monetary policy and the Irish Central Bank could not increase interest rates

Figure 7.5 Irish Credit Growth

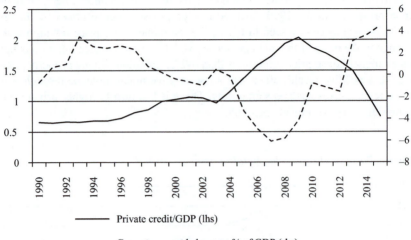

———— Private credit/GDP (lhs)

- - - - - Current account balance as % of GDP (rhs)

Sources: Credit from the Central Bank of Ireland. GDP from CSO. Current Account Balance from *OECD Economic Outlook.*

in response to rising borrowing and house prices, although other tools remained available to Irish policymakers and were not used.

With hindsight Ireland was in a very vulnerable position by the end of 2006. Rapid growth in asset prices had enabled households to borrow heavily against the value of those assets. This borrowing had been intermediated by the Irish banking sector, which would be left very exposed if the loans were not repaid and the assets the loans were secured against declined in value. The government finances looked in good shape, with a budget surplus equivalent to nearly three per cent of GDP and a gross debt to GDP ratio of only 24 per cent in 2006. However, tax revenue was very dependent on high asset prices through an excessive reliance on stamp duty and taxes on corporate profits. The imbalances had emerged very quickly, as in early 2003 the Irish economy had been in reasonable shape. It is possible that the run up to the general election in the middle of 2007 may have inhibited measures to slow economic growth down, but it is important to remember that economic statistics are only available with a lag, sometimes a substantial one. The speed with which imbalances can build up and the greater difficulties in dealing with imbalances when in a monetary union implies that there should be a stronger precautionary motive in Irish government policy than has been evident in the past.[5]

Banking Sector
In any case, by late 2007 growth was slowing and the debate was whether or not Ireland would be able to achieve a so-called 'soft landing'. By late 2008 there

was increasing evidence that a range of risks around the world had been underestimated and the growth in securitisation made it difficult to know which financial institutions were carrying this risk on their balance sheets. When Lehman Brothers, the fourth largest USA investment bank, went bust banks became much less willing to lend to each other as they were not sure of getting their money back. This affected all financial institutions, but particularly those, such as the Irish ones, that were dependent on short-term wholesale funding.

Governments around the world then faced the classic bank-run question of how to distinguish between banks that were unable to borrow because they were insolvent and banks that were only in trouble because they were unable to borrow. Alongside this was the question of which banks were systemically important enough to be worth rescuing. The idea of systemic importance is that there are some financial institutions that are important enough to the financial system and/ or the rest of the economy that they are worth saving because of their size or interconnectedness. Unfortunately, it is impossible to be sure which institutions are truly systemically important without observing what happens if they fail, and then it is too late, so central banks and financial regulators tend to play it safe when deciding which institutions to rescue, which was another reason the failure of Lehman Brothers was such a shock.

Under the apparent belief that the Irish banking system was in trouble due to the withdrawal of access to wholesale funding rather than because it had made large quantities of loans that would become non-performing as the Irish economy slowed down, in September 2008 the Irish government issued a guarantee of the liabilities of the Irish banks. However, after the guarantee was issued it rapidly became clear that the Irish banks faced solvency rather than the assumed liquidity problems, which would mean the Irish government would need to pay substantial amounts of money to the banks' creditors. How substantial only gradually became clear, and as it did so it became apparent that it was more than the Irish government could afford, and in November 2010 the Irish government had to turn to the EU, other European countries and the IMF for emergency funding via 'the bailout'.

From 2007 the Irish economy contracted sharply (Figure 7.2), as the forces that had driven the growth of the previous four years went into reverse. House prices fell, and people attempted to repay old debt rather than taking on new debt. The decline in domestic spending by households and government as revenues and wealth fell lead to lower demand for non-tradeables, again especially housing. The global recession further reduced the demand for tradeables, making it difficult for Ireland to employ the resources freed up by the shrinking of the non-tradeable sector. Irish unemployment rose and there was renewed emigration from Ireland (see Chapter 6), further shrinking the potential tax base.

It is clear that Irish government finances would have been in trouble even without the banking crisis due to their dependence on taxes linked to asset prices. As Irish economic growth and house price inflation slowed the government finances would have plunged heavily into the red (needing to borrow over ten per cent of

GDP in some years even excluding the money going to the banks). Whether this would have been enough to require a bailout without the banking crisis is unclear. On the other hand, the alternative to some form of bank guarantee would have been the collapse of the banking system, inevitably implying an even worse recession and almost certain state bankruptcy. The policy debate is largely about what should have been done over the period 2003 to 2008 and whether the objectives of the bank guarantee and the bailout could have been accomplished at lower cost. This is a study of Irish long-run growth and not the place for a detailed analysis of these other important issues.

Recovery from 2013

By 2013 the global economy was recovering and Irish debt (both household and government) seemed to be under control and the Irish economy began growing again.[6] Ireland remained throughout the downturn a relatively high income area of the EU (as measured by GDP or GNI per capita), although there have been distributional effects (see Chapter 8).

To provide some context for the Irish experience over the past ten years Figure 7.6 shows the path of output relative to the level of 2007 for a number of European countries. Ireland saw earlier and sharper falls in output but also an earlier stabilisation and a quicker recovery. The very strong Irish growth in 2015 is an indicator of how difficult it can be to interpret economic data in a small open

Figure 7.6 Output at Constant Prices, 2007–2016 (2007=100)

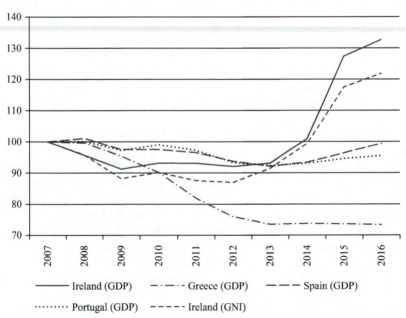

Source: DG ECFIN AMECO, https://ec.europa.eu/info/business-economy-euro/indicators-statistics/economic-databases/macro-economic-database-ameco_en

economy as this was largely due to accounting changes by large multinationals. However the growth was also partly due to a genuine increase in Irish output as unemployment fell from 14.7 per cent in 2011 and 2012 to 11.3 per cent in 2014, 9.4 per cent in 2015 and 8.3 per cent in 2016.[7] Employment tends to lag output, as firms do not immediately sack workers the moment demand declines, and similarly they do not immediately hire new workers when demand increases. In 2015 and 2016 this led to something of a disconnect between some policymakers and commentators who were proclaiming recovery based on GDP figures, and households who were seeing only limited improvements in employment and indebtedness.

The slowdown in Ireland was largely due to a collapse in domestic demand as Figure 7.7 makes clear. The decline in Irish domestic demand as people sought to reduce their borrowing was larger than the decline in output, with resources being transferred back from the non-tradeable sector into the tradeable sector, leading to an increase in exports despite the slowdown in global demand.

Figure 7.7 Irish Recovery and the Sources of Demand

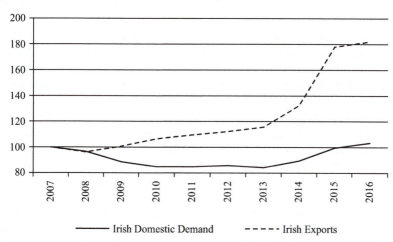

Source: Constructed from data at DG ECFIN AMECO, https://ec.europa.eu/info/business-economy-euro/indicators-statistics/economic-databases/macro-economic-database-ameco_en

In some ways the relatively rapid Irish recovery is not surprising. The crisis was caused by the rapid growth of imbalances in the economy, and given the speed with which the economy had shifted towards non-tradeables, a rapid shift back towards tradeables as incentives changed was perhaps to be expected. The legacy of the pre-crisis period is likely to remain with Ireland for some time, however, particularly in the levels of debt built up by households and the government, the damage done to the banking system and the destabilisation of Irish politics both by the mistakes made before the crisis and by perceptions that the crisis was not handled 'fairly'.

6 CONCLUDING COMMENTS

As the events of 2003 to 2008 demonstrate, poor policy choices can do a sur-prising amount of damage in a very short period of time, and there have been significant attempts to improve policymaking. These have included institutional changes such as the setting up of the Irish Fiscal Council, recruiting additional expertise into bodies such as the civil service and the Irish Central Bank, as well as increased outside scrutiny of policy through various EU bodies (see Chapters 2 and 3 for more detail). Improved policymaking does not automatically follow from more informed advice, but it is to be hoped that recent events make policy-makers more aware of, and cautious about, the downside risk of policies.

In general, the growing importance of large multinational firms for the Irish economy has made the interpretation of Irish economic data increasingly difficult. Quite small accounting changes in how multinationals allocate assets, revenues and particularly profits can have large effects on the data reported for the Irish economy without any change in the underlying activities. This in turn consid-erably complicates the task of policymakers, both in interpreting what the data means about the state of the economy and in predicting what the impacts of pol-icies might be.

As a small open economy, operating reasonably close to the world productivity frontier, Ireland's economic prospects depend to a very large extent on what hap-pens in the global economy in general and the European economy in particular. Given that Ireland is above the Western European norm for output per hour worked it is unlikely to see prolonged periods with higher economic growth than the West-ern European norm such as it saw in the 1990s. Therefore, improvements in aver-age incomes in Ireland depend firstly on global productivity growth and secondly on whether Ireland can close the remaining gap to the world productivity frontier.

Historically productivity growth amongst developed countries over the past 50 or more years has been sufficient to sustain annual income growth of around 2.5 per cent, implying a doubling of output per capita every 30 years. However, there are a number of economists who doubt growth will continue at this rate into the future. The secular-stagnation hypothesis is that many of the productiv-ity improving aspects of modern technology are already nearly fully exploited, and that further improvements in, for example, education, medicine or computing may affect living standards, but will have relatively little effect on output. Need-less to say this is controversial as only time will tell, and in any case is out of Ireland's control.

Also largely outside Ireland's control is the possibility of globalisation going at least partially into reverse. It is certainly possible that the UK leaving the EU and the election of a USA president apparently less favourably disposed to free trade could significantly raise trade barriers with some of Ireland's most impor-tant trading partners. As a small open economy Ireland is particularly vulnerable to changes in the global trading environment, particularly as it does not have its own exchange rate as a means of adjustment.

What is more under Ireland's control is its proximity to the world productivity frontier, and there are a number of policy areas of relevance. Firstly, Ireland is emerging from the recession with a high public debt to GDP ratio (about 90 per cent in 2016), and this may act as a brake on public investment in education and infrastructure for some time, with infrastructure a particular concern in the 2016 World Economic Forum competitiveness report. The impact of high debt levels may be exacerbated by new rules on tax competition, reducing Ireland's ability to raise revenue from multinationals. Secondly, while the Irish education system is above the OECD average as measured by the performance of 15 year olds in standardised tests, it is some way behind countries such as Finland, and there is evidence from surveys of Irish adults that the tests overstate Irish adult skills. Thirdly, while the encouragement of productivity improvement through FDI was effective when Ireland was a laggard, there now appears to be a weakness in that most innovative activities take place in multinationals rather than domestic firms. This weakness is recognised and has led to a variety of programmes to encourage innovation in small and medium sized enterprises but there is limited evidence yet on how successful they have been. Finally, while Ireland has become a good place to do business according to international surveys, with encouragingly low scores on product market regulation, employment protection and ease of doing business, it appears to still have too many sectors where producers are sheltered from protection, rating as about the EU average on measures of competition policy.[8]

Ireland has had something of a roller coaster ride in terms of output and income over the past quarter of a century. It has gone from having surprisingly low average incomes by Western European standards to surprisingly high and appears to have stabilised at a level above the EU average. Between about 1990 and 2000 growth was driven by improvements in productivity in which foreign direct investment and past investments in education played significant roles. There followed a period in which aggregate growth was driven by inward migration and a major expansion in credit that proved unsustainable and lead to the crisis in 2008. The Irish crisis between about 2008 and 2010 was exacerbated by global and European downturns and the Irish economy began recovering as domestic and foreign crises receded. Ireland's future growth prospects depend significantly on developments in the global economy. Given the improvement in Ireland's relative position there is now limited potential for rapid growth through catching up with other countries. The absence of strong forces for convergence makes the fine print of policymaking more important than previously, especially in light of the speed with which imbalances in the economy can build up.

Endnotes

1 A Cobb-Douglas production function is used, where $Y_t = A_t K_t^\alpha L_t^{1-\alpha}$ with $\alpha = 0.33$.

2 Using GNI rather than GDP doesn't significantly change the results although GNI growth is slightly lower, which is attributed to slightly lower TFP growth. Per capita figures also give a similar picture, although they tend to reduce the importance of hours worked, as population increase explains part of the increase in hours (Table 7.2).

3   This issue seems to be part of the background to the August 2016 European Commission decision that Apple owed the Irish government up to €13 billion in back taxes plus interest. Apple had been making relatively low royalty payments on European sales to its US headquarters, retaining much of the revenue in Europe possibly in the hope that US corporate tax rates would fall.

4   The famous description of Irish fiscal policy by the Irish Finance Minister of the early 2000s along the lines of 'When I have it, I spend it and when I don't, I don't' seems relevant here.

5   For more detail on the origins and the initial response to the Irish crisis see P. Lane, 'The Irish Crisis'. IIIS discussion paper, Trinity College Dublin 2011.

6   For further analysis see F. Ruane, 'Ireland – a remarkable recovery?' *Australian Economic Review* 49 (3), 2016.

7   It's important to note that these levels would have been significantly higher without emigration, perhaps as high as 20 per cent.

8   For a more complete analysis see N. Crafts, 'Ireland's medium-term growth prospects: a Phoenix rising?' *Economic and Social Review* 45 (1), 2014.

CHAPTER 8

Distribution and Poverty

*Michael King**

1 INTRODUCTION

Reducing inequality and eradicating poverty are key policy objectives for a small open economy like Ireland, both from a competitiveness angle and a quality of life perspective. Greater levels of equity and lower incidences of poverty afford more Irish citizens the opportunity to participate in the modern economy, reduce costly social problems and foster trust, cooperation and a greater sense of community.

Yet Ireland is characterised by significant inequalities and deep-rooted poverty. As Ireland emerges from the financial crisis, 16 per cent of Irish adults earned less than 60 per cent of the median income in 2014, the amount deemed necessary to participate fully in society. When we consider the most vulnerable groups, we find that Ireland experiences one of the highest rates of child poverty in Europe, and significant poverty among the elderly. In terms of inequality, while Ireland is not exceptional by international standards, significant inequalities exist not just in income and wealth but in education and health status.

The extent of inequality within countries varies significantly. Data from the United Nations illustrates that the ratio of income of the top 10 per cent of earners to the bottom 10 per cent of earners ranges between over 50 in Haiti, Venezuela and South Africa, countries with extreme income inequality and weak welfare systems, to less than 10 in many developed countries. In Ireland, the ratio of individual income of the top 10 per cent to the bottom 10 per cent of earners was 7.3 in 2015, but in the absence of taxation and transfers the ratio would be 45.0.

Research suggests that there is greater income inequality between countries than within countries. Estimates from the World Bank in 2014 suggest that Gross National Income (GNI) per person is 361 times higher in Norway, the world's richest economy, and 202 times higher in Ireland than in Burundi. The contrasts in income inequality are mirrored in areas such as health and education. Women are expected to live to the age of 84 in euro-zone countries compared with 48 in Swaziland and 53 in Central African Republic. Literacy rates for over 15 year olds range from very close to 100 per cent for most developed countries to 35 per cent and 39 per cent for Burkina Faso and Chad, respectively.

A child born in Central African Republic is likely to live to 52, have less than a 50-50 chance of being literate and survive with life-time earnings of €15,000, whereas a European child born into a middle to high-income family will most likely enjoy third-level education of some kind, have an opportunity to live into their 80s and enjoy life earnings of approximately €3,000,000. While the contrasts may be less extreme, statistics show that children born on the same day in different parts of the same Irish city will enjoy significantly different life expectancies, education opportunities, and future income possibilities. This brings us to the question of 'what is fairness?' To help answer this question we start with the concept of social justice.

Social justice can be seen as the extension of the legal concepts of equality and fairness into the wider aspects of society and the economy. Recognising the dignity of every human being, social justice seeks greater levels of equality and solidarity in society. At the core there are two approaches in thinking about social justice; equality of outcome and equality of opportunity. Achieving equality of outcome would mean the equalisation of income or wealth, and while the absolute equality of outcomes was tried in communist regimes in the twentieth century, all rich countries move somewhat in this direction through redistributive policies.

We can turn to the American philosopher John Rawls (1921–2002) for the rationale for seeking equality of outcome. He argued that to maximise social justice the welfare of the worst-off person in society should be increased. Rawls specifically argued that in calculating total societal welfare we should be solely concerned with the outcome for the poorest individual or family. Designing policy from this perspective could lead to very radical policy conclusions aimed at equalising income.

The second concept is the idea of equality of opportunity. Equality of opportunity is attained when all citizens enjoy an agreed norm of education and healthcare that allows citizens to participate and succeed in society. When accompanied with a basic level of income support for the poorest in society, achieving equality of opportunity is often the centrepiece of government policy.

The focus on equality of opportunity with modest income supports was endorsed by the World Bank's 2006 *World Development Report*. The report defined fairness (equity) as a situation where individuals should have equal opportunities to pursue a life of their choosing, where a person's life achievements should be determined primarily by his or her talents and efforts, rather than by pre-determined circumstances such as race, gender, social or family background and be spared from extreme deprivation in outcomes, particularly in health, education and consumption.

The rest of this chapter is structured as follows. Section 2 explores the historical reasons for the development of inequality and poverty. Section 3 outlines the case for and against pursuing greater equality and poverty reduction, illustrating the trade-offs that can be present. Section 4 discusses the nature and trajectory of inequality and poverty in Ireland and Section 5 describes the political economy of redistribution, placing the Irish welfare system in an international context.

Section 6 describes Ireland's policies that are aimed at reducing inequality and poverty, focusing on some practical examples. Section 7 concludes the chapter.

2 CAUSES OF INEQUALITY AND POVERTY

Across Countries

The obvious question for many is why is there so much poverty in the world? Why are some countries over a hundred times richer than others? A better way of asking these questions is perhaps to ask why some countries are rich. The reality of human history is that for approximately 200,000 years humans survived day-to-day initially by hunting and gathering plants and berries, before progressing to small scale farming in some regions of the world around 10,000 years ago. While some regions enjoyed concentrated but ultimately modest increases in economic well-being in the last 3,000 to 4,000 years (Egypt, Greece, the Roman empire and the Italian city states) due to innovations in finance, the development of trade routes and the concentration of political power, significant increases in income levels only began 250 years ago.

Modern economic growth began in the 1760s when the Industrial Revolution facilitated the division and specialisation of labour and began the process of urbanisation. Initially, only a small number of European countries, North America, and other European colonies enjoyed the higher living standards that accompanied the Industrial Revolution.

Hence, the birth of significant global inequalities were not the result of some regions doing badly, but others doing extraordinarily well. Economic histories continue to debate the reasons why economic growth took hold in some regions of the world and not others. While undoubtedly conditions such as abundance of natural resources, population density, proximity to trading routes and markets play important roles, it is often argued that the quality of national and local institutions, and their conduciveness to trade and investment activities, determine the relative economic performance of countries. During the last 50 years, some regions of the world have followed the path to modernity and high incomes, most notably significant parts of Asia, but others, particularly Africa, have failed to join the transformation due to a combination of geographic isolation, poor government institutions and local conflicts.

Within Countries and Across Individuals

Does this historical process tell us anything about inequality and poverty within countries such as Ireland? The answer is yes. The free market capitalism that drove the Industrial Revolution led to wage differentials within countries, between people of different levels of education, experience, and skills. As a result, significant income inequality can occur within a developed country when there are differences in skill levels, health outcomes, or indeed any characteristic that is highly rewarded in modern economies such as motivation, dependability, and conscientiousness. For example, research in the USA attributed the rise in inequality since 1970 to the increase in wages for skilled workers which came about due to technological change, increasing trade and the decline of manufacturing.

Inequality from wage differentials can be deepened by unequal ownership of capital (wealth) in the form of financial or physical assets. Income inequalities in the past can cement current inequalities through the enjoyment of significant income from investments. The evidence suggests that the importance of labour and non-labour income in inequality differs by region. In Western Europe, non-labour income is the most important factor driving inequality, whereas in North America labour income is a more important driver.

At the individual level we know a lot about inequality. We know that level of education and type of occupation are strong predictors of higher income. However, we can ask a deeper question: what accounts for differences in educational outcomes and levels of professional achievement? The answer to this question has four parts.

First, we know that everyone is born with different abilities and talents, and these play a central role in determining future success. A large body of research shows that cognitive ability is a powerful determinant of wages, schooling, participation in crime, and success in many aspects of social and economic life. In addition, recent research by Nobel Prize winning economist James Heckman documents how non-cognitive abilities (perseverance, motivation, time preference, risk aversion, self-esteem, self-control, preference for leisure) have direct effects on wages (controlling for schooling), schooling, teenage pregnancy, smoking, crime, performance on achievement tests, and many other aspects of social and economic life.

Second, who your parents are and how you are cared for in early childhood determines success in life. Empirical research shows that being born into a household with working, health conscious, educated and education-focused parents increases the likelihood of achieving higher levels of education and income. These environmental effects start in the womb. Research documents that pre-natal interventions that reduce fetal exposure to alcohol and nicotine have long-term positive effects on cognition, socio-emotional skills (such as attentiveness, motivation and self-confidence) and health. Indeed, James Heckman argues that the reason children of low-income parents often grow up to be low income has little to do with genetics and innate abilities and everything to do with the impact of the socio-emotional environment in early childhood on long-run abilities.

Third, peer and network effects play an important role in shaping the ambitions of and opportunities enjoyed by different children. Whether school or neighbourhood based, education and health conscious peers can improve a child's education and income outcomes. In addition, the availability of parental, neighbourhood or school-based networks can change career trajectory and deepen the initial inequality caused by early childhood environmental factors.

Fourth, luck in life is not evenly distributed. Some people are extremely unlucky to endure debilitating health issues that undermine their ability to reach their potential while others are extremely lucky to secure high-paying jobs. Of course an individual's ability to overcome bad luck is determined by the avail-ability of private insurance, an option not open to low-income groups, and luck in achieving a high-paying job may in fact be related to proximity to networks.

Over the life cycle inequality can also emerge when households have different attitudes to saving and investing. For example, a household that saves a sizeable proportion of income on a yearly basis can develop income from investments that raises their long-term income above their labour income. Whether invested in a dedicated pension plan or not, such savings can help maintain a high level of consumption in retirement years. Thus, inequality can emerge because of dif-ferent financial management strategies pursued by households for given levels of income.

Evolution of Inequality over Time

Does the nature of economic growth mean that inequality will continue to rise? In a seminal paper, the Russian-American economist Simon Kuznets argued that economic inequality increases over time while a country is developing, and then after a certain average income is attained, inequality begins to decrease.[1] The prediction of changes in inequality as a country develops is depicted in what is known as the Kuznets Curve (see Figure 8.1). Among many suggestions as to why this might be the case is the idea that owners of capital and workers in sectors with rising productivity benefit disproportionally in the early stages of devel-opment. As the capabilities of the state increase, however, improving education and health opportunities for all citizens, the emergence of redistributive policies gradually reduces the inequality.

Figure 8.1 Kuznets Curve

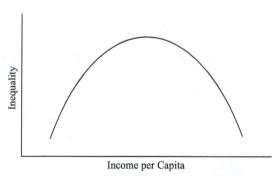

Up until 1980 there was evidence for the Kuznets curve. In the USA inequality rose in the second half of the nineteenth century and declined over the twentieth, until the 1970s when it started increasing again. In the UK inequality also rose after 1977, after almost a century of declines following the initial rise during the industrial revolution. Recent data suggests that there is in fact a natural tendency for capitalist economies to lead to 'Downtown Abbey' (high) levels of inequality, contradicting the predictions of the Kuznets curve.[2] It is argued that pre-World War I economies in Western Europe were characterised by significant inequalities; before the two wars and the great depression dragged levels of wealth back down to earth through physical destruction, capital losses and inflation.

However, since the 1970s the ratio of wealth to income has increased together with income inequality and is now approaching levels last seen before World War I. The *Economist* recently argued that the inverted U of the Kuznets curve has turned into an italicised *N*, with the final stroke pointing menacingly upwards.[3]

The central role that policy plays in determining the trajectory of inequality cannot be underestimated. Right of centre governments in the UK and the USA in the 1980s and early 1990s deliberately pursued policies of lower taxation and lower redistribution that increased inequality, undermining the predictions of the Kuznets curve. In contrast, left of centre governments in the UK after World War II and during the great depression in the US (1930s) reduced inequality through pioneering reforms in the areas of pensions and social welfare.[4]

3 ARGUMENTS FOR AND AGAINST REDUCING INEQUALITY AND POVERTY

Arguments For

If everyone has a basic standard of living, is inequality something to worry about? The answer for many is yes; and economists and political leaders from Adam Smith to Barrack Obama have been exercised by the corrosive impact inequality can have in society.[5] To make the case for reducing inequality and poverty inspiration can be taken from philosophy, economics and political science.

As mentioned in the introduction and discussed in Chapter 2, John Rawls (1921–2002) provided a philosophical justification for significant efforts at reducing inequality. In his 1971 book *A Theory of Justice*, Rawls argued that in the pursuit of social justice the welfare of the worst-off groups in society should be emphasised and policy should focus on increasing the welfare of low-income groups. Rawls argues that we would all opt for a more equal society rather than an unequal one if behind a metaphorical 'veil of ignorance' we did not know what our position in society will be. This appealing 'thought experiment' provides a strong philosophical rationale for the pursuit of greater equality; although it could be argued that as voters know their relative position on the income distribution when they vote the attractiveness of the idea may be trumped by economic self-interest in the ballot box.

Perhaps an even more convincing argument can be derived from the proposition of *diminishing marginal utility of income*. The proposition states that the effect on well-being (utility) of an additional €1 of income becomes progressively smaller as income rises. In other words, if the richest person in Ireland won €5,000 his/her well-being would not increase nearly as much compared with a low-income person winning the same amount. In terms of policy, diminishing marginal utility suggests that raising the income of poor people will raise their well-being considerably, while reducing the income of the rich by an equal amount will have comparatively little effect on their well-being. Thus redistributing from rich to poor maximises overall societal welfare; a noble objective for policymakers.

High levels of inequality also lead to externalities that undermine both well-being and income levels of all in society, including the wealthy. Intuitively, it is easy to understand how the quality of social relations can deteriorate in a more unequal society. Inequality affects our ability to identify and empathise with other people. The literature suggests that health and social problems are closely related to levels of inequality and not average income levels in developed countries; rates of mental illness are five times higher in the most unequal societies.[6] Similarly, in more unequal societies people are five times as likely to be imprisoned and six times as likely to be clinically obese. It is important to note that while this evidence cannot be strictly considered as causation, the data are suggestive of an important link. Dealing with greater levels of crime and health-care costs will affect the tax burdens of high-income groups and can lead to an inefficient waste of human talent.

In addition, levels of societal trust and sense of community are demonstrably higher in more equal societies, and while both are important to quality of life, they both play a key role in facilitating economic growth. Throughout history the societies that have flourished are those where economic transactions have taken place based on a person's word. In the absence of trust, complex business deals are no longer feasible and individuals expect betrayal in business transactions; this increases the cost of monitoring and reduces the likelihood that the transaction will occur in the first place.

Economic inequalities have important consequences for democracy. Nobel Prize winning economist Paul Krugman lamented 'Extreme concentration of income is incompatible with real democracy. Can anyone seriously deny that our political system is being warped by the influence of big money, and that the warping is getting worse as the wealth of a few grows ever larger?' Political science theory suggests that political policies chosen in a democracy should reflect the preferences of the 'median voter' or average voter and thereby allow majorities to dictate policy. However, there is evidence to suggest that tax policy of the last decade and post-crises financial sector reform fail to reflect the interests of the majority of citizens but instead have been overly influenced by wealthy individuals and corporations respectively.

In summary, strong economic arguments exist for reducing inequality and poverty in Ireland. As a small open economy, Ireland must remain competitive and succeed in export markets. First, as Ireland competes internationally on the quality of our labour force, a meritocratic society with full equality of opportunity reduces the losses from poverty when individuals do not reach their true potential. Second, Ireland needs to continue to attract the best international talent from around Europe. While high incomes undoubtedly attract some foreign-nationals to Ireland, the quality of life such as low levels of crime and social cohesion are also important.

Arguments Against

The benefits of inequality cannot be considered without reference to the costs associated with government policies designed to reduce inequality. There are costs to society incurred in the pursuit of greater equality, and concern over these costs go a long way to explaining why we do not see concerted political efforts to reduce inequality. Indeed, the history of the twentieth century is littered with examples of poorly-designed policies pursued in the name of equality of outcomes that seriously harmed economic growth prospects by ignoring the costs of taxation and redistribution. Economists call these costs the *excess burden of taxation, diminishing returns to high tax rates* and *disincentive effects* (see Chapter 4).

The excess burden of taxation, also known as the distortionary cost of taxation, is the economic loss that society suffers as a result of a tax. First discussed by Adam Smith in the eighteenth century, the excess burden of taxation occurs because individuals or firms change their behaviour when a tax is imposed. An income tax, for example, reduces the return to working an additional hour, and thereby makes it more likely that the worker will choose to enjoy leisure instead of working for some part of the week. In business, the taxation of company profits reduces the return to investment, making it less likely that the firm will undertake a project. A sales tax such as Value Added Tax (VAT) is perhaps an even more intuitive example. A sales tax on goods and services will increase the cost of the goods at the point of purchase, and hence by the basic laws of supply and demand, will reduce the number of units purchased. These are hidden losses to taxation and hence the term excess burden of taxation.

The level of excess burden for a given tax will differ between countries. For example, if citizens have high levels of work ethic, a tax on labour income will lead to a smaller reduction in the number of hours worked. High levels of work ethic have been cited as a reason why some countries, such as the Scandinavian countries, can prosper with high levels of income tax without significant losses to economic activity.

At very high levels of taxation, the excess burden of taxation can lead to diminishing returns to tax authorities. If the government increases tax rates beyond a certain point the tax base will begin to disappear. At very high rates of income taxation, people will simply choose not to work, will work in the informal economy, or will fail to declare their income to the authorities.

In a globalised world, where capital can freely move between countries, taxation on capital or company profits is perhaps the most obvious example of diminishing returns to high tax rates. If taxes on capital or company profits are increased to a high level, the capital can simply move jurisdictions. As a result, the presence of the excess burden of taxation and diminishing returns to high tax rates limits the ability of governments to tax.

212

_Q2_

An additional cost to high levels of redistribution can occur when transfers to the unemployed cause a proportion of welfare recipients to reduce their efforts to be self-reliant. Such transfers can in some cases act as a disincentive to finding paid employment. There is little disagreement that welfare payments are warranted for people who suffer from bad luck such as job loss or illness. However, welfare programmes need to be careful not to discourage the pursuit of paid employment among recipients. Any change in behaviour due to this disincentive effect is an economic loss to society.

To counter Rawls' philosophical arguments for greater redistribution, another American philosopher Robert Nozick (1938–2002) published a retort in a 1974 book *Anarchy, State and Utopia*. Nozick's theory of justice claims that whether a distribution of income, wealth or property is just or not depends entirely on how it came about. If income or wealth has been created by the fruits of individual effort, then to take property away from people in order to redistribute it violates their rights.

Nozick favours the pursuit of social justice through voluntary donations, thereby avoiding the violation of ownership rights and the losses to taxation implicit in government-led redistributive policies. Mankind has the potential to be altruistic. Adam Smith in his book *Theory of Moral Sentiments* (1759) observed that human nature led people to be altruistically concerned about the well-being of others.

The World Giving Index monitors the proportion of people in each country that give money to charity. In 2016, 73 per cent of adults in Australia and 66 per cent of adults in Ireland (10th place in the world) donated money to charity. In contrast some European countries, such as Greece (9 per cent), Lithuania (11 per cent), Bulgaria (13 per cent) and Hungary (16 per cent) do not have a tradition of giving to charity. The USA is often cited as the most generous country for the amount of private giving with about $373 billion (2 per cent of GDP) given to charities in 2015.

One reason why private giving is small can be characterised by the prisoners' dilemma of private income transfers when each person prefers that the other gives. Let's imagine a three-person society; two potential donors and one low-income individual. Both potential donors care about the welfare of the third person but would rather not bear the cost of the income transfer themselves. Each potential donor prefers the scenario where the other donor provides the income transfer to the low-income individual. This dilemma can lead to a free rider problem and will ultimately result in neither donor choosing to donate and acts as rationale for government involvement in redistribution.

4 INEQUALITY AND POVERTY IN IRELAND

In this section we explore the different dimensions of inequality and poverty, discuss different approaches to their measurement, and provide a full picture of the nature and extent of economic inequality and poverty in Ireland. We focus specifically on the concepts of equality of outcome and equality of opportunity defined in Section 1. For an alternative approach, we discuss the capabilities approach developed by the Indian economist Amartya Sen. Throughout our analysis, an attempt is made to highlight the life-cycle approach to poverty, and urban and rural differences that exist in Ireland.

Dimensions of Inequality and Poverty

Poverty and inequality can exist across four dimensions: economic, political, social, and affective. The economic sphere encompasses income, wealth, and access to services; the political sphere is associated with the distribution of influence in the political process; the social sphere is concerned with the distribution of recognition and respect in the community and finally the affective sphere concerns the distribution of love, care, and solidarity. There is a tendency for social scientists to focus on the economic and the political dimensions, and this is due in part to the availability of data, but also due to the intangible nature of the social and affective spheres.

Before focusing on the economic dimension, it is worth making a few important observations about the interconnections between the dimensions. Even within modern democracies, with the established principle of one person one vote, economic inequalities can lead to imbalances in access to political influence. This is particularly the case when private donations to political parties are not sufficiently regulated.

The relationship between income level and enjoyment of love, care, and solidarity is less straight forward. Low-income communities can be characterised by high levels of community spirit and strong family relationships. Conversely, we know wealth does not necessarily lead to personal happiness. Finally, the distribution of respect and recognition in society differs between cultures and ultimately depends on what is valued in society. In modern consumer societies, traditional reasons for respect such as integrity and community involvement can be overtaken by displays of wealth and exclusive memberships.

Inequality Outcomes

Measurement

Focusing on income inequality for both its importance to human welfare and data availability, the distribution of inequality, in a country is typically described by the Lorenz curve. Developed by the American economist Max Lorenz in 1905, the Lorenz curve is drawn with the cumulative percentage of wealth measured along the y-axis and the cumulative percentage of households measured along the x-axis (see Figure 8.2). To draw the Lorenz curve, the proportion of income earned by the poorest 10 per cent of the population is calculated, followed by each additional 10 per cent of the population until the point is reached where 100 per cent of wealth is owned by 100 per cent of the population.

The Lorenz curve simply joins the points on the graph that represent how much income is earned by each additional 10 per cent of the population. If income is equally distributed each additional 10 per cent of the population will earn an additional 10 per cent of income and since we are looking at cumulative percentages, the Lorenz curve would be a straight line emanating from the origin. This is known as the line of absolute equality and will have a slope of 45 degrees. When we plot the data for a particular country, the Lorenz curve will bow away from the line of absolute equality down to the right. The more unequal a society is, the further it will deviate away from the line of absolute equality. Changes in the Lorenz curve over time illustrate the evolution of inequality in a country.

Figure 8.2 Lorenz Curve

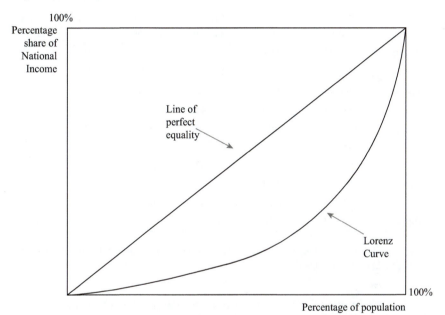

A related summary measure of inequality is the Gini coefficient. It is calculated as the ratio of the area between the Lorenz Curve and the line of absolute equality (numerator) and the whole area under the line of absolute equality (denominator). The extreme values of the Gini Coefficient are 0 and 1, although they are often presented as percentages, between 0 and 100 per cent respectively. A low Gini coefficient indicates greater equality in society, with absolute equality represented by a Gini of zero. Conversely, a Gini of 100 per cent means that the top income earner enjoys 100 per cent of all income in society. The Lorenz curve is most often used to depict the distribution of income; if data are available it can also be used to illustrate the distribution of wealth.

Income Distribution
How does Ireland perform using these different measures of inequality? Table 8.1 provides the data necessary to draw Lorenz curves for Ireland for gross income,

total taxes and net income. The table shows that before taxes the top 10 per cent earned 28.5 per cent of the income in 2013, while the bottom 10 per cent earned 2.5 per cent of all income. The taxation system equalises this somewhat. After taxes, the top 10 per cent earned 24.4 per cent of all income, while the bottom 10 per cent earned 3.2 per cent. While taxation reduces the income of all deciles, only the income share of the top 30 per cent of the distribution falls.

Table 8.1 Percentage Distribution of Household Income (2013)

	Weekly Total in Euros			Share of Total (%)		
	Gross Income	Total Taxes	Net Income	Gross Income	Total Taxes	Net Income
Bottom	135.95	7.08	128.87	2.5	0.5	3.2
2nd	212.34	9.80	202.55	3.9	0.7	5.0
3rd	266.42	23.90	242.52	5.0	1.8	6.0
4th	297.01	22.55	274.45	5.5	1.7	6.8
5th	368.04	55.05	312.99	6.8	4.1	7.7
6th	450.67	86.87	363.8	8.4	6.5	9.0
7th	545.96	123.89	422.07	10.2	9.3	10.4
8th	677.07	180.47	496.60	12.6	13.6	12.3
9th	893.03	280.03	613.00	16.6	21.0	15.2
Top	1,530.52	541.76	988.76	28.5	40.7	24.4

Source: EU-SILC 2014, www.eui.eu/Research/Library/ResearchGuides/Economics/ Statistics/DataPortal/EU-SILC.aspx

To track the evolution of Ireland inequality over time we rely on the Gini coefficient. Ireland's Gini coefficient fell from 31.9 in 2005 to 28.8 in 2009, before rising again to 30.8 in 2014. Table 8.2 illustrates that inequality declined in Ireland during the final years of the Celtic Tiger when the government increased welfare payments to low-income households and non-skilled wages increased, but rose again as welfare payments were reduced and certain sectors of the economy performed well.

Table 8.2 also places Ireland's performance in an international context, comparing Gini coefficients (after taxes and transfers) for twelve European countries, ranked by the 2014 Gini coefficient. The period was characterised by significant economic volatility, rising unemployment and destruction of wealth in many European countries. For most of the last two decades, Ireland experienced higher levels of inequality than many central European and Scandinavian countries. This seems to have moderated to some degree during the financial crisis. In 2014, Ireland was more unequal than Germany and the Scandinavian countries but slightly better than the average of the EU 15.

Table 8.2 European Comparison of Gini Coefficients (after taxes and transfers)

Country	2005	2009	2011	2014	Change 2005–2014
Spain	31.8	32.3	34.5	34.7	2.9
Portugal	38.1	35.4	35.4	34.5	−3.6
Greece	33.2	33.1	33.5	34.5	1.3
UK	34.6	32.4	33.0	31.6	−3.0
EU 15	29.9	30.3	30.9	30.9	1.0
Ireland	*31.9*	*28.8*	*29.8*	*30.8*	*−1.1*
Germany	26.1	29.1	29.0	30.7	4.6
France	27.7	29.8	30.8	29.2	1.5
Denmark	23.9	27.0	26.6	27.7	3.8
Sweden	23.4	24.8	24.4	25.4	2.0

Source: Eurostat Online database 2016.

Regional and Life-Cycle Inequalities

Regional inequalities exist within Ireland, although these have fallen since 2000. According to the Central Statistics Office, data for 2014 shows that individual residents of Dublin enjoy disposable income (after taxes and transfers) that is 12 per cent higher than the national average while residents of the southern and eastern regions enjoy disposable income that is 3 per cent higher than the national average. This is balanced by 8.7 per cent lower than average disposable income in the border, western and midland regions.

At county level, Donegal and Monaghan are the counties with the lowest levels of average disposable income whereas Dublin, Cork and Limerick are the only four counties with disposable income above the national average. Differences in standards of living are likely to be smaller when differences in the cost of living between the counties are taken into consideration. There is also a rural/urban dimension to inequality with extensive rural development policies in place to deal not only with this but also to avoid the decline of rural areas due to migration (see Chapter 9).

Inequalities can emerge at different points in the life cycle. For children, students in full-time education and the elderly, opportunities to earn money are limited and consumption is financed by parental support or the drawing down of accumulated financial wealth such as pensions.

It has been shown that in Ireland and around the world, low-income households tend to have more children. This can lead to the situation where a small number of children have access to significant resources when growing up, while more modest resources are spread more thinly over a larger number of children. Such inequality is likely to lead to very real differences in education and health outcomes.

A second inequality related to the life cycle occurs when households fail to adequately save for their retirement. This can occur as people prioritise immediate consumption while working or fail to adequately anticipate their retirement needs. This latter issue has been exacerbated by the sizeable losses incurred by private pension funds during the recent financial crisis.

Wealth Distribution
For the first time detailed data on household wealth became available after the *Household Finances and Consumption Survey* was conducted in 2013. So while, reliable data to trace changes in Irish household wealth over time do not exist, new insights into the level of wealth inequality in Ireland have been revealed.

The survey found that the median household in Ireland had total assets of €169,000 but when liabilities, mostly but not exclusively mortgage debt, is considered, the net asset position of the median household was €100,600. This wealth is heavily concentrated in homeowners, who are typically older and higher-income households. Two observations from the survey data are worth noting. First, the bottom 20 per cent of the wealth distribution had an average net asset position of minus €4,300. This is a remarkable finding. The only other country in Europe where the bottom 20 per cent had a negative asset position was the Netherlands. Second, the vast majority of wealth is owned by citizens over 45 years of age. Young adults (16–34 year olds) had a net asset position of €4,000; the lowest of the 20 European countries in the survey. In contrast the 65–74 age group in Ireland had the fifth highest net asset position in Europe with an average net wealth of €206,300.

Despite these average figures for the elderly, Ireland has large numbers of elderly in poverty (see later). The divergence in wealth levels reflects the outcome of a lifetime of differing income paths and investment decisions. This divergence can, in large part, be traced to Ireland's economic expansion between 1994 and 2007 as significant increases in returns to employment occurred in some professions and at management level while stock market and property investments produced very high returns.

Poverty Outcomes
Absolute Poverty
Poverty can be described as the state of not having enough money to take care of basic needs such as food, clothing, and shelter. At a broad level, poverty can be measured in either absolute or relative terms and is generally calculated as a head count indicator; the fraction of the population falling below a minimum standard of income. Absolute poverty is defined as the fraction of the population below some threshold of income. The simplicity of absolute poverty, and its specified income level, is undermined by the need to change the threshold income level as countries grow and the cost of living rises. For example, a measure of absolute poverty in 1960s Ireland would be out of date in the twenty-first century.

The theoretical distinction between inequality and poverty is worth noting. In our measures of inequality some households (exactly 10 per cent) must be by definition located in the bottom 10 per cent of the income distribution. As a result, stagnant inequality is consistent with falling absolute poverty, where the poorer members of society are able to enjoy a superior standard of living.

The most famous examples of absolute poverty lines are the US$1.25 a day used as part of the Millennium Development Goals (MDG). Each year, the United Nations estimates the proportion of people living under these thresholds across the globe and it has been estimated that in 2015, 800 million people lived on US$1.25 a day and over 3 billion, almost half the world's population, lived on less than US$2.50 a day.

As the absolute income thresholds of the MDGs hold little relevance for high-income countries, nationally income thresholds are established that appropriately reflect expectations about the minimum standard of living. In the USA, the Census Bureau adjusts the absolute poverty threshold each year. In 2015, an income threshold of approximately $24,250 for a family of two adults and two children under the age of 18 was used.

Relative Poverty
The alternative approach, relative poverty, occurs when people fall behind, by more than a certain degree, from the average income and lifestyle enjoyed by the rest of the society. An advantage of a relative measure of poverty is that it does not need to be adjusted as average earnings change. Ireland's first official poverty measure, 'at risk of poverty rate' is a measure of relative poverty and refers to all individuals who earn less than the threshold of 60 per cent of the median income and this measure is used by the National Action Plan for Social Inclusion and the EU.

Each of these poverty measures focus on income and such an approach can be criticised in a number of ways. First, there are limitations to income as a single identifier of poverty. Focusing on income alone fails to take into consideration household characteristics such as savings or outstanding debts. For example, monthly income may fluctuate and so poorly represent long-term income. Second, the level of past investment in consumer durables and household assets influences the extent to which current income is available for immediate needs. Third, households may be in receipt of non-cash benefits and services from the state or non-state organisations which would not be reflected in a measure of poverty based on income alone. Fourth, the non-consideration of work-related expenses such as transport and childcare may also affect the net income actually available to support living standards and avoidance of deprivation. Finally, regional differences are also important. Where prices are considerably higher in one part of the country than another, deprivation in high cost regions may not be captured by a simple income based indicator.

Reflecting these concerns, social scientists developed an approach to poverty measurement based on access to basic necessities. Basic necessities include food, heating, clothes, shelter and furniture as well as an ability to engage in family and social life. Ireland's second official poverty measure known as 'consistent poverty' is a hybrid of this approach and the at-risk of poverty rate described above. Households and individuals who are at risk of poverty (earn less than the threshold of 60 per cent of the median), and experience an enforced absence of at least two items from the official deprivation list of eleven items, are deemed to be in consistent poverty. The list of eleven essential items is presented in Table 8.3.

Table 8.3 Eleven-Item Basic Deprivation Scale

Two pairs of strong shoes	Buy presents for friends once a year
A warm waterproof overcoat	Able to keep the home adequately warm
Buy new rather than second hand clothes	Replace any worn out furniture
Roast joint (or equivalent) once a week	Gone without heating during the last 12 months
Eat meals with meat, chicken, fish (or vegetarian equivalent) every second day	Enjoy a drink/meal with family/friends monthly
	Enjoy 2+ hours entertainment in past 14 days

The absolute and relative measures of poverty discussed so far simply measure the proportion of the population falling below a minimum standard of income. They are, however, insensitive to the depth of poverty in the sense that transfers from the least poor to the most poor do not reduce poverty, but transfers from the most poor to the least poor may bring some households out of poverty. In this latter scenario, poverty may have been reduced but we cannot claim that social welfare has increased. This is known as a violation of Dalton's Principle of Transfers.[7] An alternative measure which takes into consideration the depth of poverty is the poverty-gap measure. It weights the head count measure by how far below the poverty line a given household is and has the advantage of not violating Dalton's Principle of Transfers.

Evidence
How has Ireland performed by these various measures of poverty in recent years? Ireland experienced a decline in the 'at risk of poverty' rate (threshold of 60 per cent of median income) from 20 per cent in 2003 to 14 per cent in 2009, before rising to 16.3 per cent in 2014 (see Table 8.4). A similar trend was found for consistent poverty which fell from 8.8 per cent in 2003 to 5.5 per cent in 2009, before rising to 8.0 per cent in 2014. The data suggest that the recent financial crisis and associated increases in unemployment have led to an increase in poverty. Alarmingly, if the social welfare system was stopped, all else equal, the at-risk of poverty rate would be over 50 per cent.

Research on the socio-demographic characteristics of households in poverty found similar types of households suffering from 'consistent poverty' and 'at risk of poverty'. The importance of education as a buffer against poverty is evident as those without formal educational qualifications accounted for half of income-poor households in 2007. Families headed by a person ill or disabled formed an increasing share of consistently poor households over the decade.

Table 8.4 Key National Indicators of Poverty and Social Exclusion (% of individuals)

	2003	2005	2007	2009	2011	2014
At-risk-of-poverty rate[1]:						
Including transfers	19.7	18.5	16.5	14.1	16.0	16.3
Excluding transfers	39.8	40.1	41.0	46.2	50.7	49.3
Consistent Poverty	8.8	7.0	5.1	5.5	6.9	8.0
Poverty Gap (EU Definition)	22.4	20.6	17.4	16.2	19.6	17.2

Source: EU-SILC Surveys 2003–2009.
[1] Refers to the 60 per cent threshold.

When we consider poverty over the life cycle, important results are revealed. The period of economic growth up to 2007 was characterised by falls in poverty among children, the working-age population, and the elderly. However, child poverty remains a serious problem in Ireland. By EU standards Ireland in 2015 had amongst the highest rates of child poverty, reflecting in part comparatively high birth rates in low-income households. According to Eurostat, 34 per cent of all children in Ireland are at risk of consistent poverty compared with an EU average of 28 per cent.

Inequality and Equality of Opportunity
A focus on equality of opportunity is consistent with the natural dispersion of talent and motivation in society, and a philosophy where economic outcomes should not reflect predetermined circumstances such as gender, race, place of birth, family endowments of wealth or ethnic group.

We can measure equality of opportunity with a measure of intergenerational socio-economic mobility which captures how people fare in life relative to their parents. Equality of opportunity in education, healthcare and access to employment would mean that young people's outcomes such as income or education are not determined by their parent's outcomes. If this were the case we would say there is high economic mobility between generations. We measure economic mobility with an elasticity measure, where 0 represents the desirable scenario of complete economic mobility between generations and 1 represents a complete absence of economic mobility, a situation where a child is destined for the same outcomes as their parents.

Studies of the relationship between the income levels of fathers and sons in high-income countries suggest significant differences. Elasticity estimates for Scandinavian countries and Canada range from 0.13 to 0.28 depending on the methodology used, suggesting significant levels of economic mobility between generations. In contrast, elasticity estimates for the UK and the USA range

THE ECONOMY OF IRELAND

between 0.4 and 0.6. It is no surprise that countries with more generous welfare systems and superior state services in health and education enjoy greater levels of socio-economic mobility.

Recent data from the World Bank shows that a high proportion of total inequality in Ireland can be attributable to inequality of opportunity when compared with other EU countries. In Ireland 22 per cent of inequality can be attributed to factors over which people have no control: race, gender, birthplace, parents' education and occupation. This compares with 21 per cent in the UK, 19 per cent in the US, 18 per cent in Germany, 13 per cent in France and 2 per cent in Norway.

Capability Approach to Poverty and Inequality

So far our measures of poverty and inequality have been based on access to resources. Amartya Sen's 1979 essay 'Equality of What?' challenged the focus on economic outcomes and access to resources.[8] Sen argues that these approaches do not consider a range of important aspects of deprivation such as natural/social environment characteristics (pollution and crime levels, for example), personal characteristics (illness which can reduce the ability to participate in society and enjoy material wealth, for example), and freedoms in the political and social sphere. Instead, Sen suggests that poverty be considered as the absence of capabilities or states of being such as being nourished, being loved, being able to work, having an ability to participate in democratic decision making or an ability to pursue one's dreams (see earlier discussion of various dimensions of inequality and poverty).

We can consider a number of examples that vindicate Sen's approach such as an elderly person with considerable material wealth, who is not looked after properly, reducing unnecessarily her range of capabilities or a malnourished child with a parasitic infection that may have access to sufficient levels of food but remains malnourished. The merits of the capability approach are somewhat undermined by the challenges faced in adhering to Sen's ideas in a practical sense. However, it is worth keeping in mind that it remains an important critique of the more orthodox approaches discussed in this chapter.

5 POLITICAL ECONOMY OF POVERTY AND INEQUALITY REDUCTION

Political Preferences and Systems

Political preferences for redistribution and poverty reduction vary both across and within countries. Political theory suggests as democracies emerge, there will be an increasing constituency favourably disposed to redistribution. This occurs because the small number of people who enjoy very high incomes will be outvoted by the majority of voters who earn less than the average income. An alternative theory points to an opposing force, where the initially wealthy use their disproportionate economic resources to influence political outcomes, preventing efforts towards redistribution. Cultural norms of solidarity and work ethic will also play an important role. As discussed in Section 3, political preferences for redistribution will depend not only on an understanding of the benefits of equality but also on sensitivities to the disincentive effects of high taxation and social transfers. Each of these forces combines to define a country's unique set of preferences for redistribution.

Perceptions of inequality can be garnered from globally comparable surveys such as the *World Values Survey*. The survey is conducted across a range of countries and asks respondents in 56 countries whether they believe that incomes should be made more or less equal. The results are striking; in only eight countries the mean preference was in favour of greater income equality, with 46 of the remaining 48 countries characterised by a greater preference for larger income differences as an incentive for individual effort.

The countries that favour more equal incomes include Switzerland, Iran, Germany, Chile, Slovenia, Romania, and India. These countries have Gini coefficients which range from 0.28 in Germany to 0.52 in Chile, suggesting that a preference for greater income inequality is not necessarily related to current levels of income inequality. A number of developing countries and eastern European countries, such as Ghana, Mali, Peru, Indonesia, Thailand as well as Russia and the Ukraine, report significant preferences for larger income differences as an incentive for individual effort.

In many societies, people have a strong preference for equality of opportunity over equality of outcome. When presented with the statement: '*It's fair if people have more money or wealth, but only if there are equal opportunities*' the majority of respondents agree. In Britain, the USA, and Germany, over 70 per cent more people agree than disagree with that statement.

It is possible to observe the outcome of 200 years of political preferences for redistribution in the welfare states across Europe. We distinguish between four different models. First, the Scandinavian or 'social democratic model' has a strong focus on social rights, a high degree of universality and is financed through general taxation and social insurance contributions. The Scandinavian model is considered the most generous welfare state and is associated with high levels of taxation.

Second, the 'continental' or 'social capitalism model' is also characterised by generous welfare benefits, the difference being that benefit rights are often enjoyed by those who contribute through work-based social insurance schemes. Third, the Anglo-Saxon/UK (and Irish) model is primarily needs-based and combines modest universal schemes and extensive means-tested assistance.

The fourth model, known as the southern European model, involves a more basic system of income redistribution, where the primary source of welfare is often a combination of family, private charity and the Church, rather than the state. This type of model is in operation in Portugal, Spain, Greece and the USA.

We can place these four welfare systems into a simplified left-right political spectrum. Ignoring for our purposes consideration of personal freedoms, we define the political right as a low-tax and low redistribution platform and the political left as a high-tax and generous redistribution platform. Referring to our approach taken in Section 3, the political right are more sensitive to moral hazard and welfare dependency, whereas the political left are more sensitive to those who are genuinely in need of state support. The Scandinavian and continental models could be characterised as more left of centre welfare models, while the Anglo-Saxon and Southern European models, with their more modest levels of taxation, could be considered to the right of the political spectrum.

Evidence and Position of Ireland

Categorising the Irish welfare model within the four models is less than straight-forward. During the economic expansion in the 2000s, Ireland was able to pursue the joint objectives of increases in welfare benefits and a reduction in taxes. Conversely, with the economic downturn of 2008 and the ensuing budget deficits, Ireland was faced with the prospect of tax increases and welfare cuts. In normal economic circumstances, governments operate under a resource constraint and the typical policy choice is between low taxation and low welfare or high taxation and generous welfare. In terms of the four European models, Ireland is best described as a hybrid between the Anglo-Saxon Model and the Southern European model.

Using indicators of service effort (benefits in kind as a proportion of GDP) and transfer effort (cash benefits as a proportion of GDP), Ireland can be characterised as having a low-service and transfer effort along with Greece, Spain and Portugal. Within each category a distinction can be made between transfers which are means-tested and those which are not. Ireland fits most comfortably with the Anglo-Saxon model in so far as it aims to provide universal minimum protection with an emphasis on means-testing and flat-rate rather than earnings-related provision. Ireland and the UK are both exceptional within the EU for the high proportion of means-testing. Approximately one quarter of Ireland's social expenditure was means-tested.

Preferences Over Time

When we compare welfare systems internationally a striking stylised fact emerges. Most countries' chosen balance between taxation and redistribution endures over time. Preferences seem to emanate from deep held convictions that change very slowly over time. Through survey data we can gain an understanding of the convictions of voters in different countries. In the USA only 29 per cent of respondents surveyed believe that the poor are trapped in poverty. This contrasts to 60 per cent of Europeans that share this belief. In addition, 60 per cent of Americans believe the poor are lazy, while only 26 per cent of Europeans share this belief. In fact there is no reason to believe this is the case.[9] It was found that 60 per cent of the members of the bottom quintile of the income distribution in the USA in 1984 remained in that quintile in 1993, while only 46 per cent of Germans in the bottom quintile of their income distribution remained in that bottom quintile nine years later. Besides, there is reason to believe that those in the bottom quintile of the US income distribution work far more hours than their counterparts in many European countries.

Despite the consistency in preferences for the welfare system changes can occur. The deepening of the welfare state has historically been associated with the sweeping to power of left-of-centre governments, often during times of great economic and political challenge such as the Great Depression or post-World War II. In the USA, one component of the policies pursued by Franklin Delano Roosevelt between 1933 and 1936, collectively known as the New Deal, comprised the Social Security Act of 1935. The act enshrined in USA law for the first time the right to benefits for retirees and the unemployed. In the UK, following World War II, Clement Atlee's Labour Party Government, not only established the universal public health-care system, the National Health Service, but introduced significant welfare benefits such as flat-rate pensions, sickness benefit, unemployment benefit, child benefit and funeral benefit.

Reverses to the welfare system are also possible. As noted in Section 2, the emergence of centre-right governments in the early 1980s in the USA and the UK led to an increase in inequality as welfare states were weakened and taxes reduced. A more recent example of welfare system reversal can be seen in the UK under David Cameron's conservative government (2010 to 2016).

In Ireland, the domination of centrist populist political parties since the foundation of the state has meant the slow evolution of the welfare state and the absence of revolutionary reform. The recent crisis may have provided the opportunity for a radical revision of the Irish welfare state, either a strengthening of its reach or its reduction to lessen the excess burden of taxation and disincentive effects. In the watershed elections of 2011 and 2016, Ireland elected a centrist coalition, and with little room for tax cuts and welfare state investments following the financial crisis, it seems unlikely that significant reform in either direction will be possible in the foreseeable future. Nevertheless, recent elections saw a historical peak in first preferences for left-wing parties and independents.

As Ireland emerges from the current downturn, a very serious underlying political economy issue will take centre stage in Irish politics and that is the issue of an aging population that will make up an even bigger proportion of the voting public. The aging population who have paid taxes right through their working lives will expect that, even in challenging times for the public finances, old-age pensions are maintained at reasonable levels. As the Irish population ages and people live longer, the influence of pensioners in the Irish political system will increase over time.

6 POLICY EFFORTS AND CHALLENGES

In the pursuit of social justice a number of alternative approaches can be taken by governments. The legislative framework provides the rules that underpin equal opportunity. However, the achievement of equal opportunity takes considerably more effort than the existence of legal rights. The provision of public minimum levels of education and healthcare needs to be supplemented by a minimum standard of living for all citizens to ensure that social mobility between generations is possible and people are fully rewarded for their talents and efforts irrespective of social background. This section describes Ireland's policies aimed at reducing inequality and poverty and focuses on Ireland's policy responses, social transfers in particular, towards vulnerable groups. It is worth noting that the public provision of healthcare and education remain essential to the pursuit of equality of opportunity and this aspect of health and education policies are covered in detail in Chapters 13 and 14.

Equality Legislation
The starting point for pursuing equality of opportunity is legislation. There have been several important policy and legislative changes to progress equality in Ireland over the last number of years, cumulating in the recent 2015 Marriage Equality Bill. These include the adoption of equality legislation, namely the Employment Equality Act, 1998, and the Equal Status Act, 2000, and the establishment of equality institutions, namely the Equality Authority and the Office of the Director of Equality Investigations. The Employment Equality Act outlaws discrimination in employment on nine distinct grounds such as gender, family status, marital status, age, disability, sexual orientation, religion, race, or being a member of the traveller community. The Equal Status Act goes a step further providing comprehensive legal protection against discrimination in the delivery of goods and services, whether provided by the state or private sector. Further, the establishment of the Disability Authority and the Human Rights Commission are all developments with potential to contribute to reducing poverty, inequality and discrimination.

Social Transfers
Social transfers represent the foundation of the modern welfare state (see Chapter 4) and they come in various guises each with different effects on incentives and social justice. Transfers can differ in coverage levels, either universal or targeted, and form taken, money or in-kind transfers.

Universal payments are paid regardless of a person's income or social-insurance record. Universal cash entitlements can be simple to administer, but fail to discriminate between deserving and non-deserving cases. An excellent example of a universal entitlement is child benefit which was introduced in 1944.

Effective targeting of entitlements can be considered more socially just, particularly when the savings from targeting out-weighs the administrative costs of means testing. Examples of targeted benefits provided to citizens once a means test is satisfied include the Family Income Supplement for the low paid and the One-Parent Family Payment. The jobseekers allowance involves a different form of conditionality. To receive the jobseekers allowance one must be unemployed but available for and genuinely seeking work. The weekly benefit is €188 per week. In Budget 2010 this was reduced for those under the age of 25 to encourage engagement in training and further education.

Economic theory suggests that cash transfers are preferred by recipients because it allows them to choose their preferred basket of goods. In contrast, in-kind transfers allow a paternalistic state to tilt recipients' expenditure patterns towards goods and services deemed in their interest to consume. Examples in Ireland of in-kind entitlements include the fuel allowance given to the elderly as well as the public provision of healthcare and education (see Chapters 13 and 14). If the recipient does not derive much satisfaction from the in-kind transfer provided, they would have been better off receiving the transfer in cash to spend on goods of their choosing.

Table 8.5 outlines the multi-faceted nature of the Irish welfare system. Social transfers exist for a variety of groups who have experienced adverse outcomes such as the unemployed, the low paid, individuals who experience illness or disability and bereaved partners. Groups at risk of poverty such as the elderly and lone parents are also provided for. A number of transfer schemes are subjected to a means test such as the family income supplement, the carer's allowance and the fuel allowance as well as the non-contributory pension. Another set of benefits are provided conditional on a record of Pay Related Social Insurance (PRSI) contributions made while in previous employment. This chapter now delves into policies focused on two of the most vulnerable groups at risk of poverty, namely children and the elderly.

Table 8.5 Summary of the Irish Welfare System

Group Served	Government Intervention (Type)	Complementary Policies
Unemployed	Jobseekers allowance (targeted) Back to work programmes (targeted)	Rent supplement Mortgage interest supplement Fuel allowance (means tested)
Low Paid	Family income supplement (targeted and means tested)	Minimum wage laws Fuel allowance (means tested)
Children	Child benefit (universal) Early childhood care and education (both universal and targeted) Back to school clothing and footwear allowance (targeted and means tested)	Child protection laws
Lone Parents	One-Parent family payment (targeted and means tested)	Fuel allowance (means tested)
Elderly	Contributory pensions (conditional on PRSI contributions) Non-contributory pensions (means tested)	Free travel (universal) Fuel allowance (means tested)

Group Served	Government Intervention (Type)	Complementary Policies
Widow, Widower or Surviving Civil Partner (WWSCP)	WWSCP contributory pensions (conditional on PRSI contributions) WWSCP non-contributory pensions (means tested)	Bereavement grant (conditional on PRSI contributions)
Illness	Illness benefit (targeted) Blind and invalidity pension (targeted, means tested) Back to work programmes (targeted)	Fuel allowance (means tested)
Special Groups	Disability insurance Carers allowance (targeted, means tested)	Affirmative action for minorities Fuel allowance (means tested)

Children

As children represent the future of Ireland, government intervention is essential to reduce the high poverty rates among the young. Table 8.5 details four different policies aimed at increasing equality of opportunity and reducing child poverty in Ireland, two of which will now be discussed (the others relate to education policy).

Child Benefit

As a universal entitlement, child benefit is paid to all parents in the state towards the cost of rearing a child and was increased significantly during the 2000s. The cost of child benefit to the state rose from six per cent of all social-welfare spending to ten per cent over the twenty years from 1993 to 2014. In 2016, the rate for the first and second child is €140 per child per month. With pressure on the public finances in recent years, many have advocated that child benefit become a means-tested payment. From the perspective of social justice, this would seem to be an appropriate course of action, yet the administrative and political challenges of doing so have so far prevented such a change.

Lone Parents

In 2006, the Government published a discussion paper on proposals for reforming the way the welfare system supports lone parents that is still relevant.[10] The report pointed to the fact that children of lone parents have a high probability of experiencing poverty. According to the EU-SILC survey of Ireland in 2014 almost 59 per cent of individuals in single-parent families are at risk of poverty, while 1 in 9 children live in consistent poverty. This is much higher than the national figure and compares unfavourably to rates of poverty in two-parent families. To address this phenomenon, in 1997 the government introduced the One-Parent Family Payment (OFP) which provides a payment for men and women who are bringing children up without the support of a partner.

To qualify for the lone-parent payment one must be a parent or legal guardian, not living with a spouse, civil partner or cohabiting as well as having an income of less than €425 per week and satisfy a means test. In 2014, the OFP provided a weekly payment of €188 for those unemployed or earning less than €90 per week, and €29.80 for each dependent child. If a parent or guardian is in receipt of the OFP, they cannot also be in receipt of the jobseekers allowance. There are two main differences between the OFP and the jobseekers allowance. OFP recipients receive additional payments for each child and unlike jobseekers allowance do not have to prove they are looking for work or engage in back-to-work training.

The 2006 Discussion Paper recommended that reform was required to re-orientate the incentives to encourage lone parents to enter the work force. The report argued that passive income supports alone were not sufficient to comprehensively address poverty. There were perhaps good reasons to argue that encouraging lone parents into the work place would lead to an increase in household income and act as a good example to children and their peer group. However, one might also take the alternative view that lone parents experience significant home pressures, provide an important caring role and should not be pushed into the work place. As many of the recommendations of the 2006 report have not been implemented yet, the subtle debate over whether the current OFP involves disincentive effects that ultimately condemn many one-parent families to unemployment will continue.

Elderly Population
Pensions Provision
As the Irish population greys in the next fifty years (see Chapter 6) issues of intergenerational equity will take centre stage. At present a significant part of the Irish pension system is paid for by present day taxpayers, whereby taxes paid by the working generation finance the consumption of retired generations. This is known as a pay-as-you-go system and aptly describes the public component or first pillar of the Irish pension system as well as the generous pension scheme for public sector workers involving a tax-free lump sum and commitment of a monthly pension of 50 per cent of final salary or average salary for new entrants. From the perspective of poverty reduction, the non-contributory pension provides a minimum standard of living for elderly people in the state.

The second pillar of the Irish pension system is comprised of private voluntary pensions and while just over 50 per cent of the work force have enrolled in private pensions, their financial depth even before the recent financial crisis was insufficient. It has been estimated that middle-income earners would have to save an additional 10 per cent of income per year to provide a pension of 50 per cent of pre-retirement income. The third pillar typically refers to non-pension wealth such as other financial assets or property assets that can be wound down in retirement to fund consumption.

Part of the reason for the unsustainable public pension costs and insufficient private saving for retirement involves underlying demographic changes and each raise important issues of intergenerational equity. The OECD predicts that old-age dependency rates, the ratio of old-age dependents to working-age population, will increase in Ireland from 20 per cent in 1990 to 45 per cent by 2050. This means that where the taxes of five workers were available to pay the cost of each elderly person in 1990, by 2050 OECD countries will have to rely on the taxes of two workers for each elderly person in 2050. Ireland will reach an old-age dependency ratio of 45 per cent about 20 years after the majority of western European countries, because of our high birth rates in the 1980s and significant immigration between 1993 and 2008.

In addition, the cost of healthcare has been rising faster than the overall cost of living (see Chapter 14): between 1994 and 2013, health-care costs rose by 57 per cent compared with cumulative inflation of 36 per cent. As medical treatments become increasingly sophisticated, this trend is likely to continue, putting further pressure on the standard of living of the elderly population.

Intra- and Intergenerational Inequity
The unsustainable public pension costs, the insufficient private savings, and the high personal wealth of a small number of elderly people will lead to significant issues of intra-generational and intergenerational equity in future years. Public sector workers recruited before 2013 enjoy a guaranteed pension of fifty per cent of final salary, compared with significantly lower pension provision for the vast majority of workers with private pensions. In addition, the recent financial crisis has devastated many private pension funds, reducing further the monthly pay-ments, while public sector pension funds have been unaffected. For private sector workers without private pensions, the contributory pension will only offer twenty per cent of final income if their final salary is twice the average income.

In essence, the taxpayers of today are paying taxes for the currently retired, but the pension benefits are unequally split between retired public and private sector workers. In the medium term, as the old-age dependency rate rises to EU levels Ireland will be faced with a significant transfer of resources from a shrink-ing working population, to a growing elderly population. If public sector pensions are maintained at current levels, and the non-contributory pension remains at thirty-four per cent of Gross Annual Industrial Earnings (GAIE), significantly higher taxation, and associated costs, will be required to keep the promises made to the burgeoning elderly population.

Looming Pensions Crisis
A number of policy options exist to help Ireland deal with the looming pensions crisis and associated inequities, each with implications for social justice. These include, increasing the pension age, encouraging private saving for retirement and reducing pension entitlements.

First, increasing the pension age helps reduce the old-age dependency rate by increasing the number of people in paid employment. For those looking forward to retirement this may not be a welcome prospect, but efforts in this direction have already begun. In the National Pensions Framework published in 2010, plans to increase to 66 the eligibility age for the state pension were announced. A commit-ment to gradually increase the state pension age to 68 by 2028 was also given. If you are currently under the age of 25, it would be prudent to assume that you will not receive the state pension until 70 years of age.

Second, the government can use tax policy to encourage people to save for their own retirement through private voluntary pensions. At present, taxpayers can avail of tax relief at their personal marginal rate of tax when they divert a proportion of the earnings into a private pension scheme. The current system discriminates against low earners. High earners can enjoy tax relief on pension contributions at the higher rate of tax, whereas low earners who pay tax at the lower rate can only avail of tax relief of 20 per cent.

To deal with this inequity, the National Pensions Framework proposed that the current tax relief scheme be replaced by a state contribution equal to 33 per cent tax relief for all private pension contributions but as of 2017 this has not been introduced. A complementary policy, introduced in recent years, is the mandatory offering of private pension schemes to all private sector workers over a certain minimum age.

The third approach, the reduction in state pension levels is perhaps the most controversial from the perspective of social justice, but is nevertheless a real possibility. With an estimated 10.1 per cent of GNP diverted to state pensions in 2056, if the 34 per cent of GAIE is honoured, the likelihood exists, however painful, that the state pension will have to fall. Increasing the pension age will reduce this cost to some degree, but the cost may still prove too great.

The fourth option is to renege on promises to public servants and reduce public sector pension entitlements. While this is a challenging reform from a political and legal perspective, it should be considered a viable approach. The political obstacles to reforming the public sector pension system have meant that most changes are only relevant for new entrants to the public sector.

The final policy option involves a deliberate attempt to increase the size of working-age population in paid employment through immigration or an increase in the fertility rate. Such policies will help reduce the old-age dependency rate and provide much needed revenue to pay for pension costs, but their usefulness is dependent on the availability of paid employment. The long-term solution to the looming pension crisis will likely be some combination of all four policies.

7 CONCLUSION

In most developed countries a broad political consensus prevails; policy should seek to ensure equality of opportunity accompanied by a minimum standard of living for all. As a result political competition and debate generally focuses on modest proposals, aimed at either deepening the welfare system in the pursuit of greater equality or the strengthening of individual incentives through tax reductions and smaller state benefits. Today's consensus is based both on notions of social justice that inspire redistribution and provision of public services and lessons about the distortionary effects of high levels of taxation.

Behind the consensus, the level of redistribution varies significantly across countries, and these differences can be observed in the depth of the welfare state and the associated level of taxation preferred by voters. When we compared Ireland with other countries in Section 5, we noted that Ireland is characterised by low taxation and modest levels of redistribution by European standards.

However, it is worth noting the policy of modest social transfers and the public provision of basic services is unlikely to lead to dramatic reductions in inequality and relative poverty within countries for two reasons. First, even when high-quality education and healthcare are provided to all citizens, modest social transfers fail to provide a level playing field for children in the face of significant inequalities in income and especially wealth. The cross-country evidence suggests that higher levels of redistribution are an essential ingredient, along with the provision of public services, to achieve high levels of social mobility between generations. Second, as it is possible for some members of society to reject government provision of education and healthcare, opting instead for often higher quality alternatives in private markets, the option to reject undermines attempts at achieving equality of opportunity.

In the lead-up to the economic crisis, Ireland was in the fortunate and unique position of having sufficient resources to increase social transfers while reducing taxation. While this was unlikely to continue, the speed of Ireland's downturn after 2007 and depth of the subsequent fiscal crisis has cast doubt on Ireland's ability to afford the current welfare system. The continued need to reduce Ireland's fiscal deficit is likely to overshadow concerns of inequality and poverty in the short term.

Nevertheless, while trying to balance the books Ireland should tread carefully. Lower inequality and poverty is an important cornerstone for Ireland's competitiveness, while reducing the long-term fiscal burden of challenging social problems. Of course, the primary objective of government is not to help build a high income and successful economy as an end in itself, but as a means to supporting a trusting, cooperative and self-actualised society.

Endnotes

1   S. Kuznets, 'Economic growth and income inequality', *American Economic Review*, 45 (1), 1955.
2   T. Piketty, *Capitalism in the Twenty-First Century*, Harvard University Press, 2014.
3   *Economist* magazine, 'For Richer, For Poorer', 13 October 2012. See www.economist. com/node/21564414 for details.
4   R. Kanbur, 'Income distribution and development', in A. Atkinson and F. Bourguignon, (editors), *Handbook of Income Distribution,* North Holland, Amsterdam 2000.
5   See for example J. Stiglitz, *The Price of Inequality: How Today's Divided Society Endangers our Future*, Norton Publishing, New York 2012.
6   R. Wilkinson, and K. Pickett, *The Spirit Level: How More Equal Societies Almost Always Do Better*, Allen Lane, London 2009.

7   H. Dalton, 'The measurement of the inequality of incomes', *Economic Journal*, 30 (119), 1920.
8   A. Sen, *Equality of What?* The Tanner Lecture on Human Values. Delivered at Stanford University 22 May 1979.
9   E. Glaeser, *Inequality*, NBER Working Paper 11511, Boston 2005.
10 Government of Ireland, *Proposals for Supporting Lone Parents*, Department of Social Protection, Dublin 2006.

POLICY ISSUES AT SECTORAL LEVEL

CHAPTER 9

Agriculture and Food

Alan Matthews

1 INTRODUCTION

This chapter discusses the role of the agri-food sector in the Irish economy. The agri-food sector is a complex value chain which links the procurement of agricultural raw materials produced on farms, through their processing and distribution for final consumption. The sector consists of multiple players such as farmers, input suppliers, manufacturers, importers, packagers, transporters, wholesalers, retailers, and final customers. The agri-food sector of the Irish economy has traditionally been treated as a distinct sector for economic and policy analysis, in part because of its importance as one of the key indigenous sectors in the economy and in part because of the extent of policy intervention which sets it apart from other traded sectors.

Agriculture no longer has the dominant role in economic activity which it once had, but when the contribution of the food industry is factored in, the agri-food sector remains a significant player. It accounts for 8 per cent of Irish GNP and 8 per cent of employment. The agricultural sector remains important in other ways. Together with forestry, it occupies over 70 per cent of the land area of the country; it thus has a significant impact on the physical environment and the protection of biodiversity. It is the largest single contributor to Ireland's greenhouse gas emissions accounting for 33 per cent of the total in 2015, well ahead of transport which was the next most important emitter responsible for 20 per cent. It remains the single most substantial contributor to the economic and social viability of rural areas.

At the industry level, the food and drink industry is Ireland's most important indigenous sector. Agri-food exports contributed 11 per cent of total merchandise exports in 2015 but this understates their importance relative to the rest of manufacturing; once imported inputs and profit repatriation are taken into account, the agri-food sector accounts for up to 40 per cent of net foreign exchange earnings from merchandise exports. Buoyed by rising global food prices after 2008, growth in the value of agri-food exports made an important contribution to the Irish economic recovery from the post-2008 recession. Food and drink expenditures are also important to consumers, accounting for 18 per cent of household expenditure (not including meals out). Thus agricultural and food policy is intimately linked to debates on economic competitiveness, rural development, the environment and consumer well-being.

Another reason for the interest in agricultural and food policy is the decisive influence of government interventions on the fortunes of the industry. This dependence can be highlighted in a single statistic: the income accruing to farmers from agricultural activity arises almost entirely from public policy transfers from both EU and Irish consumers and taxpayers. Agricultural production within the EU is highly protected from world market competition. EU tariffs on agricultural and food imports average around 14 per cent, compared to 4 per cent for non-agricultural goods, and for some agricultural products exceed 60 per cent and more. Total public expenditure on the agri-food sector by the Department of Agriculture, Food and the Marine (which includes some expenditure which did not accrue to farmers but excludes the transfer from consumers due to higher food prices because of tariffs) was €2.33 billion in 2015. In the same year, the value added by the agricultural sector before subsidies amounted to €2.37 billion.

This substantial government intervention in favour of a particular industry raises a series of questions. What objectives is it designed to achieve? Are these objectives justified? Is the support provided achieving these objectives? Is the support being provided efficiently? These are questions which economists are well placed to answer.

These questions are particularly pertinent at present because agricultural and food policy faces challenges on a number of fronts. Globally, demand for food continues to increase, driven partly by continuing population growth but also by improving diets as per capita incomes rise particularly in the developing world. However, there are limits on the availability of new land which can be brought into production, an increasing number of countries are facing water stress, and climate change will adversely affect yields particularly in tropical countries. At the same time, advances in plant breeding, animal husbandry, crop protection and the use of big data drive continuing increases in productivity. For many decades these increases in supply potential (shifts in the supply curve) outweighed the increase in demand (shifts in the demand curve), with the result that real food prices have declined over long periods of time. However, beginning around 2005 real agricultural commodity prices began to increase and there were significant food price spikes in 2008 and 2011. This led many observers to believe we had entered a new era of rising food prices. Since then, food prices have fallen back and the future outlook for farm and food prices remains uncertain.

Within the European Union, there is continuing debate about the future of the EU's Common Agricultural Policy and whether its current level of funding should be maintained given the new priorities and challenges facing the European Union. There is also a tension between focusing the policy on the traditional objective of supporting farm incomes or using the money to encourage farmers to adopt more sustainable production practices and to provide better environmental outcomes on managed farmland. Another area of controversy revolves around government mandates to promote the production of renewable energies and, in particular, bio-fuels. Whether it makes sense to use agricultural land resources to produce food or fuel is a hotly contested issue.

Increasing attention has also been paid to food policy. Public health advocates warn that Ireland's high rates of obesity and overweight (where we are among the four worst countries in the EU) are a factor in the prevalence of non-communicable diseases such as type-2 diabetes and heart disease. Questions are increasingly being asked about the sustainability of diets high in meat and dairy products as well as the health and environmental impacts of highly-processed foods with high levels of sugar, salt and fats. At the same time, there is evidence of growing concern among consumers about the safety and quality of food being produced. Many citizens are scandalised by the apparent high levels of food waste. There are also questions whether the food marketing chain operates in an equitable and efficient way, given the increasing levels of concentration in the food marketing chain and the possible abuse by supermarkets in particular of their growing market power.

The purpose of this chapter is to describe these challenges in more detail and to discuss the appropriate policy responses. Section 2 provides a brief overview of some salient characteristics of the Irish agricultural sector. Section 3 discusses the changing policy context for agriculture at EU and international levels. Section 4 describes the food processing and distribution sectors and examines the exercise of market power in the food chain. Section 5 explores the growing emphasis given to food safety regulation as well as the promotion of food quality. Section 6 concludes the chapter by summarising some of the conflicting tendencies at work as the agri-food sector faces into a more market-oriented and uncertain environment.

2 AGRICULTURAL SECTOR

Economic Characteristics

Agriculture has some relevant economic characteristics which help to explain why it has attracted a disproportionate share of government intervention. One is the inherent volatility of farm prices, due to the characteristics of both agricultural supply and demand. On the supply side, agricultural production is subject to natural forces such as weather conditions, pest infestations and disease risk which means production can be very volatile from one year to another. For example, the drought that hit the US maize belt in 2012, the most serious and extensive in the previous 25 years, lowered its maize production by a quarter and had significant knock-on effects on world maize prices.

On the demand side, demand for food is inelastic with respect to price; indeed, as economies around the world become more affluent, food demand becomes even less responsive to price. The share of raw material costs in the overall consumer food bill is now so low in richer societies that even a doubling in the farm-gate price of food has a relatively small impact on the prices consumers pay in shops. This means that the price changes required to ensure equilibrium between supply and demand in the face of supply shocks are further amplified. For some commodities, such as cereals, storage from one year to the next provides a possible mechanism to help smooth out the volatility in prices, but many agricultural commodities are perishable or can only be stored at great cost (such as beef) so this option is often not feasible.

The impact of price volatility is exacerbated by the particular structure of agricultural production which is dominated by family farms. Unlike in industry where artisan and craft production has been gradually replaced by increasingly large enterprises which can exploit economies of scale and scope, agricultural production in Ireland and elsewhere remains in the hands of family farms. One way in which family farms try to insure themselves against price and supply risk is through diversification (growing a range of crops and supplementing farm income with off-farm sources of income).

Although highly diversified (but low-productivity) family farms still dominate agriculture in many developing countries, in Europe price-cost pressures have encouraged greater and greater specialisation, leaving farmers more exposed to price and thus income risk. True, income variability will usually be less than price variability in response to supply shocks because output and price move in opposite directions – recall the line in Shakespeare's *Macbeth* about the farmer who hanged himself in the expectation of plenty! Nonetheless, the prevalence of price volatility means that governments are often under pressure to intervene to help farmers during market crises and periods of depressed farm prices.

Farm prices are not only volatile but over the post-war period they have tended to fall in real terms. As noted previously, this fall in relative food prices reflects the interplay of the supply of and demand for farm products. On the one hand, the supply potential of the farm sector increased as farmers gained access to a range of productive new inputs such as improved seed varieties, better fertilisers, more powerful machinery, and more effective chemicals and pesticides. However, the market for this increased output did not grow to the same extent. Growth in demand is dependent on growth in population and in per capita incomes. But the rate of population growth in industrialised countries has slowed down and in some cases has virtually ceased. While per capita incomes continue to grow, a smaller and smaller proportion of this increase is spent on food. The consequence has been a downward pressure on the aggregate price level for agricultural products relative to other commodities.

This in turn puts a downward pressure on farm incomes and has encouraged farm family members to take up non-farm job opportunities. In all industrialised countries, the share of the farm workforce in total employment has fallen significantly. In Ireland, the number of farm holdings fell from 290,300 in 1960 to 139,600 in 2013. If this adjustment process proceeds smoothly, the reduction in the numbers engaged in agriculture should ensure that farm incomes, on average, stay in line with average non-farm incomes. For various reasons, however, some farmers may find it difficult to leave farming in the face of this downward pressure on farm incomes. Unemployment may be high in the non-farm sector, or their age and skill profile can make it difficult for them to find off-farm jobs. Suitable off-farm opportunities may anyway be rather scarce in rural Ireland. Many farmers appear trapped in agriculture with low incomes. Fifty-one per cent of farmers were over 55 years of age in 2013 compared to just 42 per cent ten years previously. Government transfers to agriculture have been justified in the past as a response to this perceived problem of low average farm incomes relative to the rest of society.

Nonetheless, a puzzle remains. Why is it that farmers, among all self-employed groups, have received such preferential treatment? Arguably, small shopkeepers or pub owners also experience fluctuating incomes and have difficulty in maintaining their living standards in the face of competitive pressures, yet government does not provide support for these sectors. Farmers are able to tap into deep social values by appealing to the need to maintain domestic food production as a guarantee of national food security, and the desire to support rural areas and the rural way of life. The unmatched ability of farmer organisations to defend and lobby for their interests should not be underestimated, and there are few rural constituencies where a TD would feel safe in opposing farmer demands for more support. Thus, the reasons for the extensive government intervention in agricultural markets are found both in the particular economic characteristics of the sector but also in political economy explanations for agricultural policy (see Chapter 3).

Structural Characteristics
Climatically, Ireland is more suited to grassland than crop production. Of the total agricultural area, over 90 per cent is devoted to grass and rough grazing. Livestock and livestock products account for around three-quarters of total agricultural output. Irish agriculture is very export-oriented. The export market absorbs more than 80 per cent of dairy and beef output. Around 40 per cent of Irish agri-food exports go to the UK, around 30 per cent to the rest of the EU and 30 per cent are exported outside of the EU.

Average farm size measured in land area is 33 hectares although there is considerable diversity around this average. This average area farmed is large in EU terms, but because of the relatively low intensity of land use the average size of farm business in Ireland is at the smaller end of the EU spectrum. There is an important regional dimension to differences in farm size, with a predominance of smaller farms in the West and the North-West, and a greater proportion of larger farms in the South and East. Small farm size is frequently associated with a low-margin farming system (mainly drystock) and a predominance of older farmers, many of whom are unmarried.

The process of structural adjustment in agriculture is slow in Ireland not only because those working in farming, as mentioned earlier, tend to be relatively immobile but also because of the very limited role played by the land market. Most agricultural land is transferred within the family, a practice which is encouraged by favourable tax treatment under inheritance and gift tax rules. Very little land is sold on the open market which would enable structural adjustment to take place, allowing younger, more dynamic farmers to acquire additional land from retiring farmers. While renting of land provides an alternative mechanism for structural adjustment, land leasing in Ireland is mostly very short-term with limited guarantees of security of tenure. As a result of this dysfunctional land market, prices for agricultural land are bid to ridiculously high levels which are very hard to justify by the returns from agricultural production alone.

Income from farming compares unfavourably with average industrial earnings, although comparisons are difficult for statistical and conceptual reasons. For example, the average family farm income in 2015 was €26,303 compared to 2015 average earnings of €37,090 for workers in the construction industry. However, this comparison is not comparing like with like. The average family farm income on the nearly 40 per cent of farms which were full-time was €51,557 in 2015 (bear in mind that this figure must remunerate the capital invested in the farm and that there were an average of 1.4 family members engaged on those farms, so it is not directly comparable to the construction industry earnings figure either). Conversely, the average income from farming on the remaining 60 per cent of part-time farms was only €11,058 (the definition of full-time and part-time here refers to whether the farm has sufficient size and activity to require the time of a full-time person or not, not whether the farmer has off-farm employment). Clearly, this level of income is inadequate on its own to support a farm family.

However, on around half of these part-time farms, either the holder and/or the spouse had an off-farm job. The increasing importance of off-farm income means that average farm *household* incomes are much closer to average incomes in the non-farm economy than the figures on farm income alone would suggest. On average, farm household incomes were around 10 per cent lower than for the state as a whole in 2008, the last year for which such comparative figures were published as part of the CSO's Survey of Income and Living Conditions. However, poverty levels among farm households are not that different to non-farm households. Household survey data show that consistent poverty is generally lower among farm households than in other household groups indicating a low rate of enforced deprivation among farm families.

A closer look at the sources of agricultural factor income shows the high dependence of farming income on transfers from the non-farm sector. In 2015, income from commercial farming activity accounted for only one-third of the income accruing to the sector, with the remaining two-thirds coming in the form of subsidies and transfers from the exchequer. For some individual sectors, the dependence on public transfers is even higher. According to the National Farm Survey, the average family farm income on cattle rearing farms (associated with a suckler cow enterprise) in 2015 of €12,660 was actually exceeded by the value of direct payments and other subsidies worth €13,148. When it is recalled that the value of farm output is also inflated by high tariffs on lower-cost imports from outside the EU (see Section 3), the vulnerability of farm incomes to policy changes which might lead to lower support and protection is underlined.

241

3 AGRICULTURAL POLICY

Common Agricultural Policy (CAP)

Most countries intervene in their agricultural markets in pursuit of the objectives of price stabilisation and income support. This is also true for EU agricultural policy, the objectives of which are spelled out in the Treaty of European Union as follows:

- To increase agricultural productivity by promoting technical progress and by ensuring the rational development of agricultural production and the optimum utilisation of all factors of production, in particular labour;
- Thus, to ensure a fair standard of living for the agricultural community, in particular by increasing the individual earnings of persons engaged in agriculture;
- To stabilise markets;
- To provide certainty of supplies;
- To ensure that supplies reach consumers at reasonable prices.

These five objectives of efficient agricultural production, fair incomes for farmers, stable markets, food security, and reasonable consumer prices would be broadly acceptable to most people, though the sharp-eyed will note the ambiguity of the wording (what is a fair standard of living for farmers?, what is a reasonable price for consumers?) and that there is potential for conflict between these objectives. However, the mechanisms put in place to achieve these policy goals have prioritised the farm income objective at considerable cost to the EU budget and consumers.

The mechanisms used have changed over time. The original CAP was strongly interventionist. Farm prices within the EU were supported by a combination of policy instruments, including import tariffs, market intervention and export subsidies. For many products, this meant that internal EU prices were double, sometimes three times, the level of world market prices. As production within the EU responded to these highly favourable price incentives, the EU gradually moved from being a net food importer to a net food exporter. For a period the EU tried to remove these surpluses from the market by buying them into intervention storage (leading to the infamous butter and beef 'mountains' and wine lakes) but this was at best a temporary solution. The other alternative was to export its surplus production with the aid of significant export subsidies, to bridge the gap between the high internal producer prices and the lower world market prices. Over time, the budgetary cost of these policies became unsustainable, while the protests from the EU's international trading partners who objected to the subsidised exports as unfair competition grew louder.

The first successful attempt to tackle the malfunctioning CAP was pushed through in 1993 by then EU Agriculture Commissioner Ray MacSharry. The MacSharry reform initiated a significant reduction in support prices for the first time. Farmers were compensated by direct payments which were tied (coupled) to the level of output on each farm. These payments were accompanied by measures designed to control supply. The market regime reforms were complemented by new agri-environment, forestry and early retirement schemes for farmers, part of an expanded rural development emphasis in the CAP.

There have been further rounds of CAP reform since then, with the most recent taking place in 2013 and implemented since 2015. These reforms have followed two principal directions. The first was to make EU agriculture more internationally competitive by bringing a greater market orientation to agricultural policy. The second was to focus the CAP more on environmental objectives. We discuss each of these in turn.

More Market Orientation
While high tariff protection continues (see below), the internal price support mechanisms have been eliminated and replaced by safety-net arrangements which only kick in when market prices fall to unusually low levels. Farmers, in turn, received additional direct payments to compensate for the reduction in market support prices. Further, these direct payments to farmers have been mostly decoupled from production since another major CAP reform in 2005. In the case of *coupled* payments, a farmer must plant arable land or keep animals in order to draw down these payments. Such payments are called coupled payments because they are linked to the amount each farmer produces. A major criticism, as demonstrated by the fact that on some farms the value of income from farming was less than the direct payments received, was that many farmers were keeping livestock or growing crops simply to collect the subsidies, rather than responding to market demand.

When these payments were *decoupled*, farmers are entitled to receive a payment regardless of the area planted to crops or the number of livestock on their farm, or indeed regardless of whether they produce on their farm at all. The payment is now made per hectare of eligible agricultural area each farmer manages. This decoupling of the payment from production was a further step towards market orientation because farmers now make their production decisions based on the relative market returns from each enterprise rather than the size of the subsidy available.

An important step towards market orientation has been the removal of supply management instruments, such as milk and sugar quotas. Milk quotas were introduced in 1984 in an attempt to control the exploding budget costs of removing surplus milk production from the EU market. For Irish producers, they were a mixed blessing. Although they meant milk prices were maintained at higher levels, they stopped expansion of a sector in which Ireland is a low-cost producer and where Irish producers have a clear comparative advantage not only vis-à-vis EU competitors but also at a global level. For over thirty years, a dairy farmer wishing to expand his or her production had to purchase the quota rights from a farmer exiting the sector. In 2015, milk quotas were eliminated in the EU and

Irish dairy farmers have responded vigorously to the new opportunities, even in spite of the downturn in milk prices around that time. Similarly, sugar quotas were removed in the EU in April 2017 but this has no relevance for Ireland which ceased to produce and process sugar in 2006 when it was no longer economic to do so.

Protecting the Environment
Policy Issues
A second principal direction of CAP reform has been to integrate environmental concerns into agricultural policy (note that the original Treaty objectives make no mention of the environment). Producing food inevitably impacts on the natural environment, and these impacts can be both positive and negative. Semi-intensive management of agricultural land and the creation of stone walls and hedge boundaries have helped to encourage biodiversity as well as attractive landscapes which act as a magnet for rural tourists. On the other hand, as farming has become more specialised and intensive, and made greater use of chemical inputs and machinery, the negative impacts on the environment have become more apparent. Agriculture is one of the main sources of nitrates in groundwater and of nutrient enrichment of surface waters. Farmland habitats are disappearing with a consequent loss of species and biodiversity. The contribution of agricultural production to greenhouse gas emissions has already been mentioned.

Readers will recognise that these environmental consequences of agricultural production can be characterised as externalities. In economics, an externality is a cost or benefit that affects a party who did not choose to incur that cost or benefit. An appropriate policy response is to use regulations or market instruments (such as taxes or subsidies) to 'internalise' the externalities, so that farmers when making their production decisions take these external environmental consequences into account. Negative externalities under the 'polluter pays principle' are mostly controlled by regulation. In Ireland, for example, water quality is protected under the Nitrates Directive and the Water Framework Directive which set out rules and practices designed to minimise nutrient run-off into waterways. Another policy instrument used under the CAP is *cross-compliance*. Farmers in receipt of direct payments are required to respect standards in the areas of the environment, food safety, plant health and animal welfare, and are also obliged to keep all farmland in good agricultural and environmental condition. Apart from possible prosecution through the courts, a farmer can also lose some or all of his or her CAP payment for breach of these obligations.

However, it is not enough simply to discourage pollution and environmental damage. Farmers can also be asked to carry out activities which go beyond normal good farming practices which produce positive externalities for the rest of society. For example, farmers can plant wild bird seed on some of their arable area, or manage their land in ways which protect nearby urban areas from flooding. Farmers are not rewarded through the market for providing these benefits. In marginal farming areas, farming helps to maintain open landscapes which society values, but farming on market terms alone in these areas is often not viable. A good example is the flora-rich limestone pavements in the Burren in Co. Clare which are only maintained by winter grazing. But the winterages are undergrazed and sometimes abandoned as farmers move to indoor feeding. Under the 'provider gets principle' there is a role for government to compensate farmers for providing these services through public payments.

EU Initiatives

In recognition of the growing importance that society is placing on these environmental outcomes, new initiatives and instruments have been introduced into the CAP. Many of these are included in the CAP's Rural Development policy, also known as Pillar 2 of the CAP to distinguish it from Pillar 1 which is principally concerned with income support through direct payments and market management. They include payments to farmers in areas facing natural constraints, support for agri-environment schemes (where farmers are compensated for management practices beyond the baseline set by cross-compliance which benefit the environment, and which includes the Burren Farming for Conservation Programme), as well as support for organic farming (where environmental benefits arise because of the ban on the use of chemical inputs and the emphasis on natural practices to maintain high levels of soil fertility).

A major feature of the 2013 CAP reform was to allocate 30 per cent of the money available for direct payment to a 'greening payment' which is paid to farmers who observe a number of simple agricultural practices designed to be beneficial to the climate and the environment. For arable farmers, the practices require farmers to avoid monoculture and to have a diversified cropping pattern, as well as to have a minimum share of their arable area (currently 5 per cent) devoted to what are called 'ecological focus areas'. These are intended to be areas managed primarily for their nature value rather than for food production. For livestock farmers, the obligation is not to convert grassland into arable land in order to avoid the release of soil carbon into the atmosphere when land is ploughed.

Greenhouse Gas Emissions

The need to limit greenhouse gas emissions from agriculture will become an increasingly dominant issue in the years ahead. Ireland has ambitious emissions reduction targets under national and EU climate policy. The national transition objective is to reduce overall national emissions by 80 per cent by 2050 while aiming at climate neutrality in the agriculture and land use sector, including forestry, which does not compromise capacity for sustainable food production. Although climate mitigation policy must focus on decarbonising the energy and transport sectors, agriculture must also play its part given the sheer scale of its emissions in the Irish context. Most agricultural emissions take the form of methane (from ruminant animals and manure storage) and nitrous oxide (from manure spreading and fertiliser application). Agricultural emissions have fallen since 1990 (taken as the baseline for greenhouse gas accounting) but may well now begin to rise given the prospects for dairy expansion following the elimination of milk quotas. Emissions can be mitigated through improvements in technical efficiency in production, through technological advances in low-emission practices which can be adopted by farmers, by altering land use towards less carbon-intensive enterprises, by sequestering (absorbing) carbon in soils and biomass (particularly through afforestation), and by growing energy crops which can substitute for fossil fuels in the non-agricultural sector. Changes in food consumption patterns and reductions in food waste also have a role to play.

Unlike in the energy, heating and transport sectors where it is possible to identify technological solutions which can assist the low-carbon transition, the potential for technological solutions in agriculture is currently limited (see Chapter 12). The role of the suckler cow herd (around half of the national herd) will come under particular scrutiny. While beef cattle in Ireland convert inedible pasture into foods humans can eat and thus make a net contribution to food supply, they are also a major contributor to emissions and make a very limited economic contribution once subsidies are stripped out. A critical policy question is how to design policy instruments which can signal to farmers the negative impact of this climate externality in order to incentivise them to find ways to reduce their emissions.

In addition to being a contributor to GHG emissions and global warming, agriculture will also be impacted by climate change. Temperatures will rise which will extend the grazing season in many parts of the country. Summers will become drier and winters wetter, and there will be a greater likelihood of extreme events such as storms, droughts and floods. There is thus also a need to think ahead in terms of the necessary adaptation on farms to a changing climate.

International Constraints on Agricultural Policy

As a consequence of successive reforms, the CAP has changed very significantly. Although Pillar 1 continues to take the lion's share of the CAP budget, accounting for over 70 per cent of CAP expenditure, most of Pillar 1 expenditure is now decoupled and does not provide the same incentive for over-production as before. Nonetheless, farmers continue to benefit from high levels of external protection for some commodities (especially beef and poultry meat) which in normal years keep food prices on the internal EU market higher than world market levels – for beef the mark-up may be as high as 25 per cent. These high protection levels have come under sustained criticism from the EU's trading partners in negotiations on trade liberalisation under the auspices of the World Trade Organization (WTO).

The WTO Agreement on Agriculture to which the EU is a party and which came into force in 1995 establishes rules on the manner and amount of government support to agriculture. These rules discipline agricultural policy in three main areas: the level and type of border protection for farm products; the use of export subsidies; and the amount of domestic support to farmers. Under these rules, only tariffs can be used to protect domestic producers from low-cost imports; the EU had to replace its former 'variable levy' system of border protection with fixed tariffs. The use of export subsidies was restricted and will be prohibited completely after 2020. The EU has not used export subsidies since 2013 and had already made a commitment in the 2013 CAP reform not to use them in future in normal market situations.

With regard to domestic support to agriculture, the Agreement distinguishes between permitted and disciplined forms of support. Support that does not influence, or only minimally influences, farmers' incentives to produce is permitted and there are no limits applied (support of this kind is considered not to cause distortions to trade). Trade-distorting support, such as market price support, on the other hand, is capped. The purpose of these rules is not to prevent governments from providing support to their farmers, but to get them to do so in ways that do not stimulate production and thus lead to unfair trade competition with other countries.

The WTO Agreement on Agriculture was important in clarifying the rules which apply to different forms of farm support but it did little to reduce its overall level. A new round of negotiations to liberalise agricultural trade began in March 2000 and subsequently became part of the Doha Round of multilateral trade negotiations under WTO auspices. These negotiations have ground to a halt, in part because of disagreements between developed and developing countries over agricultural subsidies. Irish farmers viewed a possible agreement with some trepidation, as the significant tariff reductions for beef and dairy products under discussion would likely lead to lower prices, even if benefiting consumers. Efforts continue to try to strengthen disciplines on trade-distorting agricultural support – a small success was the agreement to eliminate export subsidies by 2020 agreed at the WTO Ministerial Conference in Nairobi in 2015. However, further progress may be difficult in view of the change in the USA administration in January 2017 which has adopted a more protectionist policy with respect to international trade.

While multilateral trade liberalisation under WTO auspices appears to have stalled, the EU and other countries increasingly pursue trade liberalisation through bilateral or regional free trade agreements. The EU already has an extensive network of free trade agreements as well as preferential arrangements which give exporters in third countries preferential access to the EU market. Additional agreements with Singapore, Vietnam and Canada have been concluded and were undergoing ratification in 2017. The EU is also negotiating free trade agreements with a wide range of other countries, including the United States, Japan, Australia, New Zealand and Mercosur (the common market of South America in which Brazil is the leading player). Many of these are competitive agricultural exporters and are seeking additional access for their agricultural exports, including beef, which would compete directly with Irish farmers.

However, the most important bilateral trade agreement to be negotiated by the EU affecting the Irish agri-food sector is that with the United Kingdom following Brexit. Around 40 per cent of Irish food exports by value are sold on the UK market, while the UK is an important supplier particularly of processed foodstuffs to the Irish retail sector. Unless the two sides reach agreement on a free trade agreement with full coverage of the agri-food sector, there is the prospect that tariffs could be re-imposed on this trade for the first time since both countries joined the European Economic Community in 1973.With the British decision to leave both the EU customs union and the single market, traders will in any case face additional costs in importing and exporting across the Irish Sea and also across the land border with Northern Ireland. It is widely expected that the UK will pursue a much less protectionist policy towards its own farmers after Brexit, leading to lower food prices on the UK market and lower returns to Irish firms exporting to the UK market, but the size of the adverse shock cannot be estimated until the final deal, if there is one, is in place.

The CAP after 2020

In early 2017, the EU Commissioner for Agriculture and Rural Development Phil Hogan announced a further project for the 'modernisation and simplification' of the CAP. This new attempt to reform the CAP so soon after the previous reform was justified on three grounds.

First, farmers and member states find that the rules governing the CAP supports put in place in the 2013 reform are extraordinarily complex. This makes it easy for both farmers and member states to make errors in applying for payments and in administering the schemes, which can result in significant fines for both the farmer and the member state.

Second, changes in the external environment since 2015 revealed weaknesses in the design of EU agricultural policy. The period since 2014 saw farm incomes under pressure in particular sectors, partly due to the Russian ban on certain EU food imports in that year in response to EU sanctions following Russia's intervention in the Ukraine, and partly due to commodity price cycles. There is a view that the existing CAP is not well designed to handle market volatility, and that a more extensive tool-kit of risk management instruments is needed. There is also disappointment that the new 'greening payment' which was the centrepiece of the 2013 reform actually delivered minimal changes in farming practices on the ground and thus resulted in very little environmental benefit. There is a widespread feeling that the policy could do better in this respect.

Third, there is a growing questioning of the continued value and justification for decoupled area-based direct payments. Recall that these payments were originally introduced as a compensation for market support price reductions which took place, in some cases, more than twenty years ago. They have become the major source of income on many farms, but exactly why the taxpayer should continue to fund these payments is not clear. The sums involved are not trivial. Direct payments account for over 70 per cent of the CAP budget and almost 30 per cent of the entire EU budget. Ensuring that this money is well-spent and helps to achieve important EU objectives is crucial at a time when budgets are under pressure and the value of the EU itself is under question.

For some, they are a basic income support but because they are paid on a per hectare basis most of the payments go to farms whose incomes are well above the median farm income in the Union. They are defended as a safety-net against farm income volatility, but high-value products which use little land but are often more prone to market price variability, such as horticulture, pigs and wine, get only a small share of these payments. Also, payments are made in years of high farm prices as well as low. For others, they secure the environmental benefits of farming but the payment bears no relationship to either the farmer's effort or outcomes in terms of environmental improvement. In short, decoupled payments were justified as a transitional measure to support farmers during the transition to a more market-oriented agricultural policy, but they are inequitable, ineffective and an inefficient way to address the challenges facing farmers and the food system in the coming decade.

4 FOOD PROCESSING AND DISTRIBUTION

Food Industry
Economic Importance
Few agricultural products are sold directly to the consumer – vegetables, fruit, and eggs in farmers' markets being the main examples. Most agricultural products are purchased by food processors which prepare food for final consumption for either the domestic or export markets. Total sales by the food and drinks industry amounted to over €26 billion in 2012. The gross value added by the industry (which subtracts the value of raw materials it purchases and gives a better idea of its contribution to the overall economy) amounted to €7.5 billion that year, equivalent to 6 per cent of GNP at market prices. The industry provides employment for around 52,000 people or one-fifth of the total industrial workforce.

Globally, the food industry consists of a limited number of well-known multinational food companies (Nestlé, Unilever, Kraft, Kellogg, etc.) as well as a myriad of much less well-known small and medium-sized enterprises which supply a wide variety of food products. This is reflected in the food industry structure in Ireland which consists of subsidiaries of multinational firms (for example, there is an impressive cluster of international firms, such as Abbotts, Danone and Pfizer, which together produce 15 per cent of the world's supply of infant milk formula in Ireland), some larger Irish-owned firms which have themselves become multinationals (Kerry Foods, Glanbia, Greencore, etc.) and then a large number of small and medium-sized firms which are a crucial source of employment and potentially innovation for the sector as a whole.

While there are over 650 individual food firms with more than 3 employees, the 40 largest firms each with over 250 employees account for around 40 per cent of the employment and almost 60 per cent of the output. The existence of the multinational sector creates the same need for caution in interpreting statistics on value added and productivity levels as for manufacturing as a whole. There is a pronounced dualism in the sector, to which the phenomenon of transfer pricing may contribute (see Chapter 10). Over 80 per cent of net output and exports are contributed by foreign-owned firms. Nonetheless, over 60 per cent of employment and 70 per cent of food firms are Irish-owned, and these firms account for more than half of exports by all Irish-owned manufacturing units.

Changing Markets

Building on the strong performance by the industry after the 2008 recession, the government set ambitious targets to increase both exports and food industry value added in its strategy document *Food Harvest 2025* published in 2015. These included targets to increase the value of agri-food exports by 85 per cent to €19 billion and the value added by the industry by 70 per cent to in excess of €13 billion by 2025 compared to 2012 to 2014 levels. Because of the importance of the UK market, sales are heavily influenced by the euro-sterling exchange rate. Any sharp appreciation in the value of the euro makes it difficult for the industry to maintain let alone increase its market share in the UK. Shifting sales to the euro zone would limit this exchange rate risk and has been a policy objective. The imminent prospect of Brexit will undoubtedly make these ambitious growth targets difficult if not impossible to achieve. The UK as our nearest neighbour and with substantial purchasing power will always remain a significant export market. However, Brexit will give a further incentive to diversify export markets. The ability to meet (and to document that we are meeting) exacting quality standards is a key factor in breaking into continental food supply chains, while deficiencies in language skills must also be addressed. Beyond this, the food industry faces significant challenges to improve its competitiveness, including reducing key input costs such as energy and waste, as well as improving its innovation capacity to benefit fully from emerging consumer trends.

The market for food is changing rapidly due to changing consumer demands and market structures. Changing consumer lifestyles are having a decisive influence on food demand. Increased numbers of women working in the paid labour force, reduced leisure time and the decline in the traditional family unit are changing eating habits and increasing the demand for convenience foods. Thus important growth areas for the food industry are the food ingredients business (such as dairy ingredients, meat, and by-products such as pizza toppings and meat flavourings, and other ingredients such as colourings, flavourings and malt) for pre-prepared foods, as well as the food service sector (embracing all forms of catering and eating out). Other important changes in consumer preferences are the growing concern over food safety, interest in nutrition/health/obesity management issues as well as the growing importance of ethical and food quality concerns, e.g. organic, fair trade, shop local, food miles, and animal welfare (see Section 5).

Distribution

The final element of the food chain consists of distribution, comprising wholesalers, retailers and food service firms, which provide the link between the food industry and consumers. Wholesaling involves the purchase of goods from suppliers and importers for resale to retailers and food service customers. Wholesalers provide a range of services such as storage, distribution and other services in connection with the sale of goods. The principal innovation of modern whole-saling is the emergence and growth of wholesaler-franchisors, that is, wholesal-ers which sell predominantly to retailers which are affiliated to them (symbol groups such as SuperValu, Londis, etc.). Retailers decide whether to operate as an independent retailer or under the brand of a wholesaler-franchisor. Thus, modern wholesaling is very much involved with developments at the retail level.

The wholesale level of the grocery supply chain is highly concentrated. The former Competition Authority estimated that over 95 per cent of the wholesale turnover in the Irish grocery sector is attributable to seven groups of operators. Just two firms, Musgrave and BWG Foods, together account for almost 80 per cent of grocery wholesale turnover. Six of the seven groups are wholesaler-franchisors which buy goods from suppliers for resale to retailers and which license one or more retail brands to retailers which are part of their symbol groups. The remaining group combines cash-and-carry wholesalers which are engaged in the traditional function of buying goods from suppliers for resale to independent retailers.

The grocery retail sector in Ireland is made up of the major multiples, sym-bol groups, independent retailers and speciality independents, e.g. greengro-cers, butchers, etc. The number of multiples has grown steadily, as well as their size, facilitated by the emergence of out-of-town shopping centres. Just three retail groups – Tesco, Dunnes and the Supervalu/Centra brands owned by Musgraves – have a 67 per cent share of the retail grocery market. The discount stores, Aldi and Lidl, have achieved significant market penetration over a short period of time and now control a 22 per cent market share. Independent retailers and retailers affiliated to smaller wholesaler-franchisors account for the remaining 11 per cent of grocery sales.

The other main channel for food distribution is the food service sector, defined as 'food consumed away from home', the importance of which has also been growing over time. It now accounts for over one-fifth of all expenditure on food. The channel is made up of fast-food restaurants, full service restaurants, pubs and coffee shops, hotels and institutional catering. Food is now more important than drink in sales terms for pubs. Nonetheless, the food service market in Ireland is less developed than in other European countries where the sector accounts for around one-third of consumer expenditure on food, or in the USA where the share is 50 per cent.

Market Power in the Food Chain

Price Paid to Farmers

A major issue in the food chain, not only in Ireland but across Europe, is whether the concentration of buying power in the hands of retailers gives them excessive market power to set prices and trading conditions at the expense of suppliers and farmers. Concern about the abuse of market power in the food chain is not a new issue. Since the beginning of the 1900s farmers have attempted to increase their collective bargaining power in negotiating prices with creameries, meat factories,

and grain millers. One outcome of these attempts was the co-operative movement, which still plays an important role in the Irish dairy industry.

With the rise of supermarkets these concerns have now moved further down
the food chain. In a situation where it is not unusual that the top three retailers
control 50 per cent or more of a country's grocery trade, there is a noticeable
asymmetry in bargaining power between retailers and their suppliers. The largest
food companies account for only 1 to 2 per cent of a retailer's business at national
level, but conversely a retailer may represent 20 to 30 per cent of those companies' business.

There are frequent allegations that retailers have taken advantage of this
situation of unequal dependence to increase their profit margins at the expense
of consumers and of suppliers and farmers further back the food chain through
anti-competitive practices. There are in fact two separate issues here – buyer
power vis-à-vis suppliers and seller power vis-à-vis consumers. These are separate markets and the degree of competition is not necessarily the same in each.

We first examine whether there is evidence that retailer concentration in Ireland has resulted in consumers being ripped off. Farmers are often angry when
they see prices falling at farm level but increasing to the consumer at retail level,
and blame the food chain intermediaries, particularly supermarkets, for pocketing
the difference. Indeed, the farmers' share of the retail price of food has steadily
decreased over time even for relatively simple products such as a litre of milk or a
standard loaf of bread. Between 1995 and 2009 the farmers' share of the retail price
for liquid milk fell from 42 to 33 per cent. For cheese, the share fell from 34 to 20
per cent, for pig-meat from 51 to 27 per cent, and for beef from 60 to 50 per cent.[1]

The retail price, of course, includes the cost of the marketing services added to
the raw material provided by the farmer (processing, transport, assembly, packaging, storage, and distribution). There may be good reasons why the cost of these
marketing services increases at a different pace to the cost of the raw material.
But the generally high price of food in Ireland relative to other EU countries reinforces the suspicion that competition in the retail food market is less aggressive
than it should be.

Eurostat produces regular surveys of the cost of a similar basket of food products in different EU member states. The two countries with the most expensive
food in 2015 were two Scandinavian countries, Denmark and Sweden, followed
by Austria and then Ireland. This is a slight improvement in Ireland's relative
position, as over the period 2007 to 2010 we had the second highest food prices
after Denmark. The Eurostat figures may even underestimate the high cost of food
in Ireland relative to other EU countries because the prices collected include any
VAT and other taxes. As food is mostly zero-rated for tax purposes in Ireland (in
Denmark, for example, it is subject to a VAT rate of 25 per cent) one would expect
this to be reflected in much lower retail prices than abroad. Occasional periods of
cross-border shopping (often in response to exchange rate fluctuations between
the euro and sterling) also underline that food prices here are often more expensive than in the neighbouring territory.

Explanations

Various explanations have been offered for this finding. One argument is that the cost of doing business in Ireland is, in general, higher than in other countries. Indeed, it is not just the price of food, but prices in general, which tend to be higher than the EU average. Food prices are not more out of line than other prices. The Competition Authority has highlighted the possible role of retail planning caps on the size of stores under retail planning guidelines introduced in 1982 under pressure from the independent retailers. These guidelines mean that there are no large-scale low-cost grocery retailers such as exist in Northern Ireland (the guidelines were revised in 2012 to reduce barriers to entry to the retail market but caps on the size of individual stores have been maintained).

When the Competition Authority investigated whether there was excessive profit-taking by supermarkets at the expense of consumers some years ago, it could find no evidence that this was the case. More recently, consumers have become more price-conscious and more willing to shop around and we have already noted the growing market share of the German discount chains. This change in behaviour, no doubt, has contributed to the slight improvement in Ireland's ranking in relative food prices since 2010. However, it would seem desirable, given their role in the economy, that the large vertically-integrated retailers should be obliged to report details of their profitability and turnover in Ireland, which is not the case at present, to allow charges of profit-taking to be evaluated.

The other competition policy issue concerns relationships between suppliers and wholesalers/supermarkets. Suppliers often complain about unfair practices such as the practice of seeking 'hello money'. This is the name given to the practice where supermarkets seek payments from suppliers to have their goods stocked. Processors and suppliers may be compelled to carry the cost of product discounting campaigns by retailers. Retailers may seek to use exclusive supply agreements with suppliers to withhold supplies from price-cutting rivals. Growth in the sales of own label brands is also highlighted as another possible factor leading to an increase in buyer power.

Since 2006, the Irish Government has in various ways sought to better regulate the relationship between suppliers of foodstuffs and the retailers of these products. New Grocery Goods Regulations were introduced under the Competition and Consumer Protection Act 2014 which have been in force since 30 April 2016. Since that date, all contracts between major retailers and suppliers of food and drink must be in writing and expressed in clear, understandable language. The Regulations prohibit a retailer or wholesaler from varying or terminating a contract except under the conditions specified in the contract; unilateral retrospective variations which were a feature of supermarket behaviour are not permitted. Supermarkets and wholesalers must also pay a supplier within 30 days, unless otherwise provided for in the contract. They are prohibited from seeking payments from a supplier for stocking/displaying/listing grocery goods, for promotions, marketing costs, or better positioning of shelf space, or for wastage and shrinkage – unless provided for in the contract.

The Regulations are policed by the Competition and Consumer Protection Commission (CCPC) which replaced the Competition Authority and the National Consumer Agency in 2014. It has the job of monitoring whether supermarkets and wholesalers are complying with the Regulations. It investigates complaints into potential breaches of the Regulations and can initiate prosecutions through the Courts in the event of non-compliance. A major problem with implementing previous competition provisions is the reluctance of suppliers to make a complaint for fear that it would lead to their de-listing by the supermarket. The impact of the Regulations will depend very much on the vigour of their enforcement by the CCPC.

5 FOOD SAFETY AND QUALITY

Growing Concern over Food Safety

From earliest times food has been particularly susceptible to exploitation, and there is a long history of food legislation with the purpose of preventing consumers being either cheated or poisoned! Measures for the protection of the consumer against the adulteration of food and drink are among the earliest examples of social legislation. Since then the scope of food law has been greatly widened. Examples of some of the matters now covered by legislation include the produce of diseased animals posing a threat to human health; sanitary conditions in food preparation, packaging and handling; pesticide and hormone residues in food; packaging materials which may pose a threat to health; food additives; the labelling requirements for food products; and weights and measures legislation.

Despite the undoubted improvement in food purity and in merchandising practices brought about by this legislation consumers are increasingly uneasy about the safety and quality of the modern food supply. Issues of recent concern include agrochemical residues in food, the increasing number, and diversity of food additives, the use of illegal substances in livestock production, the existence of nitrates in drinking water and genetically engineered foods. There have been sharp falls in the consumption of particular foods caused by publicity given, for example, to Bovine Spongiform Encethalopathy (BSE) in cattle ('mad cow' disease), listeria in soft cheeses, or salmonella in eggs. Consumer concerns also extend beyond the safety of food products to their production methods including genetic modification, animal welfare, and environmental and ethical concerns.

The risk of food-borne diseases has increased for a number of reasons. Best hygiene practices are not always followed in commercial and domestic kitchens. Fewer people are preparing their own food and more eating outside the home means a higher proportion of people at risk in outbreaks. The increasing demand for ready-to-go foods has resulted in food being served in a growing number of non-traditional outlets such as garage forecourts. The global distribution of food has lengthened the food chain.

The increased competition and price constraints on food producers has led the sector to seek cost reductions through ever more complex food processing and may sometimes encourage suppliers to adopt practices which have adverse health effects. The dioxin contamination of Irish pig-meat in 2008 which cost the taxpayer over €100 million was the result of an animal feed compounder using contaminated fuel oil sold as food-grade oil by a Northern Ireland supplier. In 2012 the Food Safety Authority of Ireland was the first to reveal the substitution of beef by horsemeat in frozen beef burgers which was later shown to be a wide-spread practice across Europe. Although this was an issue of fraudulent labelling rather than a health concern, it underlined the complex nature of an increasingly globalised food chain.

Fortunately, in Ireland, food problems have not emerged to the dramatic extent reached elsewhere. However, the increase in food poisoning notifications (E-coli, for instance) suggests that vigilance is essential. An E-coli outbreak in Germany in May–June 2011 caused by infected fresh vegetables from an organic farm caused the deaths of 53 people. Food production and tourism are major elements in the economy, and both depend crucially on a favourable international perception of the safety of Irish food. So along with the issue of the health and lives of its own citizens, Ireland has a vital economic interest in becoming a centre of excellence in food safety.

Economic Considerations

In economic terms, the need for governments to regulate for food safety is the result of a market failure (see Chapter 3). This arises because consumers are not necessarily in a position to determine the safety characteristics of food they consume on the basis of visual inspection alone. There is thus an asymmetry of information between the producer and consumer of food. In this, the market for food safety is like the market for used cars. Sellers have more information about the quality of the car than buyers. Because buyers often cannot tell the difference between a good and a bad used car, both good and bad cars must sell at the same price and the seller of a good car is unable to extract a premium for quality. In the same way, there is a tendency for food safety to be undersupplied by the market because consumers are not always able to distinguish between high and low food standards.

Of course, if we go to a restaurant and subsequently experience illness due to food poisoning, we are unlikely to patronise that restaurant again. Where there is the likelihood of repeat purchases, food businesses have an incentive to maintain high standards in order to maximise the likelihood of retaining our custom. The development of brand names, or supermarkets that monitor quality on our behalf, are other ways in which market institutions can respond to the asymmetry of information. However, sometimes firms themselves may be unaware of, say, the carcinogenic risk associated with a particular additive or production process.

There may also be strong externalities that justify government intervention, either on the production side (one rogue producer who fails to meet adequate food standards can put the reputation of an entire national food industry at risk) or on the consumption side (an infectious food-borne illness imposes wider costs on society that transcend those incurred by the individual consumer). This is the economic case for governments to step in to ensure that minimum food standards are maintained.

While the failure to observe adequate food standards can impose economic costs both on individuals and society at large, maintaining and enforcing these standards is also a costly exercise. For economists, this raises the question whether the benefits from a particular food regulation (in terms of the avoided cost of food illnesses or, for an exporting country, the loss of market reputation in export markets) exceed its costs. The idea that we should try to balance benefits and costs in setting food regulations suggests that trying to achieve zero risk is not the optimal strategy. Removing all risk from eating food is likely to be hugely expensive, and the economic benefit from lowering risk from a minimal to a zero risk of contracting an illness may not justify taking this extra step.

There may also be an alternative and more efficient instrument available to achieve the same degree of risk reduction, for example, by introducing more stringent product liability legislation which allows consumers to claim damages if harmed by consuming unsafe food. Governments, of course, should not take such decisions on the basis of cost benefit studies alone; moral and ethical criteria must also be taken into account. However, the economist's framework of balancing the expected benefits from risk reduction against the costs of achieving such reductions should be an important adjunct to the decision-making process in food safety regulation.

EU Food Safety Framework
Following the loss of consumer confidence in the safety of the EU food supply particularly following the BSE crisis in the 1990s, the EU completely overhauled its system of food safety regulation. A new General Food Law which brought together the general principles of food and animal feed safety was agreed in 2002. The new law made food safety and consumer protection the cornerstone of the regulatory regime. Including animal feed in its provisions was a major advance as animal feed has been the source of many food scares in the previous decade. This was supplemented by new food hygiene legislation which has been in effect since 2006. This modernises, consolidates and simplifies the previous EU food hygiene legislation and introduces a 'farm to fork' approach to food safety, by including primary production (that is, farmers and growers) in food hygiene legislation, for the first time in the majority of cases.

The general principles which now underlie food safety policy emphasise a whole food chain approach (food safety must be ensured at all stages of the food chain, from the producer through to the consumer), risk analysis (meaning that the policy is based on a scientific understanding of risk with due account for the need for precaution when scientific opinion is not yet clear), operator liability (all food sector operators are now responsible for ensuring the safety of the products which they import, produce, process or sell), traceability (all foodstuffs, animal feeds and feed ingredients must be traceable right through the food chain) and openness (citizens have the right to clear and accurate information on food and health risks from public authorities).

The General Food Law is supplemented by a large number of targeted regulations addressing specific food safety issues, such as the use of pesticides, food supplements, colouring, antibiotics and hormones in food production; rules on hygiene; food labelling; and legislation setting down procedures for the release, marketing, labelling and traceability of crops and foodstuffs containing genetically modified organisms.

A second Commission initiative was the creation of the European Food Safety Authority (EFSA) in 2002 to provide a source of independent, objective scientific advice on food-related risks. The new Authority has responsibility for the EU Rapid Alert System which links EU countries in cases of food-borne threats. The Authority's role is limited to giving its opinion, and it is up to the Commission (in conjunction with the Council and the Parliament) to initiate the required action to manage risks. The EFSA works through a series of Scientific Panels composed of independent experts who are responsible for providing scientific opinions to the Authority. Of course, scientists may disagree, and member states in the legislation establishing EFSA were reluctant to grant it the power to act as the ultimate source of food safety information. In the event of a disagreement between the EFSA and a national food safety agency, for example, it would be up to the courts to resolve this conflict.

The third initiative was to improve the EU framework for control and enforcement of food safety legislation. Enforcement of food regulations is the responsibility of national governments albeit under the oversight of the EU. An EU framework directive lays down norms and procedures relating to inspection and enforcement, and the Food and Veterinary Office of the European Commission, which is based in Grange, County Meath, controls the performance of national authorities and makes recommendations aimed at improving national control and inspection systems.

Irish Responses

In Ireland, the Food Safety Authority was set up in 1999 to ensure that food produced, distributed or marketed in the state meets the highest standards of food safety and hygiene and to coordinate food safety activities 'from farm to fork'. The Authority has functions in relation to research, advice, coordination of services and certification of food. It operates the national food safety compliance programme by means of service contracts with the agencies involved in the enforcement of food legislation (including Government Departments, Health Boards, local authorities, and the Radiological Protection Institute). In addition, the Authority works with industry and training bodies to improve, harmonise and coordinate food safety and hygiene training through the country.

Initiatives such as the National Beef Assurance Scheme and the National Sheep Identification System have been launched to ensure the identification and traceability of animals/meat. Controls on BSE remain in place to ensure that meat from confirmed cases and from herds in which cases have been located does not enter the food or feed chains. Another priority area concerns residue testing which is particularly focused on detecting illegal growth promoters in cattle and antibiotic residues in pigs. A new cross-border Food Safety Promotion Board known as Safefood has been established under the Good Friday Agreement to contribute to the improved coordination of food safety activities on the island as a whole. Its functions include food safety promotion; research into food safety; communication of food alerts; surveillance of food-borne diseases; and the promotion of scientific cooperation and linkages between laboratories.

Food Quality

Alongside food safety, consumers are showing a greater interest in food quality. What constitutes quality is very much a subjective matter, especially where food is concerned. Food quality was traditionally associated with properties that could be assessed by the senses (taste, smell, sight, and touch). These attributes, such as freshness, colour, degree of blemish or shape, are readily ascertained by consumers.

However, consumers increasingly seek to make purchases based on lifestyle or ethical considerations. They demand information on specific product or process characteristics, including the place of origin, carbon footprint, whether the farming practices are organic or not, whether the product has been modified by biotechnology, whether it meets 'fair trade' standards, and whether high animal welfare standards were adopted. Because the consumer cannot make an informed decision on these issues just by looking at a food product, he or she depends on accurate labelling. But because of the potential for fraud (e.g. passing off a product as organic in order to obtain the premium price when in fact it is not), labelling claims are either regulated by the state or may be substantiated by a credible third party.

Both public authorities and the food industry have an interest in communicating food quality characteristics to consumers. Ireland is a high-cost food producer and cannot compete on cost alone with major agricultural exporters. However, by targeting food quality characteristics where consumers have a demonstrated willingness-to-pay, the Irish food industry can hope to attract a premium price and thereby improve its competitiveness. Similarly, food retailers seek to use quality attributes as a means of product differentiation both to attract more customers to their stores and to persuade them to part with more money when they are there. As a result, there has been an explosion of quality assurance schemes both private and public aiming to provide information to consumers. Indeed, one of the problems in this area is information overload such that consumers are confused rather than informed by the plethora of labels and logos that have emerged.

An Bord Bia, as the state body charged with the marketing of Irish food abroad, operates a number of quality assurance (QA) schemes, for beef, lamb, chicken, pig-meat, eggs and horticulture, which are associated with particular production standards. A Bord Bia survey conducted in early 2009 found that more than four in five consumers in Ireland recognised its Quality Mark and almost half of respondents said that they would be much more likely to buy a product bearing the mark. In 2014 Bord Bia launched the Origin Green scheme to emphasise the environmental sustainability credentials of Irish farm produce especially for export markets. Origin Green is a voluntary programme that commits Irish food and drink producers to operate in a verifiably sustainable manner. Companies develop plans to improve sustainability in areas such as material sourcing, emissions, energy, waste, water and biodiversity. At farm level, Origin Green builds on existing on-farm QA schemes which also measure carbon footprint. By end-2015, over 485 Irish food and drink manufacturers had signed up, with 128 companies, representing over 85 per cent of exports, fully verified members. At farm level, over 45,000 beef farms, representing 90 per cent of Ireland's beef production, were QA members.

The growing demand for food safety and improved animal welfare will increasingly impact on farmers. Even in the absence of government regulation, the private sector and particularly the large retail chains are insisting that their suppliers meet stringent hygiene and safety standards. These demands will require farmers to undertake additional investments and will accelerate the process of structural change in the industry. However, they also open up additional marketing opportunities.

Instead of selling beef as a commodity product, for example, it becomes possible to produce beef for particular niche markets and to guarantee consumers that their particular requirements have been met. One fast growing market is for organic produce. Organic production in Ireland is relatively limited with 1,750 registered producers and 61,000 hectares (1.3 per cent of the agricultural land area) in organic production or in conversion in 2012. The government objective was to have 5 per cent of agricultural land under organic farming by 2012. A new Organic Farming Action Plan was launched in 2013 to increase the production level and to promote potential export markets. Farmers who wish to convert to organic production are eligible for aid under the Organic Farming Scheme which is funded through the Rural Development Programme under Pillar 2 of the CAP.

Another quality scheme operated under EU legislation is the scheme of protected Geographical Indications (GIs). A GI is an indication that is used on a good, and identifies that good as possessing a particular quality, reputation, or some other characteristic due to its geographical origin. GIs are thus a form of intellectual property. Many GIs consist of the name of the town, region or country where the goods originate from. They include indications such as PDO (Protected Designation of Origin), PGI (Protected Geographical Indication) and TSG (Traditional Specialities Guaranteed). Products which receive this recognition must be produced in the specific region, often using traditional recipes or ingredients. Similar products from other regions are not permitted to use these protected names. For example, only sparkling wines produced in the Champagne region in France may be called champagne. In this way, it is hoped that producers of these products can earn a premium based on the value that consumers attach to the name. Irish products which are protected in this way include Blaa/Waterford Blaa, Clare Island Salmon, Connemara Hill Lamb, Imokilly Regato, Timoleague Brown Pudding, Irish Whiskey, Irish Cream and Irish Poitín.

6 CONCLUSION

The agri-food sector is one of the key sectors of the Irish economy, accounting for around 8 per cent of GNP and employment. This chapter has emphasised the way in which the sector is heavily influenced by government policies promoting specific objectives. The substantial protection provided to EU agriculture means that almost all the income generated by agricultural production arises because of transfers either from consumers or taxpayers resulting from the operation of the Common Agricultural Policy. The share of budget transfers from taxpayers, which now accounts for 70 per cent of Irish farm income, is particularly striking.

Farming faces both challenges and opportunities in the future. The system of transfers is threatened by changing EU budget priorities. The future justification for decoupled payments, so important to incomes on many farms, is unclear, with many inequities between farmers themselves. The UK's exit from the EU is likely to cause an enormous negative shock as Ireland loses the advantage of selling to UK consumers behind high protective EU tariffs. Border protection may be further undermined by free trade agreements between the EU and countries with highly competitive agricultural sectors such as in South America. The adverse impact of intensive agricultural production on the environment has attracted the attention of an increasingly powerful environmental movement. Increasingly ambitious climate targets will require a change in mind-set and practices on many farms.

On the other hand, the elimination of milk quotas now allows Irish agriculture to concentrate on what it does best, namely, converting grass to milk and meat. New advances in technology will create opportunities for efficient farmers. The future outlook for food prices is uncertain, but there is at least the possibility that real commodity prices could stabilise over the medium term. The growing interest in environmental outcomes can also be a source of income on many farms, given society's willingness to pay farmers to manage land for positive externalities such as greater biodiversity and carbon storage. Over the next decade, more emphasis must be put on strengthening the competitiveness of farm production while ensuring that it lives up to ever higher consumer demands for safety and environmental sustainability.

The paradox should be noted that, at a time when government intervention in agricultural markets is being reduced, the demand for greater regulation of food markets has never been greater. While the rationale for continued agricultural support becomes less and less persuasive, the growing complexity of the food chain and fear of the consequences of new technological advances is fuelling consumer demands for greater food regulation. While a perfectly sound case for regulation can be made, it is important to bear in mind that all regulation imposes costs as well as benefits and that the task of the regulator is to find the appropriate balance (see Chapter 5). Economists are particularly well trained to assist in finding this balance through assessing the costs and benefits of alternative regulatory policies.

Endnote
1   Irish Farmers' Association, *Equity for Farmers in the Food Supply Chain*, Dublin, 2010.

Further Reading
Department of Agriculture, Food and the Marine, *Annual Review and Outlook*, latest issue (available on its website www.agriculture.gov.ie).

Department of Agriculture, Food and the Marine, 2015, *Food Wise 2025 – A 10-Year Vision for the Irish Agri-food Industry*, available at www.agriculture.gov.ie/foodwise2025/.

European Commission, Directorate-General for Agriculture and Rural Development, 2013, *Overview of CAP Reform 2014–2020*, available at ec.europa.eu/agriculture/ policy-perspectives/policy-briefs/05_en.pdf.

European Commission, Directorate-General for Agriculture and Rural Development, 2016, *Improving Market Outcomes: Enhancing the Position of Farmers in the Supply Chain, Report of the Agricultural Markets Task Force*, available at https://ec.europa. eu/agriculture/agri-markets-task-force_en.

Houses of the Oireachtas, Joint Committee on Agriculture, Food and the Marine, 2013, *Report on the Grocery Goods Sector 'Increasing equity and transparency in producer-processor-retailer relationships'*, available at www.oireachtas.ie/parliament/media/ Final-Report-on-Groceries-Goods-for-publishing-on-website.pdf.

J. Phelan and J. O'Connell, 2011, *The Importance of Agriculture and the Food Industry to the Irish Economy*, available at www.ucd.ie/t4cms/UCD%20Project%20JP-JOC.pdf. A blog which provides up-to-date commentary on agricultural policy and CAP reform issues by the author of this chapter can be found at capreform.eu.

CHAPTER 10

Manufacturing and Internationally-Traded Services

*Ciara Whelan**

1 INTRODUCTION

The world in which an economy operates has changed radically with the advances of globalisation and technological developments resulting in increased mobility of goods, people, capital and services. Ireland has demonstrated an uncanny propensity to embrace these changes in its approach to industrial policy. Irish industrial policy has been used for a reorientation of the economy to take advantage of the opportunities that the changing global environment brings.

From an agrarian based economy, Ireland embarked on a path of industrialisation in the 1930s where a policy of self-sufficiency and protectionism focused on the development of an indigenous manufacturing base. The failures of this policy became evident by the 1950s, when the focus of industrial development switched to one based on export promotion (see Chapter 1).

The period spanning the 1960s through to 2002 marked an industrial policy driven by investment criteria with the objective of pursuing export-led growth in the economy. Expansion in exporting took place in both high-value added high-technology sectors (chiefly chemicals and pharmaceuticals) which were predominantly foreign owned, and in traditional or low-technology sectors (mainly food and drink products) which were mainly populated by indigenous exporting firms. Industrial policy over this period catapulted manufacturing to the fore as a driver of economic growth and was largely responsible for the extraordinary growth rates observed during the 1990s.

The phenomenon that was the manufacturing sector began to lose ground after 2000, as exports of goods stagnated and the contribution to employment and output in the economy declined with the birth of the construction boom. After 2002 industrial policy was reoriented toward the internationally traded services sector. As globalisation and technological advancements allowed for greater scope in the international trading of knowledge-based services (such as financial, research and development (R&D), information technology (IT), consulting, legal and marketing services), industrial policy focused on these areas. Services imports and exports have increased dramatically since 2003. The composition of exports changed dramatically, as services exports became an increasingly large component of total exports in goods and services accounting for more than 50 per cent in 2015.

In the aftermath of the financial crisis in 2008, after an initial decline of exports in goods, exporting in goods began to recover, alongside the continued expansion of exports in services. Improved cost competitiveness as well as the weakening of the euro and growth in the Eurozone (aided by EU quantitative easing policies), and Ireland's capacity to attract FDI in liquid US markets after the US quantitative easing programme all played a role in this recovery.[1]

The post-financial crisis has seen a resurgence of interest in the manufacturing sector in a bid to rely less on financial and IT services and to nurture growth based on a sector that can yield high dividends in terms of productivity, jobs, linkages to other sectors, tax revenues and a terms of trade surplus.

In this chapter we will consider the factors driving these adjustments and impacts on the performance of the economy. Section 2 begins with an overview of the broad sectors of the Irish economy. Section 3 considers the role of industrial policy and rationales for state intervention. Section 4 provides an overview of the history of industrial policy, covering targets and tools, in the Irish economy. Sections 5 and 6 analyse the manufacturing sector and the internationally traded services sector in Ireland, respectively. Section 7 concludes.

2 BROAD ECONOMIC SECTORS

Economic activity can be classified into the three broad sectors of Agriculture, Industry and Services. Agriculture includes forestry and fishing as well as farming (cultivating soil, producing crops and raising livestock). Examples of industry include mining and quarrying (mineral extraction), construction, electricity and gas (the operation of electric and gas utilities, which generate, control and distribute electric power or gas), water supply and manufacturing. Manufacturing is an important subsection of industry, and refers to the transformation of raw materials from the primary sector (agriculture, forestry, fishing, mining or quarrying) or of other manufactured products into new products. Examples of manufactured goods include food, beverage and tobacco products, chemical products, machinery and transport equipment, basic semi-manufactured goods (e.g. leather, wood, paper and textiles), clothes, shoes, furniture, scientific instruments etc. Services include wholesale and retail trade (including hotels and restaurants), transport, government, financial and insurance, professional (such as legal, accounting, advertising), and personal (such as education, healthcare, and real estate services).

The relative importance of these sectors to the economy has changed with economic development. This was shown in Chapter 6 with respect to the composition of employment. Agriculture accounted for 24 per cent of total employment in 1973, declining to roughly 12 per cent in the early 1990s, and to just 5 to 6 per cent in 2015. Services' share of employment has grown steadily over the decades, from 45 per cent of total employment in 1973 to approximately 75 per cent of total employment in 2015. Industry accounted for 31 per cent of total employment in 1973, approximately 28 per cent at the turn of the century, and declined thereafter to 19 per cent in 2015.

In terms of the contribution of these sectors to the output of the economy, Figure 10.1 below illustrates the percentage contribution of agriculture, industry (including manufacturing), manufacturing only, and services sectors to gross value added (GVA) at current basic prices. GVA measures total output at basic prices less intermediate consumption at purchaser prices. This has been declining steadily for agriculture, while industry contributed an increasing share over the 1990s followed by a declining share since the turn of the century. The large changes in the relative shares of services and industry to GVA in 2015 should be treated with extreme caution however as the documented rise in value added from industry relative to services is to a large extent a reflection of a restructuring of the operations of multinationals located in Ireland. Rising industry GVA can thus partially be explained by contract manufacturing (where a company outsources its manufacturing to another company abroad).[2] Such practices are not the exclusive driver of the increase in value added from industry relative to services however, as the economy also enjoyed a boost in exports of goods manufactured in Ireland as we will see in Section 5.

While the above provides an overview of the trends in output and employment in the broad sectors of agriculture, industry, and services, beneath these

Figure 10.1 Sector Percentage Contribution to Total Gross Value Added

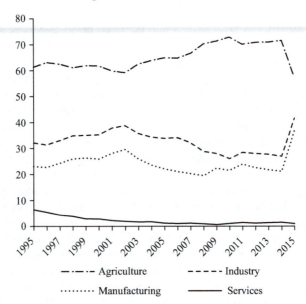

Source: Constructed from CSO, *National Income and Expenditure* Annual Results, various years.

aggregate figures there have been ongoing structural changes. In the industrial sector, manufacturing has become increasingly export oriented and specialised in high-technology sectors dominated by foreign owned firms (in terms of exporting and value added). In the services sector, structural changes have occurred due to the increasing international tradability of services. The causes and effects of these changes are examined in Sections 5 and 6, respectively.

3 RATIONALE FOR POLICY INTERVENTION

Industrial policy can be broadly thought of as interventions which enhance the business environment or induce structural change in the economy with the objectives of enhanced economic growth or societal welfare.[3] It implements policy with the objectives of improving competitiveness and growth, but can also be used as an instrument to attain wider societal goals. More recently, the concept of industrial policy has expanded from industry to also include economic activity in the services sector. This broadening of industrial policy emerged due to the linkages between industry and the services sector along with the structural changes that have emerged as a result of globalisation and the growth of internationally traded services.

At a basic level, the state has a role in ensuring a business-enabling environment through for example, the enforcement of property rights and contracts, or the design and enforcement of corporate and labour laws. Active industrial policy goes further, however, intervening in the economy to direct the nature of industrial development, or structural change, through the targeting of specific activities or sectors of the economy.

Efficiency

Interventions to enhance competitiveness and to promote economic development can be rationalised on the grounds of market failures. The levels of infrastructure (transport and utilities) and education and skills of workers affect the ability of firms to do business efficiently and competitively. If left to the market, there would be underinvestment. The high levels of investment required for infrastructure and its public good characteristics define a role for state provision.

The positive externalities from education for competitiveness and for the economy as a whole, in addition to credit market and information failures, define a rationale for education policy (see Chapter 13). Similarly the beneficial external effects from R&D and innovation on productivity and growth provide a rationale for state intervention to ensure optimal levels of investment in these activities.

Intervention in the manufacturing sector can be rationalised through the linkages it has to the primary (agriculture, forestry, fishing, mining or quarrying) and the services sectors. Growth in manufacturing generates positive employment and growth spillovers for these related sectors through increased demand. Likewise, positive externalities from trade for the economy can justify intervention in these activities through industrial policy.

Imperfect competition in the non-traded sector can lead to a loss of competitiveness in the traded sector through higher input costs, which defines a role for competition policy.

Other Policy Criteria
Industrial policy can also be implemented to achieve the goals of regional policy. Implementation can have a distributional impact by ensuring inclusive growth through targeted regional measures. It can be used to reduce regional disparities that would otherwise emerge during the process of economic development and industrialisation.

Moreover, industrial policy can be implemented to help achieve the goals of environmental policy. Negative production externalities for the environment, in terms of adverse effects on climate change for example, can define a role for industrial policy that promotes a switch to greener and more environmental production techniques.

In Ireland, industrial policy in manufacturing was driven by investment criteria with the objective of pursuing export-led growth and with embedded social welfare criteria. Interventions were thus made on the basis of promoting exports while also taking into consideration employment, linkage effects (small business, innovation), balance of trade and regional effects. The investment criteria became somewhat more diluted in terms of social benefits with the expansion of high-technology value added manufacturing, and even more so with the expansion of internationally traded services.

A consideration of environmental criteria has been noticeably absent in Irish industrial policy and one that should be embedded in future policy with the objectives of promoting cleaner and more green production techniques. Future industrial policy also needs to move beyond investment criteria rooted solely in the domestic economy. With globalisation and technological advancements there is a need to also consider the economic, social and environmental effects of policy on other economies and for world sustainable development, although this will require greater international cooperation.[4]

4 INDUSTRIAL POLICY

Overview
Ireland began to pursue an active industrial policy with the objectives of promoting structural change in the economy in the 1930s (see Chapter 1). For thirty years Ireland then pursued a policy of self-sufficiency and import substituting industrialisation. High tariffs and a prohibition of most foreign direct investment (FDI) lead to the creation of an indigenous manufacturing base. By 1949 brewing, bread and flour confectionary, and clothing were the biggest sectors of manufacturing accounting for over a quarter of total goods output.[5] Guinness, Jacobs, and the state owned Irish Sugar and Irish Steel companies were important indigenous producers in the economy.

The failures of this policy became evident in the 1950s, when the focus of industrial development switched to one based on export promotion. A series of targeted measures were phased in over the following decades to encourage exporting – initially in the manufacturing sector and more recently in the services sector. In addition to policies aimed at increasing the openness of the Irish economy in particular sectors, horizontal (general non-sectoral) interventions took place to improve competitiveness and productivity. The combined effects of these policies contributed to the development of a manufacturing base that was increasingly export oriented in both traditional and high-technology sectors, and a services sector that has become increasingly internationally traded.

Foreign exporting multinationals began to locate in Ireland, initially in more traditional sectors but later populating high-technology high value-added sectors and then the high value-added internationally traded services sectors. General Electric and Pfizer arrived in the 1960s, Ericson, Electric Corporation, Allergan and Smithkline & French arrived in the 1970s. Apple, Microsoft, Intel, Motorola, Dell, HP and IBM located subsidiaries in Ireland in the 1980s. Financial services attracted Citi, Deutschbank, HSBC in the 1990s. 2003 onward saw the arrival of Mastercard and Paypal, as well as Google, Yahoo, eBay, Amazon, Twitter and LinkedIn.[6]

Irish-owned exporting multi-nationals also developed, mainly in traditional sectors. Well-known successful exporting indigenous firms include packaging company Smurfit Kappa, food manufacturing Kerry Group, food company Glanbia, building materials firm Cement Roadstone Holdings (CRH), manufacturer of heating and home appliances Glen Dimplex and foods producer Greencore.

Horizontal Interventions
Infrastructure, education and competition policies are examples of general, or horizontal, interventions which all play a role in enhancing competitiveness and productivity and as such are important elements of overall industrial policy.

Developments in infrastructure have continued to be made in line with economic development and with regional policy in Ireland (see Chapter 3). These include transport networks (e.g. development of an improved road and motorway network), energy provision, water services, and telecommunications infrastructure (de-regulated since 1998). The state has intervened in the levels and quality of provision of infrastructure in the economy through a series of capital investment programmes and regulatory changes, facilitated by EU structural funds.

Since the 1960s there has been state investment and on-going reform in the education sector in an endeavour to enhance the overall levels and quality of education of the population. As the economy became more developed towards high-technology and knowledge intensive sectors, education policies also became targeted to ensure quality education in skills appropriate for a knowledge-intensive economy (see Chapter 13). This has led to an educated and skilled workforce in the economy.

Competition policy is recognised as being important for competitiveness. Competition legislation was first enacted in Ireland in 1953 with the Restrictive Trade Practices Act (see Chapter 5). Since then it has undergone various amendments, and was subsequently replaced by the 1991 Competition Act (and its amendments) which has at its core, the objectives of ensuring effective competition and preventing abuse of dominance in the economy.

Appropriate infrastructure, an educated workforce with the right skills, and low costs of doing business are important for all firms, but are also critical in determining Ireland's competitiveness in the attraction of FDI.

Targeted Policies
More targeted interventions can also be implemented under industrial policy to help shape the nature of the transformation of the economy. With the change in policy from protectionism and self-sufficiency towards one of openness, a range of targeted measures was implemented: reductions in tariffs, incentives to export through export tax relief and capital grants to attract green-field export-oriented FDI and to encourage new Irish owned exporting businesses. With the realisation that a move to free trade would inevitably result in structural change involving both winners (exporting firms and activity linked to these) and losers (import-competing firms), these measures were phased in over the following two decades.[7]

Trade Policy
As seen in Chapter 1, Ireland in the late 1950s had very high effective rates of protection. With the shift in focus toward export-led growth, tariffs were reduced unilaterally by 10 per cent in 1963, and again by 10 per cent in 1964. The 1965 Anglo-Irish free trade agreement phased in free trade with the UK in nearly all manufacturing products over the next ten years. Ireland became a member of GATT (general agreements on tariffs and trade) in 1967, and the EEC in 1973 leading to the removal of tariffs on nearly all manufacturing products in the community within five years. Membership of the EU also affords Ireland the benefits of EU negotiated trade agreements with countries outside of the EU.

Trade liberalisation played a fundamental role in setting Ireland onto an economic development path that was export-led. Free access to a large EU market has also been an important factor in FDI location decisions.

Tax Incentives
Tax incentives to encourage exporting have been a key part of industrial policy in Ireland. Fifty per cent tax relief on profits earned from increased manufacturing export sales was introduced in 1956, and later extended to allow for a zero per cent tax rate on profits stemming from all manufacturing exports. The late 1970s saw a phasing out of these export tax reliefs under EU rules, and its replacement by a 10 per cent corporation tax on profits for all manufacturing firms in 1980, later extended in 1987 to certain internationally-traded financial services. EU rules subsequently led to an amendment to a rate of 12.5 per cent effective from

2003, to cover all corporations in all sectors of the economy including all those in internationally traded services. Ireland continues to have one of the lowest corporation tax rates in Europe, although it collects a significant amount of tax revenue from this source (see Chapter 4). +CPT FDI on other side

Q5 The tax incentives instigated in the 1950s did provide incentives for indigenous firms to expand their exporting production. The preferential corporation tax treatment afforded to companies in Ireland compared with other countries also had a significant impact on FDI inflows in the export-oriented sector. Coupled with the horizontal interventions in infrastructure, education and competition, an English speaking population, and free access to the EU market, the attractiveness of Ireland as a location for FDI in high-technology sectors, particularly from the USA, was enhanced greatly by its corporation tax policy. Initially concentrated in the manufacturing sector, the expansion of favourable corporation tax treatment to certain financially traded services in 1987 and to all sectors of the economy in 2003 has resulted in a large increase of FDI into internationally traded services.

Calls for corporate tax reform on an international scale are mounting due to the growing problem of tax-avoidance by multinational corporations. For example, companies incorporated in Ireland but not tax resident anywhere can appear to avoid payment of tax on profits in any jurisdiction. This is evident in the recent European Commission Apple tax ruling, which deemed the preferential tax treatment afforded to Apple by Ireland to be in breach of EU state-aid rules.

Multinationals can avoid tax by shifting profits from high-tax to low-tax jurisdictions through transfer pricing, when subsidiaries in different countries charge each other for goods or services. Income can be shifted to low-tax countries by reducing prices of goods and services sold (increasing price of goods and services purchased) by subsidiaries located in high-tax locations. Transfer pricing is easier in the case of intangible goods or services (e.g. intellectual property, copyrights, patents), where it is difficult to establish what the price would be on the open market and hence the use of transfer pricing for tax avoidance.

The proposed Common Consolidated Corporate Tax Base (CCCTB) aims to reform corporate taxation throughout the EU to, among other things, tackle the issue of tax avoidance. While the CCCTB is not to affect corporate tax rates, which will still be set locally by individual countries, it will affect FDI location choice.

Grants and Supports
Beginning in the late 1950s, the Industrial Development Authority IDA (established in 1949) had the remit to encourage exports and FDI (see Chapter 1). This body administered grants to exporting manufacturing firms to encourage set-up and expansion. They included grants toward building, machinery and equipment costs, and later extended to R&D, training, and marketing costs. Such supports were available for both indigenous exporting and foreign exporting firms in manufacturing. There was an element of selectivity involved in the allocation of supports across regions: designated areas (mainly poorer peripheral regions suffering depopulation due to the decline of agriculture) were targeted to incentivise the

location of new foreign owned and indigenous plants in industrial estates across the least industrialised regions.

A review of industrial policy in the early 1980s and again in the early 1990s called for a greater focus on indigenous industry and on improving overall competitiveness, respectively. Following a restructuring of the IDA in 1994, IDA Ireland was made responsible for the promotion and development of FDI, while Forbairt was created and tasked with promoting indigenous industry.[8] Established in 1998, Enterprise Ireland (replacing Forbairt, and the Irish Export Board *An Bord Tráchtála* established in 1991), continued to focus on delivering supports for the promotion and development of indigenous enterprises. Policy has widened to include supports for indigenous non-exporting SMEs (small and medium enterprises), exporting indigenous and foreign owned firms, in industry and increasingly in the internationally traded services.

Effect: Creative Destruction

These measures had the objective of promoting export-led growth. Theoretically, one could argue that the effects of these policies induced a Schumpetarian wave of creative destruction as modelled by Aghion and Howitt.[9] The policies lead to the creation of new exporting value added products with embedded innovation in intermediate goods (mainly imported) and required a different set of skills from the labour force. Simultaneously, there was phasing out and destroying of import competing product lines.[10]

5 MANUFACTURING SECTOR

Concerted policy efforts toward export-led growth since the late 1950s resulted in an increasingly export oriented manufacturing sector, in both traditional and high-technology sectors, over the decades. With greater globalisation and technological advances, manufacturing in Ireland has progressed up the global value chain by attracting foreign investment into high value-added knowledge and skills-based activities. However, after the 'glory' days of manufacturing in the 1990s, the overall contribution of manufacturing to the economy in terms of employment and output began to decline at the turn of the century in Ireland, as in many other countries. In recent years there has been a recovery in the sector and an increasing focus on manufacturing.

Goods Exports
Overall
The opening up of the Irish economy through trade liberalisation led to a phenomenal increase in exports of goods, particularly in the 1990s with lower growth rates exhibited in the years after 2000. This is evident in Figure 10.2, which documents the movement of goods out of and into Ireland in value terms, and the increasingly favourable terms of trade.

After many years of low, sometimes negative, growth rates, in 2015 total goods exports exhibited a dramatic increase of almost 20 billion euros (a roughly 21 per cent increase on the previous year). Most of this increase (64 per cent) was driven by growth in chemicals and particularly pharmaceuticals exports. Improved cost competitiveness as well as the weakening of the euro and growth in the Eurozone (aided by EU quantitative easing policies) also contributed. Total goods exports continued to expand in 2016 (particularly chemicals, but also electrical machinery), with an increase of 4 per cent on the previous year to a value of approximately €117 billion.

Figure 10.2 Total Goods Exports and Imports (€billion)

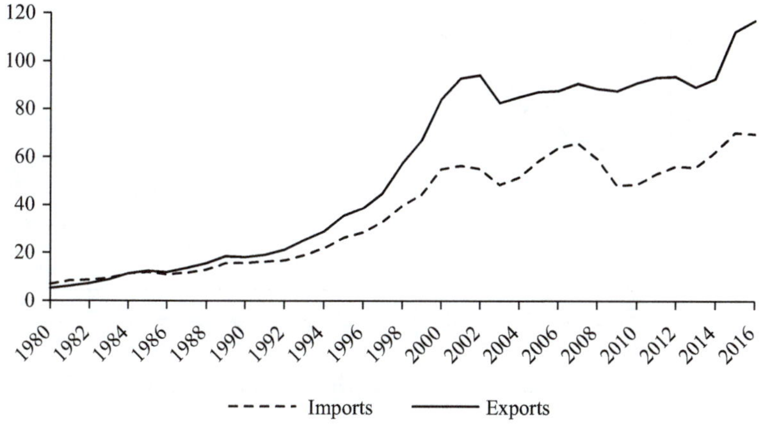

Source: Constructed from CSO, *External Trade Data*, various years.

Composition

Total goods exports include the exporting of food and live animals, beverages and tobacco, crude materials (excepting fuels), mineral fuels/lubricants, animal and vegetable oils/fats/waxes. It also includes manufactured chemicals and related products, basic manufactured goods classified chiefly by material, machinery and transport equipment, and miscellaneous manufactured goods (commodities in Standard Industrial Trade Classifications 5 through 8 respectively). Expansion in this latter group has driven most of the increases in goods exports since the pursuit of the export-led growth strategy in Ireland, as illustrated in Figure 10.3. Manufacturing of these commodity groups has become increasingly dominant in exporting, converging on and then surpassing EU and OECD figures. In 1963 exports of manufactured chemicals and related products, basic manufacturing, machinery and transport equipment, and miscellaneous manufactured goods account for 21 per cent of total goods exports. Ten years later, this had doubled to 42 per cent. By 1990 the corresponding figure was 70 per cent. In 2016 manufacturing of these goods accounted for 87 per cent of total goods exports. In contrast, exports of food and live animals as a per cent of total goods exports declined dramatically over this period (from approximately 41 per cent in 1973 to just under 9 per cent in 2016).

Figure 10.3 Manufactured Goods as Percentage of Total Goods Exports*

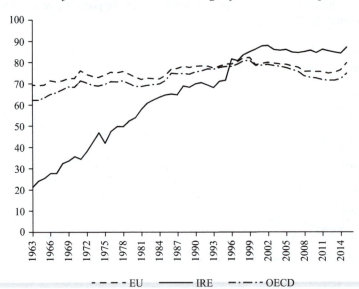

Source: Constructed from World Bank *World Development Indicators*, various years.
* Manufacturing data here covers SITC classifications 5 (chemicals), 6 (basic manufacturing goods classified chiefly by material – excluding sub-division 68 non-ferrous metals), 7 (machinery and transport equipment) and 8 (miscellaneous manufactured goods).

Moreover, the nature of exporting in manufacturing has changed over time, and has become increasingly specialised in a small number of high-technology sectors that are dominated by foreign multinational firms (see Table 10.1).[11]

In 2016 the share of total goods exports accounted for by chemical and related products was almost 57 per cent, of which exports of organic chemicals account for 20 per cent while medicinal and pharmaceutical products account for roughly 26 per cent. The share of organic chemicals increased from 6 to 20 per cent between 1980 and 2000, with little variation thereafter. Most of the growth in chemical exports since 2000 has come from the expansion of medicinal and pharmaceutical exports. These goods have increased their share of total goods exports from 6 per cent in 2000 to 26 per cent in 2016.

The increasing dominance of these sectors in exporting has come at the expense of declining shares of total food and live animals exports and more traditional manufacturing goods. From a share of total goods exports of almost 34 per cent in 1980, total food and live animals exports has fallen and in 2016 accounts for just under 9 per cent of goods exports. Machinery and transport equipment exports has fallen from 41 per cent of total goods exports in 2000 to just 16 per cent in 2016, while basic manufacturing exports classified chiefly by material have also declined over the decades to just under 2 per cent of total goods exports in 2016.

Table 10.1 Share of Total Goods Exports for Selected Manufacturing Products

	Total goods exports (€ billion)	% All chemical & related products	% Organic chemicals	% Medical & pharmaceutical	% Manufactured goods classified chiefly by material	% Machinery & transport equipment
1980	5.2	12.7	6.2	2.0	12.7	18.7
1990	18.2	15.9	6.8	4.0	8.0	31.3
2000	84.0	32.6	20.1	6.3	2.3	40.6
2010	90.9	58.6	21.7	26.4	1.6	12.4
2016	116.9	56.8	20.2	25.8	1.8	16.3

Source: CSO, derived from External Trade data, various years.

Destinations

In addition to growing specialisation of exports in a small number of high-technology products, Ireland also demonstrates some degree of specialisation in terms of exporting destinations (see Table 10.2). The opening up of the economy resulted in a steady decline in the share of all goods exports destined for the UK (from 47 per cent in 1977 down to 12.8 per cent in 2016), as exporting to other destinations developed. Table 10.2 illustrates the share of goods exports (of which roughly 85 per cent are explained by manufacturing exports from the year 2000) by destination for select years.

While the UK (Great Britain and Northern Ireland) and EU together dominate, export markets outside of these have managed to improve their relative position in very recent years. Exports of goods to the UK have been affected by the recent Brexit decision, and continue to face a significant threat with the actual withdrawal of the UK from the EU. Exports to the UK are as low as 12.8 per cent of total goods exports in 2016. Almost three times this figure denotes the share of

Table 10.2 Goods Exports by Area of Destination

	Goods Exports (€ billion)	% UK	% Other EU	% North America (USA + Canada)	% Rest of World
2000	84.0	22.5	40.8	17.4	19.3
2005	87.2	17.7	46.6	18.2	17.5
2010	90.9	15.4	42.5	24.4	17.7
2013	89.2	16.0	41.2	22.1	20.7
2014	92.6	14.8	40.2	23.2	21.8
2015	112.4	13.8	39.4	24.7	22.1
2016	116.9	12.8	38.2	26.6	22.3

Source: CSO, derived from External Trade data, various years.

exports to the rest of the EU, making it by far the most important export market for modern Ireland. The USA is the main non-EU destination for goods exports.

Output and Employment
Structural change was inevitable with the new industrial policy focus.[12] Within all manufacturing sectors (both high-technology and traditional), there was a simultaneous expansion of exporting firms alongside the decline of import-competing firms. Traditional, mainly indigenous, manufacturing sectors dominated by import-competing firms declined in employment. High-technology manufacturing sectors, predominantly owned by foreign multi-national exporting firms, expanded in employment. Overall employment levels in manufacturing declined over the 1980s, a trend which was reversed in the late 1980s leading to increasing employment levels in the years up to 2000 as expanding sectors began to dominate in the economy (see Table 10.3).

Following trends in the OECD, employment in manufacturing suffered a decline after 2000. Possible reasons for the OECD trend of declining manufacturing include saturated demand for manufacturing products, productivity growth in manufacturing, the reclassification of manufacturing firms as service firms, and the increasing internationalisation of manufacturing production.[13] The internationalisation of production can lead to the relocation of labour intensive manufacturing production and employment to lower cost locations abroad. This is less likely to be a problem for Ireland's knowledge-intensive highly-skilled high-technology manufacturing sectors, given Ireland's competitive advantage, its corporate tax regime, availability of an English speaking skilled and educated workforce, business supports and free access to the EU market.

This downward trend in Irish manufacturing employment was only halted in 2012, when employment levels began to rise once more reaching approximately 190,000 in 2014. However employment levels in both Irish and foreign owned enterprises in 2014 are still below 2008 levels (Table 10.3).

Indigenous firms account for almost 58 per cent of total manufacturing employment in 2014 (similar to 2008). Yet, as seen in Table 10.3, they account for almost 97 per cent of manufacturing enterprises (similar to 2008). The indigenous sector is populated by a very large number of small and medium sized businesses. This contrasts with the foreign-owned sector, which accounts for a relatively small number of much bigger firms in terms of employment.

Growth in manufacturing output on the other hand has been positive for decades. In the 1990s this was primarily driven by the very high growth rates in the high-technology sectors with the large influx of FDI, although these have exhibited lower growth rates since 2000.

Table 10.3 Manufacturing Sector Statistics

	Employment			
	2008	2010	2012	2014
All Manufacturing	218,792	181,611	178,700	189,966
Irish Owned	126,356	101,431	99,988	109,959
Foreign Owned	92,436	80,180	78,712	80,007
	Number of Enterprises			
	2008	2010	2012	2014
All Manufacturing	14513	14311	14533	14628
Irish Owned	14,020	13,778	14,008	14,145
Foreign Owned	493	533	525	483
	Gross Value Added (€ Billion)*			
	2008	2010	2012	2014
All Manufacturing	36.1	35.6	38.2	38.3
Irish Owned	8.6	6.7	5.6	7.8
Foreign Owned	27.5	28.9	32.7	30.5

* *Production value (excluding VAT) less intermediate consumption*

	Product % Share of Manufacturing GVA for key products			
	2008	2010	2012	2014
Basic pharmaceutical products & preparations	31.8	38.8	30.7	33.4
Chemicals & chemical products	8.5	7.0	15.3	8.1
Food products	13.2	15.4	15.9	20.1
Computer, electronic, optical & electrical equipment	13.4	9.2	8.3	7.1

Source: Census of Industrial Production (Manufacturing Enterprises) and Prodcom Statistics, various years.

The total value of products manufactured and sold (net selling value) by Irish based enterprises was in the region of €115.6 billion in 2015, of which the chemical and pharmaceutical sectors together accounted for more than half. The dominance of these sectors in manufacturing has increased over time, at the expense of more traditional sectors, as production has become increasingly specialised in these high-technology sectors.

A more effective indicator of the contribution of manufacturing to output of the economy is provided by manufacturing gross value added (GVA) at factor cost (i.e. production value (excluding VAT) less intermediate consumption) as shown in Table 10.3. Foreign-owned firms account for the vast majority (almost 80 per cent in 2014) of GVA in manufacturing. Manufacturing GVA has increased, although the experiences of foreign-owned and indigenous firms differ. With the exception of 2009, GVA for foreign owned enterprises has consistently risen yielding a 10.9 per cent increase over the period. Although increasing since 2012, the GVA for indigenous firms suffered an overall decline of 9.2 per cent over the period. Foreign owned firms thus account for an increasing proportion of GVA in manufacturing since 2008, and in 2014 account for almost 80 per cent of all manufacturing GVA.

Examining GVA by product, Table 10.3 documents the proportion of manufacturing GVA accounted for by the four biggest individual products. Jointly, chemicals and pharmaceuticals account for approximately 41 per cent of manufacturing GVA in 2014, while computer products account for roughly 7 per cent. While these products have been strong growth performers in the past, it is noteworthy that their contributions to manufacturing GVA have declined in recent years. Food products, a traditional sector, have increased their share of GVA from almost 16 per cent in 2012 to 20 per cent in 2014.

Table 10.3 clearly shows that foreign firms are extremely important in terms of their contribution to value added in manufacturing, and there has been increased specialisation of manufacturing into a small number of (foreign dominated) high value-added high-technology sectors. Yet the indigenous firms (which dominate more traditional sectors) deliver more social benefits with respect to employment. The additional effects in terms of employment, linkages to other sectors and tax returns from the specialisation in a small number of high-technology sectors are not as significant as those generated by the expansion of more traditional manufacturing.[14]

6 INTERNATIONALLY TRADED SERVICES

Introduction
The services sector makes an important and growing contribution to the economy. Services include transport, tourism and travel, communications, financial and insurance services, royalties/licences and a range of business services (e.g. advertising and market research, R&D, information technology (IT), legal, accounting,

recruitment, other professional services, other trade related services and operational leasing). As the economy grows and develops, the demand for these services increases. Globalisation and technological advancements have facilitated the outsourcing and international trading of knowledge-based services. The General Agreement on Trade in Services (GATS) identifies trade in services as including services supplied from one country to another (e.g. call centre services), consumption of services abroad (e.g. international tourism), commercial presence whereby a foreign company establishes a subsidiary or branch to provide services in another country (e.g. a domestic subsidiary of foreign insurance companies or financial companies) and individuals travelling from their own country to supply services in another (e.g. accountants, consultants).

Exports
Following trends in most developed countries, Ireland has experienced an expansion of both services imports and exports since 2003 as illustrated in Figure 10.4. In 2003 exports of goods were valued at €82.6 billion and increased to a value of €116.9 billion by 2016 (Figure 10.2). Over the same period, export in services increased from €37.1 billion up to €132.6 billion in 2016 (Figure 10.4). In 2003 imports of goods were valued at €48.5 billion and increased to a value of €69.6 billion by 2016 (Figure 10.2). Over the same period, imports in services increased from €48.2 billion up to €173.9 billion in 2016 (Figure 10.4).

Figure 10.4 Value of Services Exports and Imports (€billion)

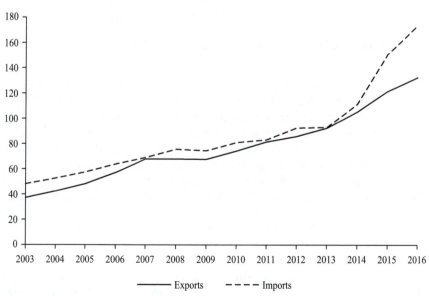

Source: Constructed from CSO, Balance of Payments Annual Series.

An analysis of the evolution of services exporting is interesting, both as an accompaniment to the role of goods exporting as a growth strategy for the economy and as an outcome of government industrial policy. The big increase in goods exports prior to 2000 and the subsequent jump in services exports thereafter have resulted in a sustained upward growth of total exports in goods and services. Exporting in goods and services has become and continues to be of paramount importance to the Irish economy, as evidenced in Figure 10.5.

Figure 10.5 Exports of Goods and Services as Percentage of GDP

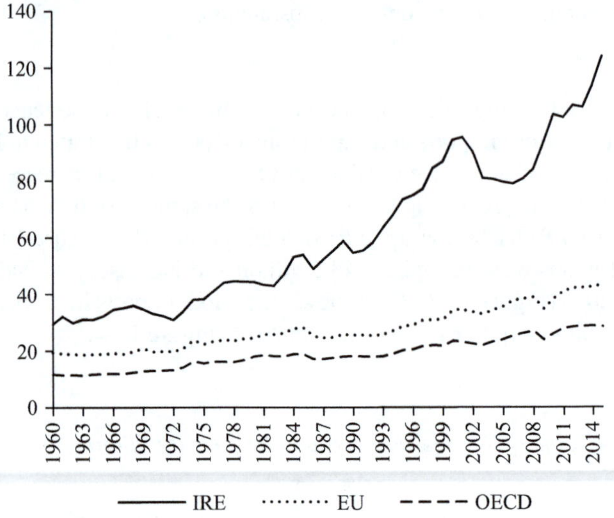

Source: Constructed from World Bank *World Development Indicators*, various years.

At the turn of the century, as the share of employment and output from manufacturing began to decline in the Irish economy and the growth in exporting of goods began to wane, internationally traded services began to dominate.

The expansion of favourable corporation tax treatment from manufacturing (initially to certain financially traded services in the late 1980s) to all sectors of the economy in 2003, and the gradual integration of services into industrial policy targets, has resulted in an inflow of FDI into internationally traded services since 2000. Export in services, particularly in financial and IT services, have increased dramatically since 2000, and has since continued on its upward trajectory to account for roughly half of total (goods and services) exports in 2015.

Composition of Exports
Table 10.4 provides a decomposition of service exports by main service type. Exports in computer services now dominate, accounting for 48 per cent of all service exports in 2016 (up from 33.9 per cent in 2003). This component includes

hardware and software-related services and data-processing services (e.g. IT consultancy and implementation, maintenance and repair of computers, web page hosting services).

Financial services suffered a steady decline in export market share in the years following the financial crisis (increasing only in 2012 and then again in 2015) it accounted for 8.5 per cent of service exports in 2016. The share of insurance services in exports declined from 21.0 to 7.1 per cent over the period. Of interest is the small but growing share afforded to exports of royalties and licences which in 2016 exceeded the shares of export services from transport, from tourism and travel and from communications.

Table 10.4 Decomposition of Services Exports by Service Type

				% Share of Services Exports				
	Insurance	Financial Services	Computer services	Royalties/ Licences	All Business Services[1]	Tourism and Travel	Transport	Other[2]
2003	20.7	9.1	33.9	0.5	18.7	9.2	4.6	3.3
2007	12.9	10.9	32.0	1.3	30.3	6.5	4.3	1.8
2011	9.9	8.1	38.6	4.4	28.7	3.7	5.3	1.3
2016	7.1	8.5	48.1	5.7	19.4	3.5	4.6	3.1

Source: CSO, Balance of Payments annual series.
[1] All Business Services include services-related merchanting, other trade related services, operational leasing, legal, accounting and other professional services, advertising and market research, R&D, architectural engineering and other technical services, and management services between affiliates.
[2] Other Services here include those related to communications (postal & courier services, and telecommunications services), repairs and processing, and other services n.e.c. (e.g. government services, personal, cultural and recreational services, construction services).

Export Destinations
There is a high degree of specialisation in traded services export destinations. From Table 10.5, we observe that the EU is still the most important destination for exports in services, with a high proportion going to the UK. Outside the EU, the USA remains an important market for services exports. However there has been a big increase in services trade with other countries outside of the EU and the USA over time, particularly with Asia. Exports of computer services and financial services are dominant in services exports to the UK. Royalties and licences is the biggest type of service export to North America in 2015, followed by exporting of computer services. Computer services was the single most important service type in exports to Asia in 2015.

While the growth in internationally traded services exports contributes to economic growth, the additional effects in terms of linkages to other sectors, employment and regional benefits are not as significant as those generated by manufacturing export expansion historically.[15] As documented in Section 3, transfer pricing of service intangibles that shift profits to Ireland for tax purposes can lead to an overstatement of the real value added to the economy.

Table 10.5 Services Exports by Country of Destination

	2003	2005	2007	2009	2011	2013	2015
Total (€ billion)	37.1	48.2	68.0	67.6	81.5	92.5	121.6
% UK	25.2	25.4	23.2	20.2	18.4	19.0	19.4
% Rest of EU[1]	37.1	42.5	41.4	43.1	39.8	36.4	34.6
% North America (USA+Canada)[2]	14.1	9.8	9.9	7.3	8.3	10.6	11.2
% Rest of world	23.6	22.2	25.5	29.3	33.5	34.0	34.8

Source: CSO, Balance of Payments annual series.
[1] Refers to EU25 (2003–2005), EU27 (2006–2011), EU28 (2011–2015) excluding the UK.
[2] USA accounts for 96 per cent of North American services exports in 2013. This declined to 90 per cent in 2015.

Some challenges lie ahead for the Irish economy. First, in the immediate term, the exit of the UK from the EU will pose a significant threat to services (and goods) exports to the UK. On a positive note, it is hoped that some of these losses to the economy from Brexit will be compensated for by the relocation of foreign direct investment from the UK to Irish shores. Secondly, there is evidence that the rapid growth in internationally traded services, particularly in computer and information services, in Ireland was fuelled by Ireland's capacity to attract FDI in liquid US markets after the US quantitative easing programme, and not by austerity-induced cost competitiveness.[16] Growth in services driven by unsustainable financing sources would indicate that the future continued expansion of internationally traded services is uncertain.

The increasing importance of internationally traded services is not unique to Ireland and has exhibited similar trends in most other developed countries. With a global increase in services trade, there is an increasing need for governments to collectively establish agreed upon rules that will govern internationally traded services. The General Agreement on Trade in Services (GATS) provides a framework for international trade in services for WTO members. The EU 2006 Services Directive, implemented by all EU countries in 2009, removed all legal and administrative barriers to services trade. The Trade in Services Agreement (TiSA), currently being negotiated by members of the World Trade Organization (WTO), endeavours to improve the rules of trade in many service areas.

7 CONCLUSION

In Ireland, industrial policy in manufacturing was driven by investment criteria with the objective of pursuing export-led growth and with embedded social welfare criteria. Interventions were made on the basis of promoting exports while also taking into consideration employment, linkages, balance of trade and regional effects. The investment criteria became somewhat more diluted in terms of social benefits with the expansion of high-technology value added manufacturing, and even more so with the expansion of internationally traded services.

Policies implemented included horizontal interventions to develop infrastructure, to improve the level and quality of education in the economy, to promote effective competition in the domestic economy. Targeted policies were implemented to actively shape the nature of transformation of the economy to one that would be export-led, with consideration to the effects on employment, linkages between sectors, balance of trade and regional distribution. Trade liberalisation policies were implemented on a phased basis. Grants and supports were provided to encourage all indigenous and foreign exporting firms, but with an emphasis on high value-added high-technology sectors and certain regions. Tax incentives were established and cemented as a key pillar of industrial policy to encourage exporting, which also encouraged inward FDI. While these policies were initially targeted at manufacturing, they later expanded to incorporate international trade in services in line with the changing global economy.

The combined effects of the policies implemented had a radical effect on the manufacturing sector, leading to the creation of new exporting value-added product lines and a phasing out of import-competing products. After a period of restructuring, growth in employment and output took off in the late 1980s and expanded further in the 1990s, largely driven by expanding exports. Manufacturing exports experienced extraordinary growth rates in the 1990s, dominated by growing high-technology mainly foreign owned sectors. At the turn of the century, growth in manufacturing exports stagnated while the overall contribution of manufacturing to employment and output declined as the property boom fuelled economy growth.

With a well-developed manufacturing base in high-technology sectors, the demand for knowledge-intensive services increased. Globalisation and technological advancements enabled greater international tradability of these services. As the manufacturing sector came to the end of its 'glory' days, internationally traded services began to dominate. Services imports and exports dramatically increased. Services exports became an increasingly large component of total exports in goods and services, although extremely specialised in a small number of service areas.

As Ireland emerges from the aftermath of the recession, the importance of the manufacturing and internationally traded services sector to our continued survival and growth has become abundantly clear. Post-financial crisis has seen a resurgence of interest in the manufacturing sector in a bid to rely less on financial and

IT services and to nurture growth based on investment criteria that can yield high dividends in terms of productivity, jobs, linkages to other sectors, tax revenues and a trade surplus. Moreover, future industrial policy needs to move beyond investment criteria rooted solely in the domestic economy. With globalisation and technological advancements there is a need to also consider the economic, social and environmental effects of policy on other economies and for world sustainable development, although this will require greater international cooperation.

Endnotes

*   This chapter builds on Chapter 9 from the 12th edition of this book which was written by Carol Newman. Many thanks to John O' Hagan, Francis O'Toole and Patrick Paul Walsh for comments and suggestions.

1   S. Brazys and A. Regan, 'These little PIIGS went to market: enterprise policy and divergent recovery in European periphery', *Perspectives on Politics* (forthcoming 2017).

2   Under this arrangement the foreign contract manufacturer supplies a service to the Irish entity and has no ownership of the product being produced. When the product is then sold to a customer abroad, it is recorded as an export of the Irish entity.

3   For a detailed discussion on the definition of industrial policy, see K. Warwick, *Beyond Industrial Policy: Emerging Issues and New Trends*, OECD Science, Technology and Industry Policy Papers, No. 2, OECD, Paris 2013.

4   P.P. Walsh, UN GSDR, Brief, Industrial Policy and Sustainable Development, 2015.

5   CSO, 'That was then, this is now, change in Ireland 1949–1999', Chapter 8, 2000.

6   P. Donnelly, 'How foreign firms transformed Ireland's domestic economy', *Irish Times*, 13 November 2013.

7   P.P. Walsh and C. Whelan (2010), 'Hirschman and Irish industrial policy'. *Economic and Social Review*, 41 (3), 2010.

8   The Industrial Development Act 1993 split the IDA into three separate bodies: IDA Ireland, Forbairt and Forfás. Forfás, the national policy advisory board for enterprise, trade, science and technology was dissolved in 2014, when the Department of Jobs, Enterprise and Innovation took on the advisory role.

9   P. Aghion and P. Howitt, 'A model of growth through creative destruction', *Econometrica*, 60, 1992.

10   For a detailed discussion on the structural change in manufacturing, see P.P. Walsh and C. Whelan, 'The importance of structural change in industry for growth', *Journal of the Statistical and Social Inquiry Society of Ireland*, 29, 2000.

11   For a full discussion on the nature of Irish goods and services exports, see S. Byrne and M. O'Brien, 'The changing nature of Irish exports: context, causes and consequences', *Central Bank Quarterly Bulletin*, 2015.

12   Walsh and Whelan, *op cit.*

13   Warwick, *op cit.*

14   N. O'Clery, 'A tale of two clusters: the evolution of Ireland's economic complexity since 1995', *Journal of the Statistical and Social Inquiry Society of Ireland*, 2016.

15   A. Regan and S. Brazys, 'Celtic phoenix or leprechaun economics? The politics of an FDI led growth model in Europe', Geary WP2017/01 UCD Dublin, 2017.

16   S. Brazys and A. Regan (2015), 'These little PIIGS went to market: austerity and divergent recovery in the Eurozone', Geary WP2015/17 UCD, Dublin, 2017.

CHAPTER 11

Energy and Environment

Eleanor Denny

1 INTRODUCTION

Energy and the environment are strongly interlinked and are critical policy concerns for governments around the world. Energy plays a role in almost every facet of society from industry, to transport, to domestic use, yet it is also responsible for over 80 per cent of global greenhouse gas emissions. The environment is a strategic and valuable asset and as such it must be protected and proactively managed to ensure it forms the basis of economic welfare and a healthy society. Balancing these two, often competing, policy agendas is at the crux of global energy policy and is the focus of this chapter.

Since the 1800s the role of energy in modern society has evolved and today energy is an essential input into almost every aspect of daily life, both for consumption and as an input to production. From lighting, heating and transport at the residential level to production processes, IT systems, communications networks, and retail and services provision, energy is considered a vital necessity without which any developed economy would grind to a halt. In fact, a reliable and safe energy supply at a sustainable cost is a basic necessity for economic development.

Ensuring a secure energy supply also has a critical political aspect from a local perspective, with the development of national energy projects and infrastructure, to high profile international politics. Conflict over the control of valuable oil supplies has been a persistent feature of international affairs since the beginning of the twentieth century. Such conflict varies in nature, from territorial disputes over the possession of oil-laden regions to struggles among the leaders of oil-rich countries to major inter-state wars over the control of vital oil zones. As oil reserves continue to be depleted, the frequency and severity of such conflict is likely to increase.

Coupled with the necessity for a safe and secure energy supply is the protection of the environment, including air, water and land quality and the sustainability of natural habitats and species. A sustainable environment is a critical component of high quality of life, with clean air and safe water being two of the most basic human needs. Given the enormous pressure the energy system places on the environment (for example through the release of harmful emissions, the consumption of vast quantities of water, the creation of harmful waste such as nuclear waste, and the impact of energy and transport infrastructure on the natural environment), it is imprudent to consider energy in isolation from environmental concerns.

This chapter examines energy and environmental issues and policy in Ireland in the context of European and global pressures. Section 2 looks at the structure of energy demand in Ireland, highlighting the three main sectors, electricity, heating and transport. A detailed discussion of the role of the state in the energy sector is also provided in addition to an analysis of the political nature of energy supplies. Section 3 looks at energy supply, in terms of diversity and security. The discussion covers energy infrastructure and renewable energy sources, in addition to contentious topics such as nuclear energy and fracking all of which have obvious environmental dimensions. Section 4 looks at the issue of pricing and competition in the energy sector, relating back to issues discussed in Chapter 5. Section 5 is devoted to four major environmental concerns, namely air quality, water pollution, waste disposal and biodiversity. Addressing the potentially disastrous consequences of global climate change is the responsibility of all nations, including Ireland. However, it should be noted that in recent years, the spread of contention with regard to climate change has been growing. This denial has come from numerous sources including contrarian scientists, fossil fuel corporations, conservative media, think-tanks and politicians, self-designated experts, climate bloggers, and many more. The motivations of these actors vary from economic, to personal to a shared opposition to government interventions and regulations. Despite this worrying trend of climate change denial, Section 5 takes as given the underlying assumption that climate change is a real and significant challenge facing the global community.

2 ENERGY SECTOR: IMPORTANCE AND ROLE OF THE STATE

One of the most significant infrastructural challenges facing the state is the provision of a secure and sustainable energy supply into the future. This requires not only investment in the underlying capital resources, for example in power stations and networks, but also in the security of energy supply, for example in indigenous fossil fuel production and renewable energy. Both of these areas, the provision of the energy sector physical infrastructure and the security of energy fuel supplies, result in the state traditionally playing a large and important role in the energy sector.

Importance and Nature of Energy Sector and Demand
Energy is generally classified by its mode of application: for electricity, heating/ cooling (of space and water) or for transportation. In Ireland, the energy landscape in each of these sectors has changed significantly over the last century as Ireland has grown from a largely agricultural society to a service, industrial and manufacturing driven economy.

Electricity

The original driver for electricity arose from a desire for people to light their homes in a cheap and safe way. The subsequent challenge was to develop an electricity system that could create electricity in a central location (at a power plant) and carry it to people's homes (across a network). In 1882 the first power plant in the world was constructed in New York and it supplied 85 customers with electricity to light their homes. It wasn't until almost 20 years later, in 1903, that Ireland's first power station was built at the Pigeon House in Dublin to supply power to the street lights around Dublin city.

In 1922 discussions began on a proposal to dam the River Shannon and by 1925 construction had begun on Ireland's first bulk power station, a hydro-electric plant in Ardnacrusha in Co. Clare, to supply electricity to the towns and cities of Ireland. Today the island of Ireland has over 32 power stations operated on coal, gas, oil and peat, 249 wind farms and a variety of smaller installations at businesses and homes. In 2015, electricity accounted for 33 per cent of all energy used in Ireland.

Heating

In terms of energy for heating, Ireland has a strong tradition of open fires in domestic dwellings which have resulted in coal and peat remaining important heat sources in the residential sector over the past century. Open fires typically have low efficiency and in order to heat the entire house are usually supplemented by oil, electric and, increasingly, gas heating systems. Significant upgrades in building regulations have led to improvements in the efficiency of the building stock in Ireland with a house built after 2010 typically using one-third of the heating energy of the average existing home.

However, Ireland still has a large stock of inefficient residential dwellings with energy use per dwelling 5 per cent above the UK average in 2010 and 26 per cent above the EU-27 average in 2010. Comparisons with the UK provide a good benchmark as the climates in both countries are similar. Other EU countries would have a much higher air-conditioning demand than Ireland and so tend to have a peak thermal energy demand in the summer months, whereas Ireland has its peak demand in winter.[1]

Reasons for Ireland's poor performance when compared to the UK and the rest of the EU include larger average dwelling sizes, a higher proportion of solid fuel use and a lack of district heating initiatives. District heating uses heat which is generated efficiently in a central location, for example using the waste heat from a power station of factory. This heat is then circulated to residential and commercial premises for both space and water heating. District heating is prevalent throughout Europe, but its uptake in Ireland has been slow. However, advances in technology and environmental drivers are likely to see an increase in the use of district heating in Ireland into the future. Residential heat demand represents approximately 45 per cent of total heat demand in Ireland, with the remainder from industry, services, and agriculture. In 2015, heat demand accounted for 33 per cent of all energy use in Ireland.

Transport
The final third of energy demand is accounted for by the transportation sector, a sector which has seen huge change in the past two decades. Economic activity is the main driver of transport demand and an increase of 190 per cent in economic output in the 1990 to 2007 period saw transport energy demand increase by 181 per cent. Much of this increase was seen in freight transportation for the construction industry and an increase in aviation demand, but the residential sector also contributed significantly. In the same period, the number of licensed private cars increased from 796,408 in 1990 to 1,882,901 in 2007, an increase of 136 per cent. By the end of 2015, this figure had grown to 1.98 million licenced private cars.

Role of State
Large infrastructural projects often necessitate the intervention of the state due to the significant capital costs and the importance of the assets to sustaining economic growth. The expected lifetime of investments in the energy sector is forty years or more, thus the wisdom of any investment decisions, for example investment in a coal-fired power station versus a nuclear station, must be considered within a similar time frame. Investments in the underlying network have even longer lifetimes. Similarly, policy decisions with a view to increasing competitiveness or decreasing emissions today must take account of the long-term legacy of these decisions.[2] The energy sector displays many types of market failure, such as monopolies, externalities and public goods, each of which prompts a role for the state in the sector.

Monopolies
The first form of market failure in the energy sector is the presence of monopolies. Due to the importance of maintaining the security of energy supply, the state traditionally took a role in sourcing, generating, transmitting, and supplying electricity and gas to end users. In other words, the state created state-owned vertically integrated monopolies such as the Electricity Supply Board (ESB) and Bord Gáis Eireann (BGE). While the energy sector has evolved significantly in recent years with the introduction of new players and increased competition (see also Chapter 5), the role of the state in all aspects of the energy industry continues to be large.

Across Europe, the provision of electricity and gas require extensive network infrastructure and, because of the huge economies of scale, these networks are considered to be natural monopolies. In 1996 the EU initiated common rules on the internal markets for electricity and gas, intended to open electricity and gas markets up to competition in all the member states.

However, these EU directives recognise that the networks element of the industry is a natural monopoly and so allow member states to continue to have a monopoly in network provision, but this company cannot participate in any other aspects of the industry. Thus, the electricity and gas networks are now separated from the traditional vertically integrated monopolies and are operated by companies which are ring-fenced from other aspects of the industry. In Ireland, these companies are

Eirgrid (high voltage electricity network), ESB Networks (low voltage electricity networks), and Bord Gáis Networks (gas interconnectors and network).

While Eirgrid, ESB Networks, and Bord Gáis Networks are now independent companies, they continue to remain under the ownership of the state. A report published in 2011 by an independent review group established to assess state assets and liabilities, states that the high voltage electricity and gas networks should remain under state ownership, as these are the most critical elements of the energy infrastructure.[3]

While the electricity and gas networks are recognised to be natural monopolies, the EU directive does require an increase in competition in the generation of electricity and the supply of both electricity and gas to end-users. With this in mind, Ireland has seen a number of new independent participants enter the electricity and gas markets in recent years such as SSE Airtricity, Energia and Flogas (competition in the energy sector is discussed further in Section 4 and also in Chapter 5). However, the state remains the dominant player in both sectors.

In fact, the ESB remains the largest undertaking in state ownership by a significant margin, accounting for over half of the state's commercial sector when measured by net assets. State participation in the energy sector also includes Bord Gáis Eireann (through the gas infrastructure but also in the electricity sector and more recently in wind power developments), Bord na Móna (with involvement in peat production, power generation and wind) and also in Coillte (which provides wood to the power generation sector and has also begun to develop interests in wind farms). Thus, the state owns three companies (ESB, Bord Gais and Bord na Móna) that have competing interests in the electricity generation sector and one (Coillte) which is developing interests in this area.

While state participation in the energy sector was traditionally required in all aspects of the industry to ensure the provision of a secure energy supply, the necessity to have such a large and competing involvement is now questionable. With this in mind, the privatisation of ESB, Bord Gáis Eireann, Bord na Móna and Coillte remains a live policy debate.

While formerly dominated by vertically integrated monopolies, the energy sector now displays increased competition (see also Chapter 5). However, it is far from perfectly competitive. Natural monopolies remain in the network aspect of the energy sector and the generation and supply elements of the industry are more like oligopolies (which retain a high level of state ownership). The potential for strategic behaviour on the part of participants in the sector remains high and thus the sector must be heavily regulated.

The state-run Commission for Energy Regulation in Ireland undertakes this role in both the electricity and gas sectors (and more recently also in the water sector). In fact, the energy sector is one of the most highly regulated of all industrial sectors. Thus, while the state's role in the provision of electricity and gas may diminish in the coming years through the sale of state assets, it will continue to play an important role in the networks element of the sector and crucially in the regulation of all aspects of the industry.

Externalities

A second reason for the involvement of the state in the energy sector is due to the fact that the energy sector is the largest contributor to greenhouse gas emissions in Ireland. The presence of externalities, such as emissions, prompts a role for government in the energy sector. In Ireland this has taken the form of subsidies for renewable generation and energy efficiency measures as well as penalties for producers of carbon dioxide (such as carbon taxes and mandatory participation in the EU Emissions Trading Scheme). Environmental issues are discussed later in Section 5.

Public Goods

A third reason for the involvement of the state in the energy sector is that the security of energy supply is an example of a marketable public good. Energy supply is considered a basic necessity and when provided for all promotes greater standards of living for all. A secure energy supply results in a lower risk of blackouts and supply interruptions which is a necessity to promote commercial activity and economic development. Thus, the benefits of a secure energy supply are enjoyed by all, even those that do not pay directly for it.

However, investments in energy infrastructure have long lead times (of up to 10 years when planning delays are taken into account) and exceptionally high capital costs. Once a power station is built it improves the security of energy supply for all but the cost is so high that no individual customer can afford to pay to incentivise an increase in generation capacity. In addition, providing energy from a single source (e.g. gas) is a threat to supply security, whereas providing energy from a diverse range of sources reduces the risk of supply interruption and increases energy security. However, market incentives are unlikely to be present to encourage private investment in a diverse range of fuels. For instance, in an era of low gas prices, free market incentives are likely to drive investment in gas-fired power plants for electricity generation despite an already heavy reliance on natural gas for electricity generation on the Irish system. There are considerable positive externalities associated with having a diverse fuel mix for electricity generation, thus the government may intervene in the free market to incentivise generation from a variety of fuels to avoid an over-reliance on any single supply.

All of these factors prompt a role for government in securing the provision of energy security from a diverse range of fuel sources. This can be done by direct involvement through the establishment of state-run vertically integrated monopolies or through regulation and incentive schemes.

Energy and Spatial Planning

In examining Ireland's energy consumption patterns, the state's role in spatial planning is a key issue. Compared to other EU countries, Ireland's planning legacy has resulted in a historical trend of low-density housing resulting in urban sprawl around major cities and large numbers of one-off housing in rural areas.

In 2014, just 4.7 per cent of Ireland's population lived in apartments, which is the lowest in the EU-28, where the average is 40 per cent.[4] This planning legacy of low density and one-off housing has important knock-on implications for energy usage in all sectors.

The most obvious implication is for the transport sector; when people live closer to their workplace, commuting distances are lower, and a public transport system can be optimised to meet the needs of the population more efficiently. In the electricity sector, our dispersed population has led to Ireland having four times the EU average length of power lines per customer. While unsightly and more costly to construct, longer lines also have the disadvantage that more energy is lost in transmission. A history of poor spatial planning decisions also has consequences for the development of new power stations, with the routing of power-lines more challenging when houses are distributed widely outside towns and villages. In the heating sector, our distributed housing impacts on the availability of mainline gas, one of the most efficient fuels available for domestic use. One-off and dispersed housing also reduces the potential for centralised district heating schemes.

The provision of electricity, heating and transportation are considered to be basic necessities in any developed society. Thus, in an era of rising oil prices, environmental concerns and competitive pressures, energy policy is a critical concern for policymakers and decisions in this area have far reaching consequences. Energy policy is generally driven by three main goals: security of supply, sustainability of prices for end-users, and environmental concerns. Each of these components will be discussed in detail in Section 3.

Politics of Energy Security
Ireland imports 88 per cent of fuel required for energy provision, of which the majority is oil and gas. As such, Ireland is highly exposed to international price and supply fluctuations in these vital resources. While not a major player on the world stage in terms of either supply of, or demand for, these fuels, our high import dependence and remote location leave Ireland particularly vulnerable to international fuel markets and therefore fuel politics.

Oil is the world's major source of primary energy, accounting for approximately 31 per cent of global energy consumption. Because it plays such a critical role in fuelling the world economy, any prolonged shortage in oil supplies can feed into a global economic recession, as occurred in 1974 (following the Arab oil embargo), 1979 (following the Iranian revolution), and 1990 (following the Iraqi invasion of Kuwait).

Petroleum is also a vital factor in the military strength of nations, as it supplies most of the energy used to power tanks, planes, missiles, ships, armoured vehicles, and other instruments of war. Vast amounts of petroleum are consumed in modern combat operations, for example, during the 1991 Gulf War, USA and allied forces consumed an average of 19 million gallons of oil per day – this is equivalent to the total daily consumption of Argentina. Because of its strategic importance in the conduct of warfare, its possession has been termed a 'national security' matter by the USA and other countries, meaning something that may require the use of military force to protect.[5]

This close connection between oil, economic growth and national security has resulted in oil-fuelled political conflict since the early stages of the industrial era. Oil driven conflict can be seen to derive from two essential features of petroleum: firstly its vital importance to the economy and military power of nations; and secondly to its irregular geographic distribution.

Natural petroleum does not occur randomly across the globe but is highly concentrated in a few large reservoirs. The largest of these, containing approximately two-thirds of the world's oil reserves, is located in the Persian Gulf area, comprised of Saudi Arabia, Iran, Iraq, Kuwait, Qatar, and the United Arab Emirates (UAE). Large reservoirs are also found in the USA, Canada, Mexico, Colombia, Venezuela, the North Sea basin (Norway and the UK), Russia, Azerbaijan, Kazakhstan, Algeria, Angola, Libya, Nigeria, China, and Indonesia. Together, these 22 countries possess more than 90 per cent of the world's conventional oil reserves.

For all of these reasons, the risk of armed conflict over valuable oil supplies is liable to grow in the years to come. Such conflict could take the form of conventional warfare involving the military forces of the major powers, as in the 1991 Persian Gulf War, or internal power struggles between competing political, ethnic, and tribal factions. Indeed, throughout the last decade, oil-related conflict of one sort or another was under way in Bolivia, Colombia, Iraq, Georgia, Indonesia, Nigeria, Saudi Arabia, and Venezuela.

In addition to exposure to conflict in oil-fuelled nations, Europe is also open to natural gas price and supply risk. While natural gas is more geographically spread than oil reserves, Europe remains heavily reliant on imported Russian gas, with Gazprom, the Russian gas monopoly currently supplying 34 per cent of European gas supplies in 2015. This dependence has been brought into the spotlight in recent years in light of conflict in the Ukraine conflict and the fact that over 40 per cent of Europe's imported Russian gas travels through Ukrainian gas pipelines.

On the flip side, however, Europe accounts for over half of Gazprom's total revenues, and around half of Russia's total budget revenue comes from oil and gas. Moscow depends on Europe for this source of revenue, and most energy analysts seem to agree that Russian leadership is unlikely to jeopardise this key income stream. Short of an actual war, the consensus appears to be, Europe's gas supplies are unlikely to be seriously threatened in the short to medium term.

Ireland has a high reliance on imported fossil fuels, which will be discussed further in Section 3. While it is unlikely that Ireland will ever be immune to international, geopolitical issues surrounding fossil fuel supplies, the growth of indigenous renewable generation and energy efficiency measures are important strategies to ameliorate this risk.

3 ENERGY SUPPLY: PERFORMANCE AND POLICY ISSUES

As one of the key inputs to economic activity, the security of energy supply into the future is a key concern. Interruptions in supply, even for short periods of time, can have very serious economic consequences. Security of supply can be considered under a number of metrics: for example, how reliant is the country on an individual fuel source, and how diverse are its energy fuel needs? How dependent is the country on imported fuel and as a result how exposed is it to price fluctuations and interruptions in imported fuel supplies? Does the country have the physical infrastructure in place to ensure delivery of energy to the end-user into the future?

Fuel Diversity

Table 11.1 illustrates the breakdown of energy demand in Ireland in 2012 by fuel type. It can be seen that Ireland's dominant fuel source is oil accounting for around 55 per cent of total energy use. This demand is primarily driven by the transport and heating sectors. Natural gas is increasing in importance, mainly driven by its usage in electricity generation and domestic heating.

Table 11.1 Ireland's Percentage Energy Usage by Type in 2015 (2008 figures in parenthesis)

	Total	Electricity	Heating[2]	Transport
Oil[1]	48 (56)	2 (7)	41 (55)	97 (99)
Natural gas	27 (27)	42 (54)	39 (29)	–
Coal	10 (9)	25 (22)	8 (7)	–
Peat	6 (5)	12 (9)	5 (5)	–
Renewable Sources	8 (3)	17 (5)	7 (4)	3 (1)
Electricity imports	0.4 (1)	1 (2)	–	–

Source: Sustainable Energy Authority of Ireland (SEAI), *Energy in Ireland Key Statistics 2015*, Energy Policy Statistical Support Unit, 2016, and Sustainable Energy Authority of Ireland (SEAI), *Energy in Ireland Key Statistics 2008*, Energy Policy Statistical Support Unit, 2009.
[1] Oil includes oil products such as diesel, petrol, and kerosene.
[2] Data shown relates to 2014 as information for 2015 was unavailable at the time of print.

As mentioned in Section 2, policymakers generally try to encourage diversity in each sector to ensure protection should there be an interruption in the supply of one fuel source. In each of the energy sectors, though, Ireland has a heavy reliance on at least one fuel type. This is particularly pertinent for the transport sector where 98 per cent of fuels are oil based, and thus this sector is heavily exposed to any potential interruptions in oil supply.

The electricity sector, as can be seen in Table 11.1, has the most diverse range of fuel types, although it has a heavy reliance on natural gas. The existing oil-fired power stations are gradually being decommissioned due to age and any new fossil fuel based power stations planned are expected to be natural gas fired. While coal and oil can be stored (albeit at a cost), natural gas storage is much more complex. Thus, this heavy reliance on natural gas for electricity production can be seen as a threat to supply security into the future. The sources of energy for the heating sector are more diversified and reflect that of the economy as a whole (see earlier), with a heavy dependence likewise on oil.

Indigenous Fuels and Import Dependency

Twinned with the challenge of diversity of fuel supplies is the reliance of a country on imported fuels. When a country can produce energy locally it provides a hedge against fluctuations in international fuel prices and interruptions in fuel supplies. It also saves on important foreign exchange outlays. Thus, policymakers try to encourage the production of energy domestically.

Ireland had an import dependency of 88 per cent in 2015, the fourth highest dependency in the EU28 and well above the EU average. The trend has been upward, the figure having been around 70 per cent twenty years ago, and reflects the fact that Ireland is not endowed with significant indigenous fossil fuel resources and has, to date, not harnessed significant quantities of renewable resources.

Oil, as seen in Table 11.1, is by far the most dominant energy source in Ireland of which 100 per cent is imported. The transport sector has the heaviest reliance on imported fuels with 98 per cent dependence on imported oil. The bulk of Ireland's oil though is sourced from politically stable countries such as the UK, Norway and Denmark. The UK continues to have ample oil potential, with proven and probable reserve estimates of 4,339 million tons in 2014. Actual oil production in 2014 was 40 million tons.[6] The impact of Brexit on UK oil production is currently unclear and will likely be impacted by future domestic oil demand in the UK (which is a function of economic growth) and the sterling-US dollar exchange rate (the US dollar is the international trading currency for oil).

Arising from membership of the EU and the International Energy Agency (IEA), Ireland must hold 90 days of oil stocks based on the previous year's imports. Under the European Communities (Minimum Stocks of Petroleum Oils) Regulations, this responsibility has been vested in an Irish state body called the National Oil Reserves Agency (NORA). NORA receives no exchequer funding and its ongoing activities are 100 per cent funded by a levy imposed on certain oil products.

According to the Department of Communications Energy and Natural Resources, if there was a 10 per cent reduction in world oil supplies (a level of disruption unprecedented since the Suez War of 1956 to 1957), it is estimated that the required 90-day reserves would last over two years, even without taking into account any demand-reduction measures.[7] Thus, in the short term, Ireland is hedged against fluctuations in oil supply. However, in the medium to long term, in order to protect itself from fluctuating supply and prices, Ireland needs to diversify further its energy mix away from oil, particularly in the transport and heating sectors.

Given Ireland's large oil stocks, interruptions to gas supply are of greater concern in the short to medium term. In 2015, just 3 per cent of Ireland's gas was produced domestically with the remaining 97 per cent imported via a pipeline to Britain. The majority of Ireland's imported gas is sourced from politically stable locations in the North Sea. It is anticipated that Ireland's production of natural gas will increase in the coming years through the continued development of the Corrib gas field and a proposed liquefied natural gas development in Co. Clare. A number of gas storage facilities are planned in Larne and Ballycotton.

In addition to domestic gas, Ireland also has an indigenous peat resource which is currently used to generate electricity at three power stations. The Irish government supports the use of peat for electricity generation through a Public Service Obligation levy on all electricity bills (see later). The justification for this support is for security of supply reasons (to reduce Ireland's dependence on imported fuels) and to support jobs in rural areas.

In a further effort to reduce Ireland's reliance on imported fuels (as well as for environmental and sustainability reasons), the Irish government has set targets for renewable energy in each of the energy consumption sectors. In the electricity sector Ireland has an ambitious target of achieving 40 per cent electricity from renewable sources by 2020, exceeding the targets of any other country worldwide. In the heating sector the target is 12 per cent by 2020 and for transport 10 per cent. Given the centralised nature of electricity supply, it is relatively easier to integrate renewable sources into this sector, hence the higher target.

Renewable Energy

Hydro generation was the earliest renewable technology used for electricity generation and underwent rapid development throughout the last century. Across the developed world few, if any, suitable economic sites remain for the further development of hydro-electricity. After hydro, wind generation is one of the most advanced forms of renewable energy and output has grown rapidly in the last fifteen years. As the market for wind energy has grown, the costs have reduced dramatically. Ambitious renewable energy targets together with reducing costs and successes to date are likely to ensure that wind energy continues to grow in electricity networks worldwide.

Given its location on the edge of the Atlantic Ocean, Ireland has a vast wind resource potential. It is anticipated that the bulk of Ireland's renewable target in the electricity sector will be met through wind generation. In 2015, wind generation represented over thirteen per cent of electricity generation on the island of Ireland, and, as a single synchronous power system, it has arguably the largest penetrations of wind power in the world at present.

Solar technology for electricity generation requires direct sunlight, and as such is not considered an economically viable option for Ireland at present. Ireland does however have large ocean energy resources for the development of wave and tidal turbines. Nevertheless, the development of ocean technology has been relatively slow with just a small number of devices at the commercial prototype stage. While the vast majority of wind turbines follow the same general design (three blades on a vertical tower), no single ocean device has emerged as the leading design. Operational challenges and access issues in the marine environment have been among the main barriers to ocean energy development to date.

Renewable technologies such as wind generation, solar, tidal and wave generation have a 'variable' output. The output of these units depends on weather conditions which cannot be controlled by the operator of the generator. For example, the amount of electricity generated by a wind turbine fluctuates as wind speed changes and that of a solar panel with the intensity of sunlight. Thus, the control of their output is limited. When significant penetrations of these forms of generation are connected to an electricity network, it can increase the challenge of providing a secure and reliable electricity supply at all times. This is a challenge that must be addressed by electricity system operators into the future as wind and other renewable energy sources increase further.

In the heating and transport sectors, the integration of renewable sources of energy is more challenging as these sectors do not generally use centralised energy supplies. For heating just 6.5 per cent of energy in 2015 was from renewable sources with the main contributor being the use of wood biomass. In the transport sector, renewable energy represented 3.3 per cent of transport energy in 2015. The share of bio-fuels in transport continues to grow year-on-year following the introduction of tax breaks in 2006. The use of electricity in the transport sector (for the Dart, LUAS and in electric vehicles) is also considered to be 'renewable' as the electricity can be generated through renewable sources.

Energy Infrastructure

In order to ensure the security of energy supply it is important to examine not only the sustainability of the fuels used (renewable versus fossil fuel) but also the adequacy of the energy infrastructure. As mentioned in Section 2, adequate infrastructure requires the intervention of the state, not only in incentivising the provision of infrastructure but also through regulation.

The main infrastructural challenges in the heating energy sector are the poor-quality existing housing stock and the availability of mains gas. While advances have been made in recent years regarding the energy usage of new-build housing (for example Part L of the Building Regulations 2008) unfortunately in many cases it was too late and did not apply to houses built at the height of the housing boom. Retrofitting existing houses with improved insulation, glazing and efficient boilers is likely to be the predominant source of infrastructural improvements in residential heating in the future.

Natural gas is one of the most efficient forms of heating. However, access to the natural gas network is required. Gas supply in Ireland is delivered via a network of approximately 12,300km of pipelines. There are two main gas entry points, one from Moffat in western Scotland which connects Ireland to the main GB gas network and the other at Inch in Co. Cork to service the Kinsale and Seven Heads gas fields. The primary source of future indigenous production of gas is from the Corrib gas field in Co. Mayo.

Currently Ireland has two electrical interconnectors to the system in Britain: one to Scotland and one to Wales. This second interconnector to Wales, known as the EastWest Interconnector, was completed in 2012 and is approximately 260km in length and has the capacity to transport enough electricity to power 300,000 homes. These two interconnectors allow Ireland to import electricity when needed and to export power when Ireland has excess generation. They significantly enhance the reliability of the Irish electricity system. It should be noted however, that capacity margins (the amount of excess supply available) are tightening in Great Britain which suggests that Ireland should carefully assess how much reliance is placed on interconnection there.

It should be noted that any new generation capacity will require the servicing and upgrade of the existing electricity network. To this effect, in 2010 the Commission for Energy Regulation announced plans to invest €3.76 billion in the Irish electricity network. The purpose of this investment is to improve the quality of electricity to customers, to allow for the development of new energy projects (such as remote wind farms) and to help attract new foreign direct investment into regions which would traditionally have been poorly serviced by the electricity network. This network upgrade plan will be financed through revenues earned by ESB networks and Eirgrid. Again, the issue of spatial planning arises in regard to the upgrade of the electricity network. Ireland's legacy of ribbon development greatly increases the challenge of routing power lines often resulting in lengthy planning delays.

Nuclear Energy
A highly controversial topic relating to energy supply security and energy infrastructure is the potential for nuclear energy in Ireland. The international nuclear debate has heightened in recent years following the events in 2011 at the Fukushima nuclear plant in Japan with widespread re-evaluation of nuclear programmes. Current Irish legislation bans the generation of electricity from nuclear sources, and it is unlikely that any Irish government would be elected with a mandate for nuclear energy in the foreseeable future. The infrastructural aspects of nuclear power for Ireland will be discussed in this section and the environmental aspects in a later section.

Nuclear fission energy is the energy that is released when an atom is split in two. In most nuclear power stations, the atom that is split is a uranium atom. The splitting uranium atoms react with each other to split more atoms creating a chain reaction. Each of these reactions releases energy in the form of heat which can then be used to generate electricity. Uranium is in abundant supply across the world, with large stocks in politically stable countries such as Canada and Australia.

The infrastructural challenges of integrating nuclear energy into the Irish electricity system are very challenging, particularly given the size of plant required, at least in the past. However, it should be noted that in recent years, there has been a move towards smaller scale nuclear units which would be more comparable in size with existing generation units. In addition, mini reactors are currently being designed and tested and the UK is investigating the potential of these small-scale units to be installed at a local level to generate hot water and electricity to the local area. It is possible that these smaller units may be suitable for the Irish system in the future.

Another infrastructural challenge of traditional nuclear generation is that it is relatively inflexible in nature. Once a nuclear plant is in operation its output cannot be varied easily due to safety concerns. This lack of flexibility would cause a challenge for the reliable operation of the Irish electricity system. With a large and growing wind penetration what Ireland needs are flexible power stations to accommodate the variable wind output, i.e. power stations which can increase their output when renewable generation is low and decrease output when renewable generation is high. Thus, as Ireland is actively pursuing the promotion of renewable energy what it needs are complementary flexible conventional power stations. The traditional, large nuclear power stations are not flexible in their operation and thus are not complementary to renewable generation on a small isolated electricity system like Ireland's. Thus, without significantly more electrical interconnection which would essentially increase the size of Ireland's electricity system, and/or significant advances in the development of small and micro-scale nuclear energy, it is likely that for the foreseeable future Ireland can either pursue nuclear or renewable sources of energy, but probably not both.

Fracking

The exploitation of shale gas using hydraulic fracturing or 'fracking' has increased dramatically in the USA over the past twenty years and by 2014 dry shale gas production had risen to 48 per cent of total dry gas production. Fracking is the process of drilling into the earth to allow a high-pressure water, sand and chemical mixture to be injected into the rock to release the gas inside. The process is carried out vertically or, more commonly, by drilling horizontally to the rock layer. The process can create new pathways to release gas or can be used to extend existing channels.[8]

While the USA and Canada have led the way in fracking, there is an increasing interest in the technique in other areas of the world with potential sites for shale gas extraction through fracking occurring across Europe. However, the extensive use of fracking in the USA, and the consideration of the process by EU Governments, has prompted heated environmental debate.

296

Environmental concerns associated with the fracking process include the vast amounts of water that are consumed in the process, which must be transported to the fracking site, at potentially significant environmental cost. The second is the worry that the potentially carcinogenic chemicals used may escape and contaminate groundwater around the fracking site. There are also worries that the fracking process can cause small earth tremors.

Commentators in Europe have also cautioned against overstating the potential benefits of fracking, saying that while the USA can produce shale gas at low cost, this is due to advantageous geological conditions and 20–30 years of experience. In essence, the shale gas revolution took place 30 years ago in the USA and it is unlikely that the EU will be able to replicate the economies of scale, with anticipated production costs 150–250 per cent higher than those in the USA.

Also, while the USA has seen a reduction in greenhouse gas emissions through the use of shale gas, this has largely come as a result of the low-cost shale gas replacing coal-fired electricity generation. It is unlikely that the EU will be able to produce shale gas at a low enough cost to push out European coal-fired generation, particularly when the USA can export its unused coal and sell it at low cost on the European markets. There are also concerns that potential methane leaks from fracking activities could counteract any CO_2 benefits.

While there may be some longer term benefits to shale gas extraction in Europe it is unlikely to make more than a few percentage points difference in the energy mix and should not be considered as the panacea for Europe's energy concerns. It is likely that renewable technologies and energy efficiency measures will have a much greater impact than pursuing shale gas extraction.

4 END-USER ENERGY PRICES AND COMPETITION

The second pillar of energy policy is the sustainability of end-user energy prices. As a key input in almost every production process, energy costs have a direct impact on Ireland's international competitiveness and indeed on living standards in Ireland, as the cheaper the energy the better-off are consumers. The provision of electricity and heating is also considered to be a basic necessity and thus it is important to protect the financially disadvantaged from excessively high prices. However, prices must also be high enough to attract investment in the energy infrastructure in Ireland into the future. Thus, energy prices are generally discussed as being sustainable; low enough so as not to adversely impact on competitiveness, living standards and vulnerable users, but also high enough to ensure continued investment in supply. Table 11.2 illustrates Ireland's end-user energy prices compared to the EU15 countries listed.

It can be seen that end-user energy prices in Ireland are among the highest in the EU. There are a number of factors that influence energy prices in Ireland including, but not limited to, imported fuel prices, electricity generating fuel mix, infrastructure investment and non-energy costs (for example, taxes levied,

Table 11.2 End User Energy Prices (including taxes) in EU 15 Countries

	Electricity Prices 2016 € per 100kWh		Gas Prices 2016 € per GJ[1]		Transport Prices Jan 2017 € per litre	
	Industrial	Domestic	Industrial	Domestic	Unleaded	Diesel
Austria	10.29	20.34	3.53	6.90	1.09	1.01
Belgium	11.15	25.44	2.57	5.47	1.32	1.19
Denmark	9.48	30.88	2.87	7.17	1.45	1.22
Finland	6.85	15.41	4.14	n/a	1.35	1.15
France	9.93	16.85	3.33	6.50	1.27	1.16
Germany	15.05	29.69	3.39	6.61	1.27	1.06
Greece	11.51	17.60	2.96	5.64	1.52	1.15
Ireland	*13.27*	*23.06*	*3.28*	*6.52*	*1.36*	*1.27*
Italy	15.26	24.13	3.12	7.31	1.53	1.38
Luxembourg	8.73	16.98	3.52	4.54	1.06	0.89
Netherlands	8.57	16.20	3.84	7.79	1.55	1.19
Portugal	11.25	23.50	3.40	9.13	1.45	1.19
Spain	11.05	21.85	2.81	6.77	1.07	1.02
Sweden	6.16	18.94	3.73	11.29	1.35	1.32
UK	13.77	19.51	2.91	5.53	1.22	1.23
Euro area	12.43	21.88	3.25	6.80	1.25	1.10
EU - 28	11.69	20.58	3.15	6.21	1.23	1.11

Source: Electricity and gas prices are from Sustainable Energy Authority of Ireland, 'Electricity and Gas Prices in Ireland, 1st Semester 2016', June 2016. Unleaded and diesel prices were obtained from the AA website in January 2017 at www.theaa.ie
[1] Domestic gas prices unavailable for Finland.

employment costs, raw material and shipping costs). Looking at each of these components in turn can help explain Ireland's high electricity prices.[9]

Imported Fuel Prices and Electricity Generation Mix

The most significant factor driving energy prices in Ireland is the instability of global oil prices which have shown dramatic fluctuations in recent years. This has particular effect in Ireland due to our high dependence on oil. In addition there is the knock-on impact that oil prices have on other energy prices, in particular natural gas, and as a consequence electricity prices.

Ireland has close to the highest overall dependency on imported fossil fuels in the EU which leaves it particularly exposed to international fossil fuel markets. In the electricity sector Ireland has the fourth highest dependency on imported fossil fuels for electricity generation in the EU-27 and the second highest dependency on imported gas for electricity generation. This reliance is one contributing factor towards Ireland's high energy prices.

Network Costs

The second largest component of end-user prices is network costs. These are charges which are used to maintain and upgrade the electricity network. This is essential in order to encourage foreign direct investment into areas with relatively weak network connection. Also, without investment in the electricity network the achievement of Ireland's renewable targets will not be possible. However, as mentioned previously, Ireland's spatial planning legacy has resulted in Ireland having four times the EU average length of power line, thus network costs are higher than those experienced elsewhere in the EU: they account for approximately six per cent of residential end-user electricity prices.

Taxes and levies

Another important driver of energy costs are non-recoverable taxes on energy (these include VAT for residential customers, energy taxes, carbon taxes and climate-change levies). In Ireland, non-recoverable taxes account for 9 per cent of the final electricity price for industrial customers and 18 per cent of the final prices for residential customers. These tax rates are lower than the EU average for both sectors (28 per cent and 34 per cent respectively).

In addition to taxes, Irish electricity consumers also pay a Public Service Obligation Levy (PSO) on their electricity bills. This levy is designed primarily to support the use of indigenous peat and renewable energy sources in electricity generation. The PSO is justified on security of supply grounds in order to support security of supply, indigenous fuels and renewables but it is one of the most contradictory policies of the Irish government in the energy area. Peat is the most inefficient fuel for electricity generation and is the highest emitter of carbon dioxide (CO_2) of all fuels used in electricity generation in Ireland. Thus, while on the one hand the government has developed ambitious targets for renewable sources of energy to reduce emissions, on the other hand it is financially supporting the use of peat, the highest emitter of CO_2.

In the transport sector, the main driver of end-user prices are international fuel price fluctuations with other factors such as exchange rates, production, and refining costs also playing a role. In Ireland taxes also form a significant component of end-user prices and in January 2017 excise rates (including carbon charges) accounted for approximately 63 per cent of final petrol prices and 58 per cent of diesel prices.

5 ENVIRONMENTAL ISSUES

So far two of the pillars of energy policy have been discussed: security of supply and sustainable end-user prices. The third energy policy pillar is environmental sustainability. Energy provision impacts on almost all facets of the environment from emissions and air pollution, to water consumption and quality, to waste generation and the natural environment. Thus, energy policy should always be considered in parallel with environmental issues. However, environmental policy is also much broader than just energy-related concerns. This section elaborates on some of the environmental issues relating to energy provision but more importantly discusses some of the broader environmental policy issues facing Ireland. Environmental policy is discussed under four headings in this section: emissions, air and water issues, waste and biodiversity.[10]

Emissions
Due to international concern about climate change, policymakers worldwide have introduced numerous instruments to help curb global emissions. Obviously a goal of zero pollution is unrealistic and undesirable since pollution is a by-product of day-to-day living. Thus, the key for policymakers is to decide upon an optimal level of operation where the costs do not exceed the benefits of pollution (material standard of living).

Paris Agreement and EU Trading Scheme
Climate change requires both an urgent and long-term response as the decisions policymakers make today will determine large scale and irreversible changes over this and subsequent centuries. In December 2015, 197 world leaders met in Paris for a meeting of United Nations Framework Convention on Climate Change (UNFCC) to set the agenda for addressing the climate change challenge. A new global agreement, known as the Paris Agreement, was reached at this meeting and it aims to hold global average temperatures to well below 2°C above pre-industrial levels and to pursue efforts to limit temperature increase to 1.5°C. It also includes aims to address the impacts of climate change, particularly on food production, and to make finance flows more consistent with a low GHG emissions goal.

The Paris Agreement is legally binding and is expected to enter into force in 2020 and progress will be determined by a regular global stocktake. By January 2017, 127 of the 197 parties who attended the UNFCC meeting in Paris have ratified the agreement. Included in the parties who have accepted and signed the agreement is the USA, who participated in the Paris meetings under President Obama. With the election of President Trump, an unapologetic climate change denier, the future of climate policy in the USA is currently in a state of uncertainty. It remains to be seen how US environmental policy will develop. However, experts suggest that state level environmental policies in the USA, rather than national level policies, are going to be more important than ever in addressing the environmental challenge.

Prior to the Paris Agreement, the most wide-reaching agreement was the Kyoto Protocol which set binding targets for 37 industrialised countries and the EU to reduce greenhouse gas (GHG) emissions. The EU committed to reducing emissions by 8 per cent below 1990 levels in the 2008 to 2012 period, a target which was achieved. Following the Kyoto Protocol target, the EU set a target for the subsequent period from 2013 to 2020, to reduce emissions to 20 per cent below 1990 levels and by 40 per cent relative to 1990 levels by 2030.

The EU aims to meet these targets by controlling emissions from large industrial sources through the *European Union Greenhouse Gas Emission Trading Scheme* (EU ETS) which commenced operation in January 2005. The EU ETS is now the largest multi-country, multi-sector GHG emission trading scheme in the world. Emissions from other non-ETS activities, such as transport, agriculture, heating and waste are addressed at a member state level under the Effort Sharing Decision.

For Ireland, policies for mitigation and adaptation to climate change are framed by United Nations, EU and national policy. These include the UNFCC, the Kyoto Protocol, the UN Paris Agreement, the EU Strategy on Adaptation to Climate Change, the EU Climate and Energy Package, the National Policy Position on Climate Change and the Climate Action and Low Carbon Development Act 2015.

In Ireland in 2014, the energy sector was responsible for over 60.0 per cent of GHG emissions in Ireland, the agriculture sector (due to emissions from livestock) accounted for 32.0 per cent of the total, followed by industrial processes and product use (5.2 per cent) and the waste sector (2.6 per cent). Ireland met its Kyoto Protocol emissions targets for the period 2008 to 2012 and has now been set a target of limiting annual GHG emissions from the ETS sector to 20 per cent below 2005 levels by 2020 in line with EU 2020 targets. For the non-ETS sector (covering transport, agriculture, heating and waste) Ireland is required to deliver a 20 per cent reduction in GHG emissions by 2020 (relative to 2005 levels).

These are considered to be onerous targets and the Environmental Protection Agency (EPA) predicts that without dramatic interventions, Ireland is projected to exceed its annual limits in 2016 and, even with additional policies, this limit will be exceeded in 2017. Total emissions are projected to be between 6 to 11 per cent below 2005 levels in 2020. The target is a 20 per cent reduction. The consequences of this underachievement are likely to be onerous financial penalties.[11]

Nuclear Energy
Omitted from Ireland's emissions reduction plans is the potential for nuclear generation. Nuclear energy was discussed previously with regard to the opportunities and challenges it presents in terms of electricity provision. Nuclear energy also has potential environmental impacts and these are discussed here.

In 2014, Ireland had the fourth highest GHG emissions per capita in the EU-28, whereas, France with the largest nuclear programme had one of the lowest CO_2 levels. However, it should be noted that nuclear energy is not 100 per cent emission free as CO_2 is released during uranium mining, transportation, decommissioning and waste treatment. Also, nuclear energy can contribute to emissions reduction in the electricity sector but alone does not assist in meeting targets in the heating and transport sectors. Nevertheless, the fact that nuclear energy allows for the generation of large amounts of electricity with minimal levels of CO_2 is the most compelling argument for nuclear power generation.

Nuclear waste and environmental and safety issues surrounding waste storage and disposal are among the most concerning aspects of nuclear power generation. Final disposal methods currently exist for low and intermediate level waste. However, there are presently no operating facilities in the world for the final disposal of high level nuclear waste products. Current practice is to store all high level waste in intermediate storage facilities based on site at the nuclear power stations.

Coupled with the environmental concerns regarding nuclear waste storage are the potential safety concerns. New nuclear power stations have far superior safety precautions than old stations with much of the operation now automated. However, the potential for accidents should be considered when examining nuclear energy. The environmental impact of an accident in Ireland is likely to be catastrophic. The prevailing winds are south-westerly so an explosive accident would almost certainly see radioactive clouds spread over land rather than towards the Atlantic. If the power station was located on Ireland's west coast, it is likely that the majority of the island would be affected by the spread of radioactivity with the radioactive clouds then spreading across Britain and into mainland Europe.

While a fully-informed scientific debate about nuclear energy is warranted in Ireland, it is unlikely as mentioned already that any Irish government would be elected with such a mandate in the foreseeable future. However, despite Ireland's legislative ban on nuclear energy, electricity generated by nuclear power is used in Ireland through the use of electrical imports from Britain. This use of nuclear power is likely to increase into the future as further interconnection to Britain is planned and the nuclear programme continues to expand there.

Air and Water Issues
Air Quality
Related to the discussion above, which focussed on carbon dioxide emissions, general air quality depends also on other pollutants such as sulphur dioxide, nitrous oxide, particulate matter and volatile organic compounds. Ireland fares very well in terms of air quality which is among the best in Europe, due largely to prevailing clean Atlantic air and a lack of large cities and heavy industry.

Air quality standards in Ireland are currently considered acceptable and we are not in breach of any EU legislative or target values. Vehicle traffic is the main cause of air quality problems in our larger towns and cities, while smaller towns with a high dependence on coal, turf and wood for home heating, can experience poor air quality at times.

In order to maintain its good record on air quality, Ireland must continue to be vigilant in meeting its international commitments and ensure that industrial emissions of pollutants continue to be rigorously controlled. Government also needs to remain committed to reducing emissions in the transport sector through measures aimed at reducing travel demand, increasing alternatives to the private car, and improving the efficiency of motorised transport.

Water Quality

One of the primary environmental challenges facing Ireland over the next decade is water quality and preservation. Ireland is fortunate in having a relatively abundant supply of fresh water with approximately 50 per cent of the land area of the state drained by just nine river systems. In 2000 the EU developed the Water Framework Directive (WFD) in response to the increasing threat of pollution and demand from the public for cleaner rivers, lakes, and beaches. This directive is unique as it establishes a framework for the protection of all waters including rivers, lakes, estuaries, coastal waters and groundwater, and their dependent wildlife/habitats under one piece of environmental legislation.

Ireland remains significantly off-target in meeting the requirements of the Water Framework Directive. Preliminary results for example from the Environmental Protection Agency indicate that there was no overall improvement in water quality over the first monitoring period (2009 to 2015) of the WFD.

In Ireland the majority of drinking water originates from surface water (82 per cent) and the remainder originates from groundwater (11 per cent) and springs (7 per cent). The most important health indicator of drinking water quality in Ireland is the presence of microbiological particles, in particular, *E. coli*. The presence of *E. coli* in drinking water indicates that the treatment process at the water treatment plant is not operating adequately or that contamination has entered the water-distribution system after treatment. The majority of supplies where *E. coli* was detected were private group water schemes, e.g. from local wells, and it is estimated that 30 per cent of all private wells are contaminated by *E. coli*. There were 439 cases of cryptosporidium contamination in public water supplies in 2015 (mostly in Westport in Co. Mayo) but overall publically supplied water continues to be at a very high quality with 99.9 per cent compliance with microbiological standards and 99.4 per cent compliance with chemical standards. Despite this good performance in public water supply, in 2016 the EPA identified 119 supplies which are in need of upgrade, improvement or replacement to ensure continued performance.

Once water is extracted, it requires treatment in order to make it suitable for consumption. As mentioned previously, given Ireland's legacy of ribbon development the water networks are radial in nature and experience high losses. It is estimated that almost half of all drinking water in Ireland is lost in transmission, one of the highest levels in Europe.

Water Charges

Water charges are currently in place for all commercial premises across Ireland and in an effort to ease pressure on water supplies it was announced in Budget 2009 that domestic water charges would be rolled out across the country. Given the high cost to the exchequer of maintaining quality water supplies, estimated at €1.2 billion per annum, the introduction of water charges was also a condition of Ireland's assistance programme from the EU-ECB-IMF.

Irish Water was established in March 2013 as a semi-state company to manage the water and wastewater services previously under the auspices of the 34 local authorities (see also Chapter 4). Irish Water began the process of installing water meters in August 2013 and the majority of Irish households have had water meters installed by 2016. Water charges were introduced in 2015 but have been a highly controversial public issue since their inception resulting in the suspension of all domestic water charges from July 2016 until at least March 2017. The issue of water charges remains a highly political issue and at present the future rates and pricing structure for domestic customers are unknown.

Water Infrastructure and Flooding

Ireland has undergone significant investment in improving the water services infrastructure (for drinking water and urban wastewater) with over €4.6 billion invested over the last decade. This has resulted in a dramatic improvement in the level of treatment of urban wastewater.

A related issue which has increased in the public consciousness in recent years is flooding. Floods are a natural and inevitable part of life in Ireland and are usually caused by a combination of events including overflowing river banks, coastal storms, or blocked and overloaded ditches. Numerous severe floods have occurred throughout the country in the last decade and it is widely anticipated that changes in rainfall patterns and rises in sea levels resulting from climate change may make such flooding incidents more frequent and severe in the future. In 2008, the government announced new flooding guidelines and all new developments must adhere to these procedures. However, unfortunately this initiative is a classic example of 'closing the stable door once the horse has bolted' as the proliferation of development before 2008 did not adhere to these guidelines with much construction taking place on natural flood plains.

Waste

Since 2012 there have been clear developments in Ireland's waste management, driven by EU and national legislation and initiative. Ireland has made progress in meeting many EU waste recycling/recovery targets but challenges remain in relation to reducing the level of waste generated and waste management (see Table 11.3).

The bulk of Ireland's waste is municipal waste which is defined as household waste, commercial waste, and cleaning waste. Packaging waste includes materials such as cardboard, paper, glass, plastic, steel, aluminium, and wood. Since 2001 Ireland has been compliant with all statutory packaging recovery targets and exceeded the EU target of 60 per cent recovery rate of packaging for 2011.

Currently 40 per cent of Ireland's municipal waste is recycled with the majority exported to Britain. There has been a significant improvement in Ireland's attitude towards recycling and a two-bin service (general waste and mix-dry recyclables bins) is provided to virtually all households with a three bin service (including organics bin) provided to 34 per cent of serviced households in 2012.

Table 11.3 Ireland's Compliance with EU Waste Legislation

	Indicator
EU Packaging and Packaging Waste Directive	All targets met
WEEE Directive, target date 2008	All targets met
End of Life Vehicles Directive, target 2015	Recycling/reuse target at risk Recycling efficiency targets met
Batteries Directive, target date 2016	Portable battery collection target at risk
Landfill Directive, target date 2016	All targets met
New Waste Framework Directive target date 2020	On track

Source: Environmental Protection Agency (EPA), *Ireland's Environment 2016, An Assessment.*

While Ireland has outperformed its waste targets in many areas, the main threat to the sustainability of waste management is infrastructural capacity. Since 2012 there has been a significant reduction in the use of landfilling with just six active landfills remaining in 2016 compared to 18 in 2012. The most significant change in Ireland's waste management practices over the past decade is that more residual waste is now used as a fuel rather than being disposed to landfill.

There is currently only one municipal waste incineration in Ireland which is in Carranstown in Co. Meath. In 2005 the EPA granted a licence for an incinerator in Ringaskiddy in Co. Cork and in 2008 a licence was issued for an incinerator at Poolbeg in Dublin. All of these developments have undergone lengthy planning delays with Bord Pleaneala refusing planning permission for the facility in Cork in 2011 and Dublin City Council voting to abandon plans for the Poolbeg facility in light of local opposition in 2014. While plans for the Cork incinerator continue to be stalled pending planning permission, the Poolbeg facility commenced construction in late 2014 and is due to be operational in 2017.

Ireland is at an important juncture in waste management with impending EU targets and penalties on the horizon. With this in mind, one of the significant developments in the waste sector in recent years has been the introduction of refuse charges in an effort to manage and reduce waste. Domestic waste charges are now levied on almost all households that use an organised refuse collection service. These charges were brought in at different times by different operators and are not uniform across the state. However, without a concerted and significant effort towards a reduction in total waste production, a continued reduction in the reliance on landfill and the development of further waste management infrastructure, Ireland is likely to face significant EU non-compliance fines in relation to waste in the coming years.

Nature and Biodiversity

The protection of the natural environment and biodiversity is of ethical and economic concern. While progress has been made in the designation of EU-protected areas in Ireland, several areas of national importance remain undesignated and significant aspects of biodiversity in Ireland are under considerable threat from unsustainable activities. Ireland has international and legal obligations to protect biodiversity which includes a commitment to halt biodiversity loss by 2020.

On a global scale, species are currently being lost at a rate of up to 1,000 times faster than the natural rate, primarily as a result of human activities. In the EU it is estimated that only 17 per cent of habitats and protected species are in a favourable state. In terms of Ireland's performance, in the period 2007 to 2013 only 9 per cent of listed habitats are considered to be in a favourable state as defined in the EU Habitats Directive (92/43/EEC).

In terms of species, Ireland's record is also poor with only 52 per cent of species listed under the Habitats Directive being reported as in a favourable state. These species include bats, seals, and certain plants. Other species, such as a number of species of fish (e.g. Atlantic salmon), molluscs and toads, are reported as being in poor to bad status. An assessment by Bird Watch Ireland suggests that of the 185 bird species that breed and/or winter in Ireland, 37 are regionally extinct and 90 are critically endangered.

The key pressures on Ireland's habitats and species are direct habitat damage through activities such as peat cutting, wetland drainage/reclamation and infrastructural development; over-grazing and under-grazing; water pollution particularly from nutrients and silt; unsustainable exploitation such as over-fishing and peat extraction; invasive alien species; and recreational pressure. Indirect pressures such as population growth and poor special development are also threats to biodiversity. Climate change is also likely to bring additional pressures on a number of species and habitats in Ireland.

Maintaining habitats and biodiversity has economic as well as ethical value with benefits to the agricultural sector (both in terms of crops and livestock), the tourism sector, in pest control, in the resulting health benefits from pest control, in the fisheries sector, water quality, recreation, and in reducing waste assimilation. Biodiversity is estimated to be worth at least €2.6 billion per annum to Ireland.

6 CONCLUSION

This chapter has examined the development of Ireland's energy provision and environmental measures over the past decade and has highlighted some of the challenges facing each of these sectors. A key message arising is the important link between energy and environmental policy. In particular, it has been highlighted how almost every facet of the energy sector (from electricity generation, to transport provision to fossil fuel extraction and to domestic consumption) has significant environmental consequences and as such it would be naive and impractical to consider energy policy in an environmental vacuum.

The chapter also emphasises the role of the state in energy provision through direct ownership of assets, in the regulation of strategic behaviour by electricity providers, in the control of emissions and in securing diversity in energy supplies. In particular, the chapter highlights the importance of energy resources on a global scale and the political conflict that has resulted from the control of fossil fuel resources worldwide. Given its island nature with relative few indigenous fossil fuel resources, Ireland has one of the highest levels of imported fossil fuels in Europe and represents an interesting case study system when it comes to the challenges of energy diversity. This chapter expands on this issue and highlights some potential solutions such as renewable energy and more controversially nuclear energy and fracking.

One of the real success stories of the economic boom was the huge improvement in transport infrastructure in Ireland, with major upgrades seen in both road networks and public transport infrastructure. However, this improvement was twinned with missed opportunities in terms of spatial planning. The housing boom did little to address the dispersed nature of the population and the poor quality of housing stock relative to our EU neighbours. The rapid construction period also left a negative legacy in terms of our environmental goals in the areas of water quality and waste management. In fact planning issues are a recurring theme throughout this chapter from the high average length of our electricity lines, to the high level of water losses, and the sustainability of waste management with delays in incinerator construction.

While Ireland continues to make progress towards its environmental targets, issues surrounding air and water quality, waste infrastructure and biodiversity protection are key areas of concern in the coming years. Ireland is also facing significant challenges in keeping up with competitors in terms of the quality of energy infrastructure, end-user energy prices and in securing a more diverse energy supply. These challenges are likely to be heightened by public opposition to necessary energy and environmental infrastructure projects such as network expansion, wind farm development and waste management infrastructure.

Endnotes

1   This section draws heavily on the Sustainable Energy Authority of Ireland (SEAI), *Residential Energy Roadmap*, available at www.seai.ie
2   A good evaluation of Ireland's energy policy in each of these areas can be found in J. FitzGerald, *A Review of Irish Energy Policy*, Research series No. 21, April 2011.
3   See *Report of the Review Group on State Assets and Liabilities*, April 2011, available at www.finance.gov.ie/viewdoc.asp?DocID=6805.
4   Housing statistics are from Eurostat, the European Commission statistical database.
5   This section draws on M. Klare, *Blood and Oil: The Dangers and Consequences of America's Growing Petroleum Dependency*, Metropolitan Books/Henry Holt, New York 2004.
6   UK oil reserves and estimated ultimate recovery for 2014, available at www.gov.uk.
7   See Department of Communications, Energy and Natural Resources, *Oil Stock Policy*, available at www.dcenr.gov.ie

8   This section draws on D. Healy, 'Hydraulic Fracturing or "Fracking": A Short Summary of Current Knowledge and Potential Environmental Impacts', A Small Scale Study for the Environmental Protection Agency (Ireland) under the Science, Technology, Research & Innovation for the Environment (STRIVE) Programme 2007–2013, 2012, available at www.epa.ie.

9   This section draws heavily on Sustainable Energy Authority of Ireland's *Price Directive for the 1st Semester of 2016*, available at www.seai.ie.

10   This section draws significantly from the Environmental Protection Agency (EPA), *Ireland's Environment 2016, An Assessment*, available at www.epa.ie.

11   Environmental Protection Agency, 'Ireland's Greenhouse Gas Emissions Projections, 2012–2030', April 2013, available at www.epa.ie.

CHAPTER 12

Housing: Supply, Pricing and Servicing

Ronan Lyons

1 INTRODUCTION

Housing is at the core of modern economies. According to the 2009 to 2010 Household Budget Survey in Ireland, housing comprised a greater share of consumer expenditure than any other category. Of the €42,150 spent by the average household in that year, nearly one-fifth was spent on housing, with another 10 per cent spent on goods and services related to housing (including fuel, light, durables and household non-durables). This compares with 16.2 per cent spent a year on food, the next largest category. For households with mortgages or private sector rents, the fraction spent on housing costs was even greater (22.5 per cent for households with a mortgage and 26.3 per cent for households in the private rented sector).

More generally, property is the dominant asset in household portfolios. Detailed information on household wealth is available from the newly established Household Finance & Consumption Survey, part of a cross-European effort to better understand household balance sheets in the wake of the Great Recession (see also Chapter 7). The typical Irish household had gross wealth of €175,500 in 2013 and debt of just over €75,000, leaving typical net wealth for Irish households of €105,000. The vast majority of Irish household wealth is held in property ('real assets') of some form, in particular the main residence (53 per cent of real assets) but also land (21 per cent) and other property (15 per cent). Compared to real assets, financial assets were a much smaller part of the typical household's balance sheet, with the majority (55 per cent) held in savings, an average of €4,500 per household. Similarly, almost 95 per cent of household debt related to either a mortgage on the main residence (72 per cent) or on another property (23 per cent). From a household perspective, then, the housing sector matters and, related to this, it is of prime importance for policymakers. The Great Recession, associated with the Global Financial Crisis of 2008, had its roots in a run-up of housing debt in the USA and elsewhere (see Chapter 7) and there is strong evidence that the same is true of the Great Depression of the 1930s.[1] Despite this, housing has remained – at least until recently – something of a neglected topic in economics and economic policymaking, falling between the two stools of micro-economics and macroeconomics.

This chapter addresses the Irish policy space relating to housing. Section 2 will outline the rationale for government intervention. Section 3 presents housing as a market, documenting the supply and demand forces at work, as well as tenure considerations. Particular attention is paid to demand shifters, with Section 4 focusing on one demand shifter, mortgage credit, which has recently been the subject of significant policy intervention, and to the elasticity of supply, which is the subject of Section 5. Section 6 focuses on non-market provision of housing, in particular social housing, through both price and supply supports. Section 7 discusses the utilities related to housing, such as water and household waste, and the policy issues arising, while Section 8 concludes.

For the purposes of clarity, it is useful to set out here the terminology that will be used in this chapter. First, the term 'property' refers to any form of real estate comprising land and a structure, including residential or commercial property, as well as land without any structures on it. The term 'housing' is used to refer specifically to residential real estate, i.e. any property used for accommodation. This is distinct from the term 'house', which is one form of accommodation, with others including apartments. A 'dwelling' will refer to something that is built on a site, whereas a 'property' refers to both the dwelling and the site. Housing prices may refer to sale prices or rental prices, thus these specific terms will be used where appropriate, while the housing price ratio refers to the annual rental price as a fraction of the sale price.

2 RATIONALE FOR STATE INTERVENTION

Due to the importance of property in the economy, understanding the rationale for the nature and extent of government intervention in the sector is critical. Two central reasons are discussed below for government intervention in the property sector, namely efficiency (and in particular externalities) and equity and information failures. Costs of government action or changes in policy are also discussed in brief.

Efficiency
As is outlined in Section 5, on the supply of housing, land is essentially fixed in supply and is immobile. Thus, it is highly susceptible to externalities. For example, a factory emitting pollutants will affect residents nearby. Alternatively, the construction of a new rail line, with stations, will have an effect on the properties close to those stations. Policymakers may expect the bulk of these effects to be positive in nature, as these properties enjoy greater access to other parts of the country as a result, although there may also be negative spillovers, e.g. traffic congestion at rush-hour or extra crime as a result of higher footfall.

The presence of such externalities can be generalised slightly to thinking about land values as reflecting a missing market. While land varies hugely in

310

value around the country, and indeed even within cities, those variations do not stem primarily from the actions of the current owner or previous owners. Instead, differences in the value of land across space reflect the actions of others, including society generally as well as government actions specifically. The presence of an employment cluster, or a consumption cluster (such as restaurants), may not reflect any specific policy actions, rather a natural tendency for agglomeration. This creates a spillover amenity enjoyed by landowners nearby. In addition, specific government actions – such as the example of a new rail line given above – may also significantly affect land values.

However, if land values are not taxed, such increases in the value of land cannot be connected to the initial investment decisions. This creates a misallocation of resources, in a regime without land taxes, compared to one with land taxes, as there may be, for example, under-investment in rail infrastructure. The same logic applies to other government actions that affect land values, including other transport infrastructure, such as motorways and airports, but also a wide range of other amenities, including parks, green space and blue-flag beaches, as well as schools, hospitals and police stations, where freedom from crime is amenity.

Equity and Information Failures
In aggregate, the demand for housing is, ultimately, very inelastic: everyone needs access to shelter on a regular basis. Housing requires resources, though. Therefore, with a spread of incomes in the economy, it is inevitable that, at any given point, there will be residents who cannot afford to cover the cost of their housing, even in a situation where housing supply is at a point close to maximum efficiency. This is the rationale for substantial government intervention, in order to ensure that all citizens have adequate housing. This can take two forms, as discussed in some detail in Section 6: boosting demand (for example, through income supports) or increasing supply (for example, through the direct construction of dwellings).

The government may also intervene to address information failures, which may undermine efficiency. It is for this reason that Ireland has had, since 2012, a public register of transaction prices for residential property. Other countries have, for similar reasons, publicly available registers of bids on residential property and maps of land ownership. The EU requirement to have an energy performance certificate, known in Ireland as a Building Energy Rating (BER), combines both informational and behavioural motivations. It is believed that such certificates will lead to more informed decision making on the part of consumers, largely through making energy consumption more salient to the consumer and providing an incentive to improve the energy efficiency of the housing stock.

A similar argument could be made for the numerous minimum standards that apply to Irish housing currently, such as requirements relating to minimum sizes, orientation, facilities (such as kitchens and bathrooms) and, in the case of apartments, requirements relating to lifts, balconies and basement car-parking. This, however, creates two tensions. The first tension is with personal freedoms, as a universal requirement for minimum sizes may prevent people from living as close to an urban centre as they otherwise would like, more central properties being dearer, *ceteris paribus*. The second tension is with social justice, as preventing the construction of smaller and cheaper homes, for example, may price out those on lower incomes, unless government subsidies are increased to compensate. More broadly, as in other policy areas, in addition to market failure, policymakers need to be aware of the scope for, and effect of, government failure.

This may include effects from changes in policy. Arguably, as explained below, regulatory and policy changes relating to mortgage credit and the taxation of construction created the dramatic property market bubble and crash seen in Ireland over the period 1995 to 2012.

3 MARKET FOR HOUSING

Since 2012, a mismatch of supply and demand has characterised the Irish housing market. It can be seen in the scarcity of student accommodation, an increasing number of homeless people, including those in work, and in the rapid increase of prices and rents in certain parts of the country. In Dublin, sale and rental prices rose by more than 40 per cent between 2012 and 2016. In other parts of the country, particularly in rural areas where tax reliefs were most generous, prices and rents have registered much more modest increases in the same period. This reflects the underlying economics of the housing market.

A Composite Good

The ability to buy and sell housing means that the sector can be thought of as a market, with price and quantity outcomes reflecting underlying supply and demand and related policy interventions. The asset-based nature of housing – in other words, its durability and the possibility of reselling it at a later date – means that demand will reflect not just demand for housing as a service (the rental component) but also the costs and/or potential gains of holding housing as an asset.

For those who own their own home, housing as a service is often termed 'implicit rent': just as a house in the rented sector has an occupier (tenant) who pays rent to an owner (landlord), it is possible to think of those who own their homes as receiving (imputed) rent payments from themselves. Put another way, the owner of a housing asset is saving on accommodation costs by not having to rent somewhere to live. This is different to someone with the same wealth but who bought a different type of asset (e.g. shares in a publicly listed company); they would still need to spend on rents.

In addition to the distinction between housing as a service and housing as an asset, a second central feature of housing is that it is a composite good, such that every individual property is unique (as the sites are, even if the dwellings are identical). Microeconomic studies of housing – in other words, where the unit of observation is the individual house, rather than the housing market – exploit this fact. They typically attempt to explain the sale or rental price of an individual property using a range of characteristics relating to the dwelling and to the location. In brief, the value of any property can be broken down into the site and what is built on it.

Specific dwelling characteristics include the size, type, age and quality of the built dwelling itself. Comparisons across dwellings need to take into account in particular the number of rooms (such as bedrooms) but more generally the full floor area. More accurate comparisons will also take into account the type of dwelling: a 70sqm apartment will face a different demand curve to a 70sqm terraced house. Similar issues arise with age – typically newer properties command a higher price but vintage premiums (e.g. for Victorian or Georgian homes) also exist. As mentioned earlier, following an EU directive, it has become mandatory for properties listed for sale or rent to include their BER and, not surprisingly, research has shown that more energy efficient homes command a price premium over less efficient counterparts, *ceteris paribus*.

The second set of characteristics that affect the value of a property relate to the plot of land. Whereas the owner has relatively complete control – subject to, for example, preservation orders – over the value of what is built on the site, they do not have any meaningful control over the value of their site. As mentioned in Section 2, this depends on a large set of factors, including proximity to the nearest city centre, to the coast, and to other amenities such as transport facilities, green space and schools, as well as distance from dis-amenities, such as pollution of any form, including noise or visual pollution, congestion and crime. The site value will also depend on factors that depend on neighbourhood characteristics, rather than geography, such as the fraction of people in the neighbourhood that have a degree or the fraction at work. The bulk of variation in housing prices comes instead from the land value, as opposed to dwelling characteristics. This is a theme for policy discussed in later sections.

Fundamentals

While the above discussion focuses on the nature of demand at the property level, i.e. what differentiates one property from another, much of the public policy focus in housing is at the aggregate or market level. When thinking at the market level, it is useful to highlight the distinction between two sets of factors affecting housing outcomes: fundamentals and asset factors. Fundamentals affect both implicit rents, and thus sale prices, as well as market rents, whereas asset factors affect the relationship between sale and rental prices. For example, an increase in average incomes of 10 per cent would be expected to increase both sale and rental prices. However, increased confidence about future economic conditions is likely to have a major demand effect only for owner-occupied properties. The three main fundamentals affecting the price of housing, both sale and rental, are household income, demographics and housing supply.

313

Household Income

Income is a key measure of underlying demand for housing and is best measured as real (i.e. inflation-adjusted) income per household. The relationship between incomes and house prices is positive: households will spend more on housing as average incomes rise or as the typical household enjoys an additional source of income. It is worth noting that a change in household income could come from a number of sources. First, it may stem from a simple increase in incomes paid to each person. Second, it may reflect greater participation in the labour force on the part of the typical household, e.g. greater numbers of women staying in the labour force, as occurred during the 1990s in Ireland. Lastly, it reflects unemployment. If 10 per cent of the working age population lose their employment, as happened between late 2007 and early 2010, this reduces the number of incomes the average household enjoys.

The positive relationship between income and accommodation costs occurs through two channels. First, even if households keep constant the fraction of their expenditure devoted to housing, an increase in income will mean more spent on housing. Without any change in housing supply, this merely pushes house prices up. Second, there is empirical evidence that housing may be what economists term a luxury good. This means that as incomes increase, the fraction of money spent on housing does not stay static, it increases. Evidence from the Irish housing market over the period 1975 to 2012 suggests that an increase in income of 10 per cent (keeping other factors, including the general price level, constant) is associated with a 12.6 per cent increase in the real price of housing.

Demographics

The second demand-side factor affecting rents, both market rents and implicit rents, is demographics. There are a number of elements to demographics that affect housing demand, including fertility rates, longevity, the age structure of the population and divorce/separation rates. These are best captured in the broadest measure of demographics, the number of persons per household. This number is typically slow-moving and has been falling from roughly four in the 1970s to less than three today. (A related concept is the headship rate, which measures the fraction of the population that heads up their own household.)

To see how the ratio of persons to households could impact house prices and rents, contrast the housing requirements of a population of four million people split into two million, two-person households with the same population split into one million households of four people each. Over the period 1980 to 2012, the number of persons in the typical Irish household fell by one. This increase in effective housing demand per head of population was associated with an increase in real house prices of roughly 40 per cent.

It is highly likely that Ireland's average household size will continue to fall over the coming decades (see Chapter 6). This could create significant demand for new homes. For example, assume that Ireland's population stays constant at 4.8m, but that the average household size falls from 2.7 (as it was in 2011) to 2.5.

This in itself would require the construction of 142,000 extra dwellings. Given roughly 14,000 dwellings were constructed in 2016, that is, the equivalent of 10 years' output from the building sector, even if population were to remain stable. Convergence to the EU average of 2.3 persons per household would require the construction of an additional 300,000 dwellings in Ireland: more than 20 years of current supply.

Supply
In terms of impact on prices and rents, housing supply works in the opposite direction to household income. An increase in the number of dwellings relative to the number of households gives the demand side of the market greater bargaining power, lowering prices and rents. Note that, perhaps slightly counterintuitively, this factor also includes net migration, as a large inflow (for example) of households into the country reduces the quantity of housing stock available to each household, thus driving down supply relative to demand.

The correct measure of supply is not the number of dwellings per household, but instead the value of the housing stock (measured annually by the Central Statistics Office in the national accounts as the real net capital stock in residential dwellings) per household. This is because not all dwellings are equal. If Ireland's housing stock has been gradually moving over time from smaller rural cottages and urban terraced dwellings to larger and/or more energy efficient homes, this increase in the quality of supply will not be reflected in a simple count of dwellings.

Research on the Irish housing market 1975 to 2012 suggests that an increase in the real value of the housing stock of 10 per cent is associated with a fall in real house prices of 8 per cent. A similar relationship between supply and rental values is likely to hold. Note that the effect is slightly less than proportional: as housing stock increases, there is a price effect but also a small quantity effect (see later).

Asset Factors
Key Concepts
It is important to highlight that a house can be thought of as an asset similar to other financial assets. The durable nature of housing means there may be a demand for housing simply because it is expected that there will be demand for housing in the future. This suggests expected capital gain as a source of housing demand, and the remainder of this section deals with the concept of user cost, of which expected capital gain is a principal component. The other asset factor that may affect demand for housing is the condition of the mortgage credit market (see later).

The yield on a financial asset can be thought of as reflecting the ratio of returns (e.g. dividends or price gains) to the price of the asset. Similarly, the yield on housing – the ratio of the annual rental price to its value if sold – can be measured and compared with other assets. The three factors outlined above – real incomes per household, real housing supply per household, and demographics – affect both sale and rental prices in the housing market. Therefore, it is unlikely that changes in any would have a significant effect on the yield (or annual return) on housing.

A fall in user cost or more relaxed credit conditions, on the other hand, will – for reasons outlined below – shift out the demand curve for property for sale and therefore increase sale prices but not rental prices. They are, thus, the principal determinants of the equilibrium yield in the property market. The yield is often considered one of the most important barometers of the health of a housing market. A yield that is 'too low' is taken to signify that sale prices have become detached from their fundamentals, as reflected in rental prices, whereas a yield that is 'too high' may mean that impediments exist to the proper functioning of the sale market.

User Cost

The user cost refers to how expensive it is to hold an asset for a given period, typically a year. It is thus a measure of the cost of capital, taking into account the opportunity cost (the interest rate), but also holding costs (such as maintenance and depreciation) and expected capital gains. This is a core concept in finance and applies also to housing due to its durable nature.

In relation to residential housing in Ireland, there are two main contributors to user cost. The first is the cost of holding housing. For owner-occupiers, this includes the nominal mortgage interest rate (before 2013, the net or after-tax rate was different to the gross or advertised rate due to mortgage interest relief), costs of maintenance and depreciation, and property taxes such as stamp duty and Local Property Tax. Most of these costs are relatively stable over time, while the most variable – the mortgage interest rate – has varied within narrow bands (roughly 3 per cent to 6 per cent) since Ireland entered the euro zone.

The second and typically more important aspect of user cost is expectations of future house prices, in other words expected capital gain. As mentioned above, interest rates and property taxes have a relatively small range over the course of the cycle. However, expectations about the annual change in house prices can vary between plus 20 per cent year-on-year (as was the case in the mid 2000s) and minus 20 per cent (as was the case in the late 2000s). This reflects the fact that expectations about sale prices for housing are to some extent adaptive, i.e. they reflect not only expected future changes in fundamentals but also momentum from recent trends.

Among the gaps in our knowledge of the housing market – not just in Ireland but indeed across the developed world – is a high-quality, high-frequency measure of housing market expectations.[2] In practice, these need to be measured in a survey format and, without surveys extending back in time, it is not possible to say definitively what the impact of expectations on housing market outcomes has been. A relatively standard assumption is that the average change in house prices over the last four years is a good measure of expected capital gains. When applied to the case of Ireland's housing bubble and crash, this suggests that the user cost rose from minus 10 per cent (with strong price appreciation, there was no cost to capital) to plus 20 per cent between 2006 and 2012, an increase in costs that was associated with a fall in equilibrium prices of approximately 45 per cent.

A negative user cost suggests almost irrepressible demand for housing, as appears to have been the case in Ireland in the final stages of the housing market bubble, and is far from healthy. A per-annum user cost of 20 per cent also is highly unhealthy and suggests a normalisation of expectations that would lead to an outward shift in demand for housing and thus a rise in price. In lay terms, this is often described as house prices 'overshooting' both on the way up and the way down and stems from adaptive expectations.

Tenure Factors

The discussion so far has mentioned sale and rental prices, implying the existence of two segments of the housing market. The presence of both sale and rental demand for property may reflect heterogeneous preferences among people of similar circumstances: some people may prefer flexibility or a more central location, and thus rent, while others may buy. In addition, the existence of rental market may reflect constrained demand, where households want to own property but are unable to do so, for some reason.

It is important to note that the boundary between these two segments is not fixed and changes with technology (broadly defined, i.e. including policy technology and financial technology) as well as with preferences. Figure 12.1 presents the fraction of households by tenure type in Ireland, at each census since 1961. It includes social housing (Section 7) as well as owner-occupied and market rental,

Figure 12.1 Fraction of Households, by Tenure Type, Ireland (1961–2011)

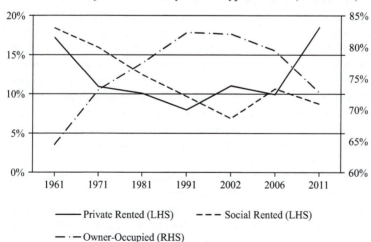

——— Private Rented (LHS)   – – – Social Rented (LHS)

— · — Owner-Occupied (RHS)

Source: Census of Ireland (various issues).

and shows a clear upward trend in owner-occupancy from 1961 to 1991. Both private market rental and social rental fell during the same period, although it is important to note that the fraction in social housing did not increase between 1991 and 2011, while the fraction in private rented accommodation rose from 8 to more than 18 per cent.

Contrary to popular perception, Ireland does not have an unusually high fraction of its population that own their home. Indeed, the homeownership rate in Ireland is one of the lowest in Europe, ranking 21st out of 28 countries. Many central and eastern European countries have significantly higher homeownership rates, due in large part to redistribution of property after the fall of the Soviet Union and its satellite states in the early 1990s.

A final note concerns the relationship between household income and yields. As outlined earlier, a higher income at household level would be expected to increase housing demand, with upward pressure on sale and rental prices. However, it may be possible that the effect is greater for sale prices than rental prices. For example, if it is the case that home ownership rates increase with incomes, then as incomes go up over time – in particular relative to the cost and supply of dwellings – this will reduce the demand for rented accommodation relative to the owner-occupied sector.

4 ROLE OF CREDIT

Commercial Property

While the bulk of the chapter focuses on residential property, one must also consider commercial property, which includes real estate used for retail, offices and industrial, among other uses. Broadly speaking, both commercial and residential sectors are subject to the same forces of supply and demand. Thus, the pattern of commercial property prices, both sale and rental, mirrors to a large extent those of residential property prices, both sale and rental, over the last generation.

Nonetheless, there are some important differences. One stems from the credit side. As a general rule, residential property is highly leveraged, i.e. there is likely to be a high fraction of debt associated with every euro of housing wealth. Given that businesses are more mobile than residents, including the option for businesses to cease to exist, commercial property is typically far less leveraged than housing. Whereas equity is a percentage claim on an asset, debt is a nominal (i.e. euro) claim. The greater role for equity in commercial property provides a larger buffer in times of falling values.

Combined with the fact that its owners and its occupiers are not households and, by and large, have separate legal status, allowing them to go bankrupt in the extreme case, commercial property is far less of a concern for public policy than residential property. Given recent Irish history, though, it is necessary to include one crucial caveat to this statement. Where a government chooses to guarantee the liabilities of its financial institutions, as Ireland did in 2009, this creates a link between the taxpayer and the performance of commercial property, in particular the development of new property. In effect, Irish banks had borrowed large sums from international capital markets and lent to developers (both commercial and residential), who could not repay when the Irish property bubble burst. When the Irish government – in an attempt to preserve the Irish financial system – guaranteed all liabilities, rather than for example just new liabilities, it made commercial property a policy issue in a way perhaps unique in modern economic history (see Chapter 7). This is unlikely to occur in future, as the principle of 'bailing in' bondholders (those who lend to banks) is now enshrined in EU policy (see Chapter 3).

Mortgage Credit Market
Returning to residential property, a fifth major factor affecting housing market outcomes is non-price conditions in the mortgage credit market. To see why non-price conditions matter, compare 2006 and 2014. In both years, average incomes were similar and financial institutions would have offered a household on an average income mortgages with similar rates. However, the conditions of borrowing were very different in those two years. In particular, a significant fraction of first-time buyers in 2006 required no down-payment on their mortgage, while many others required a deposit of less than 5 per cent. In contrast, most first-time buyers in 2014 required a deposit of at least 10 per cent, in many cases 15 per cent.

The deposit required of the typical first-time buyer is a measure of leverage, or how stretched a first-time buyer is. The higher the leverage, the less protected an asset-holder is in response to a negative price shock. If first-time buyers are required to have a 20 per cent deposit to obtain a mortgage, this means that if housing prices were to fall by 15 per cent, a family that needed to move (e.g. in response to losing a job) would have enough equity to be able to absorb the fall in house price. In contrast, if first-time buyers need no deposit, i.e. the mortgage is worth 100 per cent of the value of their home, then any fall in housing prices means that they will be unable to sell up in response to a loss of income or employment. This latter situation describes the fate of many families once the Irish housing market collapsed after 2007.

Somewhat surprisingly, given their importance in the macro-economy, long-run series on the loan-to-value (LTV) of the typical first-time buyer are not available for Ireland.[3] However, a proxy measure, the ratio of the stock of mortgages to the stock of household bank deposits, can capture the change in credit conditions over recent decades. In particular, the ratio of mortgage credit to household deposits rose by 100 percentage points, from less than 80 per cent to 180 per cent, in the decade to 2008. The evidence shows strongly that it is not just user cost that determines the equilibrium yield for housing, it is also credit conditions.

One of the reasons that credit conditions are so important is the relatively elastic nature of the demand for mortgage credit. Everything else being equal, offering more credit to a household with a given level of income allows them to access more of their future earnings and thus buy a more expensive property. Given the high income elasticity of housing, the typical household will borrow

Figure 12.2 Stylised Analysis of an Outward Shift in Credit Supply

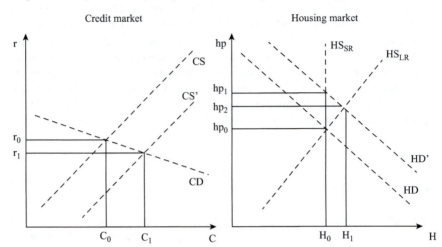

as much as it can. This relatively flat elasticity of credit demand is shown in the left-hand side panel of Figure 12.2.

An outward shift in credit supply (from CS to CS') – for example, due to a change in regulations that allows banks to lend more to borrowers – will result in a far greater proportional increase in the quantity of credit supplied than the fall in its price (interest rate). This translates into an outward shift in the demand for housing (from HD to HD', in the right-hand panel), significantly pushing up the average sale price of housing.

Central Bank Mortgage Regulations

Referring back to the five main factors affecting housing market outcomes, policy intervention in relation to the housing market typically will not be in reference to either incomes or demographics. Income is, in many senses, an outcome variable and it is unlikely that any government would attempt to stimulate income purely to alter housing market outcomes (as opposed to policy measures to stimulate income for its own sake).

Similarly, it is unlikely that policy would be designed to affect demographics purely to affect the housing market. Instead, there are three principal areas where housing market policy is undertaken: macro-prudential policy, reflecting the asset factors outlined above; housing supply; and social housing policies, reflecting equity and tenure concerns.

The term macro-prudential policy refers to regulation of the financial system that aims to reduce the risk of the financial system as a whole, particularly the risk it could pose to the broader economy (see Chapter 3). While the term is relatively new, policies that would now be characterised as macro-prudential date back at least to the 1930s response to the Great Depression, if not before.

Macro-prudential policy is typically seen as regulation relating to the financial sector, rather than the housing sector. Nonetheless, the strong overlap between housing and finance, particularly at the household level, means that the two sectors are inextricably linked. In terms of housing-related finance, the two dominant forms of macro-prudential regulation are loan-to-value and debt-to-income. Since 2015, both are in force in the Irish housing market.

In January 2015, the Central Bank of Ireland introduced proportionate limits for loan-to-value and loan-to-income for new mortgage lending, covering both 'primary dwelling houses' (PDHs, or owner-occupied homes) and buy-to-let (BTL) mortgages. For owner-occupied homes, both conditions must apply, i.e. households will only be able to borrow a certain multiple of their income provided it is also not beyond a certain multiple of their savings. On loan-to-value, there are different limits for first-time buyers and for other buyers. Since 2016, first-time buyers are required to have a maximum loan-to-value of 90 per cent. Non-first-time buyers are subject to a limit of 80 per cent LTV for their mortgages – if a family that already has a mortgage wants to borrow €400,000, they must have €100,000 in savings. BTL mortgages are subject to a more stringent 70 per cent LTV requirement.

In addition, owner-occupier mortgages are subject to a limit of 3.5 times loan to gross income (LTI). But in the case of both LTV and LTI caps, over the entire loan book of individual banks, exceptions are allowed. In particular, banks are allowed to exceed the 3.5 LTI limit on a total of 20 per cent of the value of all PDH mortgages each year. Banks are also allowed to exceed the LTV restrictions for PDH mortgages for up to 15 per cent of their mortgage book.

Issues Arising
Empirical analysis of the Irish housing market suggests that the single biggest contributor to the bubble in the run-up to 2007 was the decline in lending standards. Nonetheless, while there is widespread agreement that the broad thrust of the macro-prudential regulations is desirable, the exact nature of the Central Bank rules raises questions. All market regulation is typically designed to address a market failure and the rationale for limiting leverage by putting in place a maximum loan-to-value ratio can be described as addressing the market failure of excess leverage. It is unclear, however, why first-time and subsequent purchasers of owner-occupied property are treated differently.

Additionally, the rationale for the loan-to-income limits is unclear. First, they are tied to a particular interest rate regime. If mortgage interest rates were to rise to levels seen in the 1980s (10–15 per cent), rather than 3–6 per cent seen since the 2000s, the limits would be significantly less relevant as few banks would be willing to extend families four or five times their gross income. Consider a €350,000 property with an 85 per cent loan of roughly €300,000. At a mortgage interest rate of 4 per cent, the monthly repayment would be €1,400, whereas at 8 per cent the repayment would be almost €2,200 and at 12 per cent just over €3,000. It is not clear how a limit of borrowing relative to gross income protects lenders or borrowers.

A further complication arises given the variation in land values around the country. In early 2015, when the regulations were brought in, the value of a three-bedroomed semi-detached property varied from less than €70,000 in some areas to over €700,000 in others. This variation in house prices far exceeds the variation in incomes across space and reflects different amenities, such as access to employment, offered in different locations. It also allows households to choose housing that reflects their priorities: for some families, access to expensive urban amenities is important and this will be reflected in their spending, whereas for others, they would rather spend their income on goods, not amenities.

Under the Central Bank regulations, families that otherwise would rather spend more of their income on housing than other goods may be forced to substitute away into other goods. For example, a household whose income means they would have to borrow four times their gross income to buy in Dublin may instead be told to buy further away from Dublin, where prices are cheaper but their fuel bills larger.

5 HOUSING SUPPLY AND REGULATIONS

In Figure 12.2, short-run housing supply was shown as inelastic – it is not possible to add 5 per cent to the housing stock overnight or even over a period of many months – while the long-run housing supply curve was more elastic. The central question addressed in this section is what factors affect the shape of the long-run housing supply curve or, more precisely, the elasticity of housing supply.

For example, if demand for housing were to increase by 10 per cent over the next five years, what would be the increase in supply? In a healthy housing system, supply should also increase by 10 per cent, thus preserving sale and rental prices at the same level (adjusting for general inflation). A failure of housing supply to respond to new demand reflects a dysfunctional housing system. Between the 2011 and 2016 censuses, the Greater Dublin Area witnessed an increase in demand of almost 10 per cent but an increase in supply of less than 1 per cent, suggesting a hugely dysfunctional housing system.

Housing supply has two components. The first is the natural churn in the existing supply, which depends on tastes, as well as the natural increase or decrease in the market due to first-time buyers and deaths/executor sales. As this is just the redistribution of existing stock, the second and more important element of supply is the construction of new homes.[4] Note, however, that for the case given above, there is an asymmetry between an increase and a decrease in demand. A fall in demand by 10 per cent requires merely a reduced level of building, and if construction fails to fall fast enough, the effect on the economy is positive, in the form of reduced accommodation costs. A rise in demand by 10 per cent requires new building, which involves a wide variety of inputs and markets, including land, finance and policy as well as construction.

The focus here will be on the following two components of the cost of building new property: the cost of land, and the cost of construction on that land. Every individual site is, in some way, unique. Thus, the market for land deviates fundamentally from the textbook model of perfect competition: each site is a local monopoly, although there are likely to be close (but imperfect) substitutes nearby. In addition, land is fixed in supply.[5] This marks another key deviation from the model of perfect competition, which assumes perfectly elastic supply of a good in response to market prices. The policy implications of inelastic land are discussed below.

Setting aside land costs temporarily, the construction of new dwellings is based on a number of hard and soft parameters. At its simplest, construction will take place where the difference between the net present value of rental income and the cost of building is positive. The net present value of rental income means the value, in today's terms, of the rental service into the future and will reflect prevailing rental prices (either market or implicit, if the dwelling is to be sold), the expected rate of inflation in prices, and the rate at which future amounts are discounted. These costs include a desired profit margin, so in a competitive construction market, any positive difference between income and costs ought to be reflected in the residual factor, namely land prices.

The core concept in understanding building supply, therefore, is the break-even rent. This is the level of market or implicit rent at which all costs, including whatever 'normal' return is desired by the owners of capital, are covered. Assuming for the moment that the cost of a plot of land is residual, i.e. reflects other costs, rather than speculative, there are roughly ten key parameters determining the break-even rent associated with a dwelling. Thus, in addition to factors relating to land use, for a given level of demand, these parameters will largely determine the supply of new homes and the elasticity of new supply. They can be categorised, loosely, as being either regulatory factors or market factors.

Regulatory Factors
Five regulatory factors affecting costs are outlined below: per-square-metre costs; size restrictions; density restrictions; local authority levies; and VAT. Four of these are 'hard costs', i.e. in euro per square metre terms, while the fifth – the VAT rate – is a 'soft cost' in percentage terms. A key metric in the housing supply equation is the ratio of all hard costs to all soft costs.

Construction Costs
The central factor in determining the break-even rent is the cost of construction per square metre. In theory, construction costs could be considered a market factor. However, in the Irish case, while the cost of building materials is largely subject to global forces, the dominant element in construction costs – the hourly wage rate in construction – is heavily regulated. In addition, other regulations, such as requirements for each unit in an apartment block to have its own basement car-parking space, add to construction costs.

There is some evidence that construction costs per square metre are significantly higher in Ireland than in its peers. For example, the cost per square metre of medium density apartments in 2013 was almost 45 per cent more expensive than in Germany (€1,360/sqm vs. €950/sqm) and per-square-metre construction costs for apartments were roughly 50 per cent more expensive in Dublin than in the Netherlands and Canada. Similarly, rebuild costs by professionals suggest that, for a family home, the price of an additional square metre in Dublin is almost €1,800, compared to €1,700 in the Greater London area and €1,000 in Northern Ireland.[6] These are all industry figures, however. A policy analysis of the reason construction is so expensive in Ireland is required to address the issue of a lack of supply.

Minimum Size and Maximum Density
The second factor is the required (average or minimum) size per unit in square metres. This is set at local level currently in Ireland, but with national guidelines for all multi-unit developments. For one- and two-bedroom apartments, the minimum unit size in Dublin (in particular in Dublin City Council and in Dun Laoghaire-Rathdown) was in 2015 among the largest in Europe. This means that the minimum size was greatest in the parts of the Irish housing market that could sustain smaller units due to the presence of location-specific amenities. While larger units bring benefits reflected in higher rental values, they also add to costs. Regulatory changes brought in in late 2015 set new national maximums for apartments.

The third factor is the number of units allowed per acre. This varies widely across the country and, in Dublin City Council where pressure for agglomeration is greatest, there are guidelines for bringing about greater density but also, paradoxically, stringent limits on height. These limits vary by district within Dublin, and are typically limited to seven floors, with some areas allowed twelve floors. In some local authority areas, in particular in Dublin, the number of units is further restricted by limits on orientation and the regulated ratio of lifts/stairwells to units on each floor. For example, as is the case currently in central Dublin, a one-acre site where no solely north- or east-facing units are allowed (and where the vast majority of units must be dual-orientation) will have a smaller number of units than one where a greater mix is allowed.

Taxes
The two final regulatory factors relate to taxes. One is local authority levies, which are typically levied on a per-square metre basis. The other is the VAT rate, which is regulated nationally: construction activities are subject to a reduced 13.5 per cent VAT rate. In practical terms, as in other sectors, the VAT rate can be thought of as effectively a profit margin charged by the state.

Market Factors
Soft Costs
There are five market factors that help determine the break-even rent and thus the supply of new dwellings, for a given set of demand factors including incomes. All five are 'soft costs', i.e. in percentage terms.

The first factor is fees, with development of new dwellings incurring a range of fees, including professional, legal and compliance fees. Also included in this category (for ease of exposition) is stamp duty, although strictly speaking, this is of course a regulatory charge. These fees are in percentage terms, thus any increase in hard costs will be reflected in higher fees.

A second market factor is the interest rate (and term length) associated with site purchase and construction works. In general, this can be assumed to be determined largely at economy-wide level, although financial institutions may regard some projects as higher risk than others, which would then be reflected in the interest rate charged. Typically, Irish development projects would be funded through a mix of debt finance and equity finance (including retained earnings). The desired profit margin on equity finance is a third market factor and, as with other market factors, is a percentage addition to costs.

The above factors can be used to calculate the cost of a dwelling, including VAT and profit margins, and thus its purchase price. For owner-occupied homes, the final factor needed is a comparison of this cost with the likely purchasing power of those interested in buying the homes. This will include asset factors, including the mortgage interest rate and deposit required by buyers, as discussed above.

For rental dwellings, there are two final market factors that are relevant. The first is the desired net yield for investors. Institutional landlords will have a desired net yield, in annual terms, and this affects the relationship between the full price and the break-even monthly rent. The margin between the risk-free return and the desired return on, say, Dublin residential rental property will be largely determined by a combination of the class-specific risk premium (property compared to bonds) and the location-specific risk premium (Dublin compared to major markets).

The last factor that affects costs and the supply of new homes is the management margin. This includes service costs (management fees) and depreciation. The gross rental yield is the combination of the desired net yield and the management margin. It is used to convert the up-front break-even costs into a monthly rent, which can then be compared with ability to pay on the market.

Taking a sample development of 36 two-bedroom apartments on a one-acre site in Dublin, and excluding land costs (until the next section), the core build costs represent roughly half of total costs. The remainder would be mostly a roughly equal split between levies, profit and VAT. With no site costs, the all-in cost of perhaps €320,000 per unit in early 2017 translates into a monthly break-even rent of about €1,600 for a two-bedroom apartment. This figure, which excludes any land costs, is well above the prevailing rent for a two-bedroom apartment in Ireland (roughly €800) and in line with the rents in the most expensive areas of Dublin.

State-Provision?
Some have argued that the issue is with profit-led development and that other models, such as state provided homes or cooperative development, should be

THE ECONOMY OF IRELAND

pursued. These are certainly options to be explored but they do not eliminate the opportunity cost of capital. If the state were to invest without return, this is capital that could have been employed on other projects, for example in health, education or transport that would have delivered a social return on investment. Similarly, cooperative development (such as the German *Baugruppen*) requires the voluntary relinquishing of capital – in this case for a share in a development. It is also worth remembering that profits in a competitive market will form a relatively small share of overall costs and thus the impact on the break-even rent will be limited.

Given the apparently large discrepancy between the cost of a square metre in Ireland and in other economies, efforts to boost supply and lower the cost of accommodation are better directed at these hard costs. This is doubly so as, the lower the hard costs, the smaller the soft cost multiplier is in euro terms. For example, if profit, VAT and fees together add 30 per cent to the hard costs, a reduction in hard costs from €200,000 to €150,000 will have a knock-on effect on 'soft costs', from €60,000 to €45,000. (In practice, the all-in soft-cost multiplier is closer to 65 per cent.)

This has implications for minimum standards. While there may be an understandable desire to increase the quality of the minimum acceptable unit, this has an effect on cost. If an additional square metre costs €2,000 and the minimum one-bedroom apartment size is 55sqm (as was the case in Dublin) and not 40sqm (as in many European cities), this means that the hard costs of the smallest allowable dwelling in Dublin would be expected to be €30,000 higher. With a soft-cost multiplier of 65 per cent, this is an additional €50,000 to the full cost of the unit. Where investors seek a 5 per cent net yield, this adds €250 to the monthly break-even rent, a not insignificant additional cost for those on lower or middle incomes to bear.

Land Markets
Until now, the issue of land costs has been avoided. More specifically, it has been assumed that land costs will reflect the difference between the net present value of the market rent and the break-even costs (excluding land). This residual form of calculating land values is how many developers approach whether or not to purchase a plot of land, but it does not accurately reflect land markets.

In practice, land markets operate through a combination of such residual net-present-value calculations, reference points and speculative behaviour. Residual calculations take into account market rents and the cost of building, as outlined above. Reference points refer to, effectively, norms in pricing behaviour. For example, it may be the case that if an acre of land sold for €2.5m in one part of Dublin 2, then the holder of another site nearby will not be willing to sell for substantially less than this, regardless of the ratio of market rents to build costs. In addition to reference points, there are also speculative motives for holding land. Where there is no penalty for holding land vacant, those owning or purchasing land may do so, in anticipation of future capital gains.

A final source of uncertainty in land markets is the use to which land can be put. In countries such as Ireland, land has a use specified in local authority development plans but these are not fixed. By applying for planning permission, it may be possible to convert land from one use (e.g. industrial) to another or mixed use (e.g. office, retail or residential). Thus, land may come with option value, broadly defined.

Land Values and Taxation
A challenge for policymakers is the tendency for inertia in land use. For example, in Dublin, there remain army barracks on the same sites as in the eighteenth century, bus depots on the same sites as nineteenth century tram depots, and industrial estates on the same sites as the twentieth century. However, the demand for particular locations will change across decades. Much as labour market policy has moved from passive to active since the 1980s, it is now important that policymakers adopt a similar policy for land. In particular, the recognition of under-employed land is key, as is the identification of regulatory or policy barriers to the use of particular sites. Inertia in land use can be overcome by altering the annual user cost of a site. In many countries, such as Denmark, Estonia, and parts of Australia and the USA, this is done through a land or site value tax, which charges the owner of a site a fraction of the value of that site, if it were put to the best allowable use.

Earlier, mention was made of the inelastic aggregate supply of land. The near-perfect inelasticity of the supply of land raises an important policy implication. Unlike other forms of wealth, which may be highly mobile, land is immobile and thus it will bear the burden of taxation. Historically, land tax formed the basis of many government revenue systems. To this day, it forms one of the most valuable assets in any modern economy and thus a land tax is a de facto wealth tax, unable to be avoided by the wealthiest citizens.

In addition, though, a land tax internalises the externality associated with location-specific investments by government. For example, the construction of a new motorway linking commuter towns with a nearby city gives those towns greater market access. This will be reflected in, among other things, greater property values. Under a land value tax system, this upswing in value creates a return on the investment made by the taxpayer. The same argument applies to other social investments, including urban parks. A land value tax is an important mechanism in enabling policymakers to move from a cost-based approach to public spending decisions to one based on the ratio of social benefits to costs.

Role of NAMA
The Irish market for development land has, since 2010, been dominated by the National Asset Management Agency (NAMA). This agency was set up as a 'bad bank', to recapitalise the Irish financial system (see Chapter 3). Roughly €77bn of loans, secured against what was valued at approximately €88bn of collateral at the peak, were bought from the Irish banks for about €37bn. These are then to be sold off over time at amounts that reflect their long-term

economic value. As of early 2017, it is envisaged that NAMA will not make a loss and may make a small profit.[7]

However, NAMA's work has meant that it has become the dominant market player in development land in Ireland. Its exact role is unclear, as in theory it should be a supplier (of land) to developers but in practice, it is the stated intention of NAMA to remain as a landholder in Dublin's north docklands. In addition, land that NAMA does sell is not sold on condition of development, thus encouraging speculative landholders. The combination of all these factors means that the price of development land currently is far from the textbook case of residual valuation.

6 SOCIAL HOUSING

Rationale and Features

The final area of housing policy relates to tenure and social housing. In practical terms, one could think of households ordered from richest to poorest. The richest fraction, perhaps 70 per cent, have incomes that are both high enough and stable enough to secure a mortgage and thus they typically own their home. Of the remaining 30 per cent of households, these will be split between those in the private rented sector and those in the social housing sector.

The private rented sector has, as described above, a minimum rent below which costs are not covered. Currently in Ireland, as outlined in the previous section, it is difficult to build new accommodation at a monthly cost of less than €1,000. At the same time, households can only devote a certain fraction of their disposable income sustainably to accommodation. The rule of thumb is that a household should not spend more than one third of its disposable income on housing. Taking into account the Irish tax system, this means that a household earning €45,000 should be spending no more than €1,000 per month on housing.

The role for the state in providing social housing is, therefore, clear. Regardless of the minimum cost of providing adequate housing, there will be a segment of the population with insufficient income to cover their accommodation costs. The rationale for state intervention is therefore to ensure access to housing for all, taken as a basic human right. It is also clear from this the ideal form of state intervention: a supplement to income to ensure that accommodation costs can be met. In particular, given the rationale for intervention, the subsidy should be larger, the poorer the household. If €12,000 is needed for adequate accommodation per year, and no more than one third of after-tax income should be spent on accommodation, those households with an after-tax income of €30,000 should receive a far smaller subsidy than those with an after-tax income of €20,000.

Unfortunately, Ireland's current social housing system is such that this clarity is lacking. As with other aspects of the welfare system, the predominant form of housing subsidy, rent supplement, is a fixed amount. This hinders vertical equity while the on/off nature of the subsidy has implications for horizontal equity across working and unemployed households.

In addition, Ireland's social housing system has moved away from debt-financed publicly-funded construction of new homes. Under what is termed the Part V arrangement (after the relevant section of the Planning & Development Acts, 2000 to 2006), developers are typically required to set aside 10 per cent (previously 20 per cent) of any new development for social housing. Aside from the fact that developers were often able to get around this requirement, either directly (through payments to the local authority) or indirectly, this has the in-built feature of generating quantities of social housing that are pro-cyclical, while demand for social housing is likely to be strongly counter-cyclical. In particular, when private developers are building 8,000 dwellings a year, rather than 80,000, the provision of social housing is likely to be grossly inadequate.

Ireland's Housing Finance Agency exists precisely to lend to local authorities and voluntary housing bodies, giving the social sector access to international capital markets. In addition, the underlying collateral is strong, given that the rental payments are effectively state-guaranteed. However, the weakness (and indeed complexity) of the prevailing Differential Rent schemes, coupled with a reliance on fixed Rent Supplement subsidies, means that there is very little demand on the part of social housing providers for development capital.

Controlling the level or rate of change in rents is often considered as a tool for policymakers in relation to housing. In late 2016, the Minister for Housing introduced a system for diagnosing Rent Pressure Zones, which capped rental inflation at 4 per cent per year for areas with excessive inflation in rents. This is the equivalent of a binding price ceiling. As with all price ceilings, it means that there will be excess demand and that supply and demand will equilibrate through black market activity (such as side payments) or through non-price rationing, through for example queuing or lotteries. However, it should be remembered that high rental prices are a symptom of a lack of supply and thus controls on rental inflation may further dull the pressure for new housing supply.

A 'Human Right'?

The system outlined above is connected to policy debates about a universal basic income and about whether housing should be included in the constitution as a human right. The close juxtaposition of economic recession and rising accommodation costs in Ireland in the decade from 2006 to 2016 has led many to call for a right to housing to be included in the Irish constitution. Those who call for such a right often cite other countries or the Universal Declaration of Human Rights and the Council of Europe's European Social Charter, both of which include a right to adequate housing.

While the inclusion of a right to housing in the Irish constitution might bring about a meaningful right in practice, it is likely that this would only be so after a landmark court case, including various appeals. How that right would be made effective, in general to the populace at large and not just the plaintiffs of that particular case, would still need to be worked out. A system of subsidising households based on the gap between their means and their needs would achieve this, having the greatest impact for the lowest cost. Nonetheless, the cost of such a scheme would be sizeable: a subsidy averaging €400 per month for 500,000 households translates into an annual exposure of €2.4bn.

Such a scheme, though, would mark a further step towards a system of universal basic income, elements of which are already in place for younger (child benefit) and older citizens (pension entitlements; see Chapter 8). Technically, it would be closer to a negative income tax, where a certain threshold for subsistence is established, and redistribution is to those below that threshold. A final note on this is that it can be extended to other areas. For example, as outlined in a report published by the Housing Agency, policy supports for housing and care needs of Ireland's older people should reflect the gap between an individual household's means and the cost of its needs, both housing and care.[8]

7 SERVICING HOUSING

Introduction

As mentioned earlier, housing comprises the single largest fraction of household expenditure. Its importance also stems from it sitting at the heart of a range of complements (and substitutes). For example, a household may choose to spend 35 per cent of their monthly budget on Property A, close to their work, or 25 per cent to live further out in Property B and spend 10 per cent on transport: in this sense, Property A and transport can be seen as substitutes, while Property B and transport are clear complements.

In addition to transport services, there are a number of other services that are connected to housing. These include water, waste disposal, electricity, heating, and telecommunications (previously landline, but now principally broadband). This section briefly discusses the market structures of these services and public policy issues arising, as well as discussing the role of property taxes.

As seen earlier, each site is unique and thus a local monopoly and – even if all dwellings built on sites were identical – this means that each property is differentiated from all others. The corollary of this is that any services supplied to a property also have to be differentiated. For example, a broadband line to a property requires at least some of the line to be specific to that property. Similarly, with household waste collection, there is a cost of effort required for each bin lifted.

As discussed in Chapter 5, a system with many differentiated suppliers is unlikely to occur, where there are significant fixed costs relating to infrastructure. This is the case with water, authorised waste disposal, broadband, electricity and heating. In the case of heating and electricity, there may be lengthy supply chains, while there are likely to be capacity constraints in all utilities, affecting the elasticity of supply. Thus, it may be expected that the likely market form in many utilities related to the servicing of housing will be oligopolistic or even monopolistic.

Waste Disposal and Water

Water supply is discussed at some length in Chapter 5. Waste disposal is also covered there, but it will also be dealt with briefly here.

Historically, waste regulation and management functions were the responsibility of local governments throughout the country and the provision of kerbside waste collections to domestic households and businesses were funded through the collection of domestic property rates (see below). The abolition of rates in the 1970s left local authorities responsible for this service, without a source of revenue to pay for it. Over the following 30 years, the service became increasingly privatised, albeit with extensive use of waiver schemes to those on low incomes. This occurred in particular in response to a 1998 Department of the Environment policy statement on waste management and the associated introduction (albeit controversial) of bin charges.

The exit of public operators created something of a vacuum, with private market operators keen to secure particular affluent areas, while other less affluent areas were left with very few service providers. Many areas in Ireland suffer from congestion caused by numerous waste providers accessing the same roads, often competing with rush-hour traffic, while other areas have little or no competition, leaving local monopolies free to increase prices. Ultimately, public policy in Ireland deviated from best practice, with a reliance on 'competition in the market' rather than 'competition for the market'. Where there is likely to be a natural monopoly or wasteful costs of duplication, it may make more sense for policymakers to tender for access to a market every few years, and allow competition at the level of the district (see Chapter 5).

International experience would indicate that competition *for* the market, in the form of public tendering competitions every few years, would seem to be the most effective option. Regulators would be able to specify the terms of the tender and allow service level agreements, pricing structure and revenues to be known in advance offering clarity to market bidders.

Other Utilities

Other utilities serving households at their residence, such as broadband, electricity and heating, rely heavily on infrastructure and other fixed costs. In particular, there is potential for wasteful duplication of resources in the distribution network, while the importance of brands and consumer trust is likely to mean that supply is a natural oligopoly. In contrast, generation is likely to be much more utility-specific, with potential for market structures close to perfect competition in some utilities.

As a general rule, then, it is likely that there will be a natural monopoly in the transmission grid for a particular utility. This is true for water, electricity and gas, for example, with all suppliers using the same grid to reach the consumer. The distribution of gas and electricity relies on publicly-owned networks, which customer-facing suppliers pay to access, and was discussed at some length already in Chapter 11.

The Irish government is implementing a National Broadband Plan, to bring broadband to rural Ireland. The target is that all 1.9 million homes and businesses across Ireland will have fibre broadband by the end of 2020, with service provider *eir* estimating that 80 per cent will have access through the market. It is clear that such a scheme involves those living in high-density areas subsidising those in low-density areas. This is one of the challenges of a country as sparsely populated as Ireland. Ireland has on average fewer than 70 people per square kilometre, roughly one quarter the density of the UK and just one hundredth the population density of Singapore, which has a similar population (see Chapter 11). An issue of moral hazard arises also: if high-cost locations are subsidised by the taxpayer, a concern may arise as to whether the population will remain excessively dispersed, thus driving up the cost of living compared to other countries.

8 CONCLUSION

This chapter has reviewed the economics and policy issues surrounding the property market. Due to its policy importance, it focused almost exclusively on residential property, although the case of commercial property was discussed, in particular due to its role in Ireland's economic crisis in the late 2000s.

Housing can be understood as a market, with demand and supply forces at work. The demand forces include the fundamental forces of household income, which reflects unemployment, labour market participation and trends in per-worker incomes, and demographics, most widely reflected in the ratio of people to households. In Ireland's case, this steadily falling ratio creates a significant need for new homes each year, even in a situation where overall population is static.

In addition to these fundamentals, there are also asset factors that act as demand shifters, affecting sale prices but not rental prices, and thus the equilibrium ratio between the two. The user cost reflects, above all, expected capital gains, which are volatile and typically backward-looking. Credit conditions are another demand shifter, albeit one that was omitted from analyses undertaken in the 1990s and 2000s. The smaller the down-payment required by borrowers, the more leverage households take on. This pushes up housing prices and creates significant exposure for households, if prices were to fall.

Due to the elastic demand for credit, outward shifts in credit supply translate into more credit, rather than cheaper credit. This shifts out the demand for housing, pushing up prices, at least in the short run. At this point, the elasticity of housing supply is critical. A one-for-one response to new housing demand will leave sale and rental prices unaffected in the medium-to-long term. However, in practice, housing supply is inelastic. As discussed, it is likely that the dramatic failure of housing supply in Ireland since 2011 reflects some combination of these factors, with the break-even rent well above market rents in most of the country as of 2017.

This has implications for the provision of social housing, also. Best practice in social housing would give greatest financial support to those suffering from the largest gap between their means and their accommodation needs. Unfortunately, policy in Ireland relating to social housing relies excessively on fixed subsidies, pro-cyclical housing supply devices and then, due to the failure of these, a plethora of emergency measures. Moving towards an income-based subsidy would create even greater incentives to reduce the break-even cost of building new homes in Ireland. Moving towards greater control of rents is unlikely to solve the supply shortage.

Ultimately, there are two principal barometers of the health of a housing system. The first is the yield, or relationship between sale and rental prices. This reflects, however, not only user cost but also credit conditions and thus financial technology and confidence. Nonetheless, it remains a useful tool for policymakers to assess conditions in the housing market. The second barometer is the elasticity of supply, of both market and non-market segments. The nearly complete failure of the housing system to respond to a significant increase in demand in Ireland, particularly in the Greater Dublin Area, since 2011, represents one of the greatest challenges to policymakers over the period 2017 to 2022.

Endnotes

1   For more on the role of housing and household debt in the Great Recession (and Great Depression), see B. Eichengreen, *Hall of Mirrors*, Oxford University Press, Oxford 2014, and Mian & Sufi, *House of Debt*, University of Chicago Press, Chicago 2014.
2   An annual survey was conducted in Ireland by the ESRI, as a supplement to the Consumer Sentiment Survey 2003–2008. Since 2011, a similar consumer survey, now undertaken on an on-going basis and reported quarterly, is part of the Daft.ie Report.
3   In late February 2015, the Central Bank of Ireland launched a Household Credit Market Report but this also does not report the typical loan-to-value of first-time buyers.
4   Rather than the gross number of new dwellings built, the addition to supply each year is the amount net of obsolescence, in other words housing that has depreciated past the point at which it is habitable. While the rate of depreciation is not known with certainty, the rate of new completions was so low in 2011/2012 that in certain periods it is likely Ireland's housing stock was shrinking.
5   While there are instances, such as Singapore, where new land has been created at the edge of an existing island, the cost is sufficiently high that it is reasonable for policymakers to typically think of land as fixed in supply.
6   Sources: Turner & Townsend, 'A brighter outlook: International construction cost survey 2013'; SCSI House Rebuilding Calculator (available online at: www.scsi.ie/advice/house_rebuilding_calculator) and BCIS Public Rebuild Calculator (available online at: http://calculator.bcis.co.uk/), both accessed last 1 March 2017. Sterling figures were converted to euro using a 0.75 euro/sterling exchange rate.
7   It is worth pointing out that, in the context of all bank liabilities having been guaranteed by the taxpayer, the exact amount paid by NAMA for the loans was of secondary

importance. For example, if NAMA had paid less for the loans, and thus subsequently made a larger profit, this would have meant that taxpayers would have had to inject larger amounts into the banks.

8   Amarach Research, Ronan Lyons, Lorcan Sirr & Innovation Delivery, *Housing for Older People – Thinking Ahead,* 2016, available at www.housingagency.ie/Housing/media/Media/About%20Us/Report-Housing-for-Older-People-Thinking-Ahead-(2016).pdf.

CHAPTER 13

Education: Features, Financing and Performance

Ciara Whelan*

1 INTRODUCTION

Approximately one-third of all public sector employees are involved in education and training in Ireland, supporting over one million students in full time education across over three thousand primary schools, seven hundred post primary schools, seven universities, fourteen institutes of technology, seven teacher training institutions and a number of other third-level institutions. In addition, the state contributed to the education of over 74,000 children in pre-primary education.

The returns to education are many and include economic, social, political and environmental benefits. Economic benefits include potentially higher earnings, greater employability and lower risk of unemployment for the individual. An educated workforce can thus lead to higher income tax revenues and lower welfare payments for the economy. It can also lead to improved competitiveness resulting in economic growth and its associated benefits. A range of social and political benefits can also arise from education. It provides basic skills for participation in life and can lead to lower levels of inequality in society. Education is also correlated with greater political (more likely to vote) and social (more likely to volunteer) responsibility, better health, lower crime, more inter-personal trust and happiness in life. Educating individuals about environmental responsibility can lead to the changes in individual behaviour that are required for the future sustainability of our eco-system.

While some of these benefits accrue directly and solely to the educated individual, an educated population generates a diverse array of positive spillovers for the public good. Left to the private market, however, market failures and equity considerations would result in an education system that fails to generate optimal outcomes for society. This leads to underinvestment in education across its various dimensions.

The importance of a quality education in improving lives in an economy is evident in Goal 4 of the 2016 Sustainable Development Goals of the UN, which strives to 'Ensure inclusive quality education for all and promote lifelong learning'. This global agenda focuses on promoting equality of access to and opportunity in a high quality education system that delivers a set of relevant skills for a changing environment. In addition to literacy, numeracy and digital literacy skills for participating and contributing to an economy, a focus on educating individuals about economic, social, environmental, and political issues is important. Education is an important policy instrument in the pursuit of competitiveness, social equality, economic sustainability and good governance in an economy.

This chapter will provide an economic framework for analysing the role of government in the education sector in Ireland. Section 2 elaborates on the diverse range of benefits arising from education posited above. Section 3 provides a rationale for government intervention in education and the subsequent objectives of interventionist policy. Section 4 then examines key features and policies of the education sector in Ireland. Section 5 assesses investment in and outcomes from education in Ireland over time, and relative to the other OECD countries. Section 6 concludes.

2 BENEFITS OF EDUCATION

There are many potential benefits of education. Some of these benefits are readily measurable, while others are more difficult to quantify. Some are private benefits and accrue directly to the individual, while many are positive spillover effects that benefit society as a whole.

Several economic studies have examined the relationship between education and the individual economic returns to education in terms of earnings, employability, and risks of being unemployed.[1] This body of literature and evidence indicates that higher levels of educational attainment lead to higher earnings, greater employability, and lower risk of unemployment.[2] Examining data from OECD *Education at a Glance 2016* and its detailed underlying tables for individuals aged 25 to 64 years, we observe the degree to which these outcomes vary by educational attainment.

Based on 2014 data across OECD countries, individuals in full-time employment with tertiary education earn on average, 55 per cent more than those with upper secondary education: the equivalent figure for Ireland is 63 per cent.

Looking at employment rates across OECD countries based on 2015 data, on average the employment rate for those with tertiary education is 84 per cent, while those with upper secondary is 74 per cent (corresponding figures for Ireland are 82 per cent and 67 per cent, respectively).

Unemployment rates across OECD countries for 2015 were on average, 14.8 per cent for those with primary education, 12.5 per cent for those with lower-secondary education, 7.4 per cent for those with upper-secondary, and 5 per cent for those with tertiary education (similar trends for Ireland with corresponding figures of 18.6 per cent, 14.7 per cent, 9.6 per cent and 5 per cent, respectively).

The impact that education has on individual earnings, employability, and risk of unemployment are obvious private benefits to education. It also has as mentioned earlier additional economic benefits for society as a whole as higher earnings increase income tax revenues for the economy, while lower risks of unemployment reduces welfare payments. Another important spillover effect for society (to the extent that inequality affects societal welfare) is the role that education can play in reducing inequality in society as outlined in Chapter 8. Higher levels of inequality may lead to more crime and social unrest, or lower levels of societal trust which can be debilitating for economic growth. The fact that education is a key predictor of income as well as the risk of unemployment means that differences in educational attainment result in higher measures of income inequality. Greater equity in access to and participation in education to higher levels of attainment can have a positive social benefit for society through lower income inequality in the economy.

Education can also benefit society through its effect on productivity directly and via knowledge diffusion and innovation, as well as its cost reducing effects through a plentiful supply of skilled labour. This can enhance overall competitiveness, leading to greater economic growth and the many benefits that this brings as discussed in Chapter 7. Although it can be difficult to estimate empirically the magnitude of the spillover effect of education on growth, many studies find evidence for their existence, particularly through knowledge and innovation. We have seen in Chapter 1 the important role that the presence of a skilled and educated workforce played in the attraction of foreign direct investment and the expansion of the Irish economy in the 1990s. Education delivering the right set of skills for an evolving knowledge-based and knowledge-driven economy continues to be a driver of competitiveness for the Irish economy.

Early-years education results in improved cognitive skills (core skills that help one to learn, concentrate, to remember and problem solve) and non-cognitive skills (self-discipline, confidence, organisation, and co-operation) for the individual. It yields benefits in future education as it aids with school readiness while setting the foundation for their lifelong learning and success in future levels of education. The skills developed in early-childhood education allow individuals to engage more effectively in primary, secondary and tertiary education. This in turn can benefit teachers and other students through the positive effect on the teaching environment.

Education can also have a positive external effect on the environment. Educating individuals about environmental responsibility can lead to the necessary behaviour modification required for future sustainable development.

Education provides skills for participation and functioning in society. Literacy and numeracy skills result in an ability to read instructions, signs, warnings, notifications, terms and conditions on contracts; an ability to make daily financial transactions, manage finances, pay bills, to make saving or borrowing decisions; and an ability to express oneself or make an argument verbally or in writing. Education provides an ability to make informed decisions. At an individual level, this allows one to function in and contribute to the economy, to participate in the political process and to make choices that improve outcomes in terms of health and social responsibility. All of these can lead to greater life satisfaction for the individual.

These life skills can also generate positive spillovers that benefit society as a whole. At a societal level, an educated population leads to a society where there is an understanding of the basic rules and regulations in society, there is greater political interest in the running of society and political participation, and there are fewer problems of ill-health and crime. It is one that enjoys greater social responsibility, interpersonal trust and satisfaction in life. This can lead to better and easier governance of a more democratic society with less crime and healthier and happier individuals, which will benefit all in society.

While empirically there is evidence that education is positively correlated with the above social and political outcomes, such correlations do not imply causation. For example, it could be that unobservable characteristics of individuals with high levels of education attainment make them more likely to vote; or that healthier and happier individuals may have a greater ability to succeed in education. It can be difficult to identify the true causal relationship between education and socio-political outcomes, and hence to get a precise empirical estimate of these educational benefits.

3 RATIONALE FOR STATE INTERVENTION

As seen in Chapter 3, there is a role for state intervention on the grounds of efficiency where there are market failures, and on the grounds of equity. Both of these rationales apply to the education sector. Without state intervention, market failures would lead to underinvestment in education and less than socially optimal outcomes. Besides, without state intervention, there would not be equal access to education or equal opportunity to succeed in education.

The level of investment in education, or human capital, will be determined by the expected present value of the future stream of costs and of benefits associated with that investment. An individual deciding on whether or not to send their child to school or pre-school, or deciding whether or not to invest in higher education for themselves, will compare the associated expected costs with the expected benefits.

The costs of education are readily identifiable and measurable at both lower and higher levels of education. They include tuition fees, books, school uniforms, transport to and from place of study, and the opportunity cost of foregone earnings (beyond compulsory school age). The private benefits of education have already been elucidated. Moreover, at pre-school and school levels, attendance in education can also include the benefit accruing to the parent of foregone childcare costs. Individuals making decisions on education, either on behalf of their charges or directly for themselves, will optimally invest in education where the expected marginal costs are equal to the expected marginal private benefits.

However market failures due to imperfect information, credit market constraints, and the positive spillover effects of education, lead to under-investment
in education which justifies a role for state intervention on the grounds of efficiency. Moreover, when these failures are more pronounced for cohorts of the
population from a poorer socio-economic background, targeted intervention can
be justified on the grounds of equity to ensure equality of access to education.

Imperfect Information
As outlined in Chapter 3, the presence of imperfect information results in market
failure and inefficient outcomes. An individual deciding on whether or not to
send their child to school or pre-school, or deciding whether or not to invest in
higher education for themselves, may not have full information on the private
returns to education. They may underestimate the expected private returns either
due to a lack of knowledge as to the existence of the benefits of education, or due
to imperfect information regarding the size of these benefits. Individuals may
also place less value on the expected future benefits of education and too high
a weight on the costs of education today in terms of foregone earnings due to
imperfect information (or due to myopic or short-sighted behaviour). Imperfect
information can thus lead to underinvestment in education. The degree to which
individuals will underinvest in education due to imperfect information depends
on socio-economic demographic factors. Those from a lower income, less educated background are less likely to have full information on the expected returns
to education. Imperfect information may thus define a role for targeted education
policies to ensure optimal investment decisions are undertaken by all individuals
and to prevent inequality in education investment that may arise from this market
failure.

Imperfect information can also define a regulatory role for government in
public schools to ensure that certain standards of education are adhered to. Individuals may not have full information as to the quality of education provided
by a school or institution prior to entering and for the duration of study. In a
private market, market prices (fees) can signal quality in terms of the school's
educational outcomes and performance. In a publicly provided education system, without regulatory oversight, imperfect information can lead to low-quality
educational outcomes. The publication of school league tables arguably helps to
overcome this imperfect information problem as rank position signals quality of
education provided by a school, at least in terms of outcomes.

Credit Market Constraints
Undertaking investment in education requires access to cash reserves or credit
markets in order to finance this investment. At the tertiary level, student access
to credit markets is important for the financing of their higher level education.
We have seen that education leads to higher earnings, better employability and
lower risk of unemployment. However the returns to education will vary across
individuals. While individuals are informed as to their likely returns to education

based on their own inherent ability and effort, the banks do not have information on either the potential or willingness of applicants to repay student loans. Such asymmetric information leads to failure in the credit market as worthy students may not be able to access loans for their tertiary education if there is no collateral to guarantee the loans, and no guarantee to the bank of future employment and earnings to secure repayment of the loan. As a result, there will be underinvestment in education. This is problematic for individuals from lower income family backgrounds with insufficient resources to either provide collateral or guarantee a loan, which can lead to inequity in access to higher education. At third level, failures in the credit market due to asymmetric information provide a strong rationale for targeted policy intervention to ensure investment decisions in tertiary education are optimal and are not constrained by failure to secure credit financing, and to prevent inequality in access to tertiary education that may arise from this market failure.

At the pre-tertiary levels of education (pre-primary, primary and secondary levels), parents pay the costs of education. If education were only privately provided, then the associated tuition and related costs would be prohibitive for many parents. Only those with cash reserves and with access to credit would be able to afford pre-tertiary education for their children. The inability of parents to access loans from banks to invest in their child's schooling is due to an inability to repay the loans based on current/projected income. Failure to access credit leads to underinvestment in pre-tertiary levels of education. It can lead to inequity in the ability of individuals to access and participate in schooling and thus provides a strong argument for intervention on equity grounds.

Positive Spillovers
The previous scenarios have discussed the potential problems of under-investment in education due to imperfect information and credit market constraints. Even if such market failures were resolved, there is an overwhelming argument in favour of state intervention due to the positive spillovers of education which individuals do not take into account when making their investment decisions. These positive spillovers have been discussed at length earlier.

Such economic, social, political and environmental spillovers (or positive externalities) result in a measure of total social benefits in excess of the private benefits to education. Yet individuals will not take these spillovers into account when deciding upon investment in education. As outlined in Chapter 3, this leads to market failure as the free market yields less than the socially optimal level of investment in education. This provides an argument for government intervention on the grounds of efficiency. The state will optimally invest in education where the expected marginal social costs are equal to the expected marginal social benefits (which include private benefits plus the external economic, social, political and environmental benefits from education).

The costs of state provision of education include the actual amount of finance required, in addition to costs of financing (through higher taxation for example) and taxes foregone by those in full time education. A problem arises however in identifying precisely and in quantifying all of the positive spillovers of education. It is difficult to empirically measure the benefits that come with the smoother running of society and greater ease of governance for example. It is also hard to quantify the degree to which education actually generates additional benefits to society (over and above private benefits) through productivity improvements. Finally, as highlighted in Section 2, it can be difficult to establish a causal relationship between education attainment and many of the socially desirable outcomes correlated with education.

Given the problems inherent with empirical estimation of the external benefits of education, there is no agreement on the precise magnitude of social returns to education. The social benefits from education are higher when a greater proportion of the population is educated. It can thus take many generations to magnify social benefits. Many developed countries can trace their current standards of living back to the implementation of effective education policy in the past. If one could identify and measure all of the diverse additional benefits over and above the private benefits of education, then the argument for government intervention in education on the grounds of market failure due to positive spillovers would be strong, particularly at the pre-primary, primary and secondary levels. The argument may also be valid at higher levels of education, but the empirical evidence on high private returns to schooling at the tertiary level (in terms of earnings), along with the difficulties in measuring the extent of positive spillovers from education at this level and the high costs of state provision, can make it difficult for policymakers to make a concrete case for intervention on the grounds of externalities.

Equity Issues

We have seen that education leads to higher earnings and better employability. Disparity in the levels of education achieved will subsequently lead to differences in income. Education policy can play a key role in ensuring equality of opportunity for individuals. Ensuring an inclusive education system, with targeted policies to grant all students an equal opportunity to succeed in education, will lead to a reduction in income inequality in the economy.

As discussed, market failures relating to issues of imperfect information and credit market financing can be more pronounced for cohorts of the population from a poorer socio-economic background. This in turn can lead to greater problems of under-investment in education in these cohorts, which in turn will lead to greater inequality of participation in education in society. State intervention is therefore justified to ensure equality of access to education.

Interventions are also justified to ensure an equal opportunity to succeed in education where there is educational disadvantage or '… impediments to education arising from social or economic disadvantage which prevent students from deriving appropriate benefit from education in schools' (Section 32 (9) of the 1998 Education Act). Performance at second level education is a key determinant of access to tertiary education in Ireland. Performance at second level is in turn dependent on performance at primary. The cognitive and non-cognitive skills developed in pre-school education benefit performance outcomes in primary and secondary schooling. Targeting policy to overcome educational disadvantage at all levels of pre-tertiary schooling can help to ensure equal opportunity to perform well in schooling, and to ensure equal access to higher level education when combined with complementary targeted policies to tackle credit market constraints at this level.

4 KEY FEATURES AND POLICIES

Pre-Primary
Pre-primary education is voluntary and is mainly provided by the private sector. In spite of the growing body of literature citing the benefits of pre-school education, including the development of cognitive and non-cognitive skills in preparation for school and for successful lifelong learning, Ireland does not perform well in pre-primary education participation as evidenced in Table 13.1.

In 2014 Ireland had one of the lowest enrolment rates in the OECD for three-year olds in pre-primary education at just 46 per cent, compared with the OECD average of 69 per cent. While the enrolment rate in education for children aged four was 92 per cent in Ireland, this is comprised of 56 per cent in pre-primary education and 36 per cent in primary education. The sizeable proportion of four year olds in primary education in Ireland is in stark contrast with every other OECD country. The OECD average counts 86 per cent of four year olds in education, of which 85 per cent are enrolled in pre-primary education and just 1 per cent in primary.

Table 13.1 Enrolment Rates by Age in Pre-primary and Primary Education (2014)

	% of Age 3 pre-primary	% of Age 4 in education	of which	
			Pre-primary	*Primary*
Ireland	*46*	*92*	*56*	*36*
OECD	69	86	*85*	*1*

Source: Constructed with OECD data from: *Education at a Glance 2016.*

Where enrolment is voluntary and must be paid for privately, then in addition to underinvestment due to education spillovers, issues pertaining to imperfect information and inability to finance abound (particularly for those from a less educated and lower income background). This leads to inequity in participation. In recognition of this, in 2010 the state introduced the Early Childhood Care and Education (ECCE) scheme, which entitled children to one free pre-school year. In an endeavour to improve Ireland's performance in pre-school participation rates and enhance equality of opportunity to children at this stage of the education process, the number of years free pre-school under this scheme was extended in September 2016. This allows for up to 76 weeks of free pre-school education (compared with 38 weeks previously), which covers up to 15 hours per week over the school year. In 2016 roughly 74,000 children (about 95 per cent of eligible children) were registered for this voluntary free pre-school scheme.[3]

Primary[4]
The state provides free education to all primary and secondary (since 1967) school-going children. The provision of free education at these levels has a solid rationale in terms of the obvious positive external benefits, or spillovers, that it provides, as well as on grounds of equality of opportunity by eliminating problems of financing for those families unable to afford private education.

Compulsory education ensures an inclusive education system, which eliminates problems of non-attendance in education due to imperfect information on the private returns to education, or underinvestment due to the failure to take into account the external benefits of education. Education is compulsory in Ireland from ages six to sixteen years, although in practice nearly all five-year olds are enrolled in primary school. The fact that market failures arising from imperfect information or access to finance can be more pronounced for certain segments of the population, allows for the co-existence of fee paying and public schools in the economy.

State-funded primary schools include a majority of religious schools but also include non-denominational schools, multi-denominational schools and Gaelscoileanna (Irish language schools). Private or fee paying schools constitute a very small component of primary education in Ireland. At the primary level, in addition to the 3,262 state schools educating 553,380 children, there are just over 30 fee paying independent primary schools educating 3,727 students (less than 1 per cent of all primary students). The financing and running of these private schools are independent of the state, although there is some state assessment to ensure children receive a certain minimum education. Private primary schools are not obliged to provide the basic curriculum set out for national schools, although many do.

Second Level[4]
Second level schools include (usually denominational Roman Catholic or Protestant) secondary schools, community schools and comprehensive schools as well as non-denominational vocational schools and community colleges. Fee-paying second level schools are not independent of the state either in financing (they receive financing for teaching resources, although not for day-to-day running costs or capital projects) or from regulatory oversight. Of the 735 state-aided second level schools, only 52 are fee paying and these account for approximately seven per cent of all full-time second level students. The state has a regulatory role in the delivery of education and in ensuring quality standards of education are met in all state-aided schools.

343

Individual performance in education depends not only on inherent ability, but also the ability to fully participate in the educational programme as frequently dictated by socio-economic status or special needs. Targeted education policy at primary and second level to give children in vulnerable groups an equal opportunity of succeeding in education is important in achieving the goal of social equality. A number of initiatives have been put in place in an endeavour to eliminate educational disadvantage that can arise due to socio-economic background or special needs. The Delivering Equality of Opportunity in Schools (DEIS) scheme for example, targets designated disadvantaged schools for the provision of a number of additional supports to help students in these schools to reach their full potential in education.[5] Provision for the education of children with special educational needs is made in special schools, special classes within mainstream schools, or within mainstream classes.

As well as pursuing an education policy that is inclusive and provides equal opportunity to participate and succeed in education, an important goal of education policy is to promote lifelong learning by ensuring high quality educational outcomes and skills. In addition to literacy, numeracy and digital literacy skills for participating and contributing to an evolving economy, a focus on educating individuals about economic, social, environmental, and political issues is important. Moreover, the quality of education at primary and second level sets the foundation for the ability to achieve high quality standards of education at third level. This will be important in the creation a labour force that can contribute to the ever growing knowledge-based economy with an awareness of economic sustainability.

A number of initiatives have been undertaken to achieve these objectives at primary and secondary levels.[6] There has been an increasing emphasis on improving literacy and numeracy skills and an increasing role for the use in information technology both in the delivery of education and by students. At second level, the need to encourage creativity, innovation, independent learning and critical skills is recognised. The Junior Cycle is currently in reform, with a dual emphasis on exam and class based assessments. A complete new curriculum for maths at both junior and senior cycles, introduced on a phased-in basis in 2010 with a focus on improving student problem solving skills through increased use of applications and context, is now fully embedded into the system.

Sustainable development goals emphasise the need for an education system that incorporates awareness of economic, environmental, social and political issues.[7] At both primary and secondary levels, the principles of education for sustainable development are reflected in the curriculum of Civic Social and Political Education (CSPE), Social Personal and Health Education (SPHE), History, Geography and Science subjects, while the 1997 Green Schools initiative is a student-led programme that promotes action for the environment, There is scope for formally embedding education for sustainable development into the curricula, although the integration of education for sustainable development is more difficult at second level, due to difficulties in linking across individual subject areas taught by different teachers.

Third Level[4]

At tertiary level, education is predominantly provided by the state-funded seven universities, fourteen institutes of technology, seven teacher training institutions and a small number of other state funded third-level institutions. Third level tuition fees were abolished in publicly funded institutions for first-time full-time undergraduate students in 1996, although students must pay a substantial registration fee to cover additional costs associated with providing student services and examinations. Promoting equality of access to higher education is a key motivation for such an intervention. In addition to ensuring tuition financing of students for those unable to access education due to credit market failures, means-tested student grants for registration fees and/or maintenance are available to supplement this measure in promoting greater equality of access to higher education.

It should be noted, however, that prior to the abolition of tuition fees, means-tested tuition fees and maintenance grants were provided to qualifying students. These individuals did not gain additionally from the 1996 free tuition fees policy. The policy mainly impacted those that did not previously qualify for free fees or grants under means testing, but still had difficulty accessing credit to fund their higher level studies due to credit market failures. The empirical evidence suggests that the introduction of free tuition fees has not been successful in ensuring equality of access to higher level education, as individuals with lower socio-economic status are still less likely to attend third level.[8] Alternatives to a free tuition fees model to correct for credit market failures have become increasingly called for due to the funding crisis experienced by the third level sector (see next section). One such alternative is a student loan scheme, whereby students do not have to pay fees during their third level education but would have to repay the costs of their education as graduates once their earnings reach a certain level.

Performance at second level education is a key determinant of access to tertiary education in Ireland. Performance at second level is in turn dependent on performance at primary. The cognitive and non-cognitive skills developed in pre-primary education benefit performance outcomes in primary and secondary schooling. Inherent ability along with socio-economic status are key indicators of student performance in education. Targeting policy to overcome educational disadvantage at all levels of education, starting at pre-primary level, is thus important to ensure equal opportunity to perform well in schooling. This will in turn improve equity in access to higher level education, when combined with complementary targeted grants and subsidies policies to tackle credit market constraints at this level. At higher level, alongside means-tested grants to aid disadvantaged students, a number of specific third-level programmes have also been established to encourage participation from socio-economically disadvantaged backgrounds and of those with disabilities.[9]

As well as enhancing equity in participation at higher level education, policy has focused on ensuring high quality graduates with relevant skills for an evolving knowledge-based and knowledge-driven 'smart' economy as well as the encouragement of high-level research and innovation.[10] This is crucial to the objective of achieving greater competitiveness and economic growth. In addition to overseeing quality assurance, education policy has provided a number of initiatives to support research in third level since the late 1990s. Examples of such supports include the 1998 Programme for Research in Third Level Institutions and in 2000 the Science Foundation Ireland (SFI) (to support research in science and engineering). In 1999 the Irish Research Council for Humanities and Social Sciences was established followed in 2001 by the Irish Research Council for Science, Engineering and Technology. Both of these councils merged in 2012 to become one national body, the Irish Research Council. These endeavours provided funding to individual researchers for specific projects, with a focus on doctoral and post-doctoral students in 'fourth level' education.

While endeavours have been made to ensure high quality graduates with the relevant skills for a 'smart economy', much less effort has been made to incorporate the principles of education for sustainable development at tertiary level. Building on a primary and second level curriculum that educates for sustainable development, delivery of an education at tertiary level that fosters a combined awareness of the economic, social, political and environmental issues necessary for our sustainable development can ensure graduates that will be a force of change for the planet in their actions and in their ideas and innovations.

5 FINANCING AND PERFORMANCE

As discussed in Section 3, there are inherent difficulties in quantifying the diverse range of private benefits and positive spillovers for society as a whole that arise from education. This leads to problems in assessing in an empirical way the real benefits of education policy. In addition, while the costs of education policies are well defined and measurable, lower costs are not synonymous with improvements in education as many indicators of quality improvements necessitate greater inputs to education. With this in mind, we evaluate the sector through an examination of its inputs (financial and human resources invested) and outcomes (access and participation, and learning outcomes) in Ireland over time and relative to other OECD countries.[11] This is done against the demographic backdrop of the rising population and its drivers in Ireland, and the effects on the population of school-going age as detailed in Chapter 6.

Enrolment
Since 1967 (when free second level education was introduced), the total number of students enrolled in full time education increased steadily up to nearly 963,000 in 1988, with little change from 1988 through 1994, followed by a persistent decline until 2001. Since then, there has been a steady increase in student numbers at all levels of education up to a total of 1.1 million full-time students in 2016 (see Figure 13.1).

Figure 13.1 Number of Full-time Students Enrolled in State-aided Schools

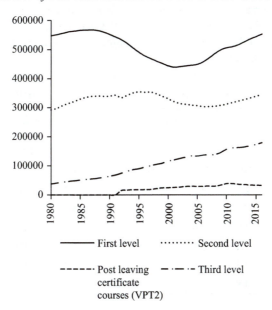

Source: Constructed from Department of Education and Skills database.

At primary level, after a period of steady decline post 1987, enrolments began to steadily increase after 2001. The numbers enrolling in primary education follow trends in the number of births in Ireland, leading to subsequent changes in second level enrolments (at least to the compulsory age of education). The numbers enrolled in full-time second level education have increased steadily from 2007. While demographics can influence enrolment numbers in tertiary education, greater accessibility to tertiary education is also an important determinant of participation rates in this non-compulsory level of education. The numbers enrolled in tertiary education have increased dramatically as illustrated in Figure 13.1. In 1980 there were 37,000 enrolled in full-time third level education. This increased to 64,000 by 1990, to 116,000 by the year 2000, and to 180,000 by 2016.

Projections into the next decade predict that the numbers enrolled in primary education will continue to rise until roughly 2020 and thereafter decline, numbers in second level will continue to rise until mid 2020s and thereafter decline, while numbers enrolled in undergraduate higher education will continue on their upward trend into the foreseeable future.

Expenditure

The OECD provides detailed comparable 2013 data on spending in primary, second and third level education across some OECD countries. As can be seen in Table 13.2, total spending (private and public) on education (excluding pre-primary), as a share of GDP in Ireland was the same as the average for OECD countries at 5.2 per cent (of which private is a small component in Ireland). At pre-tertiary levels, the expenditure share of GDP was slightly higher than the OECD average of 3.8 per cent, while at higher education levels it was less than the average of 1.6 per cent.

Table 13.2 Expenditure on Educational Institutions as a Percentage of GDP

	Total (public plus private)					Public as % total expenditure	Private as % total expenditure
	2008	2010	2011	2012	2013	2013	2013
Germany	4.2	4.5	4.4	4.4	4.3	86.6	13.4
Ireland	*5.3*	*6*	*5.7*	*5.7*	*5.2*	*95.6*	*4.4*
Netherlands	4.9	5.4	5.4	5.4	5.5	84.5	15.5
Norway	6.4	6.8	6.4	6.2	6.3	99.0	1.0
Sweden	5.3	5.4	5.3	5.4	5.4	96.9	3.1
OECD average	4.9	5.2	5.1	5.2	5.2	86.3	13.7

Source: As for Table 13.1.
Note: Public expenditure figures presented here exclude undistributed programmes.

Table 13.3 Annual Expenditure per Student by Level of Education (in equivalent USD converted using PPPs for GDP), 2013

	Ireland	OECD Ave	Ranking (OECD)
Primary	8,002	8,477	19th of 34
Secondary	10,804	9,811	14th of 33
Tertiary (including R&D)	13,663	15,772	19th of 34
Primary to Tertiary	10,065	10,493	18th of 34

Source: Department of Education and Skills, Education at a Glance 2016, OECD Indicators, *A Country Profile for Ireland.*

Expenditure per student takes into account underlying student population demographics. Examining annual expenditure per student by level of education in 2013, Table 13.3 indicates that the overall total spend per student on education (excluding pre-school) for Ireland is slightly below the OECD average and ranks 18th out of 34 countries. While expenditure per student is similar to the OECD average at primary level, it is above average at second level where Ireland ranks 14th out of 33 countries. While spend per student is higher for third level education across all countries, Ireland falls below the OECD average in this regard.

The large increase in total student enrolments at all levels of education and the failure to correspondingly increase spending in education has resulted in an overall decline over the period 2008 through 2013 at every level of education in Ireland. This is evident in Table 13.4, which details changes in the expenditure per student in pre-tertiary levels of education.

Table 13.4: Change in Total Expenditure per Student (Index: 2008 = 100)

Year	Change in expenditure		Change in student numbers		Change in expenditure per student	
	Ireland	OECD average	Ireland	OECD average	Ireland	OECD average
Pre-tertiary (primary, secondary and post-secondary non-tertiary) level						
2008	100	100	100	100	*100*	*100*
2010	107	105	103	99	*104*	*105*
2013	100	106	107	99	*93*	*108*
Tertiary level						
2008	100	100	100	100	*100*	*100*
2010	102	108	108	106	*95*	*102*
2013	86	117	120	111	*72*	*105*

Source: As for Table 13.1.

From 2008 to 2013, expenditure on pre-tertiary educational institutions increased by 6 per cent on average across OECD countries, while the number of students decreased by 1 per cent, resulting in an increase of 8 per cent in expenditure per student over this period. In contrast, in Ireland over the same period there was no increase in expenditure on pre-tertiary institutions despite a seven per cent increase in student numbers, which resulted in a decline of expenditure per student of seven per cent at pre-tertiary levels. At tertiary level these trends were more dramatic. Over the period 2008 to 2013 there was an overall increase of five per cent in expenditure per student at tertiary level on average across OECD countries, as the increase in expenditure exceeded the increase in enrolments. In Ireland, however, tertiary expenditure declined fourteen per cent over the period 2008 through 2013, while student numbers increased by twenty per cent, resulting in an overall decline in expenditure per student of twenty-eight per cent over that period. The decline in total expenditure on tertiary education is driven by a decline in public spending by the state. Over the same period student contribution charges have increased significantly, from €825 for academic year ending 2008 to €2,250 in the academic year ending 2013. The charge in 2017 is €3,000.

Total spend at pre-tertiary levels can be affected by both the numbers of students enrolled and also by teachers' salaries (the main input costs). In Ireland, teacher salaries account for 75 per cent of total current expenditure at primary level and 69 per cent at second level in 2013 (on average across OECD countries, the corresponding figures are 61 per cent at both primary and second level). At both primary and secondary levels, teacher starting salaries in Ireland are lower than the OECD average, but this is reversed for teachers with more than 15 years' experience. Teaching hours in Ireland are longer than the OECD average (at primary level, 915 hours per year compared with the OECD average of 776 hours per year, and at second level 735 hours per year compared with OECD average of 644 hours per year).

At pre-tertiary levels, pupil teacher ratios and average class sizes are important determinants of the delivery of quality education. Table 13.5 indicates a fall in the pupil-teacher ratio at primary level from 21.5 in 2000 to 16.0 in 2014. This compares with OECD average of 17.7 to 15.0 over the same period. Ireland's relative performance in this regard has improved. Average class size has remained unchanged at 24.8 over this period for Ireland, compared with a slight fall in the OECD average from 22.1 to 21.2. At second level, the pupil-teacher ratio has fallen over the same period and is similar to the OECD average. Maintenance or improvement of these measures will require additional financing at primary and second level in the coming years, particularly given the projected continued increases in student enrolments.

Table 13.5 Pupil-Teacher Ratios and Average Class Size

	1999/2000		2013/2014	
	Pupil-teacher ratio	Average class size	Pupil-teacher ratio	Average class size
Public Primary Schools				
Ireland	21.5	24.8	16.0	24.8
OECD average	17.7	22.1	15.0	21.2
Rank position (OECD)	4th highest of 27	5th highest of 23	13th highest of 34	5th highest of 28
Public Secondary Schools				
Ireland	15.9	22.7*	13.9	–
OECD average	14.3	23.6	13.3	23
Rank position (OECD)	6th highest of 24	15th highest of 23	9th highest of 30	–

Source: Department of Education and Skills, *Education at a Glance 2016*, OECD Indicators, *A Country Profile for Ireland.*
* Lower secondary only (based on DES Teacher Timetable Database).

Outcomes

Access and Participation

As discussed in Section 4, with enrolment rates of 46 per cent for three-year olds and 56 per cent for four-year olds in pre-primary education, Ireland's performance in pre-primary school participation fell short of the average experience for OECD countries in 2014. The recent change in policy which allows for an additional year free pre-school education will improve this comparison.

Beyond early education, we have already seen the dramatic rise in the numbers enrolled in full-time education since the turn of the century in Ireland (Figure 13.1). The fact that education is compulsory up to age sixteen in Ireland results in enrolment rates of 100 per cent for the population aged five to sixteen years. In 2014, enrolment rates in upper second level education were 55 per cent for the population aged 15 to 19 years, and 37 per cent in tertiary education for the population aged 20 to 24 years.

Table 13.6 provides information on educational attainment for the population aged 25 to 64 years, as well as for the population aged 25 to 34 years.

In 2015 Ireland, for the population aged 25 to 64 years, 20 per cent have below upper secondary as their highest level of educational attainment, 37 per cent have upper secondary or post-secondary non-tertiary, while 43 per cent have tertiary education. The rate of tertiary educational attainment in Ireland has increased over time (up from 29 per cent in 2005), and exceeds the OECD average of 35 per cent. This is true also for the population aged 25 to 34 years, where 52 per cent have tertiary education (up from 41 per cent in 2005) in contrast with 42 per cent average for the OECD (up from 32 per cent in 2005).

Table 13.6 Highest Percentage Level of Educational Attainment by Age Group (2015)

	Ireland		OECD	
	2005	2015	2005	2015
Educational attainment of 25–64 year-olds				
< upper secondary	35	20	29	23
upper secondary/post-secondary non-tertiary	35	37	45	43
Tertiary	29	43	27	35
Educational attainment of 25–34 year-olds				
< upper secondary	19	9	21	16
upper secondary/post-secondary non-tertiary	40	39	48	42
Tertiary	41	52	32	42

Source: As for Table 13.1.

Participation in higher level education is not equal across all groups of society however. Profiling levels of educational attainment by parents' level of education can give some indication of the degree of intergenerational mobility in education. OECD indicators suggest a rate of tertiary educational attainment among 25 to 44 year old non-students that is higher for those with better educated parents.

Learning

Quality education requires the acquisition of relevant knowledge and skills for society. The OECD PIAAC (Programme for International Assessment of Adult Competencies) 2012 survey results of adults aged 16 to 65 indicate that a sizeable proportion of adults surveyed have difficulties with basic literacy and numeracy skills: 18 per cent are at the lowest level of literacy proficiency, while 25 per cent are at the lowest levels of numeracy proficiency.

The picture improves on an analysis of skills among 15 year olds in 2015 however. The OECD PISA (Programme for International Student Assessment) 2015 results provide a measure of the proficiency of 15 year olds across reading, maths and science subjects, and the ability to apply this knowledge to problem solving.[12] Table 13.7 illustrates average scores for the OECD and Ireland in each of these disciplines. Ireland performs well and scores above the average for OECD countries in reading, mathematics and science.

Table 13.7 Average Scores for Student Performance and Ireland Rank in OECD

	2015	2012	2009	2006
Mathematics				
OECD	490	494	495	494
Ireland	504	501	487	501
Ireland Rank	*13*	*13*	*26*	*18*
Reading				
OECD	493	496	493	489
Ireland	521	523	496	517
Ireland Rank	*3*	*4*	*17*	*5*
Science				
OECD	493	501	501	498
Ireland	503	522	508	508
Ireland Rank	*13*	*9*	*14*	*16*

Source: OECD, Programme for International Student Assessment, Derived from Database.

In 2015 Ireland ranked third in reading literacy and thirteenth both in mathematics and science. While average scores for reading and mathematics in Ireland have not changed much since the 2012 results, there was a drop in average scores for Science over this period. The 2015 survey also provides information on the use of Information and Communication Technologies within school and for homework, in which Ireland performed below the OECD average.

Despite the overall performance in reading in Ireland, 2015 survey results also indicate that 10 per cent of students perform at the lowest level of proficiency, while in mathematics 15 per cent display weak performance. Performance at these levels indicates inadequate skills to participate in society or further education. While these figures are substantially lower than the corresponding OECD averages and lower than most OECD countries, they do emphasise a continued need for targeted education policy to overcome educational disadvantage.

Finally, with regard to the goal of sustainable development education, OECD *Education at a Glance 2016* Tables 1 and 2 summarise Ireland's progress toward the 2030 education targets using various indicators in the report. Ireland's performance in learning outcomes, enrolment rates in education (primary, second and tertiary levels), and equity in access to education exceed the benchmarks for the corresponding 2030 education targets. However it still has some way to go to achieving the 2030 education targets captured by measures of skills and readiness to use information and communication technologies for problem solving, measures of performance of adults in literacy, and measures of performance of students in environmental science.

6 CONCLUSION

This chapter provides an analytical framework for analysing the role of government in the education sector in Ireland. From an exploration of the diverse range of benefits that arise from education to an economic analysis of the rationale for state intervention, it becomes apparent education is good for both the individual and for society, and if left to the free market there would be both underinvestment and inequity in education.

Education is an important policy instrument in the pursuit of competitiveness, social equality, economic sustainability and good governance in an economy. This requires an inclusive education system that promotes equality of opportunity while delivering high quality educational outcomes with an awareness of the economic, social, political and environmental requirements for economic sustainability. Armed with an understanding of the rationale for government intervention and the objectives of education policy, we then examined the key features and policies of the education sector in Ireland followed by an analysis of the financing and performance of the sector. This illustrates a number of challenges that future policy needs to address.

In terms of spending on education, given the predicted continued increase in student enrolments until roughly 2020 at primary level and into the mid 2020s at second level, additional finance must be made available to maintain or improve on measures of spending per student, pupil-teacher ratios and average class sizes, and overall educational outcomes. At tertiary level there is a funding crisis and a threat to the quality of education given the sustained decline in public spending alongside increasing student numbers. With the number of enrolments at third level predicted to rise over the next decade, policy needs to implement a radical change in the financing of this sector.

While performance measures in terms of enrolment and educational attainment rates are to be applauded, there are still some issues surrounding intergenerational mobility and equity of opportunity at higher levels of education. Skills from education in terms of reading literacy and mathematical ability do rank highly among other OECD countries, though efforts in science need to be maintained to prevent a further decline in performance, digital literacy in education needs to improve, and those students not achieving an adequacy in basic reading and math skills need to be targeted to help overcome any educational disadvantage. Finally, while Ireland is on track to achieve some of the sustainable development educational targets, there is need for a concerted effort to embed education for sustainable development formally into the education programme at all levels of education and to drive toward the achievement of all the 2030 targets.

Endnotes

* This chapter builds on Chapter 13 from the 12th edition of this book which was written by Carol Newman. Many thanks to John O' Hagan, Francis O'Toole and Patrick Paul Walsh for comments and suggestions.

1 See M. Dickson and M. Harmon, 'Economic returns to education: what we know, what we don't know, and where we are going – some brief pointers', *Economics of Education Review*, 30 (6), 2011.

2 The human-capital view of education attributes higher earnings to enhanced productivity from education. It is also possible that education does not actually improve productivity, but rather is used as signalling of workers' inherent characteristics and their productive ability to potential employers – more productive individuals are likely to stay in education for longer. Empirically it is difficult to identify which theory of education is correct.

3 Figures for school year end 2016, from Pobal (2016): *Early Years, Service Profile, 2015/2016.*

4 Discussion for primary, secondary and tertiary education is based on the Department of Education and Skills database, and information provided on the Department of Education and Skills and the Citizens Information websites. Data refer to end of school year 2016 for all institutions aided by the Department of Education and Skills and so do not include fee-paying independent primary schools, which is referenced separately (in 2016 these independent schools only accounted for less than 1 per cent of all primary students). Second level numbers include those enrolled in post leaving certificate courses.

5 Such supports include DEIS grants paid to schools based on level of disadvantage and enrolment; access to the School Completion Programme, the Home School Community Liaison Scheme, the School Meals Programme, literacy and numeracy supports; and a school books grant scheme. See Department of Education and Skills website for more detailed information on these supports.

6   Discussion based on Department of Education and Skills, *Literacy and Numeracy for Learning and Life: The National Strategy to Improve Literacy and Numeracy among Children and Young People 2011–2020,* Dublin 2011, and Department of Education and Skills, *Digital Strategy for Schools 2015–2020: Enhancing Teaching, Learning and Assessment,* Dublin 2015.

7   Discussion based on Department of Education and Skills, *Education for Sustainability: The National Strategy on Education for Sustainable Development in Ireland, 2014–2020,* Dublin 2015.

8   For a detailed discussion and analysis on the effects of the free tuition fees on access to higher education, see K. Denny, 'The effect of abolishing university tuition costs: evidence from Ireland', *Labour Economics,* 26, 2014.

9   For example, UCD *Higher Education Access Route (HEAR)* and *Disability Access Route (DARE)* schemes, and TCD *Trinity Access Programme (TAP).*

10   Department of Education and Skills, *National Strategy for Higher Education to 2030,* Dublin 2015.

11   Discussion based on OECD *Education at a Glance 2016* and the corresponding Department of Education and Skills report, *Education at a Glance 2016, OECD* Indicators, *A Country Profile for Ireland.*

12   Discussion based on OECD international report on PISA 2015, *PISA Results in Focus,* and the Irish ERC national report: *Future Ready? The Performance of 15-year-olds in Ireland on Science, Reading Literacy and Mathematics in PISA 2015,* prepared by G. Shiel, C. Kelleher, C. McKeown, and S. Denner.

CHAPTER 14

Health: Funding, Access and Efficiency

*Anne Nolan**

1 INTRODUCTION

This chapter examines the health sector, a key component of Irish economic activity and the subject of much recent policy discussion. In terms of its economic impact, current expenditure on the health services accounted for 11.6 per cent of GNI and 12.9 per cent of total employment in 2014. The public sector accounts for approximately 70 per cent of total health expenditure in Ireland. Over the period 2000 to 2009, public health expenditure more than doubled in real terms. As a result of the economic crisis, public health expenditure fell sharply by nearly €1.5 billion between 2009 and 2013, but has since recovered to reach €14.6 billion in 2016 (Figure 14.1).

The scale of the reduction in public health expenditure during the economic crisis created unprecedented challenges for the Irish health system, most notably in terms of ensuring the delivery of safe and effective health services in the context of declining budgets. During the crisis, the oversight of the EU-IMF 'Troika' focused attention on costs in the Irish public health service, with major policy changes implemented in the areas of pay and pharmaceuticals. More recently, the policy debate has focused on issues around access, and the most appropriate method for financing a universal healthcare system. As the economy recovers, a particular challenge for a labour-intensive sector such as health will be managing demands for increased pay on the part of health sector staff.

The remainder of this chapter focuses on the themes of access and efficiency in the context of discussions on key issues with regard to the health services in Ireland. Section 2 discusses the rationale for government intervention in the financing and delivery of health services (see also Chapter 3). Section 3 outlines the key features of the Irish health service, in terms of governance and organisational structure, entitlements, financing and delivery. Section 4 examines how the Irish health service compares with other OECD countries in terms of expenditure, outcomes, financing and delivery structures. Section 5 focuses on the financing of primary care services in Ireland, as well as the current role of private health

Figure 14.1 Public Health Expenditure in Ireland: 1997–2016 (deflated by CPI)

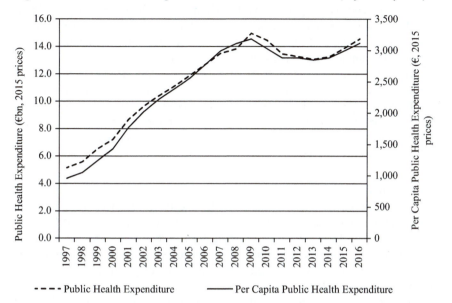

- - - - Public Health Expenditure   ——— Per Capita Public Health Expenditure

Sources: For expenditure data see Department of Health, *Health in Ireland Key Trends*, various issues. Data on population and the CPI are from the CSO.

insurance in the Irish healthcare system. Section 6 discusses the issue of cost containment in the health sector. Section 7 concludes the chapter.

2 WHY GOVERNMENT INTERVENTION?

Despite the fact that the private sector accounts for approximately 30 per cent of healthcare finance (see Section 3), and is heavily involved in the provision of health services in Ireland, the public sector remains the main agent responsible for the finance and delivery of health services in Ireland. Chapter 3 discusses the rationale for government intervention in the economy in general. In terms of the health service, efficiency concerns relating to asymmetric information, uncertainty and the existence of externalities, as well as equity or distributional concerns motivate government involvement in healthcare.

Asymmetric Information
The nature of the relationship between producers and consumers in healthcare is distorted by asymmetric information. Patients are essentially buying the provider's knowledge and/or information when they consume healthcare. In comparison with other goods and services, information acquisition on the part of the consumer

in healthcare markets is made more difficult by the nature of the product. Learning by experience is complicated by the fact that every illness episode is different and the consumer cannot sample the service before purchase or is unlikely to have had prior experience of the same service. In addition, the information is often technically complex, involving many years of study.

The relationship has often been characterised as a principal agent one; due to the high costs of acquiring such technical information, the patient relies on the healthcare provider to act in their best interests in terms of diagnosis and treatment decisions. The presence of asymmetric information justifies a role for government in improving consumers' information and regulating the behaviour of healthcare professionals.

Uncertainty

Healthcare markets are also characterised by uncertainty, i.e. lack of information about the future. Ill-health is inherently unpredictable, both in terms of financial costs and physical and emotional suffering. This necessitates a role for insurance in offering the consumer protection against uncertainty. However, the problems of adverse selection, moral hazard and cream-skimming may arise in a private health insurance market.

Adverse selection arises when the insurer cannot distinguish between low and high risks, because individuals purchasing health insurance have better information about their risk status than the insurer. Insurers must therefore base the premium on the risk pool that includes both low and high risks. Low-risk individuals will not purchase health insurance because the premium does not reflect their risk status leaving only high-risk individuals in the risk pool. This can make the fund unsustainable. The solution is to have compulsory insurance or risk-related premiums. However, due to concerns that high-risk individuals would be denied access to healthcare under a private health insurance system with risk-rated premiums, most governments intervene to provide free or heavily subsidised health insurance for the population for most basic public health services.

Moral hazard, where an individual's behaviour is affected by their insurance status, may arise in the form of excessive utilisation of services. It may also arise in the form of less preventive activities. User fees, which aim to make patients more aware of the resource implications of their decisions, are often used to temper the moral hazard effects of free or heavily subsidised healthcare. However, the degree to which user fees are effective in changing behaviour has been questioned, and there are well-documented adverse impacts on access (see also Section 5).

A final problem associated with a private-insurance market is that of cream-skimming. Insurers seek to encourage low-risk persons to insure with their company. In the market for car insurance for example, premiums are substantially higher for high risk groups such as the young, those with penalty points, etc.

In Ireland, the government strictly regulates the behaviour of the major private health insurers in an attempt to prevent cream-skimming through the principles of open enrolment (no one can be refused cover), community rating (all individuals face the same premium) and lifetime cover (once insured, an individual's policy cannot be terminated). Section 5 discusses the role of private health insurance in the Irish healthcare system in greater detail.

Externalities

The healthcare sector may also be characterised by the presence of externalities when private costs or benefits are out of line with social costs or benefits. The standard solution to an externality is to levy a Pigouvian tax in the case of goods or services that produce negative externalities or to offer a subsidy in the case of goods or services that produce positive externalities.

Free childhood vaccinations against infectious diseases and excise taxes on cigarettes are examples of government intervention in the health sector due to the presence of externalities. A vaccinated population confers a positive externality on society while second-hand cigarette smoke confers a negative externality on society; in the absence of government intervention vaccination levels would be less than the socially-optimal level while smoking levels would be greater than the socially-optimal level. Of course, the efficacy of taxes in changing behaviour to reflect the socially-optimal level depends on the price elasticity of demand for the good/service, the availability of substitutes, budget share, etc. (see also Chapter 4).

An alternative strategy for internalising the costs associated with a negative externality is a minimum price; current legislation in relation to alcohol consumption in Ireland proposes the introduction of a minimum unit price (MUP). Proponents argue that a MUP would be particularly effective in tackling consumption of alcohol that is cheap relative to its strength. However, opponents argue that increased taxation is more effective as the proceeds of the tax are realised by the state; with MUP, some of the benefits are realised by retailers.

Equity

Apart from efficiency concerns, the desire to ensure that healthcare should be distributed equitably across the population motivates government intervention in the sector. However, there is much discussion over what is meant by equity in the context of the health services.[1] Is the objective equality of opportunity (i.e. access to healthcare) or equality of outcome (i.e. health status)?

Equality of opportunity implies that access to healthcare should be distributed on the basis of need for care, not on the basis of non-health related attributes, such as ability to pay (which is the case for many other commodities). But how do we define access? Most empirical studies proxy access by utilisation, arguing that access to health services is equitable if utilisation rates are similar, even after controlling for need factors such as age, gender and health status. However, it is obvious that even if everyone enjoys the same access to healthcare, persons in equal need may end up consuming different amounts of care (and types of care) due to differing tastes and preferences, differing ability to navigate the system, etc.

Nonetheless, the principle of access according to need rather than ability to pay is an accepted principle in most countries, and has motivated recent policy changes in the Irish context (see Section 3 for further details).

An additional issue concerns the progressivity of funding sources, i.e. most governments subscribe to the view that health services should be financed in relation to ability to pay (those on higher incomes should pay a higher proportion of their incomes in taxation, social insurance contributions, etc.). Such thinking motivates government involvement in the financing of healthcare services, offering free or subsidised healthcare services to those on low incomes or in particularly vulnerable situations.

3 KEY FEATURES OF IRISH HEALTH SERVICE

Governance and Organisational Structure

The Irish healthcare system has undergone substantial organisational reform on numerous occasions in the past decades (and Section 3 discusses proposals for further organisational reform). At present, the key bodies in the current system are the Department of Health, the Health Service Executive (HSE) and the Health Information and Quality Authority (HIQA).

The main role of the Department of Health is to advise the Minister and Government on the strategic development of the health system. HIQA was fully established in 2007 and is an independent agency responsible for developing standards, monitoring compliance and carrying out investigations in residential services for children, older persons and persons with disabilities. Legislation that is currently being drafted will provide for the extension of its remit to the private health service. HIQA is also responsible for carrying out health technology assessments (HTAs) in Ireland.

The HSE, which was established in January 2005, is responsible for the delivery of health and social care services in Ireland. Many services are provided directly (e.g. public health nursing), while others are provided under contract with the HSE by self-employed health professionals, private healthcare providers, voluntary hospitals and voluntary/community organisations.

Eligibility for Free Public Health Services

All individuals who are ordinarily resident in Ireland are granted either full or limited eligibility for public healthcare services. Individuals with full eligibility, termed 'medical cardholders' or 'public patients', are entitled to receive all health services free of charge under the General Medical Services (GMS) Scheme. This includes GP services, prescribed medicines, all dental, ophthalmic and aural services, maternity services, in-patient services in public hospitals and specialist treatment in out-patient clinics of public hospitals. However, from 1 October 2010, medical cardholders are required to pay a fixed charge per prescription item (currently €2.50 per item, up to a maximum of €25 per family per month). At the

Figure 14.2 Public Health Cover (percentage of the population, 1990–2016)

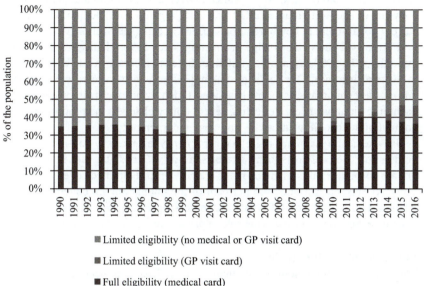

■ Limited eligibility (no medical or GP visit card)

■ Limited eligibility (GP visit card)

■ Full eligibility (medical card)

Sources: For data on medical and GP visit card, see PCRS, *Statistical Analysis of Claims and Payments*, various issues; and HSE, *Monthly Performance Reports*, various issues. Data on population are from the CSO.

end of December 2015 approximately 37 per cent of the population had a medical card (see Figure 14.2).

The remainder of the population, those with limited eligibility ('non-medical cardholders' or 'private patients'), are entitled to free maternity services, in-patient services in public hospitals (subject to a €80 charge per day up to an annual maximum of €800), specialist services in out-patient clinics (again, subject to a €80 charge per day up to an annual maximum of €800), assistance towards the cost of prescribed medicines over a monthly limit of €144 per family (under the Drugs Payment Scheme) and assistance towards the cost of prescribed medicines for certain chronic conditions (under the Long Term Illness Scheme) or high cost treatments (under the High Tech Drugs Scheme). In most cases, they must pay in full for GP consultations and all dental, ophthalmic and aural treatments. However, those who satisfy an income means test are eligible for a GP visit card (introduced in 2005), which grants the recipient access to free GP services only (other entitlements are the same as those with limited eligibility).

Eligibility for a medical card is decided on the basis of an income means test. The income thresholds for the GP visit card are 50 per cent higher than those for the standard medical card. In special circumstances, such as a cancer diagnosis, an individual who is otherwise ineligible on the basis of income may be granted a medical card or GP visit card. As of November 2015, approximately 6 per cent of medical cards, and 10 per cent of GP visit cards, were issued on a 'discretionary' basis.[2] In 2015, all those aged 70 years and over, and all children under the age of six years of age, were granted a GP visit card, regardless of income. This reflects current government policy in relation to free GP care (see Section 3).

Figure 14.2 shows the change in coverage since 1990. Medical card cover fell throughout the 1990s as income guidelines failed to increase in line with increases in average incomes. Due to rising unemployment, medical card coverage rose during the economic crisis, but has since fallen again due to improvements in economic circumstances. Reflecting recent policy changes, the proportion of the population with a GP visit card is now just under ten per cent.

Private health insurance in Ireland is primarily taken out by non-medical cardholders to cover the costs of private or semi-private hospital care in public and private hospitals (although many plans are now offering limited cover for primary care). At present, just under 46 per cent of the population are covered (see also Section 4). Medical and GP visit cardholders may also take out private health insurance. Section 5 discusses the role of private health insurance in greater detail.

Financing of Health Services
There are three main sources of finance in the Irish healthcare system: public resources, out-of-pocket payments by individuals and private health insurance. In 2013, general government resources (primarily taxation) accounted for approximately 68 per cent of total Irish health expenditure. Out-of-pocket payments by individuals (e.g. GP fees by non-medical cardholders) accounted for a further 17 per cent. Despite the fact that 46 per cent of the population hold private health insurance, it accounted for only 13 per cent of total financing in Irish healthcare.

After the onset of the recession in 2008, the proportion of total health expenditure accounted for by public resources decreased, while that contributed by direct out-of-pocket payments by individuals and private health insurance increased. This reflected the increasing reliance on out-of-pocket charges as a financing mechanism in the Irish health service as a response to the economic crisis. However, this trend was contrary to that observed in other OECD countries, where the share of public funding increased in order to safeguard access to public health services during the crisis.

Delivery of Health Services
While the state is heavily involved in the financing of health services in Ireland, it mainly leaves the delivery of health services to the private sector, with the hospital and primary care sectors providing particularly good examples of the intermix between the public and private sectors in the financing and delivery of health services in Ireland.

Public hospitals also provide private healthcare. Consultants employed in public hospitals may treat private patients in the same public hospital (depending on their contract). This has led to concerns over a two-tier system of access to public hospital care, with those with private health insurance or who can pay privately able to gain faster access to public hospital care.

Primary care services are mainly provided by independent professionals (e.g. GPs, pharmacists, dentists, etc.) who may be contracted to provide services in the public sector, in addition to services provided to private patients (approximately 90 per cent of GPs also have contracts to provide services to medical cardholders). The Primary Care Reimbursement Service (PCRS) undertakes the reimbursement of providers for GP, dental, optical and pharmaceutical services supplied to medical cardholders as well as the reimbursement of pharmacists for services provided to non-medical cardholders under the various community drugs schemes.

The Irish healthcare system therefore has a mixture of a universal public health service and a fee-based private system. Some services are publicly funded and delivered (e.g. treatment as a public patient in a public hospital), some are publicly funded but privately delivered (e.g. GP consultations by medical cardholders), some are privately funded and delivered (e.g. GP consultations by non-medical cardholders), while some are privately funded but publicly delivered (e.g. non-medical cardholders must pay a modest charge for treatment in public hospitals). This complex mixture has implications for the allocation of resources both between the public and the private sector and between different types of care (see Section 5 for further discussion).

Proposals for Reform[3]

The 2011 *Programme for Government* provided for a major reform of the Irish healthcare system. The most significant commitments related to the introduction of a system of universal health insurance (UHI), the introduction of free GP care for the entire population, the abolition of the HSE, the establishment of independent hospital trusts and reform of the financing mechanism for public hospitals (from block budgets to activity-based funding or 'money follows the patient').

By far the most significant proposal concerned the commitment to move towards a system of UHI. Under the proposals, all individuals would be insured for a standard package of care from one of a group of competing private insurers. This system of UHI was closely modelled on the Dutch system. A White Paper published in April 2014 outlined the proposed UHI model. However, in 2015 in response to the publication of a study by the Economic and Social Research Institute (ESRI) of the potential cost implications of the proposed UHI model, the government abandoned this model, but remained committed to universal healthcare. The current *Programme for Government* (published in May 2016) does not mention UHI; however it does note that further work is required to identify the best way to finance universal healthcare.

The 2016 *Programme for Government* also committed to the development of an All-Party Oireachtas Committee, tasked with the development of a single long-term vision for healthcare over a ten-year period with cross party consensus. The Committee on the Future of Healthcare was established in June 2016 and was due to report in April 2017.

The proposal to move towards the provision of free GP care services for the entire population represented a major policy change in terms of the financing of primary care services in Ireland. In the initial proposal, free GP care for all was to be introduced on a phased basis, with free care extended to those on the Long Term Illness Scheme in year one and to those on the High Tech Drugs Scheme in year two, with subsidised care extended to all in the next phase, followed by access to free care to all in the final phase (i.e. by 2016). These targets were not met, and in October 2013, the government announced that free GP care would instead be extended to particular population age groups. In 2015, all those aged 70 years and over, and all children under the age of six years of age, were granted a GP visit card.

Major changes in the financing of Irish healthcare would also have significant implications for how healthcare in Ireland is delivered. One of the most important changes proposed is the eventual abolition of the HSE. HSE ownership and management of public hospitals would end, with public hospitals owned and managed by independent hospital trusts, and the purchasing role of the HSE would transfer to a new purchasing agency. Seven hospital groups have been established to date. Under the current proposals, hospitals would no longer receive fixed budgets but would be paid instead for the services they provide and the number of patients they treat ('money follows the patient'), thereby incentivising them to treat more patients and to be reimbursed according to the complexity of treatment.

4 IRISH HEALTHCARE SYSTEM IN COMPARATIVE CONTEXT

Health Expenditure

Table 14.1 illustrates that Ireland, along with most other OECD countries, experienced an increase in the share of national income devoted to health over the

Table 14.1 Health Expenditure as a Percentage of GNI[1], Selected OECD countries, 2000–2014

	2000	2005	2010	2014	% aged over 65 (2014)
Denmark	8.3	9.0	10.3	10.2	18.2
Finland	6.9	8.0	8.8	9.4	19.3
Germany	9.9	10.2	10.8	10.8	20.8
Ireland	*6.8*	*8.8*	*12.6*	*11.6*	*12.6*
Netherlands	6.9	9.4	10.3	11.0	17.3
Sweden	7.4	8.2	8.2	10.9	19.3
UK	5.9	7.0	8.3	10.0	17.4
USA	12.3	14.4	16.2	16.1	14.5

Sources: OECD, *Health Statistics 2015,* OECD, Paris 2016; European Commission, *AMECO Macro-Economic Database,* (available at: http://ec.europa.eu/economy_finance/db_indicators/ameco/index_en.htm) [accessed 30 January 2017].
[1] While health expenditure is usually expressed as a proportion of GDP, the large divergence between Irish GDP and GNP/GNI figures means that, for comparative purposes, it is more appropriate to express health expenditure as a proportion of GNP/GNI.

period 2000 to 2014. The share has increased at a faster pace in Ireland than in many other OECD countries; of the eight countries presented in Table 14.1, Ireland moved from having the second-lowest share of national income devoted to health in 2000 to the second-highest in 2014. This is despite the fact that Ireland has a relatively young population by international standards, although there is much debate in the literature about the extent to which an ageing population is a significant driver of health expenditure (see also Section 5).

Healthcare Financing

Table 14.2 presents the sources of finance for selected OECD countries for 2013. In terms of public sources of finance, countries such as Germany and the Netherlands rely much more heavily on social insurance contributions than general government sources, such as taxation, for their revenue. Social insurance contributions, which are compulsory and generally shared between the employer and employee, tend to be earmarked for specific purposes; in Ireland the 'health levy' (since replaced by the universal social charge) contributed less than one per cent of total healthcare finance prior to its abolition in 2011. As in other countries, revenue from general taxation in Ireland is not earmarked specifically for the health services, which means that it must compete with other areas for public funds.

Due to universal eligibility for free public health services in many countries, the share of total expenditure funded through private sources (out of pocket payments by individuals, private insurance payments and other sources of finance, e.g. voluntary donations) is much smaller than that accounted for by public sources. However, there can be considerable heterogeneity across different types of care; for example, in Ireland, dental care services are predominately privately-financed,

Table 14.2 Sources of Finance for Total Health Expenditure for Selected OECD countries[1] (percentage of total health expenditure, 2013)

Country	General government	Social insurance	Out of pocket payments	Private insurance	Other private sources
Denmark	84	0	14	2	0
Finland	61	14	19	2	4
Germany	7	70	13	9	1
Ireland	67	0	17	13	2
Netherlands	7	80	5	6	1
UK	83	0	10	3	4
USA	48	0	12	35	5

Source: OECD, *Health at a Glance 2015,* OECD, Paris 2016.
[1] Data for the USA does not distinguish between general taxation and social insurance contributions.

while acute hospital services are predominately publicly-financed. For residential long-term care services, a combination of public and private financing applies under the Nursing Home Support Scheme, with individuals contributing 80 per cent of their income (and 7.5 per cent of the value of assets/savings for a maximum of three years), and the state contributing the balance.

The USA is a clear outlier in terms of the share of private financing. The Affordable Care Act (ACA), enacted in 2012, is designed to ensure near-universal health insurance in the USA through a substantial expansion of Medicaid (the existing public health insurance scheme for those on low incomes), tax credits that will cap premium contributions as a share of income for people purchasing private health plans through new state insurance exchanges, and new insurance market rules that will prevent health insurers from denying coverage or charging higher premiums to people with pre-existing health conditions. By 2015, the percentage of uninsured working-age adults had declined following the full implementation of the ACA. However, the new administration has signalled its attention to repeal the ACA, although there is as yet no clarity on its replacement.

As Table 14.2 illustrates, out-of-pocket payments are now more important than private insurance as a source of finance for all countries examined except the USA. However, there are concerns that as governments come under increasing pressure to fund public health services, and out-of-pocket payments become more important as a source of revenue, a greater share of the funding burden will fall on those in ill-health (see Section 5 for a discussion of equity issues surrounding user fees in healthcare).

Health Outcomes
Levels of expenditure provide little or no guidance as to whether this expenditure is efficiently and effectively spent or distributed equitably across different sectors of the population. As the ultimate objective of health policy is to improve population health, it is useful to examine where countries rank in terms of health outcomes and whether there is any correlation between such measures and health expenditure.

Table 14.3 outlines the weak association between health expenditure and health-outcome indicators such as life expectancy and infant mortality. Most striking is the case of the USA which spends by far the most per capita on health among the eight countries examined, yet performs poorly in terms of life expectancy and infant mortality.

In an attempt to quantify the contribution of the health sector more accurately, the concept of amenable or avoidable mortality has been developed to assess the quality and performance of health systems. Amenable mortality refers to deaths from conditions considered amenable to healthcare, such as treatable cancers, diabetes, and cardiovascular disease. A recent study across 16 high-income countries found that 24 per cent of deaths under the age of 75 could be classified as 'avoidable'. In a study of 31 OECD countries, deaths from causes amenable to medical intervention were found to have fallen substantially over the period 1997 to 2007, with the largest decline observed for Ireland, although Ireland was still ranked 17th out of 31 OECD countries in terms of amenable mortality in 2007 (with a low ranking indicating 'better' performance).[4]

Table 14.3 Total Health Expenditure Per Capita and Health Outcome Rankings, Selected OECD Countries, 2013

Country	Expenditure	Male life expectancy	Female life expectancy	Infant mortality
Denmark	5	6	7	3
Finland	7	7	1	1
Germany	4	5	4	4
Ireland[1]	6	4	5	5
Netherlands	2	2	3	7
UK	8	3	6	6
USA	1	8	8	8

Source: For data on expenditure (total health expenditure per capita expressed in USA $ PPP), male and female life expectancy (at birth) and infant mortality (per 1,000 live births) see OECD, *Health at a Glance 2015*, OECD, Paris 2016.
[1] Expenditure data refer to 2012.

In the debate about the role of health expenditure in improving population health, the literature highlights the fact that the 'social determinants of health', i.e., factors such as diet, exercise, genetic inheritance, lifestyle, education, social status, income distribution, social support and housing, and their complex interactions, may be more important in determining the level and distribution of health outcomes than simple health expenditure. The recent increases in resources devoted to health promotion and prevention (e.g. through the smoking in the workplace ban, breast-cancer screening, promotion of healthy eating, etc.) reflects this realisation that lifestyle factors are also crucial in influencing population health outcomes.

In an attempt to evaluate the impact of health policy on health systems performance and outcomes, a recent study examined health policies across 43 European countries. The results showed that Ireland was ranked 11th out of 43 European countries in terms of health policy performance, with Ireland scoring well in terms of policy in relation to tobacco control, but poorly in relation to policy on child safety (e.g. measles immunisation).[5]

More recently, research has focused on the impact of the financial and economic crisis on health systems performance and health outcomes. In general, there is no simple answer to the question of how financial and economic crises impact on health outcomes, behaviours and inequalities. An important study in the USA in the early 2000s found that total mortality and most causes of mortality exhibited a pro-cyclical fluctuation over the period 1972 to 1991, with suicides representing an important exception, although more recent evidence finds little relationship between the economic cycle and mortality.[6]

5 FINANCE AND ACCESS

While the proportion of private financing in Irish healthcare is not unusual inter-nationally (Table 14.2), what sets Ireland apart from other OECD countries is the large proportion of the population that must pay out-of-pocket for primary care, particularly GP care. In addition, despite its relatively small contribution to overall health sector financing in Ireland, private health insurance has important implications for equity and efficiency in the Irish system, particularly in terms of the interaction of public and private care in public hospitals.

User Fees and Access to Primary Care

While the proportion of the population eligible for free GP services has increased recently, and currently stands at approximately 46 per cent of the population, the fact remains that over 50 per cent of the Irish population must pay out-of-pocket for GP (and other primary care) services. In Ireland, those without a medical or GP visit card pay approximately €50 each time they visit their GP. While the 2011 *Programme for Government* made a commitment to introduce universal free GP care, the commitment has since been rowed back somewhat with free GP cover due to be extended to those aged 7–18 only in addition to the existing under 6s and over 70s. In 2012, the WHO noted that Ireland was the only EU health system that did not offer universal coverage of primary care, while a 2010 study noted that those without medical or GP visit cards in Ireland faced the highest user fees for GP care in the EU.[7]

User fees are payments at the point of use and can take a number of different forms, including co-payment (a fixed fee per service), co-insurance (a fixed per-centage of the cost of the service) and deductible (full cost of the service up to a certain threshold). For example, in Ireland, medical cardholders pay a co-payment of €2.50 per prescription item, while non-medical cardholders face a deductible of €144 per month for prescription medicines. The primary motivation for user fees in public healthcare is to reduce moral hazard behaviour among consumers of healthcare services. A secondary motivation is to generate revenue. However, there is extensive empirical evidence that user fees discourage both necessary as well as unnecessary healthcare utilisation. This research highlights also the neg-ative equity implications of user fees. While demand for healthcare is relatively price inelastic, those on lower incomes have a higher price elasticity than those on higher incomes. Therefore, any increase in the cost of healthcare will have a greater deterrent effect on the poorer sections of society. As a consequence, most European healthcare systems rely more heavily on pre-payment for healthcare, either via taxation or social insurance contributions, as the predominant financing mechanism for healthcare services.

Role of Private Health Insurance
Private health insurance in Ireland is primarily taken out by non-medical card-holders to cover the costs of private or semi-private hospital care in public and private hospitals. Increasingly, the major insurers have started to offer (limited) cover for primary care expenses, usually in the form of a fixed amount per visit (subject to an annual maximum number of visits). Private health insurance in Ireland essentially provides cover for services already available free of charge (or heavily subsidised) in the public sector. It therefore fulfils elements of a duplicative role, in contrast to other countries where its role is strictly supplementary to that of the public system (e.g. Canada). The proposed system of UHI was in part a response to the frequent criticisms of the two-tier system of care in public hospitals that is supported by the current role of private health insurance in Ireland.

Apart from a small number of restricted membership private health insurance schemes, there are four main private health insurance companies in Ireland: VHI Healthcare, Laya Healthcare, Irish Life Health (previously Aviva) and Glo Health. At the end of 2015, VHI Healthcare accounted for fifty-one per cent of the private health insurance market, while Laya Healthcare had a twenty-six per cent share, Irish Life fourteen per cent, Glo Health five per cent and the restricted membership schemes accounted for the remaining four per cent.

To prevent cream-skimming or risk selection, the government strictly regulates the behaviour of the major private insurers in the Irish market via the principles of open enrolment (no one can be refused cover), community rating (all individuals face the same premium) and lifetime cover (once insured, an individual's policy cannot be terminated). However, in practice risk selection can take place in more subtle ways (market segmentation, selective advertising, etc). For example, targeting certain groups of people, such as employees in a particular sector, may be a form of risk selection.

A stable community-rating system means that a risk-equalisation scheme (which aims to remove differences in insurers' costs that result from differing risk profiles among members) must be implemented. The scheme provides for a system of age-related health credits in respect of those over the age of 60 that help to meet their higher claims costs. The health credits vary by age, sex and by level of cover. The credits are funded by a community-rating health insurance levy paid by health insurers.

In May 2015, lifetime community rating (LCR) was introduced in an attempt to ensure sustainability in the market. Under LCR, community rating is modified to reflect the age at which a person takes out private health insurance. Late entry loadings are applied to the premiums of those who join the market at age 35 or over (2 per cent per annum).

Despite the introduction of LCR, price inflation in private health insurance premia remains a concern; in the year to December 2016, the price of private health insurance increased by 6.5 per cent, in comparison with overall health prices which increased by just 1.2 per cent. Recent policy changes are likely to put further pressure on consumers. In Budget 2014 the government announced that the amount of the private health insurance premium that qualifies for tax relief will be limited to €1,000 for adults and €500 for children, while legislation was enacted in mid 2013 to allow for increased charges for private patients treated in public hospitals.

Partly in response to the introduction of LCR, but also as a result of an improving economy, the proportion of the population with private health insurance cover has been increasing recently, although has not yet returned to the level in 2006, when nearly 52 per cent of the population had private health insurance. Currently, 46 per cent of the population are covered.

6 CONTROL OF HEALTHCARE EXPENDITURE

As illustrated in Table 14.1, total current health expenditure now accounts for nearly twelve per cent of national income in Ireland, in comparison with just under seven per cent in 2000. Many of the determinants of health expenditure are outside of the control of government, such as demographic change and increasing consumer expectations. However, there are measures that can be taken to limit the growth of healthcare expenditure, and there is much debate on the merits of the different approaches. Before outlining the various measures, it is worth discussing the determinants of healthcare expenditure in greater detail.

Determinants of Healthcare Expenditure
Cross-country comparisons of the determinants of health expenditure typically focus on three main factors, namely national income, population age structure and institutional features of the healthcare system. National income is consistently found to be one of the most important drivers of health-expenditure increases; it is estimated that 90 per cent of the variation in health expenditure across countries is due to differences in GDP per capita. Related to the role of national income is the influence of rising consumer expectations (see also the discussion on Wagner's Law in Chapter 3).

While the potential impact of demographic change (in terms of both the size and age structure of the population) on health expenditure has been widely discussed, cross-country comparisons of health expenditure growth typically find that population ageing explains only a small proportion of health expenditure growth over time. There are a number of competing hypotheses about the potential effect of increased life expectancy on healthcare expenditure, with no consensus as yet on whether an increasing, decreasing or stable proportion of the additional years of life will be spent in ill-health. An important driver of healthcare expenditure is the 'end-of-life' cost and to the extent that population ageing simply delays such costs, the impact on population ageing on health expenditure may be limited. In addition, there is some evidence to suggest that the end-of-life cost is lower for those who die at older ages, although the costs of long-term care do increase. In this context, the net impact of population ageing on future health expenditure is complex and difficult to predict.

Similarly, the impact of the increasing prevalence of chronic disease on future healthcare expenditure is difficult to estimate. Approximately 80 per cent of total health expenditure relates to the treatment of chronic disease, and this proportion is likely to increase with population ageing and adverse trends in diet, exercise and obesity. While increasing rates of chronic disease may increase the demand for healthcare, changing models of care (i.e. a movement away from acute, episodic care to more preventive care in the community) may mean that the overall impact on healthcare expenditure is more modest.

On the supply side, factors such as rising healthcare prices, technological change, the regulatory regime governing behaviour in the healthcare sector and the incentives facing healthcare providers are all important drivers of healthcare expenditure. Empirical evidence suggests that the contribution of technological change to health expenditure growth is large and significant (and often greater than that of population ageing), but it must be remembered that many technological advances are hugely beneficial for human health and well-being.

In this context, health technology assessment (HTAs) has an important role in adjudicating on the costs and benefits of new technologies. In Ireland, HIQA has responsibility for carrying out HTAs for new treatments and interventions (e.g., vaccinations, screening), while the National Centre for Pharmacoeconomics (NCPE) carries out pharmaceutical HTAs. Every new pharmaceutical seeking reimbursement under the various state drugs schemes is assessed by the NCPE; pharmaceuticals with major budgetary implications for the state are sent forward for a formal HTA. The NCPE then issues a recommendation to the Minister for Health in relation to reimbursement. Recently, a number of high-profile cases (e.g., Orkambi for the treatment of cystic fibrosis) have highlighted the opportunity cost involved in public funding of high-cost treatments.

In Ireland, labour costs account for approximately 50 per cent of health expenditure (in the acute hospitals sector, the proportion is closer to 70 per cent); therefore changes in the level and type of employees have implications for spending on health services. Related to this is the concept of Baumol's disease (see also Chapter 3) whereby public-sector employees demand wage increases in line with those of their private-sector counterparts. While in the private sector (the 'progressive' sector), wage increases are accompanied by improvements in productivity, in labour-intensive sectors such as health, education and public administration (the 'non-progressive' sectors), productivity improvements are harder to implement.

The financial incentives facing healthcare providers, which are largely determined by how they are paid for the services they provide, have important implications for healthcare expenditure. Taking the example of GPs, in a fee-for-service
system, GPs receive a fee for each consultation, while in a capitation system, they
receive a payment that is risk-adjusted for the health needs of the patient (e.g.
by age and sex). Fee-for-service payments promote activity, although there are
concerns that doctors can engage in demand-inducement behaviour under such a
system. While capitation payments incentivise the provision of preventive care,
unless the capitation payment is appropriately risk-adjusted, such payments can
give doctors an incentive to engage in 'cream-skimming' behaviour. There are
therefore trade-offs involved in choosing one method over another. However,
cross-country comparisons have found that healthcare expenditure is higher in
countries with fee-for-service systems than in those with capitation systems, controlling for other determinants of expenditure such as national income, population
age structure, etc.

Expenditure Control Measures
Essentially, there are three broad approaches to achieving sustainable levels of
public health expenditure; increasing revenue, lessening the obligations of the public system via changes to public health cover, and increasing efficiency. In the current economic environment, the degree to which public revenue can be increased
(via taxation or social insurance contributions) is limited, although Budget 2017
committed to the introduction of a tax on sugar-sweetened drinks in 2018.

Shifting the responsibility for financing healthcare to individuals via new or
increased user fees, while attractive for a government trying to limit public health
expenditure, does not necessarily lead to lower total health expenditure. User
fees discourage both necessary as well as unnecessary healthcare utilisation and
are disproportionately borne by the poorer, sicker members of society. Even with
exemptions for vulnerable population groups, the level of user fees needs to be
sufficiently high, and the administrative costs of collection sufficiently low, to
generate significant revenues. However, where the objective is to discourage the
consumption of low-value care (e.g. branded pharmaceuticals where a generic
equivalent is available), user fees can be an appropriate strategy and this is the
logic behind the system of reference pricing and generic substitution.

Measures that seek to enhance the efficiency of the health sector offer a
more appropriate mechanism for ensuring long-term sustainability of healthcare
expenditure. Reforming the way in which providers are paid for the services they
provide is becoming increasingly common, with many countries shifting the
financial risk of healthcare from insurers/government to providers via capitation
or other prospective forms of provider payment. In some cases, contracts include
pay-for-performance elements in an attempt to encourage behaviour on the part
of providers that is aligned with health policy objectives, although there is limited
evidence on the effectiveness of such payments in terms of health outcomes, cost
control and quality.

With the increasing incidence of chronic disease, the provision of healthcare is increasingly focusing on health promotion and prevention rather than on the traditional roles of diagnosis and treatment, in particular through an expanded role for GP and other primary care services. International comparisons show higher health expenditure in countries with weaker primary care. The supply of primary care doctors and better primary healthcare is associated with lower total expenditure on healthcare, in part due to better preventive care and consequent lower rates of hospitalisation.

Greater use of electronic health records and associated technologies has been suggested as an important mechanism to improve quality and efficiency in healthcare. In 2013, the government published an eHealth Strategy, outlining priority projects relating to a national health identifier, ePrescribing, online referrals and scheduling, telehealthcare, etc. In 2013, Ireland scored slightly below the EU average in terms of the deployment of ICT in GP and hospital settings.

At a sectoral level, pay and pharmaceuticals have been the focus of much recent policy discussion in relation to sustainability. In 2013, legislation for a system of reference pricing and generic substitution was enacted, with 48 products currently subject to the legislation. A new pricing agreement with pharmaceutical manufacturers was negotiated in 2016, with the state estimating that savings of €600m over the four-year period of the agreement will be achieved. After a series of pay cuts in 2010 and 2013, during 2017, pay that was cut in 2013 will be restored to public sector staff.

7 CONCLUDING COMMENTS

In this chapter, an overview of the financing and delivery of health services in Ireland, as well as key policy issues, was provided. After a period of substantial budget reductions during the economic crisis, public health expenditure has begun to increase again. However, an ageing and growing population, with increased demands and expectations, poses considerable challenges for the state in ensuring sustainability. Measures that seek to enhance the efficiency of the health sector (e.g., reforming provider payment) offer the greatest potential for ensuring long-term sustainability of the healthcare system.

Access issues continue to dominate public and policy discussion, and were reflected in the proposals on universal health insurance and free GP care contained in the 2011 *Programme for Government*. More recently, the debate has moved on to consider the concept of universal healthcare, with the financing mechanism just one aspect of the design feature of a universal healthcare system. The proposals in relation to the abolition of the HSE and the establishment of all hospitals as not-for-profit, independent entities have the potential to radically change the manner in which Irish health services are financed and delivered, but there have been delays in implementation.

Endnotes

*　The author thanks John O'Hagan and Francis O'Toole for comments on an earlier version of the chapter. All views expressed are those of the author and are not necessarily shared by Trinity College Dublin or the Economic and Social Research Institute (ESRI).

1　S. Smith, 'Equity in healthcare: the Irish perspective', *Health Economics, Policy and Law*, 6 (2), 2011.

2　Calculated from HSE, *November Performance Report Supplementary Commentary*, HSE, Dublin 2015.

3　For further reading see M. Wren, S. Connolly and N. Cunningham, *An Examination of the Potential Costs of Universal Health Insurance in Ireland*, ESRI, Dublin 2015; M. Wren and S. Connolly, *Challenges in Achieving Universal Healthcare in Ireland*, ESRI, Dublin 2016; S. Burke et al., 'From universal health insurance to universal healthcare? The shifting health policy landscape in Ireland since the economic crisis', *Health Policy*, 120 (3), 2016.

4　E. Nolte and M. McKee, 'Variations in amenable mortality – trends in 16 high-income nations', *Health Policy*, 103 (1), 2011.

5　J. Mackenbach and M. McKee, 'A comparative analysis of health policy performance in 43 European countries', *European Journal of Public Health*, 23 (2), 2013.

6　C. Ruhm, 'Are recessions good for your health?' *Quarterly Journal of Economics*, 115 (2), 2000; C. Ruhm, 'Recessions, healthy no more?', *Journal of Health Economics*, 42, 2015.

7　See T. Evetovits, *Health System Responses to Financial Pressures in Ireland: Policy Options in an International Context*, WHO Brussels, 2012; D. Kringos et al., 'The strength of primary care in Europe: an international comparative study', *British Journal of General Practice*, 63, 2013.

Index

United Nations
  Framework on Climate Change 300–1
  Universal Declaration of Human Rights
    329
USA
  Affordable Care Act (ACA) 366
  businesses 27, 194
  common currency 70
  exports to 274
  New Deal 225
  protectionist policies 247
  Truth in Lending Act 120
utilities
  government ownership 80
  and housing 330–1

VAT 99, 107–8, 212, 252
vehicle insurance and tax 101, 109, 121
vehicles 101, 294
vertical equity 48

wages 83, 169–71
  differentials 208
  minimum wage 121, 171–2
  restraint 23–4, 26, 194
  wage agreements 24, 82, 83, 170
Wagner's Law 86
waste 102, 304, 305, 331

water 283, 297, 331
  charges 77, 99, 138–40
  infrastructure 304
  quality 42, 303
Water Framework Directive (WFD) 138, 244, 303
wealth 197, 214, 218
Wealth of Nations, The 93
weaving 9, 10, 12
welfare 43, 58, 74, 87, 220
  abuse of 166
  and housing 328
  and industrial policy 266
  payments 98, 337
  recipients 213
  spending 16, 20, 87
  structure 11
Whately, R. 50
Whitaker, T.K. 21
wind 285, 287, 293
women 154, 157, 185, 192, 250
woollen industry 5, 6, 9
World Bank 65
  Doing Business 84
  World Development Report 206
World Trade Organisation (WTO) 65, 117, 118, 247, 280
World Values Survey 223
World War II 19–20